GCSE

Geography

Complete Revision and Practice

Contents

Section 1 — Tectonic Activity

Section 2 — Rocks and Resources

Section 3 — Weather and Climate

Section 4 — The Living World

Section 5 — Rivers

Section 6 — Glaciation

Section 7 — Coasts

Contents

Section 8 — Population

Section 9 — Urban Environments

Section 10 — Rural Environments

Section 11 — Development

Section 12 — Industry

Section 13 — Globalisation

Section 14 — Tourism

Exam Skills

Published by CGP

Editors:
Claire Boulter, Ellen Bowness, Karen Wells.

Contributors:
Rosalind Browning, Paddy Gannon, Barbara Melbourne, Helen Nurton, Sophie Watkins, Dennis Watts.

Proofreading:
Sharon Keeley.

ISBN: 978 1 84146 374 2

With thanks to Laura Jakubowski for copyright research.

With thanks to iStockphoto.com for permission to reproduce the photographs used on pages 23, 30, 35, 42, 43, 45, 46, 47, 53, 73, 77, 96, 106, 107, 111, 128, 145, 155, 205 and 235.

With thanks to Science Photo Library for permission to reproduce the photographs used on pages 12, 15, 26 and 119.

Images of Sri Lankan coastline on page 16 © UPPA/Photoshot.

Map of UK geology on page 20 reproduced by permission of the British Geological Survey. © NERC. All rights reserved. IPR/122-32CT.

Graphs of rainfall and sunshine hours on page 32 adapted from Crown Copyright data supplied by the Met Office.

Graph of the last 1000 years of climate change on page 36 reproduced with kind permission from Climate Change 2001: Synthesis Report. A Contribution of Working Groups I, II and III to the Third Assessment Report of the Intergovernmental Panel on Climate Change, Figure SPM-10b. Cambridge University Press.

Graph of the last 150 years of climate change on pages 36, 40 and 93 adapted from Crown Copyright data supplied by the Met Office.

'Map of drought risk on page 45 © 'UCL Global Drought Monitor'.

Mapping data on pages 76, 79, 97, 110, 230, 231 and 237 reproduced by permission of Ordnance Survey® on behalf of HMSO © Crown copyright (2010). All rights reserved. Ordnance Survey® Licence No. 100034841.

Data used to compile the UK population density maps on pages 86 and 225 from Office for National Statistics: General Register Office for Scotland, Northern Ireland Statistics & Research Agency. © Crown copyright reproduced under the terms of the Click-Use Licence.

Data used to compile the UK average rainfall map on page 86 from the Manchester Metropolitan University.

Image of Rhône Glacier in 2008 on page 93 © Juerg Alean, Eglisau, Switzerland, http://www.glaciers-online.net.

Data used to produce the Rhône Glacier graph on page 93 from the Swiss Glacier Monitoring Network.

Data used to construct the UK population pyramid on page 134 © Crown copyright reproduced under the terms of the Click-Use Licence.

World Population Graph on page 141 reproduced with kind permission from Jean-Paul Rodrigue (underlying data from the United Nations).

Data used to compile the table on page 178 (except GNI per capita data) © Central Intelligence Agency

Data use to compile the pie charts on page 179 © World Trade Organisation, http://stat.wto.org/CountryProfile/WSDBCountryPFView.aspx?Language=E&Country=AU,BE,CA,CN,TH,UG,GB,UY,ZM,NI

Data used to compile the graph on page 179 from Human Development Report 2009 © United Nations, 2009. Reproduced with permission.

Data use to compile the map on page 184 © www.ustr.gov

With thanks to Ellen Bowness for the desert and polar bear images on page 217.

With thanks to Mr Steve Ellingham for the image of trekking in the Himalayas on page 217.

Data used to compile the UK tourism graph on page 221 from Office for National Statistics: General Register Office for Scotland, Northern Ireland Statistics and Research Agency. © Crown copyright, reproduced under the terms of the Click-Use Licence.

Data used to construct the flow map of immigration on page 229 - Source International Passenger Survey, Office for National Statistics © Crown copyright reproduced under the terms of the Click-Use Licence.

Every effort has been made to locate copyright holders and obtain permission to reproduce sources. For those sources where it has been difficult to trace the copyright holder of the work, we would be grateful for information. If any copyright holder would like us to make an amendment to the acknowledgements, please notify us and we will gladly update the book at the next reprint. Thank you.

Groovy website: www.cgpbooks.co.uk
Printed by Elanders Ltd, Newcastle upon Tyne.
Jolly bits of clipart from CorelDRAW®

Based on the classic CGP style created by Richard Parsons.

Tectonic Plates

The Earth's surface is made of huge floating plates that are constantly moving.

The Earth's Surface is Separated into Tectonic Plates

1) At the centre of the Earth is a ball of solid iron and nickel called the core.
2) Around the core is the mantle, which is semi-molten rock that moves very slowly.
3) The outer layer of the Earth is the crust. It's very thin (about 20 km).

Crust
Outer core
Inner core
Mantle

4) The crust is divided into lots of slabs called tectonic plates (they float on the mantle). Plates are made of two types of crust — continental and oceanic:

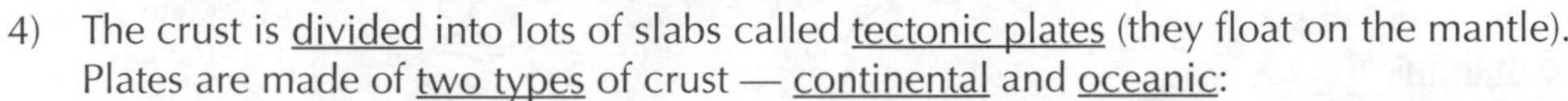

- Continental crust is thicker and less dense.

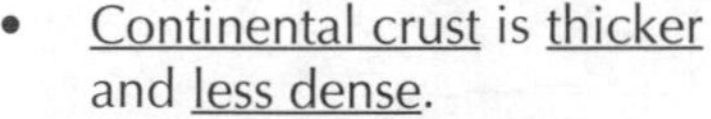

- Oceanic crust is thinner and more dense.

5) The plates are moving because the rock in the mantle underneath them is moving.
6) The places where plates meet are called boundaries or plate margins.

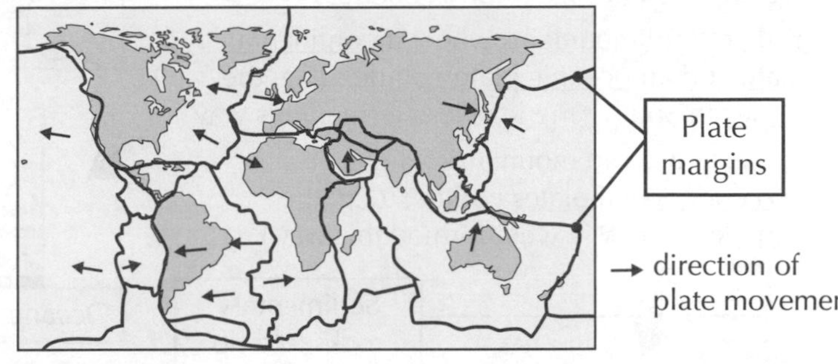

There are Three Types of Plate Margin

1 DESTRUCTIVE MARGINS

Destructive margins are where two plates are moving towards each other, e.g. along the east coast of Japan.

- Where an oceanic plate meets a continental plate, the denser oceanic plate is forced down into the mantle and destroyed. This often creates volcanoes and ocean trenches (very deep sections of the ocean floor where the oceanic plate goes down).
- Where two continental plates meet, the plates smash together, but no crust is destroyed (see next page).

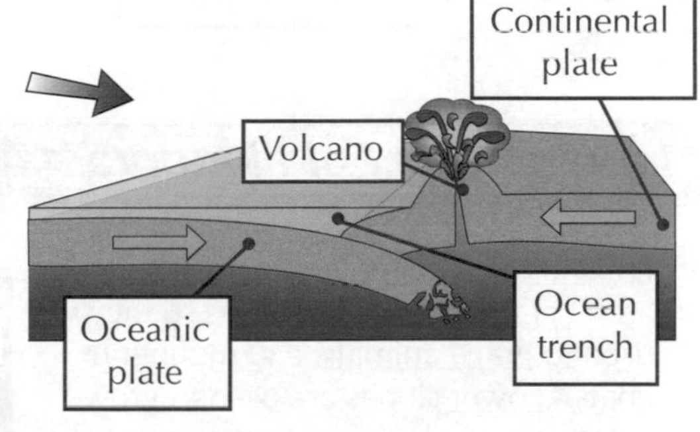

2 CONSTRUCTIVE MARGINS

Constructive margins are where two plates are moving away from each other, e.g. at the mid-Atlantic ridge. Magma (molten rock) rises from the mantle to fill the gap and cools, creating new crust.

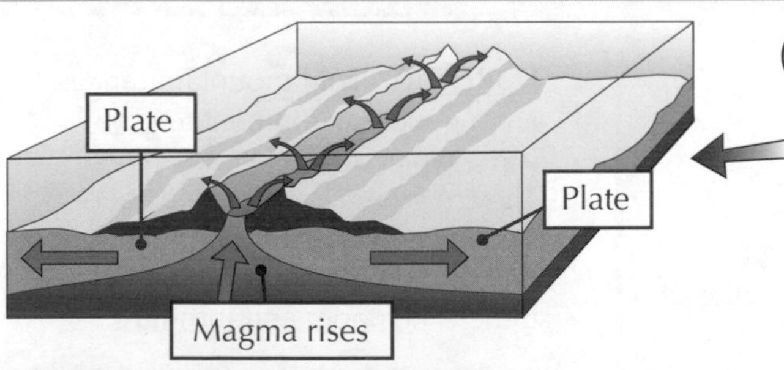

3 CONSERVATIVE MARGINS

Conservative margins are where two plates are moving sideways past each other, or are moving in the same direction but at different speeds, e.g. along the west coast of the USA. Crust isn't created or destroyed.

Plates moving sideways past each other

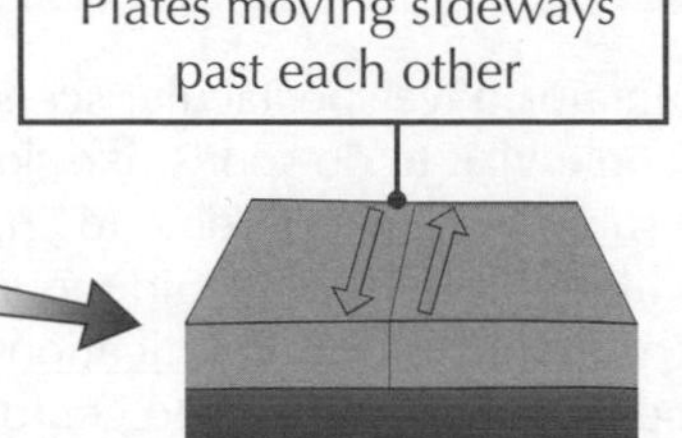

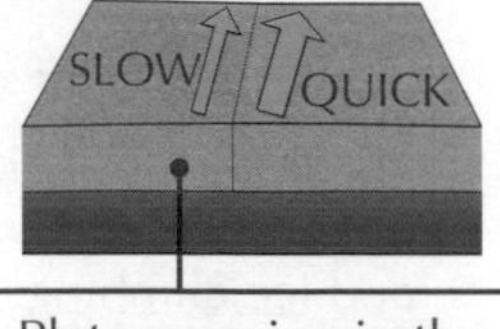

Plates moving in the same direction at different speeds

Earth's structure = core, then mantle, then crust on the outside

Make sure you understand the Earth's structure and what tectonic plates are or you'll struggle later on in the section. Practise sketching and labelling the diagrams at the bottom to learn the types of margin too.

Fold Mountains

Get ready for the first landform created by plate movement — fold mountains.

Fold Mountains are Formed when Plates Collide at Destructive Margins

1) When tectonic plates collide the sedimentary rocks that have built up between them are folded and forced upwards to form mountains.
2) So fold mountains are found at destructive plate margins and places where there used to be destructive margins, e.g. the west coast of North America.
3) You get fold mountains where a continental plate and an oceanic plate collide. (E.g. the Andes in South America were formed this way.)
4) You also get fold mountains where two continental plates collide. (E.g. the Himalayas in Asia were formed this way.)

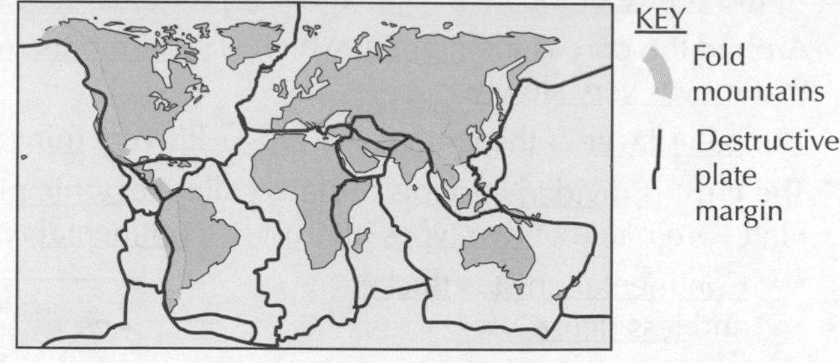

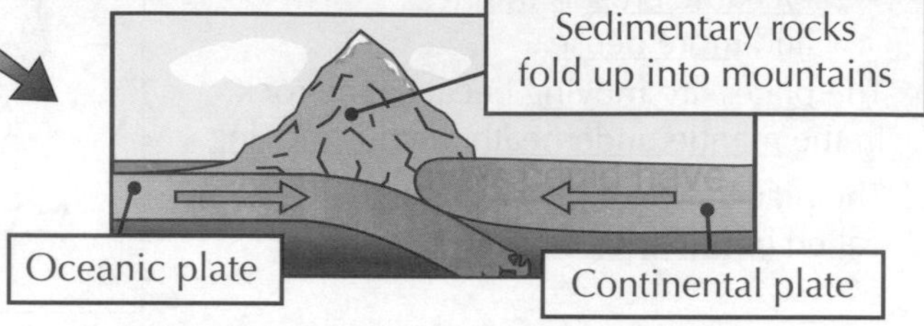

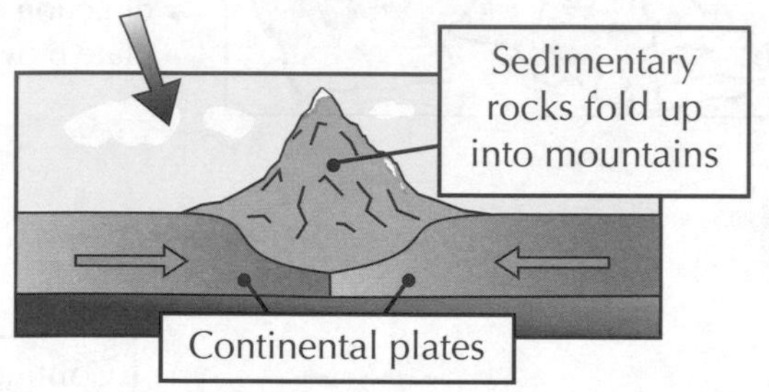

5) Fold mountain areas have lots of very high mountains, which are very rocky with steep slopes. There's often snow and glaciers in the highest bits, and lakes in the valleys between the mountains.

Humans Use Fold Mountain Areas for Lots of Things

FARMING: Higher mountain slopes aren't great for growing crops so they're used to graze animals, e.g. mountain goats. Lower slopes are used to grow crops. Steep slopes are sometimes terraced to make growing crops easier.

HYDRO-ELECTRIC POWER (HEP): Steep-sided mountains and high lakes (to store water) make fold mountains ideal for generating hydro-electric power.

MINING: Fold mountains are a major source of metal ores, so there's a lot of mining going on. The steep slopes make access to the mines difficult, so zig-zag roads have been carved out on the sides of some mountains to get to them.

FORESTRY: Fold mountain ranges are a good environment to grow some types of tree (e.g. conifers). They're grown on the steep valley slopes and are used for things like fuel, building materials, and to make things like paper and furniture.

TOURISM: Fold mountains have spectacular scenery, which attracts tourists. In winter, people visit to do sports like skiing, snowboarding and ice climbing. In summer, walkers come to enjoy the scenery. Tunnels have been drilled through some fold mountains to make straight, fast roads. This improves communications for tourists and people who live in the area as it's quicker to get to places.

Fold mountains are found along destructive plate margins

Yep, fold mountains are pretty much what they say they are — mountains made by folding. Make sure you know the different ways that humans use them and how they've adapted to the conditions in them, e.g. by terracing slopes.

Fold Mountains — Case Study

Brace yourself for the first case study of many. Make sure you learn the specific facts for good marks in the exam.

The Alps is a Fold Mountain Range

Location: Central Europe — it stretches across Austria, France, Germany, Italy, Liechtenstein, Slovenia and Switzerland.

Formation: The Alps were formed about 30 million years ago by the collision between the African and European plates.

Tallest peak: Mont Blanc at 4810 m on the Italian-French border.

Population: Around 12 million people.

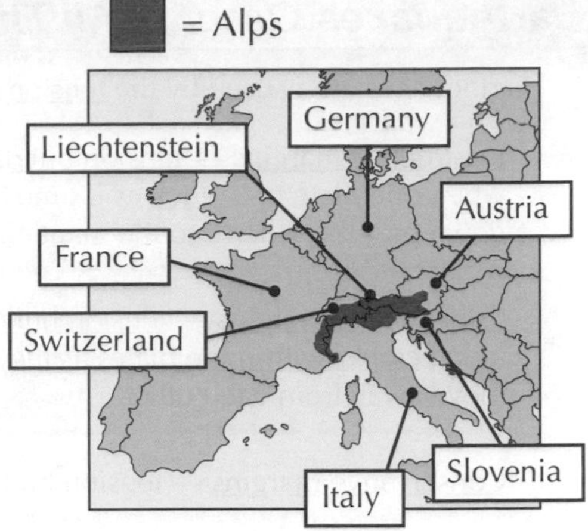

People Use the Alps for Lots of Things

FARMING

1) The steep upland areas are used to farm goats, which provide milk, cheese and meat.
2) Some sunnier slopes have been terraced to plant vineyards (e.g. Lavaux, Switzerland).

TOURISM

1) 100 million tourists visit the Alps each year making tourism a huge part of the economy.
2) 70% of the tourists visit the steep, snow covered mountains in the winter for skiing, snowboarding and ice climbing. In the summer tourists visit for walking, mountain biking, paragliding and climbing.
3) New villages have been built to cater for the quantity of tourists, e.g. Tignes in France.
4) Ski runs, ski lifts, cable cars, holiday chalets and restaurants pepper the landscape.

HYDRO-ELECTRIC POWER (HEP)

1) The narrow valleys are dammed to generate HEP, e.g. in the Berne area in Switzerland. Switzerland gets 60% of its electricity from HEP stations in the Alps.
2) The electricity produced is used locally to power homes and businesses. It's also exported to towns and cities further away.

MINING

Salt, iron ore, gold, silver and copper were mined in the Alps, but the mining has declined dramatically due to cheaper foreign sources.

FORESTRY

Scots Pine is planted all over the Alps because it's more resilient to the munching goats, which kill native tree saplings. The trees are logged and sold to make things like furniture.

People Have Adapted to the Conditions in the Alps

1) STEEP RELIEF: Goats are farmed there because they're well adapted to live on steep mountains. Trees and man-made defences are used to protect against avalanches and rock slides.
2) POOR SOILS: Animals are grazed in most high areas as the soil isn't great for growing crops.
3) LIMITED COMMUNICATIONS: Roads have been built over passes (lower points between mountains), e.g. the Brenner Pass between Austria and Italy. It takes a long time to drive over passes and they can be blocked by snow, so tunnels have been cut through the mountains to provide fast transport links. For example, the Lötschberg Base Tunnel has been cut through the Bernese Alps in Switzerland.

The Alps stretch across seven countries

As with all case studies learn the facts and figures — the examiners go all giddy and throw marks at you when they read them. In the exam you could be asked how people use the Alps and how they've adapted to the conditions there.

Earthquakes — Cause and Measurement

Plates can get stuck against each other. When they become unstuck you get earthquakes.

Earthquakes Occur at All Three Types of Plate Margin

1) Earthquakes are caused by the tension that builds up at all three types of plate margin:

Destructive margins — tension builds up when one plate gets stuck as it's moving down past the other into the mantle.

Constructive margins — tension builds along cracks within the plates as they move away from each other.

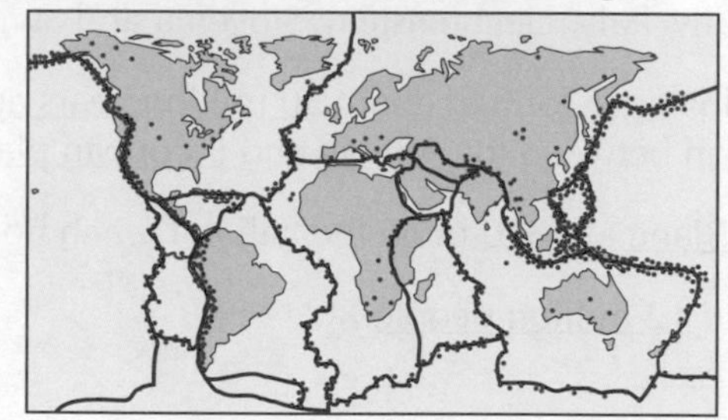

See page 1 for more on plate margins.

Conservative margins — tension builds up when plates that are grinding past each other get stuck.

2) The plates eventually jerk past each other, sending out shock waves (vibrations). These vibrations are the earthquake.
3) The shock waves spread out from the focus — the point in the Earth where the earthquake starts. Near the focus the waves are stronger and cause more damage.
4) The epicentre is the point on the Earth's surface straight above the focus.
5) Weak earthquakes happen quite often, but strong earthquakes are rare.

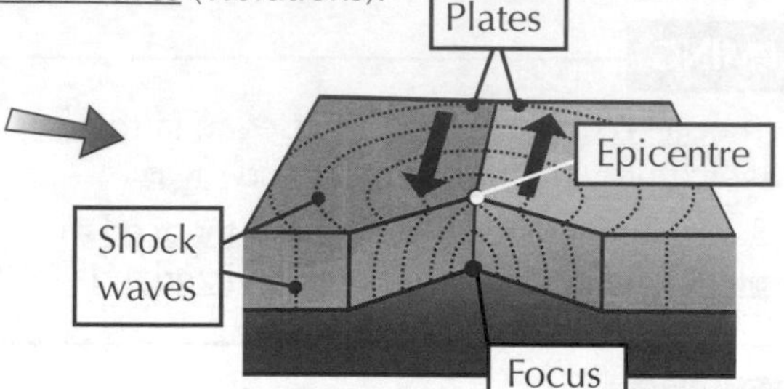

Earthquakes can be Measured

Earthquakes can be measured using two different scales:

1 The Richter scale:

1) This measures the amount of energy released by an earthquake (called the magnitude).
2) Magnitude is measured using a seismometer — a machine with an arm that moves with the vibrations of the earth.
3) The Richter scale doesn't have an upper limit and it's logarithmic — this means that an earthquake with a magnitude of 5 is ten times more powerful than one with a magnitude of 4.
4) Most people don't feel earthquakes of magnitude 1-2. Major earthquakes are above 5.

Seismometer reading

2 The Mercalli scale:

1) This measures the effects of an earthquake.
2) Effects are measured by asking eye witnesses for observations of what happened. Observations can be in the form of words or photos.
3) It's a scale of 1 to 12.

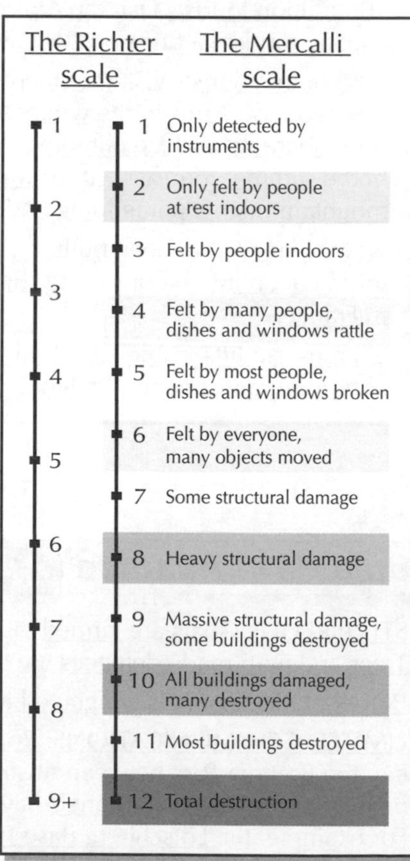

The Richter scale measures magnitude, the Mercalli scale measures effects

Lots of earthquakes happen around the world every day, but they're not usually big enough to cause damage. Be sure that you know the difference between an earthquake's epicentre and its focus before you move on to the next page.

Impacts of Earthquakes

Earthquakes have loads of serious impacts...

Earthquakes have Primary and Secondary Impacts

The primary impacts of an earthquake are the immediate effects of the ground shaking.
The secondary impacts are the effects that happen later on.
Here are a few examples of the possible impacts:

Tsunamis are a series of enormous waves caused when huge amounts of water get displaced — there's more about them on page 16.

Primary impacts

1) Buildings and bridges collapse.
2) People are injured or killed by buildings and bridges collapsing.
3) Roads, railways, ports and airports are damaged.
4) Electricity cables are damaged, cutting off supplies.
5) Gas pipes are broken, causing leaks and cutting off supplies.
6) Telephone poles and cables are destroyed.
7) Underground water and sewage pipes are broken, causing leaks and cutting off supplies.

Secondary impacts

1) Earthquakes can trigger landslides and tsunamis — these destroy more buildings and cause more injuries and deaths.
2) Leaking gas can be ignited, starting fires.
3) People are left homeless.
4) People may suffer psychological problems if they knew people who died or if they lose their home etc.
5) There's a shortage of clean water and a lack of proper sanitation — this makes it easier for diseases to spread.
6) Roads are blocked or destroyed so aid and emergency vehicles can't get through.
7) Businesses are damaged or destroyed, causing unemployment.

The more settlements built and businesses set up in an area, the greater the impact because there are more people and properties to be affected by an earthquake.

The Impacts are More Severe in Poorer Countries

Here are a few reasons why:

1) There's more low quality housing in poorer countries. Low quality houses are less stable, so they're destroyed more easily by earthquakes.
2) The infrastructure is often worse in poorer countries. Poor quality roads make it harder for emergency services to reach injured people, which leads to more deaths.
3) Poorer countries don't have much money to protect against earthquakes, e.g. by making buildings earthquake proof. They also don't have enough money or resources (e.g. food and emergency vehicles) to react straight away to earthquakes, so more people are affected by secondary impacts.
4) Healthcare is often worse in poorer countries. Many hospitals in poorer countries don't have enough supplies to deal with lots of casualties after an earthquake, so more people die from treatable injuries.

People Continue to Live in the Areas where Earthquakes Happen

Here are some of the reasons why people don't move away from earthquake prone areas, e.g. California:

1) They've always lived there — moving away would mean leaving friends and family.
2) They're employed in the area. If people move they would have to find new jobs.
3) They're confident of support from their government after an earthquake, e.g. to help rebuild houses.
4) Some people think that severe earthquakes won't happen again in the area, so it's safe to live there.

Impacts are worse in poorer areas

Earthquakes seem pretty exciting to the outsider, but they can be life-threatening for the people that experience them. All the different impacts affect both richer countries and poorer countries, but they're more severe in poorer countries.

Reducing the Impacts of Earthquakes

Unfortunately earthquakes don't have an 'off' button, but the impacts they have can be reduced.

There are Many Ways of Reducing the Impacts of Earthquakes

Prediction

1) It's currently impossible to predict when an earthquake will happen. If you could, it would give people time to evacuate — this would reduce the number of injuries and deaths.

2) There can be clues that an earthquake is about to happen though. For example, lots of small tremors, cracks appearing in rocks and strange animal behaviour (e.g. rats abandoning nests).

3) It's possible to predict where future earthquakes may happen using data from past earthquakes, e.g. mapping where earthquakes have happened shows which places are likely to be affected again — these places can prepare themselves for the impacts of an earthquake.

Building techniques

1) Buildings can be designed to withstand earthquakes, e.g. by using materials like reinforced concrete or building special foundations that absorb an earthquake's energy.

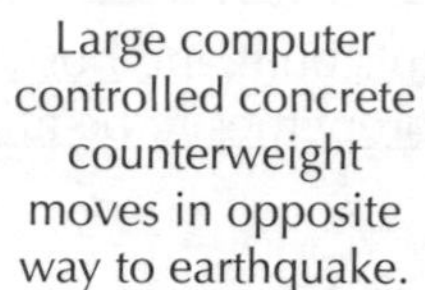
Large computer controlled concrete counterweight moves in opposite way to earthquake.

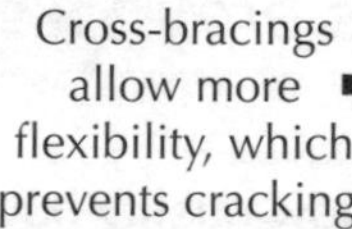
Cross-bracings allow more flexibility, which prevents cracking.

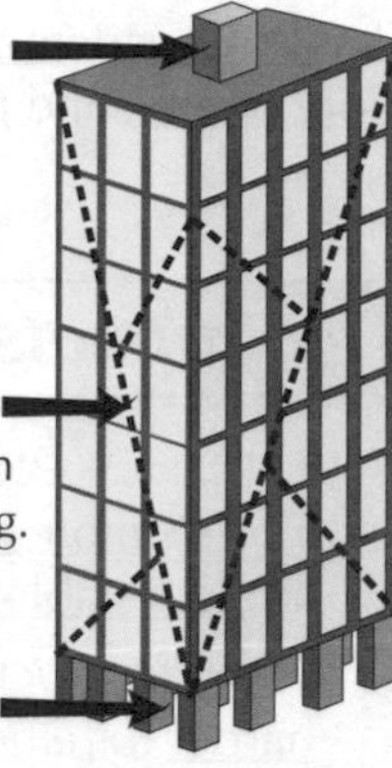
Rubber shock absorbers in foundations

2) Constructing earthquake-proof buildings reduces the number of buildings destroyed by an earthquake, so fewer people will be killed, injured, made homeless and made unemployed.

Planning

1) Future developments, e.g. new shopping centres, can be planned to avoid the areas most at risk from earthquakes. This reduces the number of buildings destroyed by an earthquake.

2) Firebreaks can be made to reduce the spread of fires (a secondary impact, see previous page).

3) Emergency services can train and prepare for disasters, e.g. by practising rescuing people from collapsed buildings and by stockpiling medicine. This reduces the number of people killed.

4) Governments can plan evacuation routes to get people out of dangerous areas quickly and safely after an earthquake. This reduces the number of people killed or injured by things like fires.

Reducing the Impacts of Earthquakes

Education

1) Governments and other organisations can educate people about what to do if there's an earthquake (e.g. stand in a doorway) and how to evacuate. This reduces deaths.

2) People can be told how to make a survival kit containing things like food, water, a torch, a radio and batteries. The kits reduce the chances of people dying if they're stuck in the area.

Aid

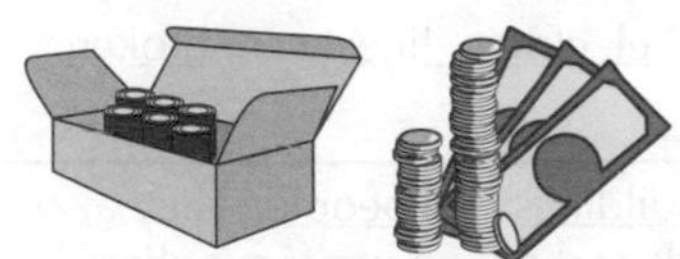

1) Poorer countries that have been affected by earthquakes can receive aid from governments or organisations — it can be things like food, water, money or people (e.g. doctors or rescuers).

2) Aid helps to reduce the impacts, e.g. money aid is used to rebuild homes, reducing homelessness.

*Some **Strategies** are **More Sustainable** than **Others***

Sustainable strategies meet the needs of people today without stopping people in the future meeting their needs. A strategy is not sustainable if it's not effective, as it doesn't meet the needs of people today. A strategy is also not sustainable if it's expensive or it harms the environment, as it stops people in the future meeting their needs.

Here's a bit on the sustainability of strategies to reduce the impact of earthquakes:

1) Predicting earthquakes is not an effective strategy, so it's not sustainable.
2) The other strategies above are sustainable — they're all effective and environmentally friendly, but some are more sustainable than others.
3) The ones that are more sustainable are basically the more cost-effective ones, e.g. good planning is usually more effective than aid at reducing impacts and it's much cheaper.
4) Some strategies are expensive (e.g. constructing earthquake-proof buildings), but they can be more sustainable than other strategies because in the long term less money and resources are used rebuilding.

Sustainable strategies are effective and environmentally friendly

If you could predict exactly when an earthquake will happen you'd make yourself a lot of friends, but top scientists think it's just too difficult to do. Anyway, it's worth knowing about the other strategies too and their sustainability.

Earthquakes — Case Studies

And you thought I'd forgotten all about the case studies.

Rich and Poor Parts of the World are Affected Differently

The effects of earthquakes and the responses to them are different in different parts of the world. A lot depends on how wealthy the part of the world is. In the exam, you're likely to be asked to compare an earthquake in a rich part of the world with one in a poor part of the world.

Earthquake in a rich part of the world:

Place: L'Aquila, Italy
Date: 6th April, 2009
Size: 6.3 on the Richter scale
Cause: Movement along a crack in the plate at a destructive margin.
Cost of damage: Around $15 billion

Earthquake in a poor part of the world:

Place: Kashmir, Pakistan
Date: 8th October, 2005
Size: 7.6 on the Richter scale
Cause: Movement along a crack in the plate at a destructive margin.
Cost of damage: Around $5 billion

	Rich (L'Aquila, Italy)	Poor (Kashmir, Pakistan)
Preparation	• There are laws on construction standards, but some modern buildings hadn't been built to withstand earthquakes. • Italy has a Civil Protection Department that trains volunteers to help with thing like rescue operations.	• No local disaster planning was in place. • Buildings were not designed to be earthquake resistant. • Communications were poor. There were few roads and they were badly constructed.
Primary effects	• Around 290 deaths, mostly from collapsed buildings. • Hundreds of people were injured. • Thousands of buildings were damaged or destroyed. • A bridge near the town of Fossa collapsed, and a water pipe was broken near the town of Paganica.	• Around 80 000 deaths, mostly from collapsed buildings. • Hundreds of thousands of people injured. • Entire villages and thousands of buildings were destroyed. • Water pipelines and electricity lines were broken, cutting off supply.
Secondary effects	• Aftershocks hampered rescue efforts and caused more damage. • Thousands of people were made homeless. • Fires in some collapsed buildings caused more damage. • The broken water pipe near the town of Paganica caused a landslide.	• Landslides buried buildings and people. They also blocked access roads and cut off water supplies, electricity supplies and telephone lines. • Around 3 million people were made homeless. • Diarrhoea and other diseases spread due to little clean water. • Freezing winter conditions shortly after the earthquake caused more casualties and meant rescue and rebuilding operations were difficult.
Immediate response	• Camps were set up for homeless people with water, food and medical care. • Ambulances, fire engines and the army were sent in to rescue survivors. • Cranes and diggers were used to remove rubble. • International teams with rescue dogs were sent in to look for survivors. • Money was provided by the government to pay rent, and gas and electricity bills were suspended.	• Help didn't reach many areas for days or weeks. People had to be rescued by hand without any equipment or help from emergency services. • Tents, blankets and medical supplies were distributed within a month, but not to all areas affected. • International aid and equipment such as helicopters and rescue dogs were brought in, as well as teams of people from other countries.
Long-term response	• The Italian Prime Minister promised to build a new town to replace L'Aquila as the capital of the area. • An investigation is going on to look into why the modern buildings weren't built to withstand earthquakes.	• Around 40 000 people have been relocated to a new town from the destroyed town of Balakot. • Government money has been given to people whose homes had been destroyed so they can rebuild them themselves. • Training has been provided to help rebuild more buildings as earthquake resistant. • New health centres have been set up in the area.

The cost of damage in wealthy areas is greater, but the effects are not as severe

The amount of damage an earthquake does, and the number of people that get hurt, is different in different parts of the world. Learn as many facts and figures as you can for an earthquake in a rich country and one in a poor country.

Worked Exam Questions

This exam question is exactly like the type you'll get in the real exam — except it's got the answers written in for you already. They show you what you should be writing — pretty handy.

1 Study **Figure 1**, which shows the Earth's tectonic plates.

(a) Name the type of plate margin labelled A in **Figure 1**.

Constructive plate margin.

(1 mark)

(b) The San Andreas Fault is labelled B in **Figure 1**. Crust is neither formed or destroyed at this plate margin. What is this type of plate margin called?

A conservative plate margin.

(1 mark)

Figure 1

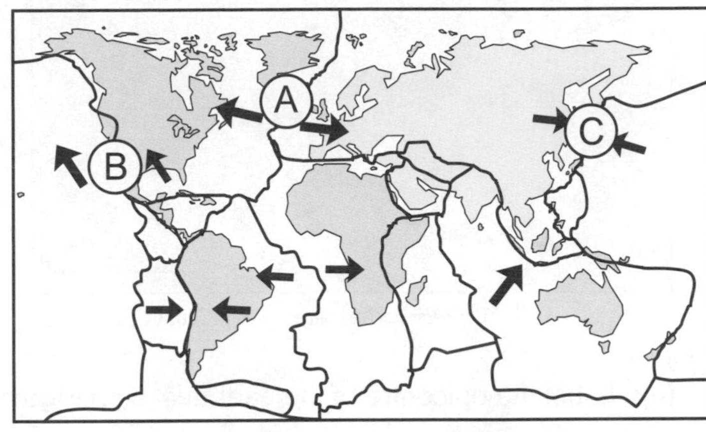

Key 〉 Plate margin → Plate movement

(c) At the plate margin labelled C in **Figure 1**, continental crust meets oceanic crust. Describe how continental crust is different from oceanic crust.

For two marks you need to give two differences.

Continental crust is thicker than oceanic crust.

Continental crust is less dense than oceanic crust.

(2 marks)

Figure 2

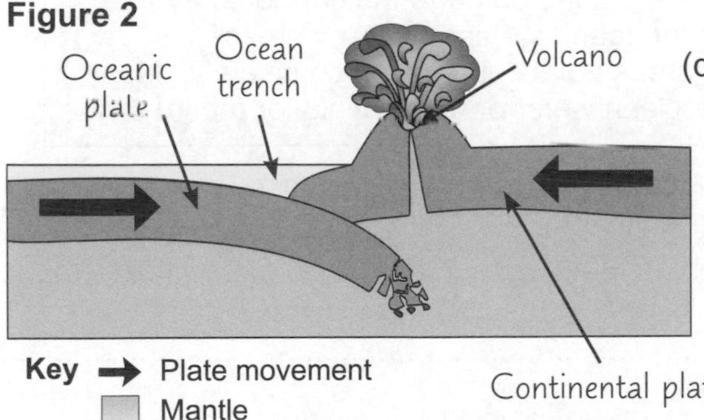

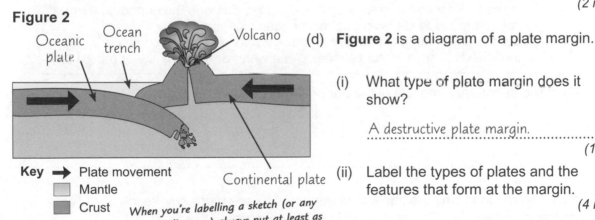

Key → Plate movement
Mantle
Crust

When you're labelling a sketch (or any photo or diagram) always put at least as many labels as there are marks available.

(d) **Figure 2** is a diagram of a plate margin.

(i) What type of plate margin does it show?

A destructive plate margin.

(1 mark)

(ii) Label the types of plates and the features that form at the margin.

(4 marks)

(e) (i) At which type of plate margin can fold mountains be found?

Destructive plate margins.

(1 mark)

(ii) Describe how fold mountains are formed.

When tectonic plates collide the sedimentary rocks that have built up between them are folded and forced upwards to form fold mountains.

(2 marks)

Exam Questions

1 Study **Figure 1**, which shows the focus of the 1994 Northridge earthquake in California, USA.

Figure 1

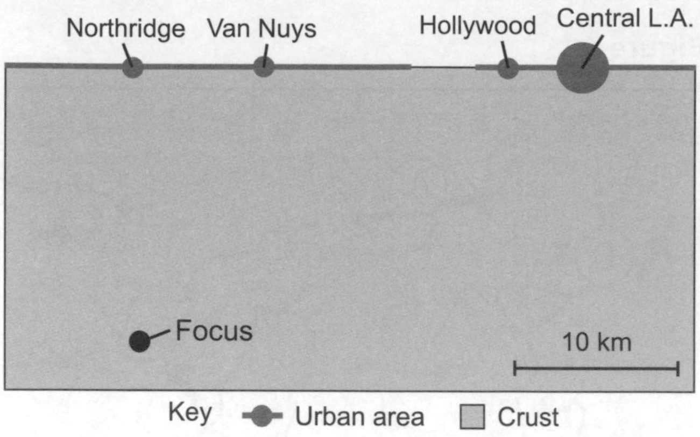

(a) (i) Define the term 'focus'.

....

....

....

(1 mark)

(ii) How deep in the Earth was the focus of this earthquake?

....

(1 mark)

(b) Label the epicentre of the earthquake on **Figure 1**.

(1 mark)

(c) What is the name of the scale that is used to measure the magnitude of an earthquake?

....

(1 mark)

2 Study **Figure 2**, an extract from a news report on the 2005 earthquake in Pakistan.

Figure 2

> The earthquake is thought to have killed 19 000 people and left many more injured. Rescue operations continue but the damage the earthquake has caused to roads is preventing rescue teams getting to many areas. Landslides mean that some rural areas have been cut off completely. Many thousands remain without shelter, clean water or medical aid for a third day.

(a) Give two secondary impacts of the earthquake described in **Figure 2**.

....

....

(2 marks)

(b) Give two reasons why the impacts of earthquakes are more severe in poorer countries, like Pakistan, than in richer countries.

....

....

....

....

(4 marks)

(c) Describe one way of reducing the impacts of earthquakes.

....

....

(2 marks)

Volcanoes

Volcanoes are caused by the movement of tectonic plates.

Volcanoes* are Found at *Destructive* and *Constructive Plate Margins

1) At destructive plate margins the oceanic plate goes under the continental plate because it's more dense. (This also creates an ocean trench.):
   - The oceanic plate moves down into the mantle, where it's melted and destroyed.
   - A pool of magma forms.
   - The magma rises through cracks in the crust called vents.
   - The magma erupts onto the surface (where it's called lava) forming a volcano.

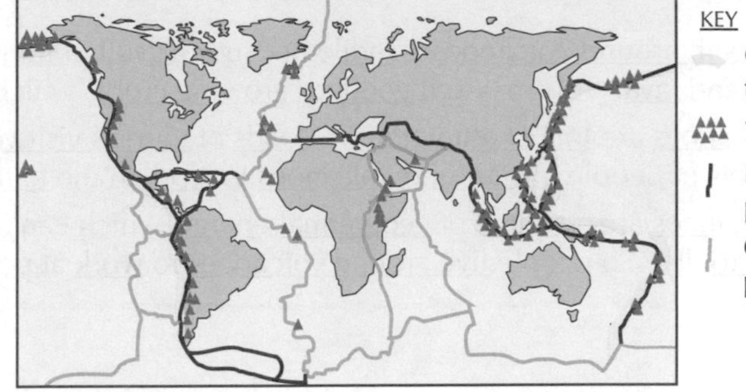

2) At constructive margins the magma rises up into the gap created by the plates moving apart, forming a volcano.
3) Some volcanoes also form over parts of the mantle that are really hot (called hotspots), e.g. in Hawaii.

*There are **Different Types** of **Volcano***

1) Composite volcanoes (E.g. Mount Fuji in Japan)

   Made up of ash and lava that's erupted, cooled and hardened into layers.
   The lava is usually thick and flows slowly.
   It hardens quickly to form a steep-sided volcano.

Steep-sided volcano
Vent
Layer of lava
Layer of ash

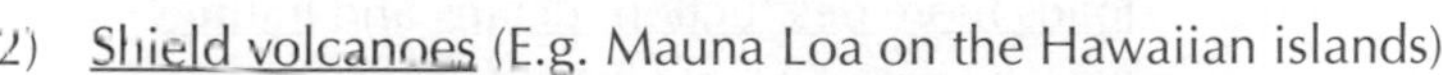

2) Shield volcanoes (E.g. Mauna Loa on the Hawaiian islands)

   Made up of only lava.
   The lava is runny. It flows quickly and spreads over a wide area, forming a low, flat volcano.

3) Dome volcanoes (E.g. Mount Pelée in the Caribbean)

   Made up of only lava.
   The lava is thick. It flows slowly and hardens quickly, forming a steep-sided volcano.

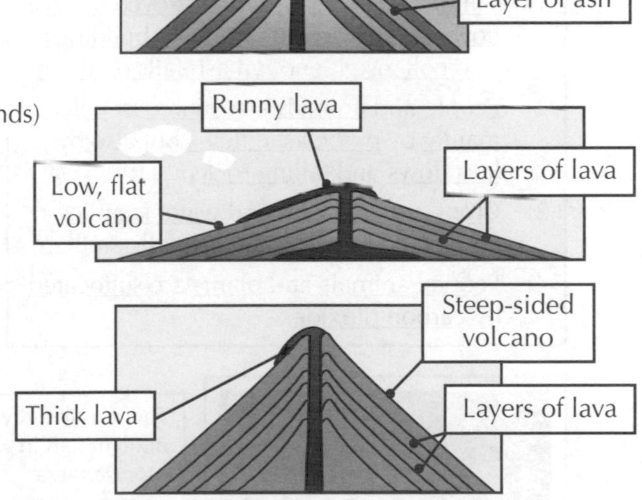

Volcanoes* and *Earthquakes* are *Tectonic Hazards

1) Tectonic hazards are natural hazards cause by the movement of tectonic plates.
2) A natural hazard is a naturally occurring event that has the potential to affect people's lives or property.
3) When natural hazards do affect people's lives or property they're called natural disasters.

How volcanoes form is a favourite topic in exams

It's a good idea to learn an example for each of the different types of volcano — examiners love real life stuff.
Also, you'll never have to draw a map like the one above, but you should have an idea of where volcanoes occur.

Impacts of Volcanoes

People living near a volcano can be seriously affected if it erupts, but plenty of people keep living near them.

Lots of People Live Close to Volcanoes

The reasons why people continue to live around volcanoes despite the hazards are exactly the same as why people keep living in areas prone to earthquakes (see page 5). But there are a few reasons why people choose to live close to volcanoes:

1) The soil around volcanoes is fertile because it's full of minerals from volcanic ash and lava. This makes it good for growing crops, which attracts farmers.
2) Volcanoes are tourist attractions — loads of tourists visit volcanoes so lots of people live around volcanoes to work in the tourist industry.
3) Volcanoes are a source of geothermal energy, which can be used to generate electricity. So people live around volcanoes to work at power stations.

Mount St. Helens (USA), Nevado del Ruiz (Colombia) and Mount Etna (Sicily) are volcanoes that have erupted recently.

Volcanic Eruptions have Primary and Secondary Impacts

The primary impacts of a volcanic eruption are the immediate effects of a volcano spewing out lava, ash, rocks and gas (e.g. carbon dioxide and sulphur dioxide), as well as pyroclastic flows. The secondary impacts are the effects that happen later on.

Pyroclastic flows are extremely fast moving flows of ash, rock and gas that move down the sides of a volcano.

Here are a few examples of the possible impacts:

Primary impacts

1) Buildings and roads are destroyed by lava flows and pyroclastic flows — buildings also collapse if enough ash falls on them.
2) People and animals are injured or killed, mainly by pyroclastic flows but also by lava flows and falling rocks.
3) Crops are damaged and water supplies are contaminated when ash falls on them.
4) People, animals and plants are suffocated by carbon dioxide.

BERNHARD EDMAIER / SCIENCE PHOTO LIBRARY

This was the city of Plymouth in Montserrat (a poorer country) — it was buried under ash and mud after a volcanic eruption in 1997.

Secondary impacts

1) Mudflows (also called lahars) form when volcanic material mixes with water, e.g. from heavy rainfall or snow melt. Mudflows cause loads more destruction, deaths and injuries.
2) Fires are started by lava flows and pyroclastic flows, which then spread.
3) People may suffer psychological problems if they knew people who died or if they lose their home etc.
4) People are left homeless.
5) There's a shortage of food because crops are damaged.
6) There's a shortage of clean water.
7) Roads are blocked or destroyed so aid and emergency vehicles can't get through.
8) Businesses are damaged or destroyed, causing unemployment.
9) Sulphur dioxide released into the atmosphere causes acid rain.

The impacts of volcanic eruptions are more severe in poorer countries than in richer countries for exactly the same reasons why earthquakes are more severe in poorer countries — have a look back at page 5.

Primary impacts are ones caused directly by the eruption

Secondary impacts are the ones that happen later on. Volcanic eruptions cause various nasty impacts and you should be clear on which are primary and which are secondary. Learn a few examples of each to dazzle the examiners.

Reducing the Impacts of Volcanoes

It's impossible to stop a volcano erupting, but there are ways to reduce the impacts.

There are **Many Ways** of **Reducing** the **Impacts** of **Volcanic Eruptions**

Prediction

1) Unlike earthquakes, it's possible to roughly predict when a volcanic eruption will happen. Scientists can monitor the tell-tale signs that come before a volcanic eruption.
2) Things such as tiny earthquakes, escaping gas, and changes in the shape of the volcano (e.g. bulges in the land where magma has built up under it) all mean an eruption is likely.
3) Predicting when a volcano is going to erupt gives people time to evacuate — this reduces the number of injuries and deaths.

Planning

1) Future developments, e.g. new houses, can be planned to avoid the areas most at risk from volcanic eruptions. This reduces the number of buildings destroyed by an eruption.
2) Firebreaks can be made to reduce the spread of fires.
3) Emergency services can train and prepare for disasters, e.g. by practising setting up emergency camps for homeless people. This reduces the number of people killed.
4) Governments can plan evacuation routes to get people away from the volcano quickly and safely. This reduces the number of people injured or killed by things like pyroclastic flows or mudflows.

Building techniques

1) Buildings can't be designed to withstand lava flows or pyroclastic flows, but they can be strengthened so they're less likely to collapse under the weight of falling ash.
2) The lava from some volcanoes can be diverted away from buildings using barriers.
3) Both of these reduce the number of buildings destroyed, so fewer people will be killed, injured, made homeless and made unemployed.

Education

1) Governments and other organisations can educate people about how to evacuate if a volcano erupts. This helps people get out of danger quickly and safely, which reduces deaths.
2) People can be told how to make a survival kit containing things like food, water, a torch, a radio, batteries and dust masks. The kits reduce the chance of people dying if they're stuck in the area.

Aid

1) Poorer countries that have been affected by a volcanic eruption can receive aid from governments or organisations — it can be things like food, water, money or people (e.g. doctors).
2) Aid helps to reduce the impacts, e.g. food aid stops people going hungry.

Some **Strategies** are **More Sustainable** than **Others**

There's a definition of a sustainable strategy on page 6. Have a read of this bit about the sustainability of strategies to reduce the impact of volcanic eruptions:

1) All of the strategies are sustainable because they're all effective and environmentally friendly.
2) Some are more cost-effective than others though, so are more sustainable.
3) Predicting eruptions needs special equipment and trained scientists, which makes it expensive, but if it's accurate it saves a lot of lives.
4) Building techniques can be very expensive, but can save money if they stop building destruction.

Predicting an eruption gives people time to evacuate

Getting people away from a volcano that's about to erupt really helps to save lives. It doesn't stop buildings being destroyed though, so a range of strategies is needed. Make sure you learn what they are and understand which are more sustainable.

Volcanic Eruption — Case Study

It's that time again, yep, case study time. Cram your memory full of these facts (the cause of the eruption, impacts and responses — don't think just learning the name and date will cut it).

The Soufrière Hills Volcano in Montserrat Erupted in 1997

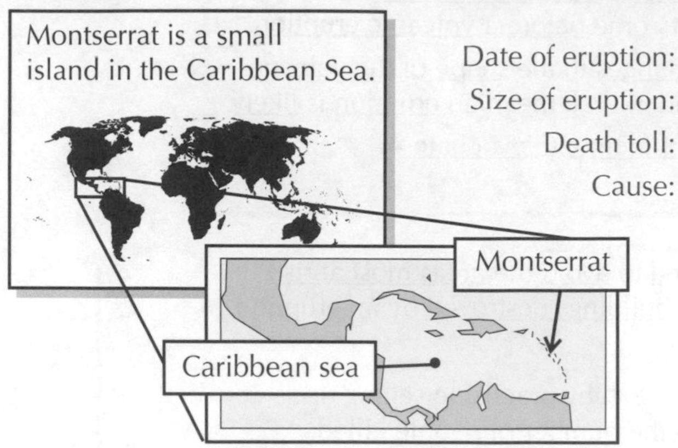

Montserrat is a small island in the Caribbean Sea.
Montserrat
Caribbean sea

Date of eruption: June 25th 1997 (small eruptions started in July 1995).
Size of eruption: Large — 4-5 million m^3 of rocks and gas released.
Death toll: 19 killed
Cause:
1) Montserrat is above a destructive plate margin, where the Atlantic plate is being forced under the Caribbean plate.
2) Magma rose up through weak points under the Soufrière hills forming an underground pool of magma.
3) The rock above the pool collapsed, opening a vent and causing the eruption.

There were Primary and Secondary Impacts

Primary impacts

1) Large areas were covered with volcanic material — the capital city Plymouth was buried under 12 m of mud and ash.
2) Over 20 villages and two thirds of homes on the island were destroyed by pyroclastic flows (fast-moving clouds of super-heated gas and ash).
3) Schools, hospitals, the airport and the port were destroyed.
4) Vegetation and farmland were destroyed.
5) 19 people died and 7 were injured.

Secondary impacts

1) Fires destroyed many buildings including local government offices, the police headquarters and the town's central petrol station.
2) Tourists stayed away and businesses were destroyed, disrupting the economy.
3) Population decline — 8000 of the island's 12 000 inhabitants have left since the eruptions began in 1995.
4) Volcanic ash from the eruption has improved soil fertility.
5) Tourism on the island is now increasing as people come to see the volcano.

Immediate responses

1) People were evacuated from the south to safe areas in the north.
2) Shelters were built to house evacuees.
3) Temporary infrastructure was also built, e.g. roads and electricity supplies.
4) The UK provided £17 million of emergency aid (Montserrat's an overseas territory of the UK).
5) Local emergency services provided support units to search for and rescue survivors.

Long-term responses

1) A risk map was created and an exclusion zone is in place. The south of the island is off-limits while the volcano is still active.
2) The UK has provided £41 million to develop the north of the island — new docks, an airport and houses have been built in the north.
3) The Montserrat Volcano Observatory has been set up to try and predict future eruptions.

Make sure you know at least two facts from each box on this page

The eruption on Montserrat wasn't all bad, well... it was mostly bad, but there were some positive impacts — the ash improved the soil fertility and lots of tourists now go to gawp at the volcano (which brings money into the area).

Supervolcanoes

Supervolcanoes — it's a brand new topic so an exam question's likely.

Supervolcanoes are Massive Volcanoes

Supervolcanoes are much bigger than standard volcanoes. They develop in a handful of places around the globe — at destructive plate margins or over parts of the mantle that are really hot (called hotspots), e.g. Yellowstone National Park in the USA is on top of a supervolcano. Here's how they form at a hotspot:

1) Magma rises up through cracks in the crust to form a large magma basin below the surface. The pressure of the magma causes a circular bulge on the surface several kilometres wide.
2) The bulge eventually cracks, creating vents for lava to escape through. The lava erupts out of the vents causing earthquakes and sending up gigantic plumes of ash and rock.
3) As the magma basin empties, the bulge is no longer supported so it collapses — spewing up more lava.
4) When the eruption's finished there's a big crater (called a caldera) left where the bulge collapsed. Sometimes these get filled with water to form a large lake, e.g. Lake Toba in Indonesia.

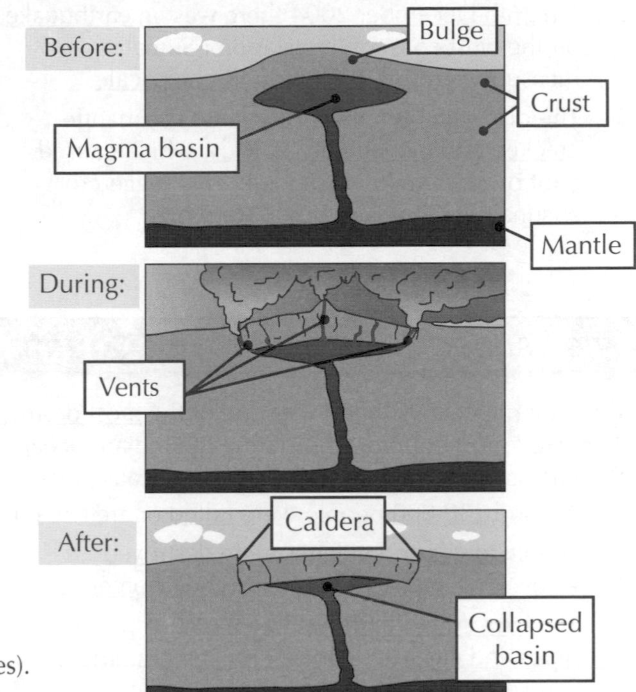

You need to know the characteristics of a supervolcano:

- Flat (unlike normal volcanoes, which are mountains).
- Cover a large area (much bigger than normal volcanoes).
- Have a caldera (unlike normal volcanoes where there's just a crater at the top).

When a Supervolcano Erupts there will be Global Consequences

Fortunately there are only a few supervolcanoes and an eruption hasn't happened for tens of thousands of years, e.g. the last one to erupt was the Lake Toba supervolcano 74 000 years ago. When there is an eruption though, it's predicted that an enormous area will be affected:

The predicted plume of ash from a supervolcanic eruption in Yellowstone National Park.

1) A supervolcanic eruption will throw out thousands of cubic kilometres of rock, ash and lava (much more than normal volcanoes, which usually produce a couple of cubic kilometres).
2) A thick cloud of super-heated gas and ash will flow at high speed from the volcano, killing, burning and burying everything it touches. Everything within tens of miles will be destroyed.
3) Ash will shoot kilometres into the air and block out almost all daylight over whole continents. This can trigger mini ice ages as less heat energy from the sun gets to Earth.
4) The ash will also settle over hundreds of square kilometres, burying fields and buildings (ash from normal volcanoes usually covers a couple of square kilometres).

Supervolcanic eruptions have huge impacts

Supervolcanoes are very different beasts from dome or shield volcanoes. They form in a slightly different way and have way bigger impacts. Oh, and you may want to reconsider your decision to move to Yellowstone National Park.

Tsunamis — Case Study

As if volcanoes and earthquakes weren't bad enough, if they happen out at sea they can cause tsunamis.
A tsunami is a series of enormous waves caused when huge amounts of water get displaced.

An **Earthquake** caused a **Tsunami** in the **Indian Ocean** in **2004**

1) There's a destructive plate margin along the west coast of Indonesia in the Indian Ocean.
2) On 26th December 2004 there was an earthquake off the west coast of the island of Sumatra measuring around 9.1 on the Richter scale.
3) The plate that's moving down into the mantle cracked and moved very quickly, which caused a lot of water to be displaced. This triggered a tsunami with waves up to 30 m high.

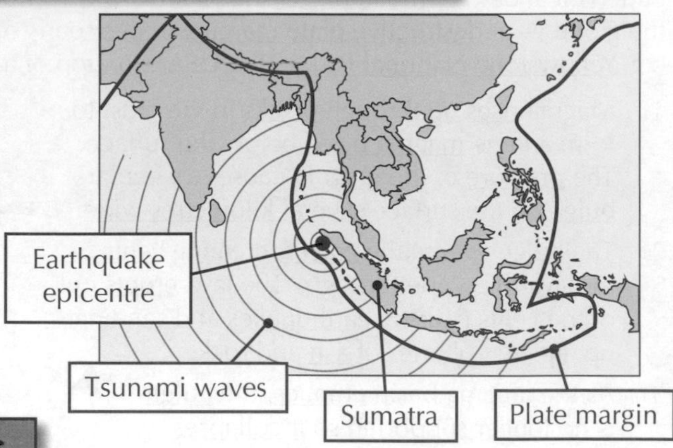

The Tsunami **Affected Many Countries**

The Indian Ocean tsunami was one of the most destructive natural disasters that's ever happened.
It affected most countries bordering the Indian Ocean, e.g. Indonesia, Thailand, India and Sri Lanka.
The effects of the tsunami were so bad because there was no early warning system:

1) Around 230 000 people were killed or are still missing.
2) Whole towns and villages were destroyed — over 1.7 million people lost their homes.
3) The infrastructure (things like the roads, water pipes and electricity lines) of many countries was severely damaged.
4) 5-6 million people needed emergency food, water and medical supplies.
5) There was massive economic damage. Millions of fishermen lost their livelihoods, and the tourism industry suffered because of the destruction and because people were afraid to go on holiday there.
6) There was massive environmental damage. Salt from the seawater has meant plants can't grow in many areas. Mangroves, coral reefs, forests and sand dunes were also destroyed by the waves.

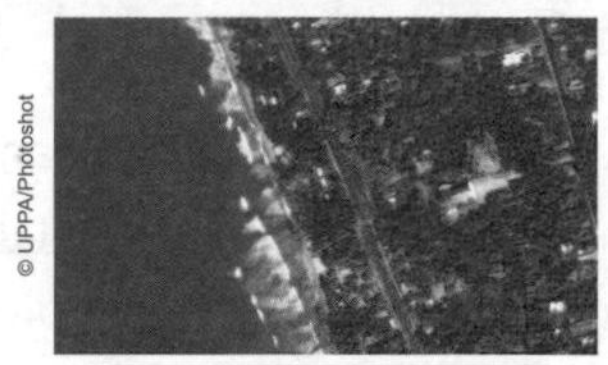

Sri Lankan coastline before the tsunami

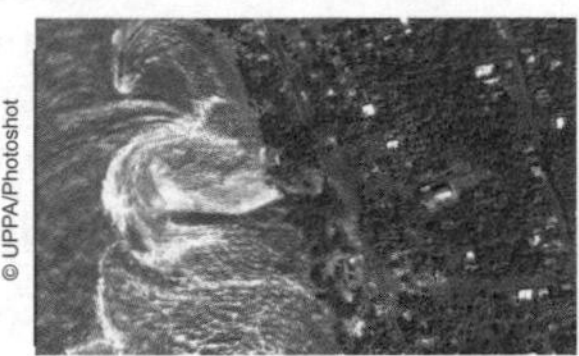

Sri Lankan coastline during the tsunami

The **Response** Involved a lot of **International Aid**

Short-term responses:

1) Within days hundreds of millions of pounds had been pledged by foreign governments, charities, individuals and businesses to give survivors access to food, water, shelter and medical attention.
2) Foreign countries sent ships, planes, soldiers and teams of specialists to help rescue people, distribute food and water and begin clearing up.

Long-term responses:

1) Billions of pounds have been pledged to help re-build the infrastructure of the countries affected.
2) As well as money, programmes have been set up to re-build houses and help people get back to work.
3) A tsunami warning system has been put in place in the Indian Ocean.
4) Disaster management plans have been put in place in some countries. Volunteers have been trained so that local people know what to do if a tsunami happens again.

A tsunami is a series of large waves

Tsunamis can wreak as much havoc as the earthquakes or volcanoes that cause them. Some tsunamis are tiny and only affect short bits of coastline, but others (like the Indian Ocean one above) affect huge areas, causing huge impacts.

Worked Exam Questions

Wow, an exam question — with the answers helpfully written in. It must be your birthday.

1 Study **Figure 1**, which shows the Earth's tectonic plates and the distribution of volcanoes.

Figure 1

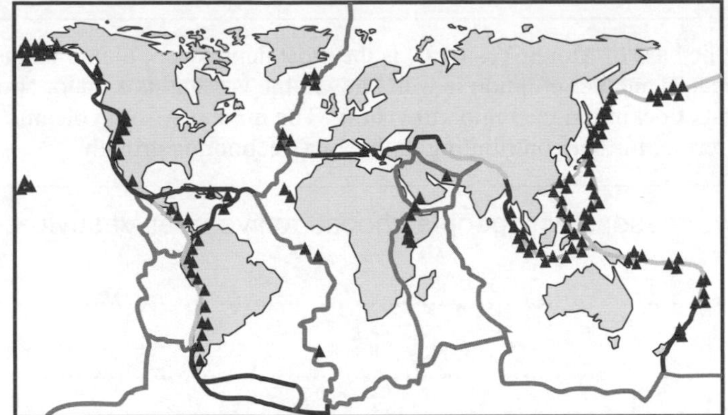

Key

Volcanoes

Destructive plate margin

Constructive plate margin

Conservative plate margin

(a) Describe and explain the global distribution of volcanoes.

When describing the distribution of something talk about the general pattern and any anomalies.

Volcanoes are found along constructive plate margins and destructive plate margins. Some are also found away from plate margins, e.g. in Hawaii. They're found at constructive plate margins because magma rises up into the gap created by the plates moving apart, forming a volcano. They're found at destructive plate margins because as the oceanic plate moves down into the mantle it melts and a pool of magma forms. The magma rises through cracks in the crust and erupts onto the surface. Volcanoes are found in places like Hawaii because they're over hotspots (really hot parts of the mantle).

(6 marks)

(b) Contrast the characteristics of shield volcanoes and composite volcanoes.

'Contrast' means write about the differences.

Shield volcanoes are low and flat, whereas composite volcanoes are steep sided. Composite volcanoes are made of layers of lava and ash, whereas shield volcanoes are made of layers of lava only. The lava that comes out of shield volcanoes is runny, whereas the lava that comes out of composite volcanoes is thick. Ash is released from composite volcanoes, but not from shield volcanoes.

(4 marks)

(c) Suggest two ways in which the effects of supervolcanoes are different from volcanoes.

Try to include specific facts where you can, e.g. the area that ash will settle over.

A supervolcano will produce far more ash, rock and lava than a volcano (thousands of cubic metres compared to a few). Ash from a supervolcanic eruption will settle over a much larger area than ash from a normal volcano (hundreds of square kilometres compared to a couple).

(2 marks)

Exam Questions

1 Study **Figure 1**, an extract from an article about Mount Vesuvius in Italy.

Figure 1

The Bay of Naples, located at the base of Mount Vesuvius, is the most densely populated volcanic region in the world. Although the threat of another eruption is well known, the volcano is a major source of income for the area, with tourists flocking to the region to visit it. The minerals from volcanic ash and lava make the land extremely fertile, further contributing to the area's economic growth.

(a) Using **Figure 1**, give two reasons why people choose to live near Vesuvius.

....

....

(2 marks)

(b) Describe three primary impacts that an eruption of Mount Vesuvius could have on Naples.

....

....

....

(3 marks)

(c) Scientists monitor tiny earthquakes on Mount Vesuvius to try to predict when the volcano will erupt next. Suggest one other way that scientists could monitor a volcano to predict when it will erupt.

....

(1 mark)

(d) Is prediction a sustainable strategy for reducing the impacts of volcanoes? Explain your answer.

....

....

(2 marks)

(e) For a volcanic eruption you have studied, describe the cause and the primary and secondary impacts.

....

....

....

....

....

....

....

(8 marks)

Revision Summary for Section 1

This section may be filled with disasters, but if you've taken it all in there won't be any kind of disaster in the exam. I know it looks like there's a lot of questions here, but you'll be surprised how much you just learnt. Try them out a few at a time, then check the answers on the pages.

1) Describe the Earth's internal structure.
2) Name the type of plate margin where two plates are moving towards each other.
3) What is an ocean trench?
4) Name the type of plate margin where two plates are moving sideways against each other.
5) Give three ways that humans use fold mountain areas.
6) a) Name one range of fold mountains.
   b) Describe three ways humans use the area.
   c) Describe how people have adapted to the conditions of the area.
7) What causes earthquakes?
8) What's the point in the Earth called where an earthquake starts?
9) What does the Mercalli scale measure?
10) What is the difference between the primary impacts and the secondary impacts of an earthquake?
11) Give three examples of a primary impact of an earthquake.
12) Describe one way buildings can be designed to withstand an earthquake.
13) Describe one way that planning can reduce the impacts of earthquakes.
14) Describe how education can reduce the impacts of earthquakes.
15) Why is prediction not a sustainable strategy for reducing the impacts of an earthquake?
16) a) Name a richer country and a poorer country where an earthquake caused a disaster.
   b) Describe two primary impacts and two secondary impacts of each disaster.
   c) Describe two responses to each earthquake.
17) Name the two types of plate margin that volcanoes are found at.
18) Which type of volcano is made up of layers of ash and lava? Name an example.
19) Which type of volcano is formed when the lava is runny? Name an example.
20) Give three examples of a secondary impact of a volcanic eruption.
21) How do scientists try to predict volcanic eruptions?
22) Describe two planning strategies that reduce the impact of a volcanic eruption.
23) a) Name a volcanic eruption and state when and where it happened.
   b) Describe two negative primary and two negative secondary impacts of the eruption.
   c) Give two positive impacts of the eruption.
   d) Give two immediate responses and two long-term responses.
24) Where do supervolcanoes form?
25) Give one way that a supervolcano is different from a normal volcano.
26) Give one predicted effect of a supervolcanic eruption.
27) What causes a tsunami?
28) Give an example of a tsunami and describe two of its effects.

Types of Rock

There are three types of rock — igneous, sedimentary and metamorphic.
Rock type depends on how the rock was formed.

Igneous Rocks are Formed from Magma that's Cooled Down

All igneous rocks are formed when molten rock (magma) from the mantle cools down and hardens.
There are two types depending on where the magma has cooled down:

The mantle is a layer of molten rock deep in the Earth.

1 INTRUSIVE igneous rocks, e.g. granite

1) These form when magma cools down below the Earth's surface.
2) The magma cools down very slowly, forming large crystals that give the rocks a coarse texture.
3) Large domes of cooled magma form domes of igneous rock called batholiths.
4) Where the magma has flowed into gaps in the surrounding rock it forms dykes (in vertical gaps) and sills (in horizontal gaps).

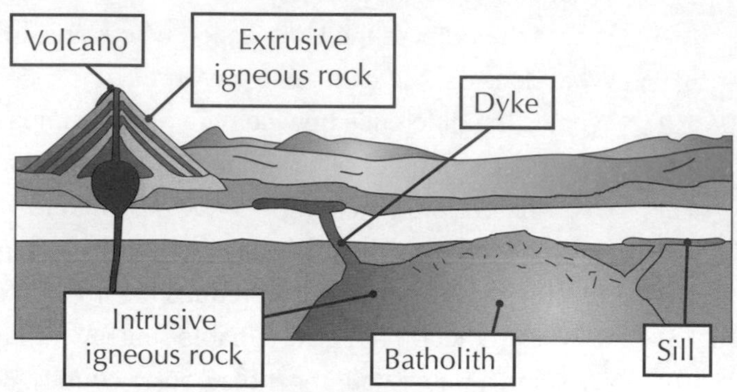

2 EXTRUSIVE igneous rocks, e.g. basalt

1) These form when magma cools down after it's erupted from a volcano onto the Earth's surface.
2) The magma cools down very quickly, forming small crystals that give the rocks a fine texture.

Sedimentary Rocks are Formed from Compacted Sediment

Sedimentary rocks are formed when layers of sediment are compacted together until they become solid rock.
The process of compaction is called lithification. Here are a couple of examples:

1) Carboniferous limestone and chalk are formed from calcium carbonate. Layers of tiny shells and skeletons of dead sea creatures are deposited on the sea bed and compacted together over time.
2) Clays and shales are made from mud and clay minerals. The particles have been eroded from older rocks, deposited in layers on lake or sea beds then compacted together.

Sedimentary rocks often contain fossils.

Metamorphic Rocks are Formed by Heat and Pressure

Metamorphic rocks are formed when other rocks (igneous, sedimentary or older metamorphic rocks) are changed by heat and pressure:

1) Rocks deep in the Earth are changed by the pressure from the weight of the material above them.
2) When tectonic plates collide, rocks are changed by the massive heat and pressure that builds up.
3) Magma from the mantle heats the rocks in the crust, causing them to change.

The new rocks are harder and more compact, e.g. limestone becomes marble and clay becomes slate.

This map shows the location of the three rock types in the UK.

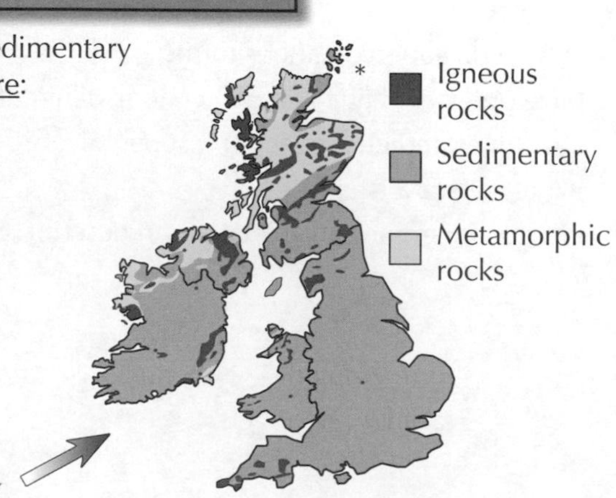

It's easy to get the different rock types mixed up, so be careful

Use the names to help you remember how they're formed — sedimentary is from sediment, metamorphic is rock that's morphed (changed) and igneous is, well, the other one. It's a good idea to know an example for each type too.

The Rock Cycle

You might think once a rock exists then that's it — but they can change from one type into another.

*The **Formation** of all **Rock Types** is **Linked** by the **Rock Cycle***

The rock cycle shows how igneous, sedimentary and metamorphic rocks are formed, and how one type is changed into another:

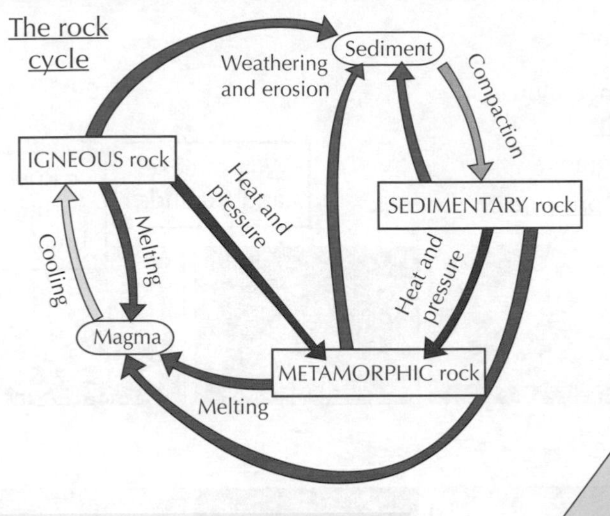

1) Weathering (the breakdown of rocks) of all three rock types creates loose sediment.
2) This makes it easier for erosion (the removal of rock) to occur.
3) The sediment is transported away (e.g. by rivers) and deposited on the sea bed.
4) Sediment is compacted on the sea bed through lithification to form sedimentary rocks.

The rock cycle in a landscape

Erosion and transport
Sediment
Deposition and compaction
Weathering
IGNEOUS rock
SEDIMENTARY rock
Cooling
Heat and pressure
Magma
METAMORPHIC rock
Melting

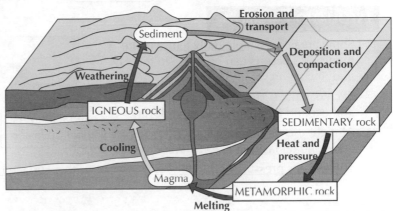

5) Heat and pressure (e.g. from overlying layers of rock) can change any rock type to new metamorphic rock.
6) Melting of any rock type (e.g. in the mantle) creates magma. When magma cools, igneous rocks are formed.

*Geological **Time** is on a much **Larger Scale** than **Human Time***

Geological period	Began, million years before present
Quaternary	2.6
Tertiary	65
Cretaceous	145
Jurassic	215
Triassic	245
Permian	285
Carboniferous	360
Devonian	410
Silurian	440
Ordovician	505
Cambrian	585

Humans evolved

Chalk formed in the UK

Clay formed in the UK

Carboniferous limestone formed in the UK

Granite formed in the UK

These are the major periods when each of these rocks formed — some of them formed at other times too.

It takes a very long time for rocks to form and go through the rock cycle.

1) The table on the left shows all the most recent geological periods (you don't need to learn their names).
2) The rocks found in the UK today were all formed many millions of years ago.
3) Humans (Homo sapiens) have only been around for the last 200 000 years, so the rock cycle is on a totally different time scale to human time.

Check that you know how rocks change

The rock cycle can look quite confusing the first time you come across it, but just take it one step at a time and you'll be fine. Before you move on, make sure you can draw it and explain how one rock type can be changed into another.

Weathering

Weathering is the breakdown of rocks where they are (the material created doesn't get taken away like with erosion). There are three types — mechanical, chemical and biological.

Mechanical Weathering — Rocks are Broken Down by Physical Processes

Mechanical weathering is the breakdown of rocks without changing their chemical composition.
Here are two types of mechanical weathering:

FREEZE-THAW weathering

1) In some areas (e.g. upland Britain in winter), the temperature is above 0 °C during the day, and below 0 °C at night.
2) During the day, water gets into cracks in rocks, e.g. granite.
3) At night, the water freezes and expands, which puts pressure on the rock.
4) The water thaws the next day, releasing the pressure, then refreezes the next night.
5) Repeated freezing and thawing widens the cracks and causes the rock to break up.

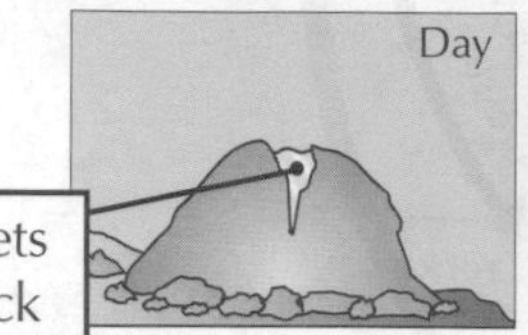
Day
Water gets into crack

Night
Water freezes and expands

Rock eventually breaks up

EXFOLIATION weathering

1) Some areas have a big daily temperature range, e.g. deserts can be 40 °C in the day and 5 °C at night.
2) Each day the surface layers of rock heat up and expand faster than the inner layers.
3) At night the surface layers cool down and contract faster than the inner layers.
4) This creates pressure within the rock and causes thin surface layers to peel off.

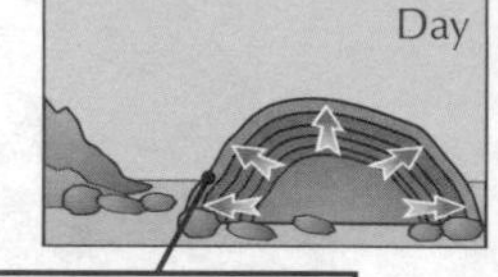
Day
Surface layers heat up faster

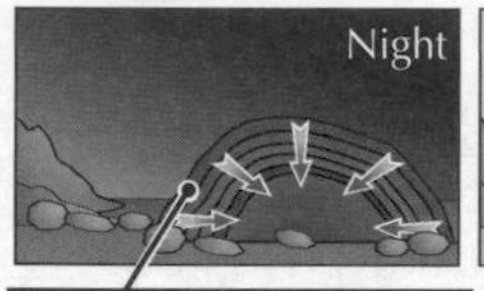
Night
Surface layers cool down faster

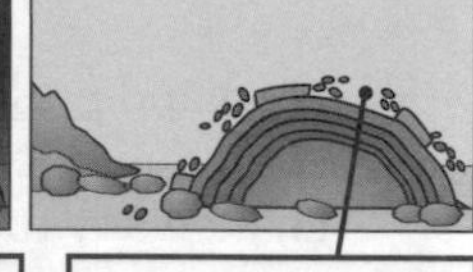
Surface layers peel off

Exfoliation is also known as onion skin weathering.

Chemical Weathering — Rocks are Broken Down by Being Dissolved

Chemical weathering is the breakdown of rocks by changing their chemical composition.
Here are two types of chemical weathering:

SOLUTION weathering

1) Some minerals that make up rocks are soluble in water, e.g. rock salt.
2) The minerals dissolve in rainwater, breaking the rock down.

CARBONATION weathering

1) Rainwater has carbon dioxide dissolved in it, which makes it a weak carbonic acid.
2) Carbonic acid reacts with rocks that contain calcium carbonate, e.g. carboniferous limestone, so the rocks are dissolved by the rainwater.

Biological Weathering — Rocks are Broken Down by Plants and Animals

Biological weathering is the breakdown of rocks by living things:

1) Plant roots break down rocks by growing into cracks on their surfaces and pushing them apart.
2) Burrowing animals may loosen small amounts of rock material.

Learn the difference between mechanical, chemical and biological weathering

You could also be asked about the different types of mechanical and chemical weathering, so cover the page and check you know the details. Also, freeze-thaw weathering crops up in other topics so it's well worth learning it properly.

Rocks and Landscapes

The type of rock in an area affects the type of landscape that forms.

Granite Landscapes have Tors and Moorland

1) Granite has lots of joints (cracks) which aren't evenly spread (they're closer together in some bits).

2) Freeze-thaw and chemical weathering wear down the parts of the rock with lots of joints faster because there are more cracks for water to get into.

3) Sections of granite that have fewer joints are weathered more slowly than the surrounding rock and stick out at the surface forming tors, e.g. Bowerman's Nose.

4) Granite is also impermeable — it doesn't let water through.

5) This creates moorlands — large areas of waterlogged and acidic soil, with low-growing vegetation.

Bowerman's Nose

Chalk and Clay Landscapes have Escarpments and Vales

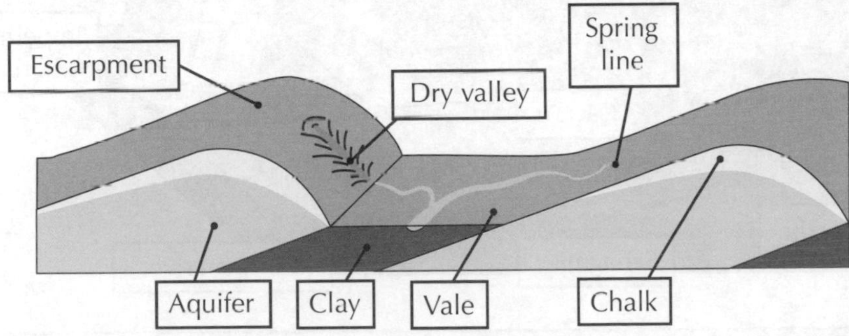

Escarpments are also called cuestas.

1) Horizontal layers of chalk and clay are sometimes tilted diagonally by earth movements.
2) The clay is less resistant than the chalk so is eroded faster.
3) The chalk is left sticking out forming escarpments (hills). Where the clay has been eroded it forms vales — wide areas of flat land.
4) Escarpments have steep slopes (called a scarp slope) on one end, and gentle slopes (dip slope) on the other.
5) Chalk is an aquifer — a permeable rock that stores water.
6) Water flows through the chalk and emerges where the chalk meets impermeable rock (e.g. clay). Where the water emerges is called a spring line.
7) Areas of chalk can also have dry valleys — valleys that don't have a river or stream flowing in them because the water is flowing underground.

The type of landscape depends on the permeability and resistance of the rock

There's a fair bit to learn on this page, I'll grant you that, but it's all pretty straightforward stuff. Scribble down the diagram and label it, then turn over the page for another type of landscape.

Rocks and Landscapes

Here's another type of landscape — this one is found in limestone areas.

Carboniferous Limestone forms **Surface** and **Underground** Features

Rainwater slowly eats away at carboniferous limestone through carbonation weathering (see page 22). Most weathering happens along joints in the rock, creating some spectacular features:

1) Limestone pavements are flat areas of limestone with blocks separated by weathered-down joints.

2) Swallow holes are weathered holes in the surface.

3) Caverns form beneath swallow holes where the limestone has been deeply weathered.

A limestone pavement

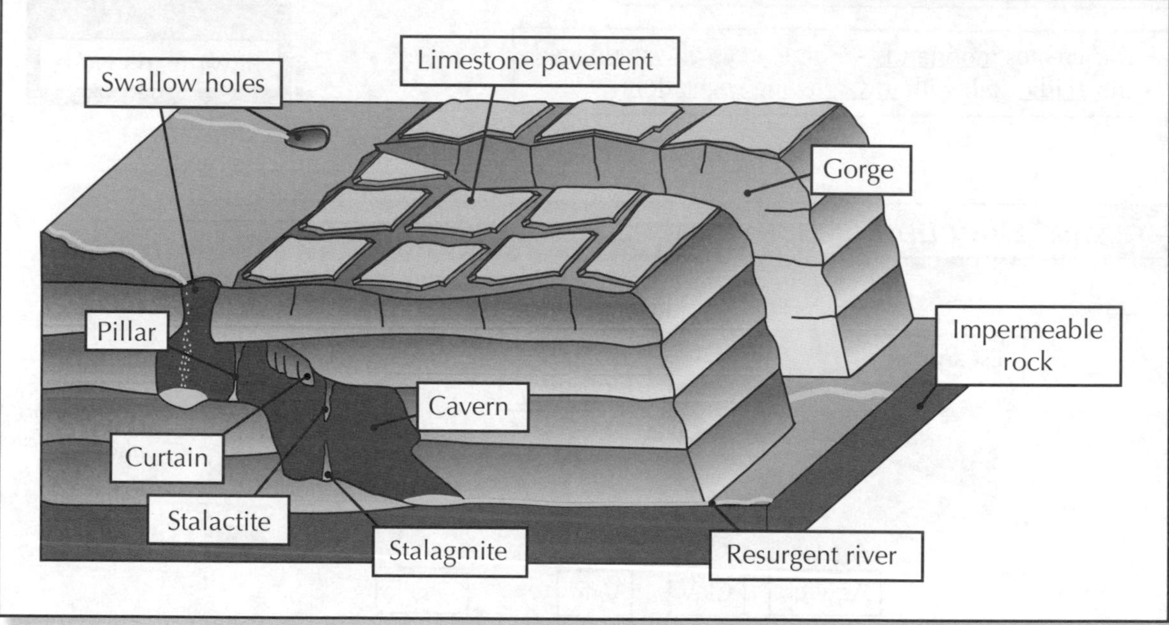

4) Limestone gorges are steep sided gorges formed when caverns collapse.

5) Limestone is permeable, so limestone areas also have dry valleys and resurgent rivers (rivers that pop out at the surface when limestone is on top of impermeable rock).

6) Water seeping through limestone contains dissolved minerals. When the water drips into a cavern the minerals solidify and build up over time to produce stalactites (on the ceiling) and stalagmites (on the ground).

7) When stalagmites and stalactites meet in the middle they form a pillar. When water flows in as a sheet a curtain builds up.

Learn what goes on above and below the ground

This is the third type of landscape for you to learn. Make sure you can draw a simple version of the diagram and explain how all the features form. Don't forget that stalactites hang from the ceilings of caves, like tights on a washing line.

Using Landscapes — Case Studies

Find out here how people use rock landscapes for resources, farming, tourism and water supplies.

Granite Areas are *Used* for *Stone, Tourism, Farming* and *Water*

1) Granite is quarried and used as a building stone for things like flooring and worktops.
2) Tourists are attracted to the features of granite landscapes, e.g. tors and moorland (see page 23).
3) There are opportunities for rearing livestock on granite areas, but the land isn't great for arable farming (growing crops) or dairy farming because the soils are acidic and waterlogged.
4) Granite's impermeable so granite areas are good places to build reservoirs.

Case Study — Dartmoor, Devon

1) Dartmoor has lots of granite quarries, e.g. Meldon Quarry. Granite from Dartmoor was used to build Nelson's Column.
2) Millions of people visit Dartmoor every year to enjoy the features of the granite landscape, e.g. Bowerman's Nose and Hound Tor are popular attractions.
3) In 2000, there were over 290 000 hectares of land used for rearing livestock (only 900 hectares of land were used for arable farming).
4) There are 8 reservoirs in Dartmoor, e.g. Burrator Reservoir supplies water to Plymouth.

Chalk and *Clay Areas* are *Used* for *Cement, Tourism, Farming* and *Water*

1) Chalk is quarried and used to make cement, which is then used to make building materials like concrete.
2) Tourists are attracted to the features of chalk and clay landscapes, e.g. escarpments and vales (see page 23).
3) There are opportunities for arable farming, livestock rearing and dairy farming on chalk and clay areas (clay vales are wide, flat, grassy areas).
4) Chalk is an aquifer — a permeable rock that holds water.
5) Aquifers are often used as a source of drinking water — water is taken out through wells and is also pumped out of the rocks.

Case Study — The Lincolnshire Wolds, Lincolnshire

1) In 2001, 438 000 tonnes of chalk were quarried from Lincolnshire.
2) The Wolds are an Area of Outstanding Natural Beauty — many tourists come to the Wolds for the scenery and activities like walking, e.g. along the Viking Way (a long-distance footpath).
3) Around 80% of the Wolds is used as farmland to grow crops.
4) There's a major chalk aquifer underneath the Wolds — it supplies water to Lincolnshire.

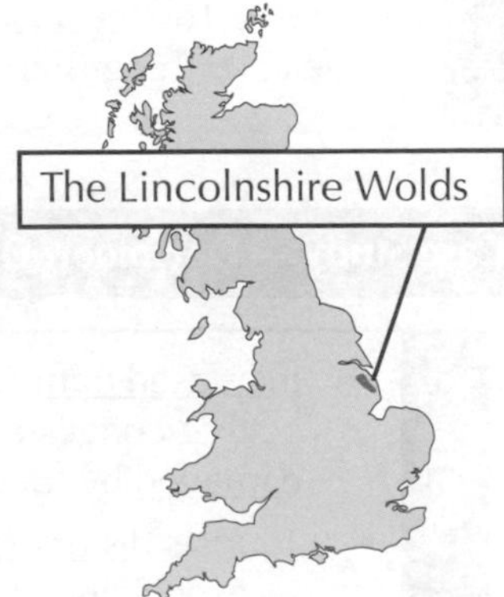

Granite — bad for crops, good for stylish kitchens...

Learning plenty of details of case studies will be really helpful in the exam. Examiners like you to refer to real-life examples, so make sure you remember some juicy facts and figures for each one.

Using Landscapes — Case Studies

Don't worry if you're getting a little bit rocked out, you're halfway through this section now. There's just limestone area uses, a bit of tourism and some quarrying to go.

Limestone Areas are Used for Stone, Cement, Tourism and Farming

1) Limestone is quarried and used as a building stone to make things like floors and walls, e.g. in churches.
2) Limestone is also used to make cement.
3) Tourists are attracted to the features of limestone landscapes, e.g. limestone pavements, gorges and caverns (see page 24).
4) There are opportunities for dairy farming or rearing livestock on limestone areas. There are also opportunities for arable farming (growing crops), but in some places the soil is quite alkaline.

Case Study — The White Peak, Peak District

1) Tunstead Quarry near Buxton produces about 5.5 million tonnes of limestone every year.
2) The cement processing plant inside Tunstead Quarry makes about 800 000 tonnes of cement each year.
3) Thor's Cave is a limestone cavern in the Manifold Valley, Staffordshire — it's popular with cavers, walkers and climbers.
4) The White Peak is mainly used for intensive dairy farming.

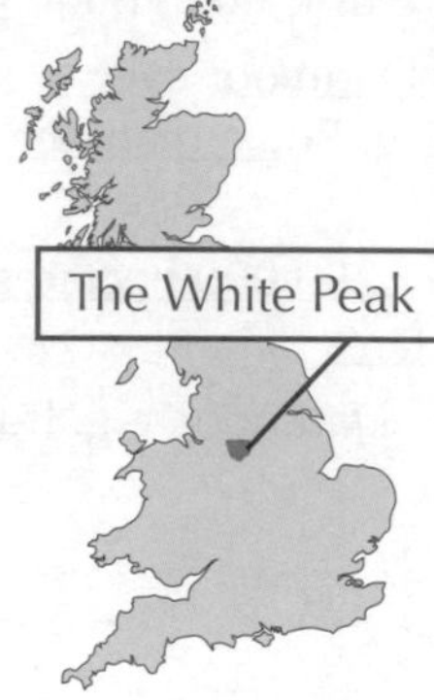

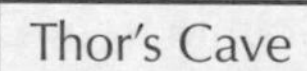

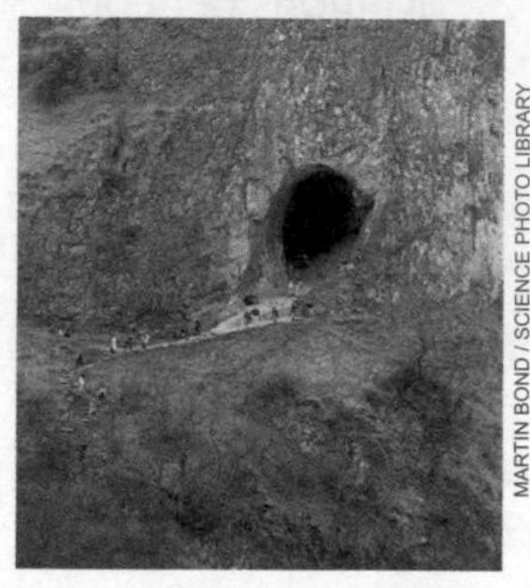

Tourism in Any Area has Costs and Benefits

COSTS

- Large numbers of people can cause footpath erosion and littering around attractions.
- Lots of tourists cause traffic congestion.
- People may be attracted into the tourist industry from jobs like farming, causing a decline in traditional jobs.
- Many tourists own second homes in rural areas. They're absent through most of the year, so things like local shops close down.

BENEFITS

- Tourism creates jobs and brings money into the local economy.
- Farmers can diversify their business to get extra income from tourism, e.g. using buildings for camping barns or running bed and breakfasts.
- New businesses may be set up in the area to cater for the tourists, e.g. souvenir shops or hotels.

Case Study — Dartmoor, Devon

COSTS

- Increased traffic means the narrow roads are getting congested. Grass verges are being damaged by tourists parking on them.
- Tourists disturb grazing animals on the moor — especially when dogs are let loose.

BENEFITS

- 4.5 million tourists visit Dartmoor every year. This creates around 3000 jobs.
- In 2003 tourism generated £120 million for the local economy.

Tourism can be both good and bad

Make sure you can write about the costs and benefits of tourism. Don't just learn the general points though — check you know some specific facts so you'll have plenty to say if you get a case study question on it.

Quarrying Impacts — Case Study

Quarrying supplies us with stone for loads of different uses, but it has a big impact on the environment.

Quarries Have Advantages and Disadvantages

A quarry is basically a massive pit in the ground that rock is taken from. Quarries bring advantages to some people and disadvantages to other people. This means people disagree about things like where they should go, or if we should have them at all. Here's a table so you can see both sides of the story:

	Advantages	Disadvantages
Economic	Quarries employ lots of local people — this brings more money into the local economy.	Tourists could be put off from visiting an area that has a quarry because they're noisy and they're an eyesore — this reduces the amount of money made from tourism.
Economic	When a quarry's built, good transport links are also built for the trucks that carry the stone — an improved infrastructure will attract other businesses and boost the local economy.	When a quarry is closed down it costs money to make them safe, e.g. by filling in holes and putting up warning signs.
Social	Some quarries are used by schools and colleges for educational visits.	People are annoyed by the heavy traffic caused by slow vehicles leaving quarries.
Social	Quarries that have been closed down can be used for recreation, e.g. for climbing.	Quarries are a very dangerous environment — people could be harmed or killed in them.
Environmental	The landscape is often restored after quarries are closed down — this can create new habitats and attract new species of wildlife to an area.	While they're operating the quarries have a massive impact on the environment — habitats are destroyed and the resources in the landscape are depleted.

Whatley Quarry is a Limestone Quarry in Somerset

Whatley Quarry is one of the largest quarries in the UK. It produces around 5 million tonnes of rock every year. Have a look at the economic, social and environmental advantages and disadvantages of Whatley Quarry:

Advantages

Economic

The quarry employs a lot of people — around 100 people work at the quarry full-time.

Social

1) The quarry has a study centre — around 4000 people from schools and colleges visit every year.
2) The quarry has donated stone to build a cycle track in the local area.

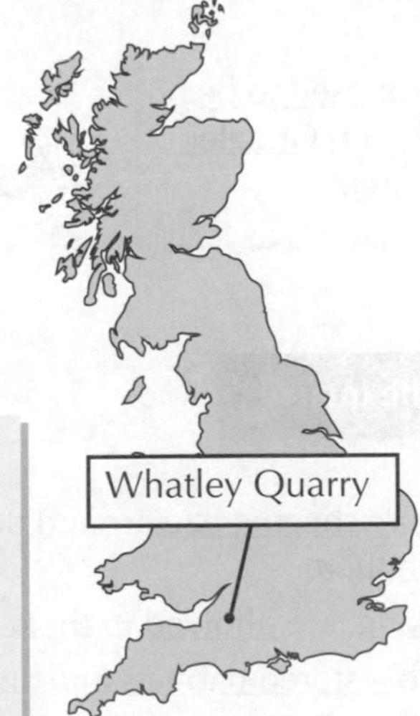

Disadvantages

Environmental

1) Each blast removes around 25 000 tonnes of rock from the quarry — this creates a lot of noise and disrupts wildlife.
2) The quarry is around 1.5 km long and 0.6 km wide — it's destroyed a large area of habitat.

Social

A man was killed in an industrial accident at the quarry in 2008.

Don't dig yourself into a hole with this lot...

Plenty of advantages and disadvantages to learn here — don't skimp on them though and learn just one or two. If you get a question on this in the exam you might have to write about both sides of the story in detail.

Quarrying Management — Case Study

This is another quarry case study, but it's different to the one on the previous page — this time it's about sustainable management...

The Sustainable Management of Quarries is Important

1) Sustainable management is all about meeting the needs of people today, without hindering the ability of people in the future to meet their own needs.
2) It involves getting what we want without damaging or altering the environment in an irreversible way.
3) Quarries need sustainable management because they could seriously damage the environment, e.g. by destroying habitats and local wildlife.

Llynclys Quarry is a Limestone Quarry in Shropshire

Llynclys Quarry is a quarry in Shropshire that covers 65 hectares of land. Some quarries are abandoned when the resources are exhausted, but Llynclys Quarry is being sustainably managed in areas where extraction has finished. This minimises the environmental impact of the quarry.

Here are some of the sustainable management strategies being used:

Sustainable management strategies

1) Areas of the quarry where work has finished are being restored to the grassland, shrubland and woodland habitats that used to exist before quarrying started. About 14% of the quarry has been restored so far.

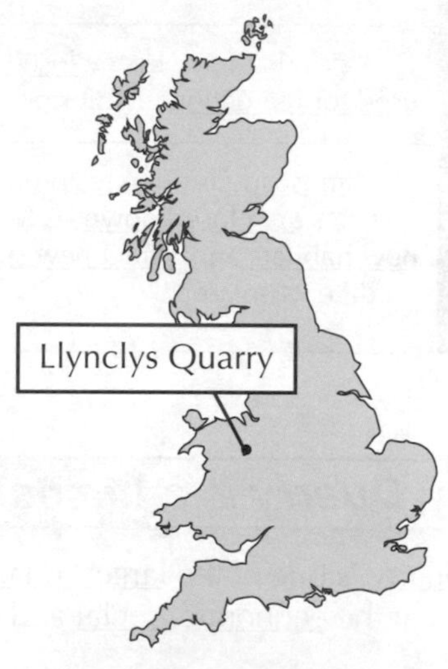

2) A wetland habitat has been created at the quarry. This encourages lots of different species to live in the area, e.g. the insects living in the wetland are a food supply for bats.

3) The habitats are attracting animals that used to be in the area before it was a quarry, e.g. the Grizzled Skipper butterfly has returned to the area.

New land uses in restored parts of the quarry

1) Some parts are used for farming — sheep graze around the wetland, which also controls the growth of vegetation there.
2) Recreational activities, e.g. walking, are allowed in the restored parts of the quarry.
3) Tourism has been boosted — the restored habitats and an annual open day are attracting a lot of visitors to the quarry.

Sustainable management of quarries involves reducing their environmental impacts

The hardest thing about the Llynclys Quarry case study is saying the quarry's name, so you don't have any excuse for not getting to grips with the different sustainable management strategies used there.

Worked Exam Questions

Exam questions are the best way to practise what you've learnt. After all, they're exactly what you'll have to do on the big day — so work through this worked example very carefully.

1 Limestone is a sedimentary rock, which forms as part of the rock cycle. Study **Figure 1**, which shows the rock cycle.

Figure 1

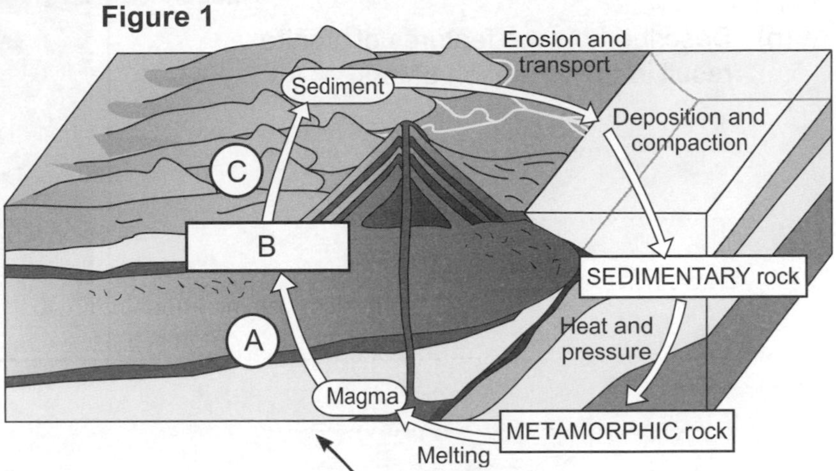

The rock cycle can be shown in lots of different ways so it might not look like this in your exam.

(a) Process A acting on magma creates rock type B. Name the process labelled A and the rock type labelled B in **Figure 1**.

A: cooling

B: igneous rock

(2 marks)

(b) How are rocks such as limestone broken down by biological weathering?

Biological weathering is the breakdown of rocks by living things, e.g. plant roots can break down rocks by growing into cracks on their surfaces and pushing them apart and burrowing animals can also loosen small amounts of rock material.

This question is worth three marks, so put some examples in your answer.

(3 marks)

(c) Describe the formation of stalactites and stalagmites in limestone areas.

Water that drips into limestone caverns contains dissolved minerals. The minerals solidify and build up over time to produce stalactites (on the ceiling) and stalagmites (on the ground).

(2 marks)

(d) Tourists are attracted to the scenic landscapes in limestone areas. Describe the costs and benefits of tourism in such areas.

One of the benefits of tourism is that it creates jobs, bringing money into the local economy. New businesses may be set up in the area to cater for tourists, e.g. souvenir shops or hotels. Farmers in the area can diversify their business to get extra income from tourism, e.g. camping barns. However, new jobs in the tourism industry can attract people away from traditional jobs like farming, causing them to decline. Also, lots of tourists cause traffic congestion and large numbers of people can cause footpath erosion and littering around attractions.

(6 marks)

The question's just asking you to describe, so all you need to do is say what the costs and benefits of tourism are. It's worth six marks though, so you need to describe several different impacts. Make sure you talk about both the costs and the benefits.

Exam Questions

2 Study **Figure 2**, which is a photograph of a granite landscape.

(a) Label **Figure 2** to show the characteristics of the landscape.

(3 marks)

Figure 2

©iStockphoto.com/Lachlan Currie

(b) Describe how the features of granite result in the formation of tors.

....

....

....

....

....

....

....

....

....

(6 marks)

(c) Granite areas are used for quarrying.

(i) Describe other ways that granite landscapes can be used.

....

....

....

(3 marks)

(ii) Describe the economic, social and environmental advantages and disadvantages of a quarry that you have studied.

....

....

....

....

....

....

....

....

(8 marks)

Revision Summary for Section 2

Some of this section is fairly straightforward, but there are a lot of rock names and landforms to remember. So it's time to get down to the serious business of answering questions. If you get stuck then have a flick back through the pages, but remember — don't move on to the next section until you can answer each question.

1) a) How are igneous rocks formed?
   b) Name the two types of igneous rock.
2) What are sedimentary rocks formed from?
3) Describe how metamorphic rocks are formed.
4) What part does weathering play in the rock cycle?
5) What part does erosion play in the rock cycle?
6) Put these rock types in the order that they formed in the UK:
   carboniferous limestone, chalk, granite, clay.
7) What is mechanical weathering?
8) a) Describe how freeze-thaw weathering takes place.
   b) Describe how exfoliation weathering takes place.
9) What is chemical weathering?
10) Describe how solution weathering takes place.
11) Describe how carbonation weathering takes place.
12) What are moorlands?
13) How do chalk escarpments form?
14) What is a vale?
15) What is an aquifer?
16) Where does a spring line form?
17) Give two surface features of a carboniferous limestone landscape.
18) What is a resurgent river?
19) How do pillars form in limestone caverns?
20) a) Name a granite area.
    b) Give the main type of farming carried out in the area.
21) a) Name a limestone area.
    b) Give two uses of the limestone produced in the area.
22) a) Give one economic disadvantage of quarries.
    b) Give one social advantage of quarries.
23) a) What is sustainable management?
    b) Why is the sustainable management of quarries important?
24) a) Give one example of sustainable management during the extraction of rock at a named quarry.
    b) Give two examples of sustainable management after the extraction of rock at a named quarry.

UK Climate

You may think it rains a lot in the UK (and you'd be right)... Well, now's your chance to find out why.

The UK has a Mild Climate — Cool, Wet Winters and Warm, Wet Summers

Temperature

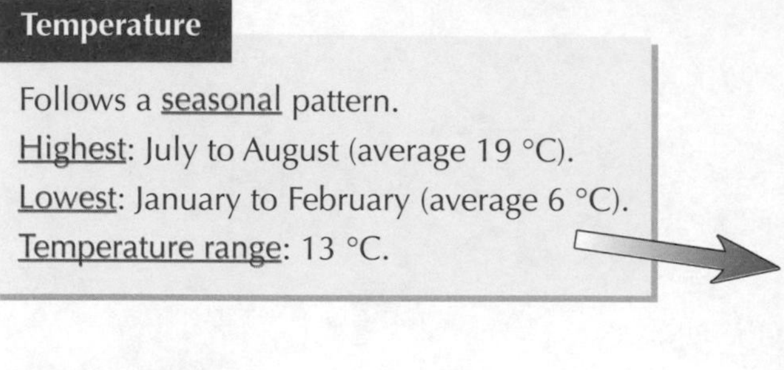

Follows a seasonal pattern.
Highest: July to August (average 19 °C).
Lowest: January to February (average 6 °C).
Temperature range: 13 °C.

Precipitation

Follows a seasonal pattern.
Highest: October to January (120 mm per month).
Lowest: April to July (70 mm per month).
Fluctuates: February to March.

Sunshine hours

Follows a seasonal pattern.
Highest: May to August (170-180 hours per month).
Lowest: December to January (40 hours per month).

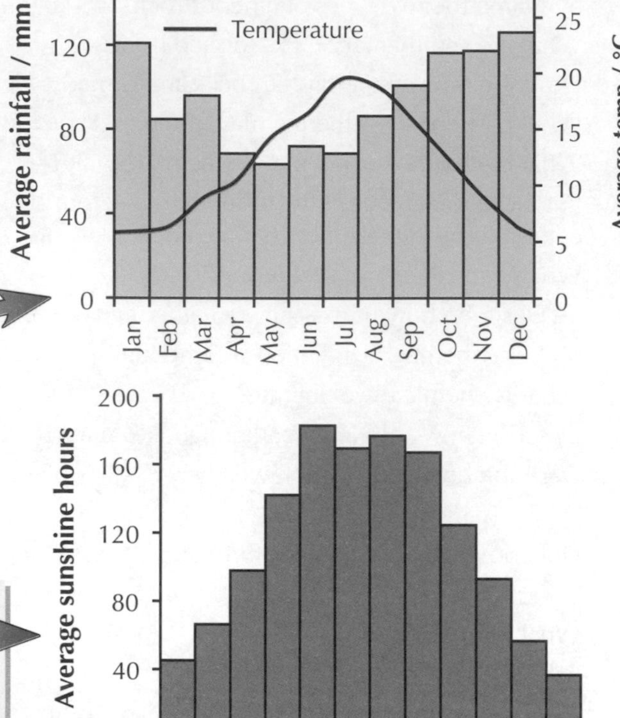

There are Five Main Reasons Why the Climate Varies Within the UK

1 LATITUDE (how far north or south of the equator a place is)

- The higher in latitude you go, the colder it gets. The Sun is at a lower angle in the sky, so its heat energy is spread over more of the Earth's surface — each place receives less heat energy than at lower latitudes.

- Southern parts of the UK are warmer than northern parts because of their lower latitude.

2 WINDS

- The UK's most common (prevailing) winds are from the south west. They bring warm, moist air, which makes the UK warm and wet.

- The west of the UK gets more of the warmth and rain than the east because the winds come from the south west.

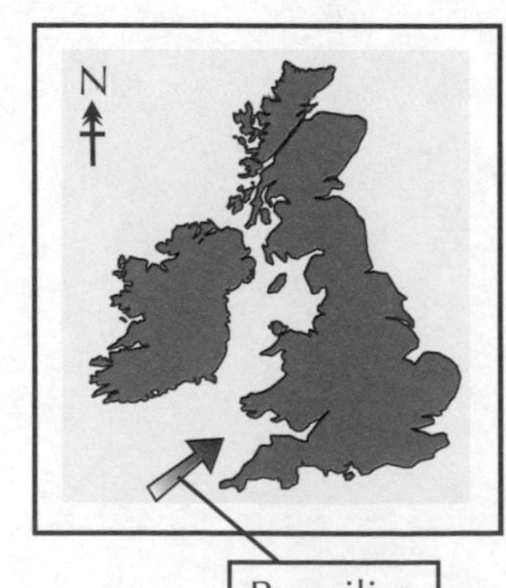

UK Climate

3 DISTANCE FROM THE SEA

- Areas near the sea are warmer than inland areas in winter because the sea stores up heat and warms the land.

- Areas near the sea are cooler in summer because the sea takes a long time to heat up and so cools the land down.

- The west of the UK gets warmed more than the east because of a warm ocean current coming from the south west called the North Atlantic Drift.

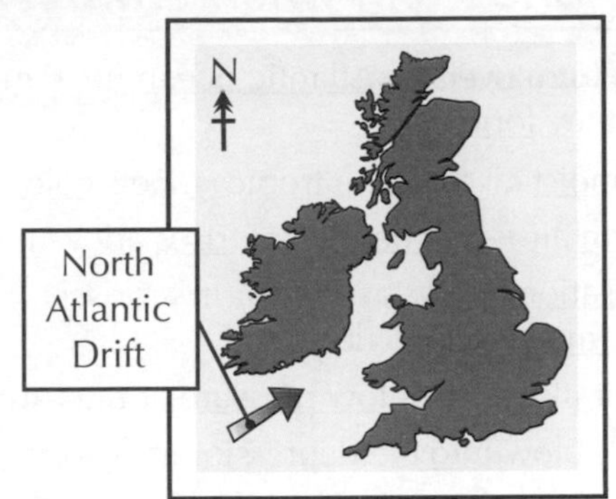

4 PRESSURE

- Low pressure weather systems have lots of rainfall because the air is rising and water vapour is condensing. High pressure systems have dry weather because the air is falling.

- Low pressure weather systems come from the west, so the west of the UK is wetter.

5 ALTITUDE (how high the land is)

- The higher up you go the colder it gets because the air is thinner so less heat energy is trapped.

- Higher areas get more rainfall as air is forced upwards and the water vapour condenses into rain clouds.

- So high altitude parts of the UK (e.g. Snowdonia) are colder and wetter than low altitude areas.

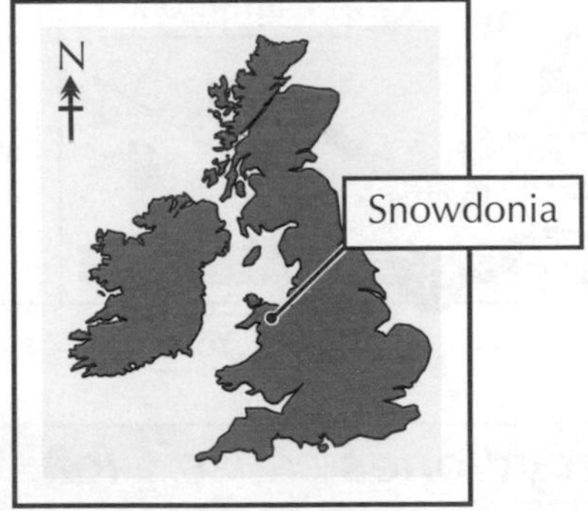

Some of these factors also explain why the climate of the whole of the UK is mild:

- It's not really hot or really cold because it's a mid-latitude country, and it has the North Atlantic Drift.
- The UK has both dry and rainy weather because it gets both high and low pressure weather systems.

Close the book and see how many of these reasons you can remember

There's quite a lot to remember about why the climate varies in the UK, but it'll be worth your while — if you get a question about why two places in the UK have different climates you'll have this stuff nailed and you'll be laughing.

Depressions and Anticyclones

Depressions are low pressure weather systems and anticyclones are high pressure weather systems — they cause different weather. There's a depression or an anticyclone over the UK most of the time.

Depressions Form when Warm Air Meets Cold Air

Depressions form over the Atlantic ocean, then move east over the UK. Here's how they form:

1) Warm, moist air from the tropics meets cold, dry air from the poles.
2) The warm air is less dense so it rises above the cold air.
3) Condensation occurs as the warm air rises, causing rain clouds to develop.
4) Rising air also causes low pressure at the Earth's surface.
5) So winds blow into the depression in a spiral (winds always blow from areas of high pressure to areas of low pressure).
6) A warm front is the front edge of the moving warm air. A cold front is the front edge of the moving cold air.

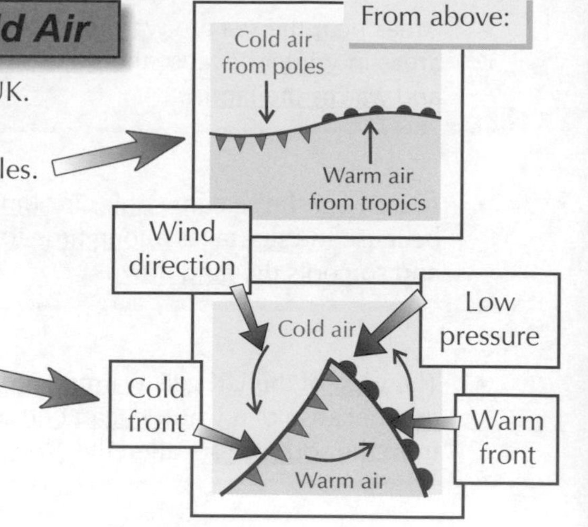

Depressions Cause a Sequence of Weather Conditions

When a depression passes overhead you get a particular sequence of weather conditions. Imagine you're stood on the ground ahead of the warm front and the depression's moving towards you.

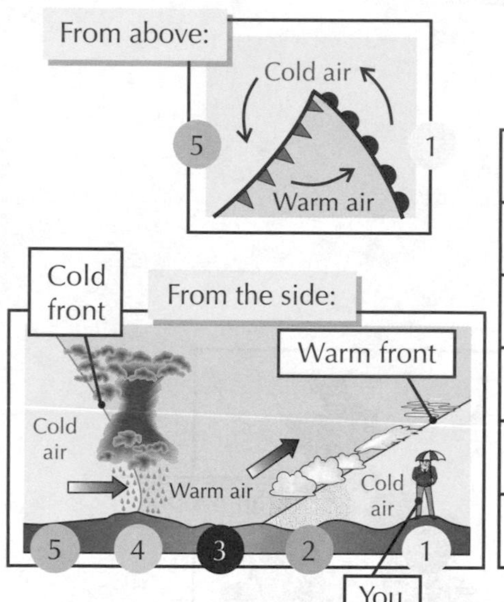

	5 Cold air overhead	4 As the cold front passes	3 Warm air overhead	2 As the warm front passes	1 Ahead of the warm front
Rain	Showers	Heavy showers	None	Heavy	None
Clouds	High, broken	Towering, thick	None	Low, thick	High, thin
Pressure	Rising	Suddenly rising	Steady	Falling	Falling
Temperature	Cold	Falling	Warm	Rising	Cool
Wind speed	Decreasing	Strong	Decreasing	Strong	Increasing
Wind direction	NW	SW to NW	SW	SE to SW	SE

Wind direction is given as the direction the wind comes from.

Anticyclones cause Clear Skies and Dry Weather

Anticyclones also form over the Atlantic ocean and move east over the UK. Here's a bit about them:

1) Anticyclones are where air is falling, creating high pressure and light winds blowing outwards.
2) Falling air gets warmer so no clouds are formed, giving clear skies and no rain for days or even weeks.
3) In summer, anticyclones cause long periods of hot, dry, clear weather. There are no clouds to absorb the Sun's heat energy, so more gets through to the Earth's surface causing high temperatures.
4) In winter, anticyclones give long periods of cold, foggy weather. Heat is lost from the Earth's surface at night because there are no clouds to reflect it back. The temperature drops and condensation occurs near the surface, forming fog. (It doesn't heat up much in the day because the Sun is weak.)

Depressions cause wet weather, anticyclones cause dry weather

Make sure you don't get depressions and anticyclones muddled up — they're complicated things, so it's really worth taking your time to learn this. Check that you can remember the weather they cause and the reasons why.

Extreme UK Weather

Extreme weather might not be something you'd usually associate with the UK, but it's becoming a lot more common.

Weather in the UK is Becoming More Extreme

1) It's raining more — the summer of 2007 was the wettest summer on record.
2) The rainfall is more intense, especially in winter — in some parts of Scotland the volume of rain that falls on wet winter days has gone up by 60%.
3) Temperature is increasing — the highest ever UK temperature was recorded in 2003 (38.5 °C).

More extreme weather has led to more extreme weather events in the last 10 years in the UK:

1) There was major flooding caused by storms and high rainfall in the south east in 2000, Cornwall in 2004, Cumbria in 2005 and 2009, the Midlands in 2007 and Devon in 2008.
2) Strong winds (combined with high tides) caused flooding in Norfolk in 2006.
3) High temperatures led to a heatwave and drought conditions in the summer of 2003.

Extreme Weather has Impacts on lots of Different Things

PEOPLE'S HOMES AND LIVES

- Floods damage homes and possessions, which can cost a lot to repair or replace.
- Businesses can be damaged by floods, so people can lose their income.
- Water use can be restricted during droughts, e.g. using hosepipes can be banned.
- Increased rainfall may mean water supplies are increased.

©istockphoto.com /Andy Green

AGRICULTURE

- Droughts can cause crop failures.
- Increased rainfall can mean higher crop yields.
- A warmer climate means farmers can grow new crops, e.g. olives.

HEALTH

- Flooding can cause deaths by drowning.
- Heatwaves can cause deaths by heat exhaustion.
- Milder winters may reduce cold-related deaths.

TRANSPORT

- Floods can block roads and railways, disrupting transport systems.
- High temperatures can cause railway lines to buckle, so trains can't run properly.

There are Three ways of Reducing the Negative Impacts

1) PREPARING — individuals and local authorities can do things to prepare for extreme weather before it happens. For example, flood defences along rivers can be improved and education programmes can tell the public the best ways to cope with floods, droughts or heatwaves.
2) PLANNING — emergency services and local councils can plan how to deal with extreme weather events in advance, e.g. they can make plans for how to rescue people from floods and where to have shelters.
3) WARNING — warning systems give people time to prepare for extreme weather. For example, the Environment Agency issues flood warnings so people can prepare and evacuate.

Extreme weather can have positive impacts as well as negative ones

Extreme weather doesn't necessarily mean one-off events like floods or storms — longer term changes can also be extreme. Make sure you're clear about the impacts of extreme weather and how the negative impacts can be reduced.

Global Climate Change — Debate

We British like to talk about the weather, so global climate change should give us plenty to go on...

The Earth is Getting Warmer

Climate change is any change in the weather of an area over a long period. Global warming is the increase in global temperature over the last century. Global warming is a type of climate change and it causes other types of climate change, e.g. increased rainfall. Here's a bit about the evidence for global warming:

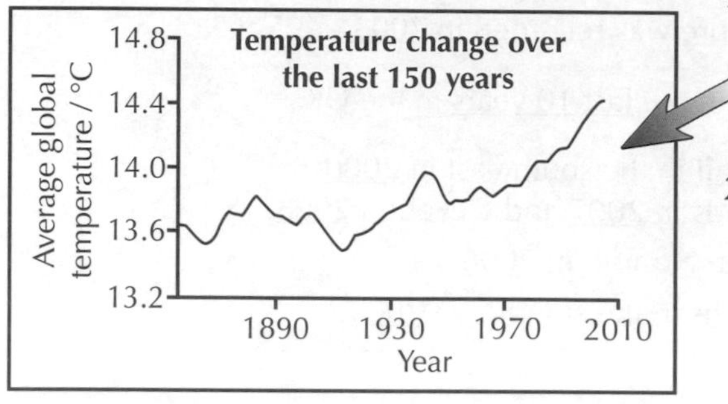

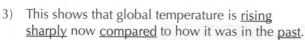

1) Global temperature has been measured using thermometers for the last 150 years. During the last 100 years, average global temperature has risen by about 0.9 °C. Average UK temperature has risen by about 1 °C.
2) Scientists have also reconstructed the climate over the last 1000 years using things like historical records, tree rings and cores taken from ice sheets.

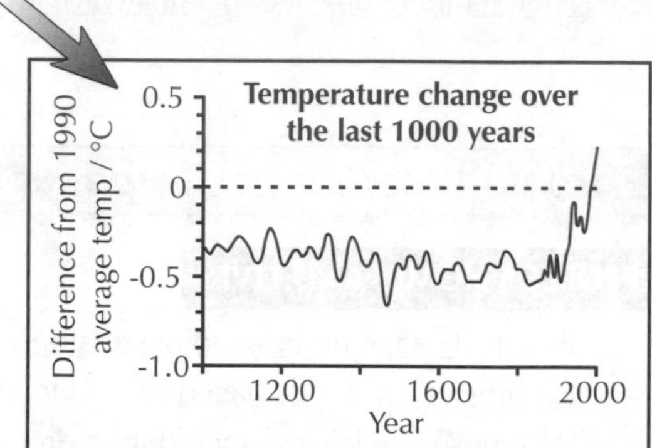

3) This shows that global temperature is rising sharply now compared to how it was in the past.
4) There's some other evidence too:
   - The ice sheets are melting because global temperature is increasing — the Greenland Ice Sheet lost an average of 195 km^3 of ice every year between 2003 and 2008.
   - Sea level is rising — increasing temperature causes ice on the land to melt and the oceans to expand. Sea level has risen 20 cm over the past century.

A few people argue that some of the evidence for global warming is a bit dodgy though. E.g. they say temperature measurements have shown an increase in temperature because human settlements have got closer to where a lot of the measurements are taken. Human settlements are warmer than natural environments because man-made surfaces like concrete absorb and radiate more heat energy.

An Increase in Greenhouse Gases is Causing Global Warming

There's a scientific consensus (general agreement) that global warming is caused by human activity:

1) An increase in human activities like burning fossil fuels, farming and deforestation has caused an increase in the concentration of carbon dioxide (CO_2) and methane (CH_4) in the atmosphere. For example, CO_2 has gone up from 280 ppm (parts per million) in 1850 to around 380 ppm today.
2) CO_2 and CH_4 are greenhouse gases — they trap heat reflected off the Earth's surface.
3) Greenhouse gases keep the Earth warm because they trap heat. Increasing the concentration of greenhouse gases in the atmosphere means the Earth heats up too much — causing global warming.

Here are some examples of other things that can cause climate change:

1) Variations in solar output — the Sun's output of energy isn't constant. In periods when there's more energy coming from the Sun, the Earth gets warmer.
2) Changes in the Earth's orbit — the way the Earth orbits the Sun changes, which affects how much energy the Earth receives. If the Earth receives more energy it gets warmer.

Temperature has increased rapidly over the last 100 years

The climate is changing — global warming is happening, it's just that a handful of people think some of the evidence isn't great. There are other things that cause climate change, but let's face it, we humans better take the rap this time.

Global Climate Change — Impacts

Global climate change will have economic, social, environmental and political impacts on the world and on the UK. That's quite a few impacts, but then, the climate's pretty important you know.

Climate Change will have **Economic Impacts**...

1) Climate change will affect farming in different ways around the world:
   - In higher latitudes, warmer weather will mean some farmers can make more money — some crop yields will be increased, and they'll be able to grow new types of crops to sell.
   - In lower latitudes, farmers' income may decrease because it's too hot and dry for farming.
2) Climate change means the weather is getting more extreme. This means more money will have to be spent on predicting extreme weather events, reducing their impacts and rebuilding after them.
3) Industries that help to reduce the effects of climate change will become bigger and make more money.

IN THE UK...

Farmers will be able to grow new crops in the warmer climate, e.g. olives.

More money will have to be spent on coping with more extreme weather conditions, e.g. to pay for more flood defences.

...**Social Impacts**...

1) People won't be able to grow as much food in lower latitudes (see above). This could lead to malnutrition, ill health and death from starvation, e.g. in places like central Africa.
2) More people will die because of more extreme weather events.
3) Hotter weather makes it easier for some infectious diseases to spread. This will lead to more ill health and more deaths from disease.
4) Some areas will become so hot and dry that they're uninhabitable. People will have to move, which could lead to overcrowding in other areas.

Don't forget — global warming is a type of climate change.

IN THE UK...

There could be fewer cold-related deaths, but more deaths caused by hot weather, e.g. from heat exhaustion.

Diseases that don't exist in the UK at the moment could become common, e.g. malaria.

...**Environmental Impacts**...

1) Global warming is causing sea level to rise, so some habitats will be lost as low-lying coastal environments are submerged.
2) Rising temperature and decreased rainfall will mean some environments will turn into deserts.
3) The distribution of some species may change due to climate change (species can only live in the areas where the conditions suit them best). Species that can't move may die out.

IN THE UK...

Flooding and sea level rise is threatening some coastal habitats, e.g. in the south east and Norfolk.

The distribution of some species in the UK may change, e.g. it's thought beech trees will become more common in Scotland.

...and **Political Impacts**

1) Water will become more scarce in some places. Competition over water could lead to war between countries.
2) Climate change may cause people to move (see above). This means some countries will have to cope with increased immigration and emigration.
3) Governments are under pressure to come up with ways to slow climate change or reduce its effects.

IN THE UK...

The government has had to set up a new political department to come up with ways to slow climate change and reduce its impacts — the Department for Energy and Climate Change.

Nobody knows exactly what the impacts of climate change will be

Scientists can make predictions about areas that are likely to get warmer or colder, wetter or drier, but they can't be certain. You should check that you know the probable impacts in different parts of the world, including the UK.

Global Climate Change — Responses

Most of the responses to climate change involve cutting emissions of greenhouse gases like CO_2. This can be done globally, nationally and locally, so everyone gets a slice of the fun.

The Kyoto Protocol is a Global Response

Most countries in the world have agreed to monitor and cut greenhouse gas emissions by signing an international agreement called the Kyoto Protocol:

1) The aim is to reduce global greenhouse gas emissions by 5% below 1990 levels by 2012.
2) Each country is set a target, e.g. the UK has agreed to reduce emissions by 12.5% by 2012.
3) Another part of the protocol is the carbon credits trading scheme:
   - Countries that come under their emissions target get carbon credits which they can sell to countries that aren't meeting their emissions target. This means there's a reward for having low emissions.
   - Countries can also earn carbon credits by helping poorer countries to reduce their emissions. This means poorer countries will be able to reduce their emissions more quickly.
4) Not all countries have agreed to the Kyoto Protocol though — the USA hasn't agreed yet, and they have the highest emissions of any country in the world (22% of global CO_2 emissions in 2004).

There are also National and Local Responses to Climate Change

NATIONAL RESPONSES

1) **TRANSPORT STRATEGIES**
Governments can improve public transport networks like buses and trains. For example, they can make them run faster or cover a wider area. This encourages more people to use public transport instead of cars, so CO_2 emissions are reduced.

2) **TAXATION**
Governments can increase taxes on cars with high emissions, e.g. in the UK there are higher tax rates for cars with higher emissions. This encourages people to buy cars with low emissions, so emissions are reduced.

LOCAL RESPONSES

1) **CONGESTION CHARGING**
Local authorities can charge people for driving cars into cities during busy periods, e.g. there's a congestion charge to drive into central London during busy times of the day. This encourages people to use their cars less, which reduces emissions.

2) **RECYCLING**
   - Local authorities can recycle more waste by building recycling plants and giving people recycling bins. Recycling materials means less energy is used making new materials, so emissions are reduced.
   - Local authorities can also create energy by burning recycled waste, e.g. Sheffield uses a waste incinerator to supply 140 buildings with energy.

3) **CONSERVING ENERGY**
   - Local authorities give money and advice to make homes more energy efficient, e.g. by doing things like improving insulation. This means people use less energy to heat their homes, because less is lost. Emissions are reduced because less energy needs to be produced.
   - Individuals can also conserve energy by doing things like switching lights off and not leaving electric gadgets on standby.

Climate change can be tackled at a range of levels

Climate change is a global problem, so the response to deal with it needs to be on a global scale. That means everyone has to do their bit, from world leaders down to folk like us. Now, better go and turn my computer off...

Worked Exam Questions

Working through exam questions is a great way of testing what you've learned and practising for the exam. This worked example will give you an idea of the kind of answers examiners are looking for.

1 Study **Figure 1**, which is an article about the climate of the UK.

Figure 1

UK feels the heat of climate change

Average temperature in the UK is increasing. Between 1995 and 2004, the UK had six of the ten warmest years since 1861. The hottest temperatures ever recorded in the UK were in August 2003 — it reached 38.5°C in Faversham (Kent). In the same month, Greycrook reached 32.9°C — a new record for Scotland.

Rainfall is also increasing — the summer of 2007 was the wettest on record and rainfall is also becoming more intense.

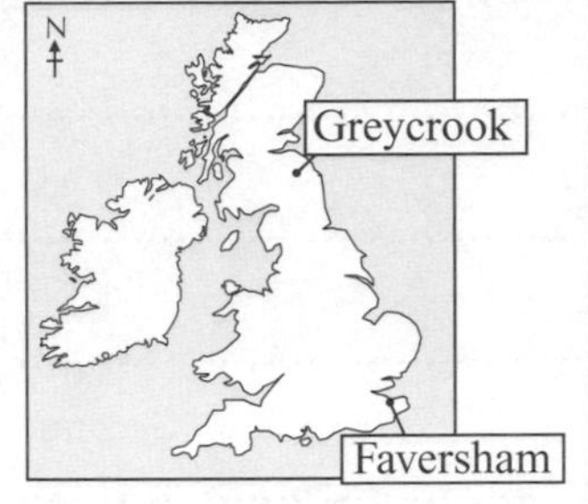

(a) Faversham and Greycrook are similar distances from the sea and at similar altitudes. Explain the difference in temperature between Faversham and Greycrook.

Greycrook had a lower maximum temperature because it is at a higher latitude. At higher latitudes the sun is at a lower angle in the sky, so its heat is spread over more of the Earth's surface.

(2 marks)

(b) (i) Suggest two extreme weather events that the changes described in **Figure 1** could cause.

Floods and heatwaves.

Make sure you only suggest events that could be caused by the conditions discussed in Figure 1 — it's no good saying blizzards when the article doesn't mention snow.

(2 marks)

(ii) Describe two negative impacts of extreme weather on transport.

Read the question carefully — here you should only mention impacts on transport.

Floods can block roads and railways, disrupting transport systems.

High temperatures can cause railways lines to buckle so trains can't run properly.

(2 marks)

2 Study **Figure 2**, which shows the average air pressure in Derby over a period of six weeks.

Figure 2

Week	1	2	3	4	5	6
Pressure (mbar)	990	998	1008	1004	1036	1006

(a) In which week did an anticyclone pass over Derby?

Week 5.

(1 mark)

(b) Explain the differences in weather caused by anticyclones in summer and in winter.

You need to describe what the differences are before you explain them.

In summer, anticyclones cause long periods of hot, dry weather and in winter they cause prolonged periods of cold, foggy weather. They cause hot and dry weather in summer because there are no clouds to absorb the Sun's heat energy so more gets through to the Earth's surface. They cause cold and foggy weather in winter because heat is lost from the Earth's surface at night because there are no clouds to reflect it back. The temperature drops and condensation occurs near the surface, forming fog.

(4 marks)

Exam Questions

1 Study **Figure 1**, which shows global temperature between 1860 and 2000.

(a) Describe the change in average global temperature shown by the graph.

Figure 1

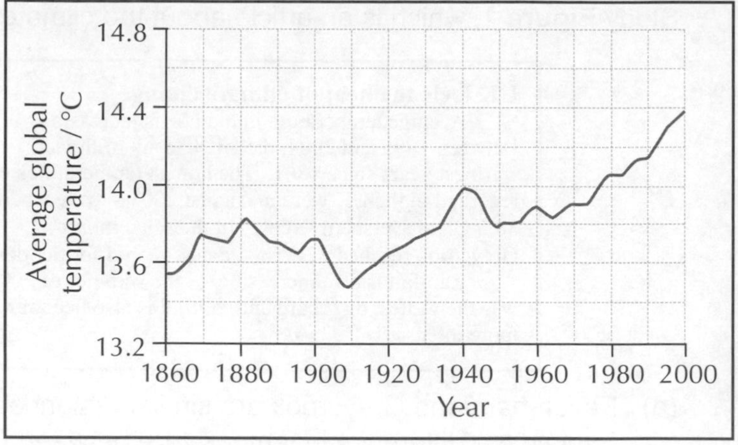

Average global temperature / °C

Year

....

....

....

....

....

....

(2 marks)

(b) What is global warming?

....

....

(1 mark)

(c) Give two environmental impacts of global warming.

....

....

....

(2 marks)

(d) Responses to the threat of climate change need to be international, national and local. Suggest some local responses and explain how they reduce the threat of climate change.

....

....

....

....

....

....

....

....

(6 marks)

Tropical Storms

Tropical storms are intense low pressure weather systems. They've got lots of different names (hurricanes, typhoons, tropical cyclones, tropical revolving storms and willy willies), but they're all the same thing.

Tropical Storms **Develop** over **Warm Water**

Tropical storms are huge storms with strong winds and torrential rain. Scientists don't know exactly how they're formed, but they know where they form and some of the conditions that are needed:

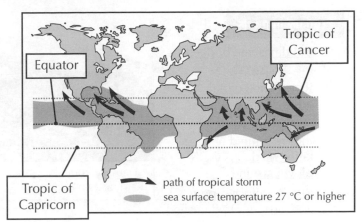

1) Tropical storms develop above sea water that's 27 °C or higher.
2) They happen when sea temperatures are highest, so they happen at different times in different places. For example, tropical storm season is August to October in the Atlantic, and May to December in the north east Pacific.
3) Warm, moist air rises and condensation occurs. This releases huge amounts of energy, which makes the storms really powerful.
4) They move west because of the easterly winds near the equator.
5) They lose strength as they move over land because the energy supply from the warm water is cut off.
6) Most tropical storms occur between 5° and 30° north and south of the equator, e.g. in the Atlantic and the Indian Ocean (any further from the equator and the water isn't warm enough).
7) The Earth's rotation deflects the path of the winds, which causes the storms to spin.

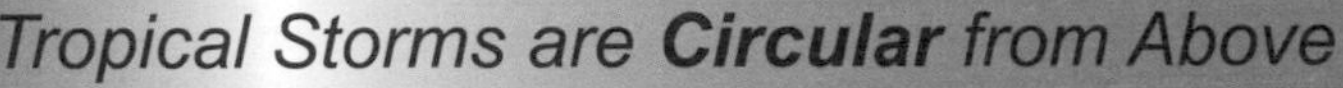

Tropical Storms are **Circular** from Above

1) Tropical storms spin anticlockwise and move north west (in the northern hemisphere).
2) They're circular in shape and can be hundreds of kilometres wide.
3) They usually last between 7 and 14 days.
4) The centre of the storm's called the eye — it's up to 50 km across and is caused by descending air. There's very low pressure, light winds, no clouds and no rain in the eye.

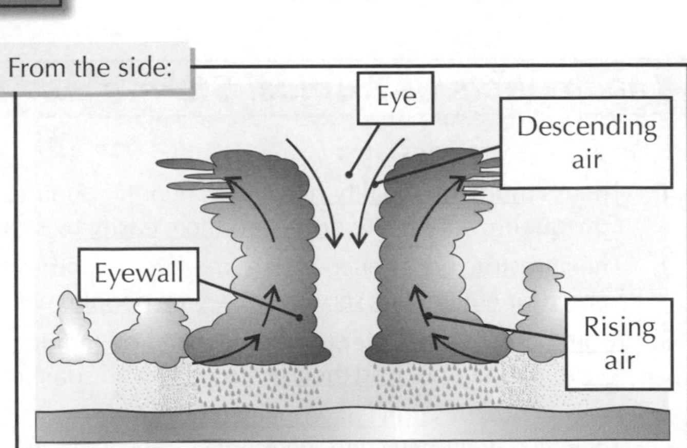

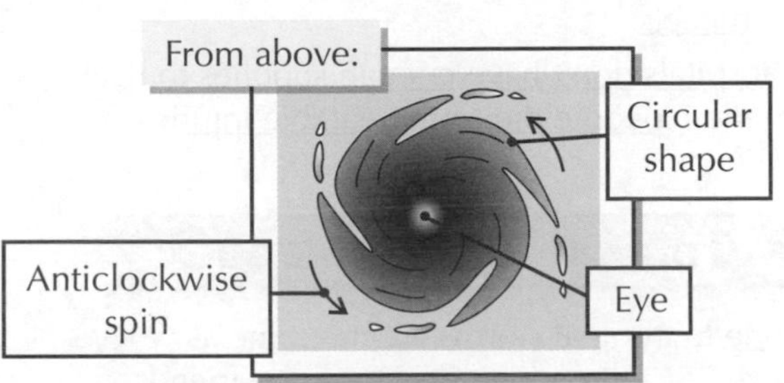

5) The eye is surrounded by the eyewall, where there's spiralling rising air, very strong winds (around 160 km per hour), storm clouds and torrential rain.
6) Towards the edges of the storm the wind speed falls, the clouds become smaller and more scattered, and the rain becomes less intense.

Tropical storms form at low latitudes

Since all the top scientists haven't worked it out yet, you don't need to know exactly how a tropical storm forms, but in the exam you might be asked about where they're found, why they're found there and their characteristics.

Impacts of Tropical Storms

Knowing where tropical storms form is one thing, but in the exam you might well be asked about their impacts.

Tropical Storms have Primary and Secondary Impacts

The primary impacts of a tropical storm are the immediate effects of strong winds, high rainfall and storm surges. The secondary impacts are the effects that happen later on. Here are a few examples of the possible impacts:

Storm surges are large rises in sea level caused by the low pressure and high winds of a storm.

Primary impacts

1) Buildings and bridges are destroyed.
2) Rivers and coastal areas flood.
3) People drown, or they're injured or killed by debris that's blown around.
4) Roads, railways, ports and airports are damaged.

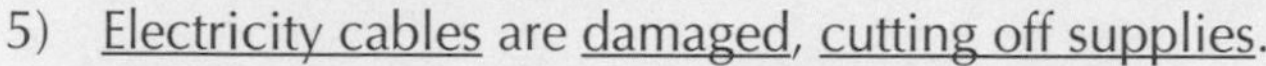

Damage from Hurricane Katrina, 29th August 2005.

©iStockphoto.com/Chad Purser

5) Electricity cables are damaged, cutting off supplies.
6) Telephone poles and cables are destroyed.
7) Sewage overflows due to flooding. The sewage often contaminates water supplies.
8) Crops are damaged and livestock is killed.
9) Heavy rain makes hills unstable, causing landslides.
10) Beaches are eroded and coastal habitats (e.g. coral reefs) are damaged.

Secondary impacts

1) People are left homeless.
2) There's a shortage of clean water and a lack of proper sanitation — this makes it easier for diseases to spread.
3) Roads are blocked or destroyed so aid and emergency vehicles can't get through.
4) Businesses are damaged or destroyed, causing unemployment.
5) There's a shortage of food because crops are damaged and livestock has died.
6) People may suffer psychological problems if they knew people who died.

The more settlements built and businesses set up in an area, the greater the impact because there are more people and properties to be affected by a tropical storm.

The Impacts of Tropical Storms are More Severe in Poorer Countries

Here are a few reasons why:

1) There's more low quality housing in poorer countries. Low quality houses are destroyed more easily by strong winds and flooding.
2) The infrastructure is often worse in poorer countries. Poor quality roads make it harder for emergency services to rescue people, which leads to more deaths.
3) More people in poorer countries depend on farming. If crops and livestock are destroyed lots of people will lose their livelihoods, and some might starve.
4) Poorer countries don't have much money to protect against tropical storms, e.g. by building flood defences. They also don't have enough money or resources (e.g. food and helicopters) to react straight away to tropical storms, so more people are affected by secondary impacts.
5) Healthcare is often worse in poorer countries. Many of the hospitals don't have enough supplies to deal with the large numbers of casualties after a tropical storm, so more people die from treatable injuries.

People Continue to Live in the Areas where Tropical Storms Happen

The reasons why people don't move away from areas that are prone to tropical storms are the same as why people don't move away from areas prone to earthquakes (see page 5) — they don't want to leave friends, they've got a job in the area, they don't think a tropical storm will happen again so it's safe etc.

Make sure you know the difference between primary and secondary impacts

Tropical storms pretty much wreak havoc in the areas they hit — boats get tossed into trees, hills go for a slide and the winds are so strong you can't stand upright... They can affect areas hit for years afterwards, especially in poor countries.

Reducing the Impacts of Tropical Storms

Tropical storms can cause loads of damage, but luckily there are lots of strategies for reducing their impacts.

There are Many Ways of Reducing the Impacts of Tropical Storms

Prediction

©iStockphoto.com

1) When and where tropical storms will hit land can be predicted. Scientists use data from things like radar, satellites and aircraft to track the storm. Computer models are then used to calculate a predicted path for the storm.
2) Predicting where and when a tropical storm is going to happen gives people time to evacuate — this reduces the number of injuries and deaths. It also gives them time to protect their homes and businesses, e.g. by boarding up windows so they don't get smashed.

Planning

1) Future developments, e.g. new houses, can be planned to avoid the areas most at risk (e.g. right on the coast). This reduces the number of buildings destroyed by winds or flooding.
2) Emergency services can train and prepare for disasters, e.g. by practising rescuing people from flooded areas with helicopters. This reduces the number of people killed.
3) Governments can plan evacuation routes to get people away from storms quickly. This reduces the number of people injured or killed by things like flying debris or floodwater.

A hurricane evacuation route sign in Florida, USA.

Building techniques

1) Buildings can be designed to withstand tropical storms, e.g. by using reinforced concrete or by fixing roofs securely so they don't get blown off. Buildings can also be put on stilts so they're safe from floodwater.
2) Flood defences can be built along rivers (e.g. levees) and coasts (e.g. sea walls).
3) All of these reduce the number of buildings destroyed, so fewer people will be killed, injured, made homeless and made unemployed.

Education

1) Governments and other organisations can educate people about how to prepare for a tropical storm (e.g. by stockpiling water and food) and how to evacuate. This helps reduce deaths.
2) People can be told how to make a survival kit containing things like food, water and medication. The kits reduce the chance of people dying if they're stuck in the area.

Aid

Governments or organisations often send aid to countries hit by tropical storms, e.g. food, bottled water, tents. This helps to reduce the impacts, e.g. food aid stops people going hungry.

Some Strategies are More Sustainable than Others

There's a definition of a sustainable strategy way back on page 7.
Here's a bit on the sustainability of strategies to reduce the impact of tropical storms:

1) All of the strategies are sustainable because they're all effective and environmentally friendly.
2) Some are more cost-effective than others though, so are more sustainable.
3) Predicting tropical storms needs special equipment (e.g. radars) and trained scientists, which makes it expensive, but if it's accurate it saves a lot of lives.
4) Building techniques can be very expensive, but can save a lot of money if they stop building destruction.

Advance warning, good planning and education help to minimise damage

Prediction means you know if you have to do some serious plywood DIY and hightail it out of there. Good evacuation planning means you can hightail quickly and safely. Other things help make sure you've got a house to come back to.

Tropical Storms — Case Studies

Tropical storms can wreak quite a lot of havoc. Here are a couple of case studies...

Tropical Storms have Different Effects in Different Places

The effects of tropical storms and the responses to them are different in different parts of the world. A lot depends on how wealthy the part of the world is. Here are a couple of case studies, so you can cash in those marks when you get asked to compare two case studies in the exam.

Tropical storm in a rich part of the world:

Name: Hurricane Katrina
Place: South east USA
Date: 29th August, 2005

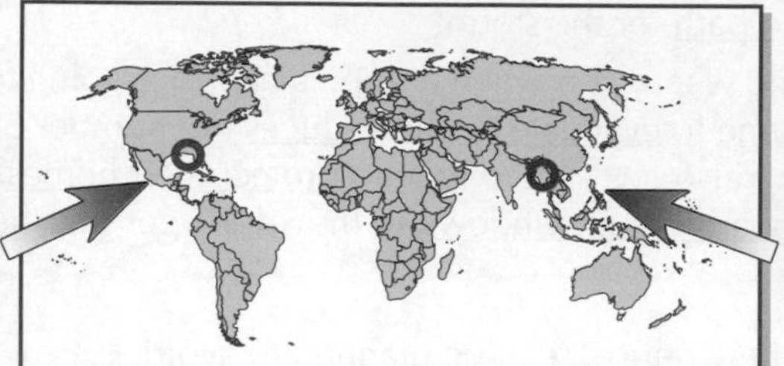

Tropical storm in a poor part of the world:

Name: Cyclone Nargis
Place: Irrawaddy delta, Burma
Date: 2nd May, 2008

	Hurricane Katrina	Cyclone Nargis
Preparation	• The USA has a sophisticated monitoring system to predict if a hurricane will hit (e.g. by using satellite images of the Atlantic) — so people were warned. • Mississippi and Louisiana declared states of emergency on 26th August — they set up control centres and stockpiled supplies. • 70-80% of New Orleans residents were evacuated before the hurricane reached land.	• Indian and Thai weather agencies warned the Burmese Government that Cyclone Nargis was likely to hit the country. Despite this, Burmese forecasters reported there was little or no risk. • There were no emergency or evacuation plans.
Social effects	• More than 1800 people were killed. • 300 000 houses were destroyed. • 3 million people left without electricity. • One of the main routes out of New Orleans was closed because parts of the I-10 bridge collapsed.	• More than 140 000 people were killed. • 450 000 houses were destroyed. • 2-3 million people were made homeless. • 1700 schools were destroyed.
Economic effects	• Total of around $300 billion of damage. • 230 000 of jobs were lost from businesses that were damaged or destroyed. • 30 offshore oil platforms sunk or went missing. This increased the price of fuel. • Shops in New Orleans were looted by residents in the days after the hurricane.	• Total of around $4 billion of damage. • Millions of people lost their livelihoods. • 200 000 farm animals were killed, crops were lost and over 40% of food stores were destroyed.
Environmental effects	• The hurricane caused the sea to flood parts of the land. This destroyed some coastal habitats, e.g. sea turtle breeding beaches.	• Coastal habitats such as mangrove forests were damaged. • The salinity (salt content) of soil in some areas has increased because of flooding by sea water. This means it's more difficult for plants to grow.
Short-term response	• During the storm the coast guard, police, fire service, army and volunteers rescued over 50 000 people. • About 25 000 people were given temporary shelter at a sports stadium (the Louisiana Superdome) immediately after the storm.	• Burma's Government initially refused to accept any foreign aid. Aid workers were only allowed in 3 weeks after the disaster occurred. • The UN launched a massive appeal to raise money to help respond to the disaster.
Long-term response	• The US government has spent over $800 million on rebuilding flood defences. • Around $34 billion has been set aside for the re-building of things like houses and schools.	• Burma is relying on international aid to repair the damage — fewer than 20 000 homes have been rebuilt and half a million survivors are still living in temporary shelters.

Richer countries tend to fare better during tropical storms

When you compare the two, it's clear that the impacts were worse in Burma and the long-term response has been a bit more organised in the USA. Get both case studies etched into your memory and you'll be ready for anything.

Drought

We're nearly at the end of this section — there are just three lovely pages on drought left to go...

Drought is when Conditions are Drier than Normal

1) A drought is a long period (weeks, months or years) when rainfall is below average.
2) Water supplies, e.g. lakes and rivers, are depleted during a drought because people keep using them but they aren't replenished by rainfall. Also, droughts are often accompanied by high temperatures, which increase the rate of evaporation, so water supplies are depleted faster.
3) The length of a drought is different in different places, e.g. the worst drought in Britain since records began lasted 16 months, whilst droughts in African countries can last for more than a decade.
4) Here are a few of the climatic conditions that cause periods of drought:

> 1) Droughts are caused when changes in atmospheric circulation mean it doesn't rain much in an area for years, e.g. this happens in Ethiopia.
> 2) Changes in atmospheric circulation can also make the annual rains fail (e.g. monsoon rains don't come when they normally do in places like India).
> 3) Droughts are also caused when high pressure weather systems (called anticyclones) block depressions (weather systems that cause rain), e.g. this happens in the UK.

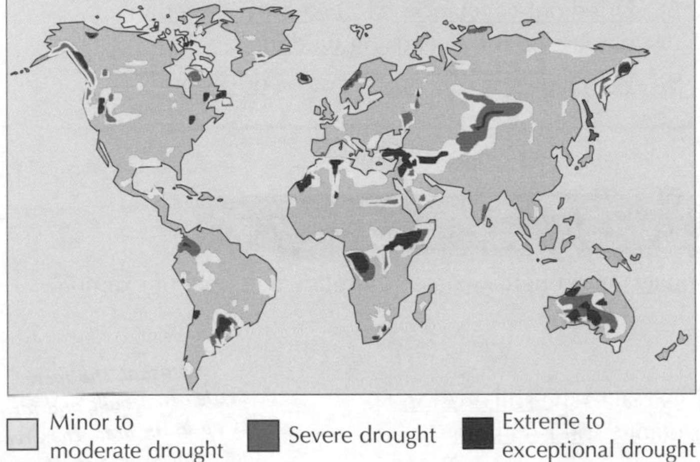

5) The map on the left shows the areas of the world that were affected by drought in November 2008.
6) Areas most at risk from drought are north-eastern Africa, the Sahel, southern Africa, the Middle East, Australia and parts of eastern South America and Indonesia.

People Continue to Live in the Areas where Droughts Happen

The reasons why people don't move away from areas that are prone to droughts are similar to why people don't move away from areas prone to earthquakes (see page 5) — they've always lived there, they've got a job in the area, they don't think a drought will happen again soon etc.

©iStockphoto.com/Klaas Lingbeek-van Kranen

Droughts and Tropical Storms are Climatic Hazards

Climatic hazards are natural hazards caused by the weather.

> *A natural hazard is a naturally occurring event that has the potential to affect people's lives or property.*

Global warming could cause droughts to become more severe and widespread

Now you know what droughts are and how they happen. As the climate changes some areas will get hotter and drier, and droughts will become more severe. Have a look back at page 37 to get an idea of the possible impacts of this.

Impacts of Droughts

You guessed it, it's time to have a think about the impacts of droughts...

Droughts have Primary and Secondary Impacts

The primary impacts of droughts are the immediate effects of low rainfall and reduced water supplies. Secondary impacts are the effects that happen later on. Here are some examples of the possible impacts:

Primary impacts

1) Vegetation dies (including crops).
2) People and animals die from dehydration.
3) Aquatic animals (e.g. fish) die because lakes and rivers dry up.
4) Soil dries out and is easily eroded by the wind and rain.

©iStockphoto.com/Morley Read

Secondary impacts

1) Animals die from starvation because there's no vegetation.
2) There's a shortage of food because crops have failed and livestock has died, so people die from starvation.
3) Soil erosion is increased because there's less vegetation to hold it together. This causes desertification — where land becomes unsuitable for growing vegetation.
4) There are conflicts over water supplies.
5) People move out of the area to find water.
6) Farms close, causing unemployment.
7) People may suffer psychological problems, e.g. stress from losing their business.
8) Dried out vegetation can be easily ignited, e.g. by lightning, causing wildfires.
9) Winds pick up dry soil, causing dust storms.

Some Human Activities Increase the Impacts of Droughts

Some of the things that humans do make the impacts of droughts worse. Here are a couple of examples:

Overgrazing

Overgrazing reduces vegetation in an area. This makes the soil erosion caused by droughts even worse — with fewer plants, soil isn't held together as strongly so it's eroded more easily.

As usual, the more settlements built and farms set up in an area, the greater the impacts because there are more people and businesses to be affected by drought.

Excessive irrigation

Irrigation is where water is artificially supplied from rivers or lakes to farmland to increase crop production. However, excessive irrigation depletes rivers and lakes, which increases the impact of drought because there's less water. Also, when irrigation water evaporates, salts are left in the soil (this is salinisation). Crops don't grow well in salty soil, so this also increases the impact of drought.

The Impacts of Droughts are More Severe in Poorer Countries

Droughts happen all over the world, but they have a greater impact in poorer countries. Here's why:

1) More people in poorer countries depend on farming. If crops and livestock die lots of people will lose their livelihoods and some might starve.
2) Poorer countries have less money to prepare for droughts or respond to them, e.g. they can't afford to build reservoirs (see the next page), so the impacts of a drought are more severe.

Make sure you understand how different factors affect the impacts of droughts

The stuff on this page isn't too tricky so it'll be nice and easy to remember. Then you'll know all about human activities that make the impacts of drought a lot worse, and why droughts have a greater impact in poorer countries.

Reducing the Impacts of Droughts

Droughts cause some pretty nasty problems. Luckily there are various ways to reduce their impacts.

There are Many Ways of **Reducing the Impacts** of **Droughts**

Prediction

1) Droughts can be predicted a short time before they happen by monitoring rainfall, soil moisture and river levels.
2) When a drought is predicted, things can be done to reduce the impacts, e.g. banning hosepipes, rationing water or moving people out of areas that will be worst affected.

Farming techniques

1) Drought-resistant crops (ones that need little water) can be grown, e.g. millet, sorghum and olives.
2) More efficient methods of irrigation can be used. For example, drip irrigation delivers small volumes of water directly to crop roots (reducing the amount lost by evaporation).

©iStockphoto.com/Lucas Cavalheiro

Drip irrigation

3) These techniques reduce the demand on water supplies and make food production more reliable.

Water conservation

1) People can conserve water by reducing the amount they use in their homes, e.g. by installing low volume flush toilets, and by having showers instead of baths.
2) People can also install water butts at home to collect rainwater and use it to wash their car or water their garden.
3) These reduce the demand on water supplies, so more water is available during a drought.

Increase water supplies

1) Reservoirs and wells can be built to increase water supplies.
2) These make more water available during a drought, reducing deaths from dehydration, reducing conflicts over supplies and making food production more reliable.

Reservoirs are man-made lakes that store water — they're created behind dams that are built across rivers.

A rural well

Aid

Aid can help reduce the impacts of drought in more than one way:

- Emergency aid (like food and water tankers) can stop people dying from dehydration or starvation.
- Aid can be used to fund development projects, e.g. building wells or water pipes, to make more water available during droughts.

Some **Strategies** are **More Sustainable** Than Others

There's a definition of a sustainable strategy back on page 7. Here's a bit about the sustainability of strategies to reduce the impact of drought:

1) Most of the strategies are sustainable because they're effective and environmentally friendly. Building wells can deplete groundwater supplies, which means there's less water for people in the future, so sometimes they're not sustainable. Building reservoirs can reduce other people's water supply downriver. This means it's not sustainable as it doesn't meet the needs of people alive now.
2) As usual, some are more sustainable than others because they're more cost-effective, e.g. buying pipes for drip irrigation can be expensive, but it saves a lot of water and can be more cost-effective than emergency aid.

Remember these five ways of reducing the impacts of droughts

I hope this section has quenched your thirst for knowledge about weather and climate because I've got nothing else to tell you. Check how much you remember by having a go at the questions on the next few pages.

Worked Exam Questions

To get you into the exam mood, here's a big exam question with the answers written in. Before you read the answers, have a think about how you might answer these questions if they came up in the exam.

1 Study **Figure 1**, which shows a leaflet from an emergency disaster relief charity.

Figure 1

Drought in Ethiopia - You Can Help

We take water for granted, but in Ethiopia it hasn't rained for months. Because of a lack of water, huge areas of crops have failed and farmers have lost thousands of animals to starvation. Some people have already died of dehydration and others are fearing the weeks ahead without food. Whole communities are leaving their homes in a desperate search to find enough water to survive. Those who stay and try to farm their land have to deal with ever-decreasing amounts of fertile soil as it's dried out and blown away by the winds. Many commercial farms have closed completely, leaving thousands without work.

(a) Describe the climatic conditions that cause periods of drought.

There are 2 marks available, so you need to put in a bit of detail.

Droughts are caused when changes in atmospheric circulation mean it doesn't rain much in an area, e.g. by making annual rains fail. They are also caused when high pressure weather systems called anticyclones block depressions, which cause rain.

(2 marks)

(b) Using **Figure 1**, describe two primary and two secondary impacts of the drought.

Primary Crops have died from a lack of water.

People have died from dehydration.

Secondary Animals have died from starvation.

People may die from starvation because there's a shortage of food.

There are lots of impacts mentioned in the article — you could say that soil has dried out so it's easily eroded by winds (primary), that people have moved out of the area to find water (secondary) or that farms have closed, causing unemployment (secondary). Make sure you stick to impacts that are mentioned though.

(4 marks)

(c) Explain one way in which human activities can increase the impact of drought on an area.

Overgrazing means the soil erosion caused by droughts is made worse. It reduces vegetation in an area so the soil isn't held together as strongly and can be eroded more easily.

(2 marks)

(d) (i) Suggest one way of predicting droughts.

Monitoring soil moisture levels. *(or monitoring rainfall/river levels)*

(1 mark)

(ii) Explain how prediction can help to reduce the impacts of drought.

Prediction gives people/authorities a chance to prepare for the drought, e.g. by banning hosepipes, rationing water or moving people out of areas that will be worst affected.

(2 marks)

Exam Questions

1 Study **Figure 1**, which shows a cross section of a tropical storm.

Figure 1

(a) (i) Label **Figure 1** to show the characteristics of a tropical storm.
(4 marks)

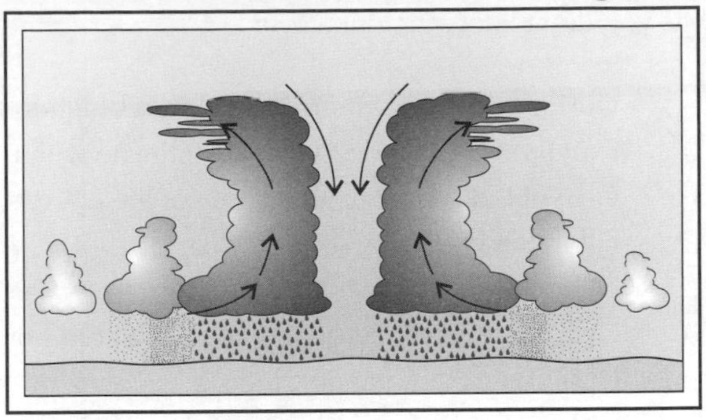

(ii) Give two other characteristics of tropical storms.

....

....

....

....
(2 marks)

(b) Suggest one reason why people choose to live in areas affected by tropical storms.

....
(1 mark)

(c) Describe two possible secondary impacts of tropical storms.

....

....
(2 marks)

(d) (i) Give one strategy for reducing the impacts of tropical storms.

....
(1 mark)

(ii) Explain whether the strategy described in (i) is sustainable or not.

....

....
(2 marks)

(e) Using case studies of tropical storms in rich and poor parts of the world, compare the short and long-term responses.

....

....

....

....

....

....
(6 marks)

Revision Summary for Section 3

Well, wasn't that a blast of fresh air from the prevailing wind. Weather and climate is a pretty complicated section, so don't worry if it didn't sink in first time round. Give these questions a whirl to see whether your weather knowledge is up to the task. If you're still confused, then look back through the section and give the bits you don't know the once over.

1) During what months are temperatures highest in the UK?
2) Explain why latitude causes the climate within the UK to vary.
3) Give one reason why the whole of the UK has a mild climate.
4) Fill in the blanks below:
   Depressions form when _______ _______ air from the tropics, meets _______ _______ air from the poles.
5) Describe the weather conditions as a cold front passes overhead.
6) Describe what an anticyclone is.
7) Give one piece of evidence for the weather becoming more extreme in the UK.
8) Give two impacts that extreme weather has on the homes and lives of people in the UK.
9) Describe one way that the negative impacts of extreme weather in the UK are being reduced.
10) What is climate change?
11) Give one piece of evidence for global warming.
12) How do greenhouse gases cause global warming?
13) Give one economic impact and one social impact of climate change on the world.
14) Give one social impact and one political impact of climate change in the UK.
15) How much does the Kyoto Protocol aim to reduce greenhouse gas emissions by?
16) Describe one national response to climate change.
17) Give one condition that's needed for tropical storms to form.
18) Describe the distribution of tropical storms.
19) In what part of a tropical storm are there no clouds overhead?
20) Describe four primary impacts of tropical storms.
21) Give three reasons why the impacts of tropical storms are more severe in poorer countries.
22) Describe two ways buildings can be designed to withstand a tropical storm.
23) Why is it expensive to predict tropical storms?
24) a) Name one tropical storm that happened in a rich part of the world.
    b) Give three effects of this tropical storm.
    c) Give one long-term response to this tropical storm.
25) What is a drought?
26) Name two areas that are at risk from drought.
27) Give one reason why people continue to live in the areas where droughts happen.
28) What is a climatic hazard?
29) Describe five secondary impacts of a drought.
30) Why are the impacts of drought greater in more populated areas?
31) Describe one reason why the impacts of droughts are more severe in poorer countries.
32) Give two examples of how people can conserve water at home to reduce the impacts of droughts.
33) Explain how aid can be used to help reduce the impacts of droughts.

Ecosystems

Welcome to a new section — get ready to learn all about ecosystems.

An Ecosystem Includes all the Living and Non-Living Parts in an Area

1) An ecosystem is a unit that includes all the living parts (e.g. plants and animals) and the non-living (physical) parts (e.g. soil and climate) in an area.

EXAMPLE

A hedgerow ecosystem includes the plants that make up the hedgerow, the organisms that live in it and feed on it, the soil in the area and the rainfall and sunshine it receives.

2) The organisms in ecosystems can be classed as producers, consumers or decomposers.

3) A producer is an organism that uses sunlight energy to produce food.

EXAMPLE continued

The producers include hawthorn bushes and blackberry bushes.

4) A consumer is an organism that gets its energy by eating other organisms — it eats producers or other consumers.

EXAMPLE continued

The consumers include thrushes, ladybirds, spiders, greenfly, sparrows and sparrowhawks.

5) A food chain shows what eats what. A food web shows lots of food chains and how they overlap.

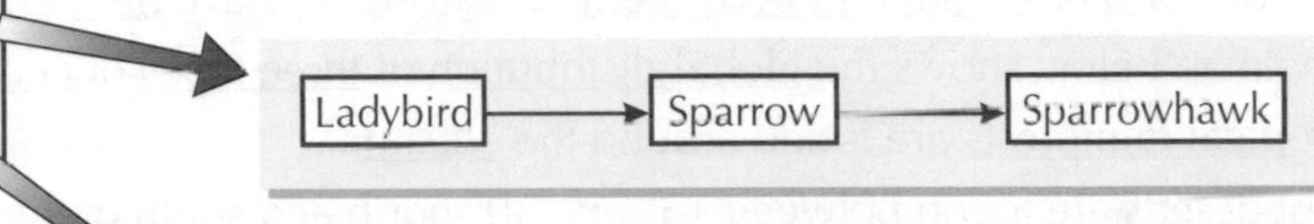

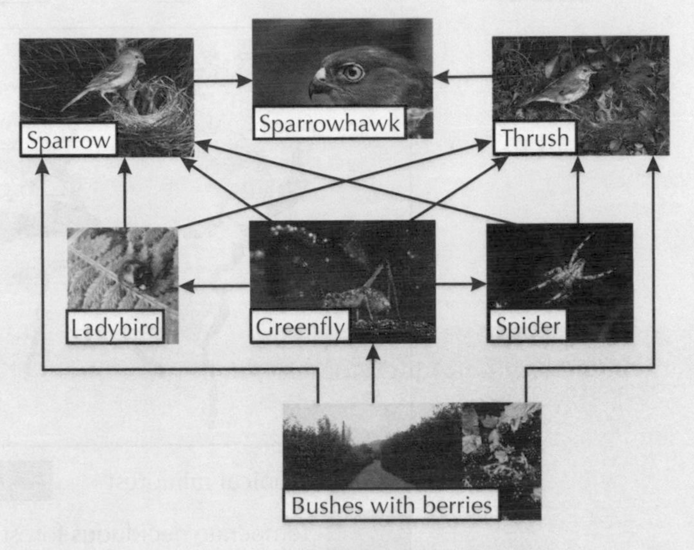

6) A decomposer is an organism that gets its energy by breaking down dead material, e.g. dead producers, dead consumers or fallen leaves. Bacteria and fungi are decomposers.

7) When dead material is decomposed, nutrients are released into the soil. The nutrients are then taken up from the soil by plants. The plants may be eaten by consumers. When the plants or consumers die, the nutrients are returned to the soil. This transfer of nutrients is called the nutrient cycle.

Food webs show multiple interlinked food chains

Examiners are really keen on definitions, so make sure you learn all the ones on this page — they're an easy way to pick up marks in the exam. (Knowing an example for things like ecosystems, producers, food chains, etc. doesn't hurt either.)

Ecosystems

All the parts in an ecosystem are linked together, so if one part changes it can have major consequences. Also, there are loads of different types of ecosystem in the world.

A Change to One Part of an Ecosystem has an Impact on Other Parts

Some parts of an ecosystem depend on the others, e.g. consumers depend on producers for a source of food and some depend on them for a habitat (a place to live). So, if one part changes it affects all the other parts that depend on it.

Here are two hedgerow examples:

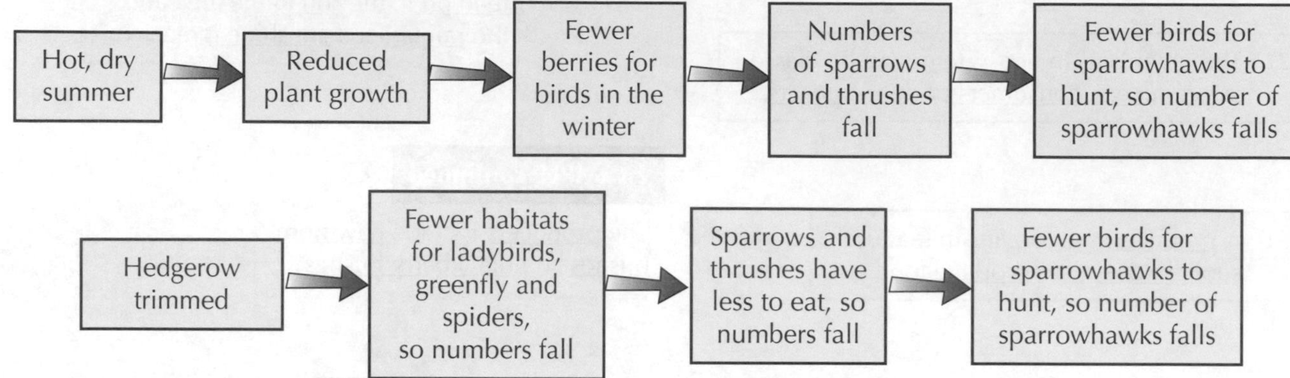

Hot, dry summer
Reduced plant growth
Fewer berries for birds in the winter
Numbers of sparrows and thrushes fall
Fewer birds for sparrowhawks to hunt, so number of sparrowhawks falls
Hedgerow trimmed
Fewer habitats for ladybirds, greenfly and spiders, so numbers fall
Sparrows and thrushes have less to eat, so numbers fall
Fewer birds for sparrowhawks to hunt, so number of sparrowhawks falls

Different Parts of the World Have Different Ecosystems

1) The climate in an area determines what type of ecosystem forms. So different parts of the world have different ecosystems because they have different climates.
2) The map below shows the global distribution of three types of ecosystem.
3) Tropical rainforests are found around the equator.
4) Hot deserts are found between 15° and 30° north and south of the equator where there's less rainfall.
5) Temperate deciduous forests are found between 40° and 60° north and south of the equator in places where there are four distinct seasons.

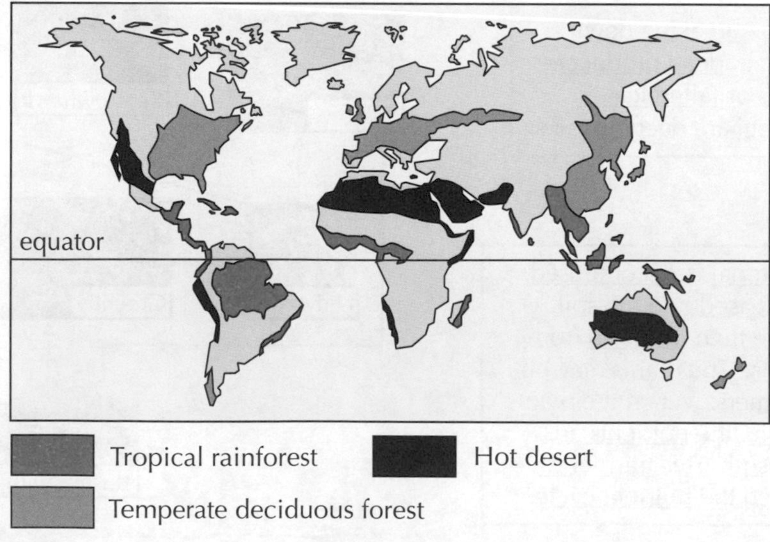

equator
Tropical rainforest
Hot desert
Temperate deciduous forest

The climate in an area determines the type of ecosystem found there

A small change to part of an ecosystem can have a big effect on the other parts — wherever in the world it is. Shut the book and write down the hedgerow examples, and sketch a rough map of where the three types of ecosystems are found.

Ecosystems — Tropical Rainforests

Let's have an in-depth look at tropical rainforests...

Hot, Wet Climates have Tropical Rainforests

AREAS

Central America, north and east South America (the Amazon), central Africa and south east Asia.

CLIMATE

A tropical rainforest has a hot, wet climate with no definite seasons.

SOIL

The soil isn't very fertile as heavy rain washes nutrients away. There are nutrients at the surface due to decayed leaf fall, but this layer is very thin as decay is fast in the warm, moist conditions.

VEGETATION STRUCTURE

There are three tree layers and a shrub layer:

The canopy layer is a continuous layer of trees around 30 m high.

The undercanopy layer trees are about half the height of the canopy layer.

40 m — Emergents — 30 m — Canopy — 20 m — Undercanopy — 10 m — Shrub layer

The tallest trees (called emergents) reach around 40 m and poke out of the canopy layer. They only have branches at their crown where most light reaches them.

The shrub layer is nearest the ground at around 10 m high. Very little light reaches this level.

PLANT ADAPTATIONS

1) Plants are adapted to the heavy rainfall — they have thick, waxy leaves that have pointed tips. The pointed tips (called drip-tips) channel the water to a point so it runs off — that way the weight of the water doesn't damage the plant.

2) Tall trees have big roots called buttress roots to support their trunks in the very shallow soil.

3) Climbing plants, such as lianas, use the tree trunks to climb up to the light.

4) The trees are deciduous — they drop their leaves in drier periods to reduce water loss.

Tree with buttress roots

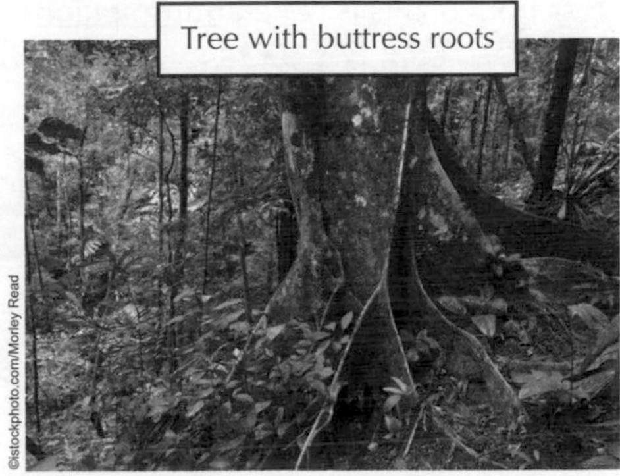

Rainforests — hot and wet with four layers of vegetation

Make sure you know about the climate, soil, vegetation structure and plant adaptations for the rainforest ecosystem. Cover the page and scribble down what you know to check. And give yourself bonus marks for getting the tree layer diagram right.

Ecosystems — Hot Deserts

From hot and wet, to hot and dry...

Hot, Dry Climates Have Hot Deserts

AREAS

North Africa, the Middle East, south west USA, large parts of Australia.

CLIMATE

There's very little rainfall. When it rains also varies a lot — it might only rain once every two or three years. Temperatures are extreme — they range from very hot in the day (e.g. 45 °C) to very cold at night (e.g. 5 °C).

SOIL

It's usually shallow with a coarse, gravelly texture. There's hardly any leaf fall so the soil isn't very fertile.

VEGETATION STRUCTURE

Plant growth is pretty sparse due to a lack of rainfall. Plants that do grow include cacti and thornbushes.

PLANT ADAPTATIONS

1) Plant roots are either extremely long to reach very deep water supplies, or spread out very wide near the surface to catch as much water as possible when it rains.

2) Cacti have swollen stems to store water and a thick waxy skin to reduce water loss (water loss from plants is called transpiration).

3) Cacti and some bushes also have small, spiky leaves to reduce water loss.

4) The seeds of some plants only germinate when it rains — the plants grow, flower and release seeds in just a few weeks, which makes sure they only grow when there's enough water to survive.

Hot and dry = thornbushes and cacti

There aren't many plants growing in hot deserts so this is a nice easy page to learn. Also, the plant adaptations tend to be based around trying to get as much water as possible, or trying to keep what they've got — learn them.

Ecosystems — Temperate Deciduous Forests

On to the last of the three types of ecosystem now, and this one should be familiar if you've ever been to the British countryside...

Mild, Wet Climates Have Temperate Deciduous Forests

AREAS

Most of Europe (including the UK), south east USA, China, Japan.

CLIMATE

This ecosystem has four distinct seasons — spring, summer, autumn and winter. The summers are warm and the winters are cool. There's rainfall all year round.

SOIL

The soil is deep and very fertile because there's a thick layer of leaf fall.

VEGETATION STRUCTURE

There are three plant layers:

The top layer is made up of trees (e.g. oak) that grow to around 30 m tall.

At the middle level (shrub layer) there are smaller trees, e.g. hawthorn. They're about 5 to 20 m tall.

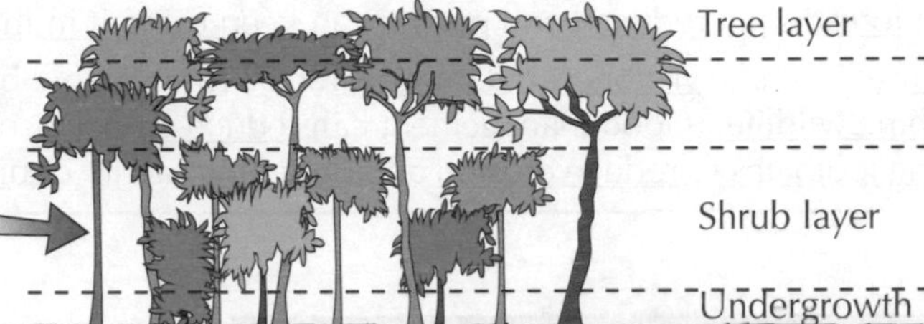

At ground level there's a layer of undergrowth including brambles, mosses, lichens, ferns and flowering plants.

PLANT ADAPTATIONS

1) The trees are deciduous (they drop their leaves in autumn and re-grow new ones in spring). This reduces water loss from leaves in the months where it's harder to get water from the soil because it may be frozen and there's not much light for photosynthesis.

2) Wildflowers (e.g. bluebells) grow on the forest floor in spring before the trees grow leaves and block out the light.

Temperate deciduous forests are found where there are four seasons

This is a fairly straightforward page, but you still need to learn it — to figure out if you've absorbed all the facts try drawing a table of climate, soil, vegetation structure and plant adaptations. If there are any blank boxes read the page again.

Temperate Deciduous Forest — Case Study

Now you know all about the <u>deciduous forest ecosystem</u> it's time to look at how it's <u>used</u> and <u>managed</u>.

Deciduous Forests are Used for Many Things

Forests don't just look pretty — they can be <u>used</u> for <u>loads of things</u>. For example:

1) <u>Timber</u> — <u>trees</u> are <u>cut down</u> and the <u>wood</u> is <u>sold</u> to <u>make money</u>.
2) <u>Timber products</u> — the <u>wood</u> can be <u>processed</u> to make <u>products</u> such as <u>fencing</u> and <u>furniture</u>.
3) <u>Recreation</u> — forests are used for <u>walking</u>, <u>cycling</u> and <u>other outdoor activities</u>.

If a forest is going to be <u>used</u> in the <u>long-term</u>, it has to be <u>managed</u> in a way that's <u>sustainable</u>, i.e. in a way that allows people <u>today</u> to get the things they need, but <u>without stopping</u> people in the <u>future</u> from getting what they <u>need</u>.

Forests can be Carefully Managed to Conserve Them For The Future

Here are some examples of <u>sustainable management strategies</u>:

1) <u>Controlled felling</u> — instead of clearing all the trees in an area, <u>only some trees</u> are <u>cut down</u>, e.g. trees <u>over</u> a <u>certain age</u> or just <u>one species</u>. This is <u>less damaging</u> to the forest than <u>felling all</u> the trees in an area because the <u>overall forest structure</u> is kept. This means the forest will be able to <u>regenerate</u> so it <u>can be used in the future</u>.

   Controlled felling is also called selective logging.

2) <u>Replanting</u> — where trees are <u>felled</u>, they're <u>replaced</u> by <u>planting new trees</u>. This makes sure that <u>overall</u> the <u>amount</u> of <u>forest</u> is <u>not reduced</u> and people can <u>keep using it in the future</u>.
3) <u>Planning for recreational use</u> — lots of <u>visitors</u> can <u>damage</u> a forest, for example by causing <u>erosion</u>, <u>dropping litter</u> and <u>disturbing wildlife</u>. Good management can <u>reduce damage</u> so <u>use can continue in the future</u>, e.g. by <u>paving footpaths</u> to <u>reduce erosion</u> and <u>providing</u> plenty of <u>bins</u> to <u>reduce litter</u>.

Case Study — The New Forest in Hampshire

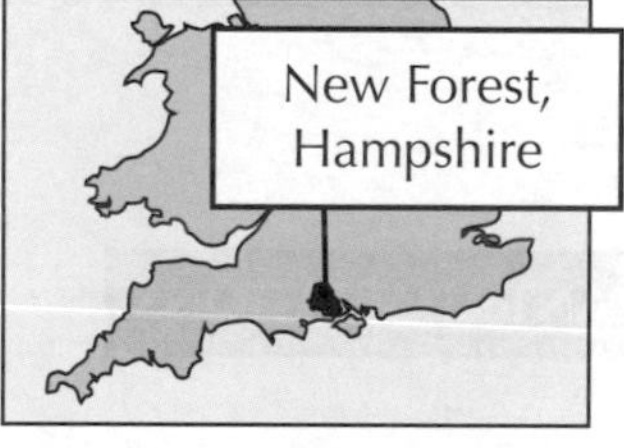

1) The New Forest is a <u>National Park</u> that covers <u>375 km</u>^{2}.
2) It's used for <u>timber</u>, <u>timber products</u>, <u>farming</u> and <u>recreation</u>.

- The New Forest produces around <u>50 000 tonnes</u> of <u>timber</u> a year.
- <u>Local mills</u> make <u>fencing products</u> out of the timber from the New Forest.

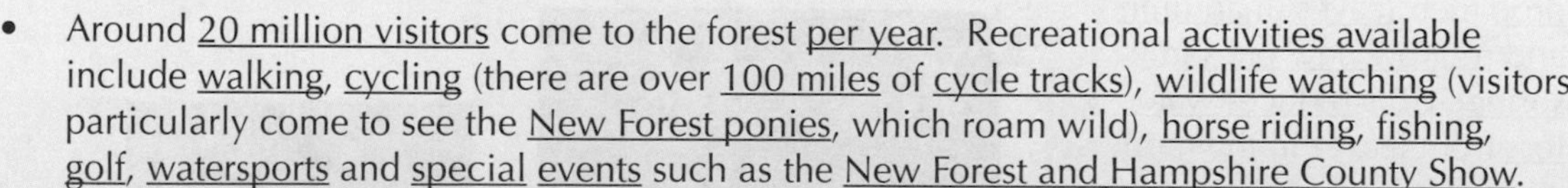

- Around <u>20 million visitors</u> come to the forest <u>per year</u>. Recreational <u>activities available</u> include <u>walking</u>, <u>cycling</u> (there are over <u>100 miles</u> of <u>cycle tracks</u>), <u>wildlife watching</u> (visitors particularly come to see the <u>New Forest ponies</u>, which roam wild), <u>horse riding</u>, <u>fishing</u>, <u>golf</u>, <u>watersports</u> and <u>special events</u> such as the <u>New Forest and Hampshire County Show</u>.

3) The forest is <u>managed</u> to make sure the way it's <u>used</u> is <u>sustainable</u>:

- Areas <u>cleared of trees</u> are either <u>replanted</u> or <u>restored to other habitats</u> like heathland.
- <u>Walkers</u> and <u>cyclists</u> are encouraged to stick to the <u>footpaths</u> and <u>cycle paths</u> to limit damage to surrounding <u>habitats</u>. Also <u>dogs aren't allowed near wildlife breeding sites</u> at certain times of year. These measures help to <u>conserve wildlife</u> so it's still there for future generations.
- <u>Recreational users</u> are encouraged to <u>act responsibly</u> (e.g. close gates, take litter home by information at the <u>National Park Forest Centre</u> and <u>local information points</u>.

Deciduous forests are mostly used for timber and recreation

There's quite a lot of info on this page, so <u>learn the details</u> one chunk at a time. Make sure <u>sustainable management</u> is as clear as crystal before you move on too (it pops up later on in the section and is a favourite exam topic).

Worked Exam Questions

Here's a typical exam question with the answers filled in to help. They won't be there on the real exam though, so you'd better learn how to answer them yourself...

1 Study **Figure 1**, which shows temperature and rainfall data for an area of temperate deciduous forest.

Figure 1

Month	Average temperature / °C	Average rainfall / mm
January	2	64
February	5	42
March	6	33
April	12	42
May	19	45
June	19	48
July	21	69
August	19	62
September	12	45
October	10	55
November	4	65
December	2	52

Quote data from the figure to back up your answer.

(a) Use **Figure 1** to describe the climate of this temperate deciduous forest.

The climate is cool in winter (e.g. 2 °C in January) and warm in summer (e.g. 19 °C in August). There's rainfall all year round but it varies from 33 mm to 69 mm per month.

(2 marks)

(b) Describe the global distribution of temperate deciduous forests.

Temperate deciduous forests are found between 40° and 60° north and south of the equator. They're found in most of Europe, south east USA, China and Japan.

(2 marks)

(c) Describe the vegetation found in a temperate deciduous forest.

The question asks about vegetation in general so you can include the vegetation structure and plant adaptations.

There are three layers of vegetation. The top layer is made up of trees, like oak, that grow to around 30 m tall. The middle shrub layer is made up of smaller trees, like hawthorn, that are between 5 and 20 m tall. At ground level there's an undergrowth layer made up of small plants, e.g. brambles and ferns. The vegetation is adapted to the climate in several ways, e.g. trees are deciduous, which reduces water loss from leaves in months when it's harder to get water from the frozen soil and there's not much light for photosynthesis. Also, wildflowers grow on the forest floor in spring before the trees grow leaves and block out the light.

Add in examples of vegetation where you can.

(6 marks)

(d) Explain what the soil is like in a temperate deciduous forest.

The soil is deep and fertile because there's a thick layer of leaf litter produced when the trees lose their leaves.

(2 marks)

Exam Questions

1 Study **Figure 1**, which shows a coastal food chain.

Figure 1

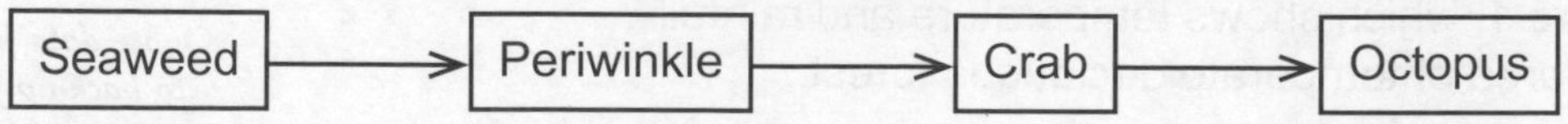

Seaweed → Periwinkle → Crab → Octopus

(a) Which of the organisms in the food chain shown in **Figure 1** is the producer?

....

(1 mark)

(b) Give an example of a consumer from the food chain shown in **Figure 1**.

....

(1 mark)

(c) Explain how the organisms in the food chain shown in **Figure 1** might be affected if a disease reduced the crab population.

....

....

....

(3 marks)

2 Study **Figure 2**, which shows climate data for a hot desert.

Figure 2

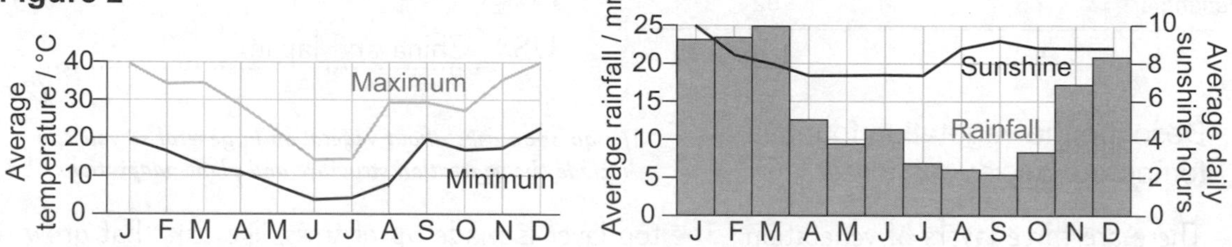

Average temperature / °C: 0, 10, 20, 30, 40; Maximum; Minimum; J F M A M J J A S O N D

Average rainfall / mm: 0, 5, 10, 15, 20, 25; Average daily sunshine hours: 0, 2, 4, 6, 8, 10; Sunshine; Rainfall; J F M A M J J A S O N D

(a) What is the average maximum temperature for December?

....

(1 mark)

(b) With reference to **Figure 2**, describe the characteristics of the hot desert climate.

....

....

....

....

(4 marks)

(c) Describe the characteristics of the soil in hot deserts.

....

....

(2 marks)

Tropical Rainforest — Deforestation

Removal of trees from forests is called deforestation. It's happening on a huge scale in many tropical rainforests. Let's start with the causes, then move on to some impacts...

There are *Five* Main *Causes* of *Deforestation*

Farming — forest is cleared to set up small subsistence farms or large commercial cattle ranches. Often the "slash and burn" technique is used to clear the forest — vegetation is cut down and left to dry then burnt.

Commercial logging — trees are felled to make money.

Mineral extraction — minerals (e.g. gold and iron ore) are mined and sold to make money. Trees are cut down to expose ground and to clear access routes.

Population pressure — as the population in the area increases, trees are cleared to make land for new settlements.

Road building — more settlements and industry (e.g. logging and mining) lead to more roads being built. Trees along the path of the road have to be cleared to build them.

Deforestation has *Economic* and *Political Impacts*

ECONOMIC

1) Logging, farming and mining create jobs.

2) A lot of money is made from selling timber, mining and commercial farming.

POLITICAL

There's pressure from foreign governments to stop deforestation.

There's more about the impacts of deforestation on the next page.

'Slash and burn' — a brutal way to clear a forest

A bit of a serious page this one, but one that's not too difficult to learn — there are just five main causes and a couple of economic and political impacts, so there's no excuse for not knowing them like the back of your hand.

Tropical Rainforest — Deforestation

You've just read about some of the impacts of deforestation, but there are more to learn, so read on...

Deforestation also has Environmental and Social Impacts

ENVIRONMENTAL

1) Fewer trees means fewer habitats and food sources for animals and birds. This reduces biodiversity as organisms either have to move or become extinct.

2) With no trees to hold the soil together, heavy rain washes away the soil (soil erosion).

3) If a lot of soil from deforested areas is washed into rivers it can kill fish, make the water undrinkable and cause flooding (as the riverbed is raised so it can't hold as much water).

4) Without a tree canopy to intercept (catch) rainfall and tree roots to absorb it, more water reaches the soil. This increases the risk of flooding and reduces soil fertility as nutrients in the soil are washed down into the earth, out of reach of plants.

5) Without trees there's no leaf fall — so no nutrient supply to the soil, which makes it less fertile.

6) Trees remove CO_2 from the atmosphere when they photosynthesise, so without them less CO_2 is removed. Also, burning vegetation to clear forest produces CO_2. So deforestation means more CO_2 in the atmosphere, which adds to global warming.

7) Without trees, water isn't removed from the soil and evaporated into the atmosphere. So fewer clouds form and rainfall in the area is reduced. Reduced rainfall reduces plant growth.

SOCIAL

1) The quality of life for some local people improves as there are more jobs.

2) The livelihoods of some local people are destroyed — deforestation can cause the loss of the animals and plants that they rely on to make a living.

3) Some native tribes have been forced to move when trees on their land have been cleared.

4) There can be conflict between native people, landowners, mining companies and logging companies over use of land.

Deforestation can have some devastating effects

Deforestation is a tricky topic because although it has some positive impacts it has quite a lot of negative ones too. Examiners will expect you to know both, so make sure you can reel off plenty of them in the exam.

Tropical Rainforest — Sustainable Management

It's not all doom and gloom for rainforests. In fact, this page is dedicated to the ways to manage them.

Tropical Rainforests can be Sustainably Managed

Rainforests can be managed in a way that's sustainable, i.e. in a way that allows people today to get the things they need, but without stopping people in the future from getting what they need.
Here are some of the ways it can be done:

1) SELECTIVE LOGGING

1) Only some trees (e.g. just the oldest ones) are felled — most trees are left standing.
2) This is less damaging to the forest than felling all the trees in an area. If only a few trees are taken from each area the overall forest structure is kept — the canopy's still there and the soil isn't exposed. This means the forest will be able to regenerate so it can be used in the future.
3) The least damaging forms are 'horse logging' and 'helicopter logging' — dragging felled trees out of the forest using horses or removing them with helicopters instead of huge trucks.

EXAMPLE: Helicopter logging is used in the Malaysian state of Sarawak.

2) REPLANTING

1) This is when new trees are planted to replace the ones that are cut down.
2) This means there will be trees for people to use in the future.
3) It's important that the same types of tree are planted that were cut down, so that the variety of trees is kept for the future.
4) In some countries there are environmental laws to make logging companies replant trees when they clear an area.

See the next page for more ways to manage rainforests sustainably.

3) REDUCING DEMAND FOR HARDWOOD

1) Hardwood is a general term for wood from certain tree species, e.g. mahogany and teak. The wood tends to be fairly dense and hard — it's used to make things like furniture.
2) There's a high demand for hardwood from consumers in richer countries.
3) This means that some tropical hardwood trees are becoming rarer as people are chopping them down and selling them.
4) Some richer countries are trying to reduce demand so fewer of these tree species are cut down, which means they'll exist for future generations to use.
5) Strategies to reduce demand include heavily taxing imported hardwood or banning its sale.
6) Some countries with tropical rainforests also ban logging of hardwood species.

4) EDUCATION

1) Some local people don't know what the environmental impacts of deforestation are. Local people try to make money in the short-term (e.g. by illegal logging to overcome their own poverty.
2) Educating these people about the impacts of deforestation and ways to reduce the impacts decreases their effect on the environment.
3) Also, educating them about alternative ways to make money that don't damage the environment, e.g. ecotourism (see the next page), reduces their impact.
4) Both of these things mean that the rainforest is conserved and so will be there for future generations to use.
5) Education of the international community about the impacts of deforestation will reduce demand for products that lead to deforestation, e.g. hardwood furniture. It will also put pressure on governments to reduce deforestation.

Sustainable management — planning for the future...

I did say it wasn't all doom and gloom. You need to really get your head around what sustainable management is and how it makes sure that there are lots of trees, animals and insects for future generations.

Tropical Rainforest — Sustainable Management

The previous page described some sustainable management strategies for rainforests. And here are some more...

Tropical Rainforests can be Sustainably Managed

1) ECOTOURISM

1) Ecotourism is tourism that doesn't harm the environment and benefits the local people.
2) Ecotourism provides a source of income for local people, e.g. they act as guides, provide accommodation and transport.
3) This means the local people don't have to log or farm to make money. So fewer trees are cut down, which means there are more trees for the future.
4) Ecotourism is usually a small-scale activity, with only small numbers of visitors going to an area at a time. This helps to keep the environmental impact of tourism low.
5) Ecotourism should cause as little harm to the environment as possible. For example, by making sure waste and litter are disposed of properly to prevent land and water contamination.
6) Ecotourism helps the sustainable development of an area because it improves the quality of life for local people without stopping people in the future getting what they need (because it doesn't damage the environment or deplete resources).

EXAMPLE: Tataquara Lodge is a tourist lodge in the Brazilian rainforest. The lodge has 15 rooms and offers activities like fishing, canoeing, wildlife viewing and forest walks. Waste is disposed of responsibly and it runs lights using solar power.

2) REDUCING DEBT

1) A lot of tropical rainforests are in poorer countries, e.g. Nigeria, Belize and Burma.
2) Poorer countries often borrow money from richer countries or organisations (e.g. the World Bank) to fund development schemes or cope with emergencies like floods.
3) This money has to be paid back (sometimes with interest).
4) These countries often allow logging, farming and mining in rainforests to make money to pay back the debt.
5) So reducing debt would mean countries wouldn't have to do this and the rainforests could be conserved for the future.
6) Debt can be cancelled by countries or organisations, but there's no guarantee the money will be spent on conservation.
7) Conservation swaps (debt-for-nature swaps) guarantee the money is spent on conservation — part of a country's debt is paid off by someone else in exchange for investment in conservation.

EXAMPLE: In 1987 a conservation group paid off some of Bolivia's debt in exchange for creating a rainforest reserve.

3) PROTECTION

1) Environmental laws can be used to protect rainforests. For example:
   - Laws that ban the use of wood from forests that are managed non-sustainably.
   - Laws that ban illegal logging.
   - Laws that ban logging of some tree species, e.g. mahogany.
2) Many countries have set up national parks and nature reserves within rainforests. In these areas damaging activities, e.g. logging, are restricted. However, a lack of funds can make it difficult to police the restrictions.

See the previous page for a definition of sustainable management.

Ecotourism — an environmentally friendly way to see the sights...

Don't forget — the basic idea is that anything that allows people today to get what they need whilst stopping the rainforest being damaged or its resources being depleted is sustainable management.

Tropical Rainforest — Case Study

The Amazon is the largest rainforest on Earth, but it's shrinking fast due to deforestation.

Deforestation is a Problem in the Amazon

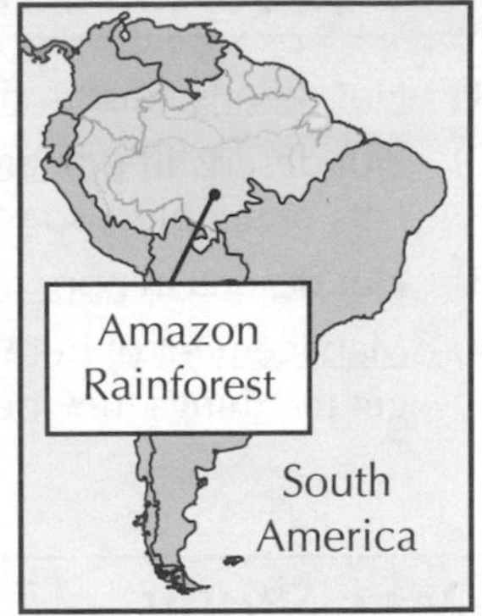

The Amazon covers an area of around 8 million km², including parts of Brazil, Peru, Colombia, Venezuela, Ecuador, Bolivia, Guyana, Suriname and French Guiana. However, since 1970 over 600 000 km² has been destroyed by deforestation. There are lots of causes — for example, between 2000 and 2005:

1) 60% was caused by cattle ranching.
2) 33% was caused by small-scale subsistence farming.
3) 3% was caused by logging.
4) 3% was caused by mining, urbanisation, road construction, dams and fires.
5) 1% was caused by large-scale commercial farming (other than cattle ranching).

Deforestation in the Amazon has Many Impacts

ENVIRONMENTAL	• Habitat destruction and loss of biodiversity, e.g. the number of endangered species in Brazil increased from 218 in 1989 to 628 in 2008. • The Amazon stores around 100 billion tonnes of carbon — deforestation will release some of this as carbon dioxide, which causes global warming.
SOCIAL	• Local ways of life have been affected, e.g. some Brazilian rubber tappers have lost their livelihoods as rubber trees have been cut down. • Native tribes have been forced to move, e.g. some of the Guarani tribe in Brazil have moved because their land was taken for cattle ranching and sugar plantations. • There's conflict between large landowners, subsistence farmers and native people, e.g. in 2009 there were riots in Peru over rainforest destruction and hundreds of native Indians were killed or injured.
ECONOMIC	• Farming makes a lot of money for countries in the rainforest, e.g. in 2008, Brazil made \$6.9 billion from trading cattle. • The mining industry creates jobs for loads of people, e.g. the Buenaventura Mining Company in Peru employs over 3100 people.

Several Sustainable Management Strategies are being Used

1) Some deforested areas are being replanted with new trees, e.g. Peru plans to replant more than 100 000 km² of forest before 2018.
2) Some countries are trying to reduce the number of hardwood trees felled, e.g. Brazil banned mahogany logging in 2001 and seizes timber from illegal logging companies.
3) Ecotourism is becoming more popular, e.g. the Madre de Dios region in Peru has around 70 lodges for ecotourists — 60 000 people visited the region in 2007.
4) Most countries have environmental laws to help protect the rainforest, e.g. the Brazilian Forest Code says that landowners have to keep 50-80% of their land as forest.
5) Some countries have national parks, e.g. the Central Amazon Conservation Complex in Brazil is the largest protected area in the rainforest, covering around 25 000 km². It's a World Heritage Site that's home to loads of ecosystems and animals like black caimans and river dolphins.
6) Reducing debt has helped some countries conserve their rainforest, e.g. in 2008 the USA reduced Peru's debt by \$25 million in exchange for conserving its rainforest.

The Amazon Rainforest — fading fast...

Lots of facts and figures for you to learn here, some of them pretty shocking too. It's good to know that there are strategies being put in place to protect the Amazon — make sure you know them for the exam.

Hot Deserts — Case Study

Hot deserts aren't totally deserted — some people live and work there.

Hot Deserts Provide Economic Opportunities

1) Hot deserts exist in rich and poor areas of the world.
2) Hot deserts in rich areas are usually used for things like commercial farming, mining and tourism. Lots of people also retire there (retirement migration).
3) Hot deserts in poor areas are usually used for hunting and gathering and farming.
4) Management of both rich and poor deserts needs to be sustainable — i.e. to allow people today to get the things they need, but without stopping people in the future from getting what they need.

Case Study — The Kalahari Desert is a Relatively Poor Region

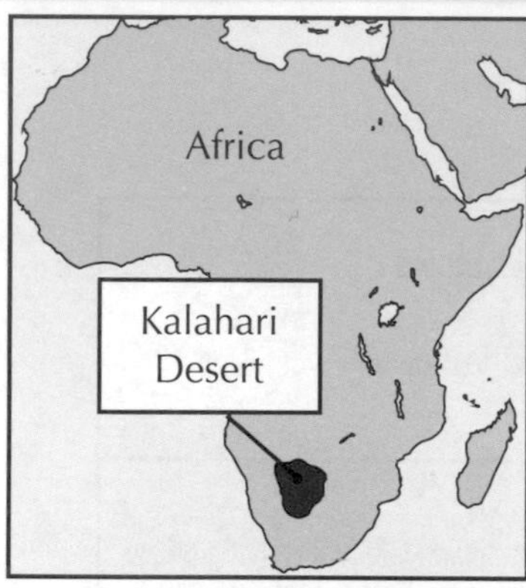

1) The Kalahari Desert has an area of 260 000 km^2. It covers most of Botswana and parts of Zimbabwe, Namibia and South Africa.
2) It gets little rain (about 200 mm per year). The only permanent river in the area is the Boteti River. However, temporary streams and rivers form after rain. The low rainfall in the area means that droughts are a problem.
3) The Kalahari is very sparsely populated, but there are native people that live there, e.g. the San Bushmen and the Tswana. Some native people still hunt wild game (e.g. antelope) with bows and arrows and gather plants for food.
4) Farming cattle, goats and sheep is a big industry in the Kalahari, e.g. in 1998 there were 2.3 million cattle in Botswana. Some grazing land is irrigated using groundwater from boreholes.
5) There's lots of mining in the area — there are coal, diamond, gold, copper, nickel and uranium mines, e.g. the Opara Diamond Mine in Botswana.
6) Some uses of the Kalahari have negative impacts:

   1) Overgrazing of land has caused soil erosion, and irrigation has depleted groundwater supplies.
   2) Fences put up by farmers have blocked migration routes of wild animals, e.g. wildebeest. The animals can't move to where the grazing is best so some die from starvation.
   3) Mining and farming have led to native people being forced off their land.
   4) Mining uses a lot of water from boreholes. This is depleting groundwater supplies.

7) Here are a few of the management strategies being carried out in the Kalahari:

   1) Some places are trying to conserve water. E.g. in Windhoek in Namibia people are charged for the volume of water they use. This encourages them to use less. This is more sustainable because water supplies aren't depleted as much and so more will be there in the future.
   2) Water supply all over the Kalahari is being increased by building dams and drilling more boreholes. This allows more farming and reduces the effects of drought, but isn't sustainable because it depletes groundwater supplies even more.
   3) Several game reserves have been created to provide areas for the native people to live and to protect wildlife. For example, the Central Kalahari Game Reserve in Botswana was set up in 1961 as a refuge for the San Bushmen. This is sustainable because it conserves the way of life of the native people and conserves the wildlife for future generations.
   4) Some agricultural fences have been removed to allow animals to migrate. This is sustainable because fewer wild animals die so they will still be around in the future.

The Kalahari Desert — dry and depleted...

The basic gist of this page is that hot deserts are used for loads of things, some of which have negative impacts and are unsustainable. The case study of the Kalahari shows this, but also how it can be managed sustainably — learn it.

Hot Deserts — Case Study

Just one more case study to go for this section — another hot desert, this time in a rich area.

*Case Study — The **Mojave Desert** is a **Relatively Rich Region***

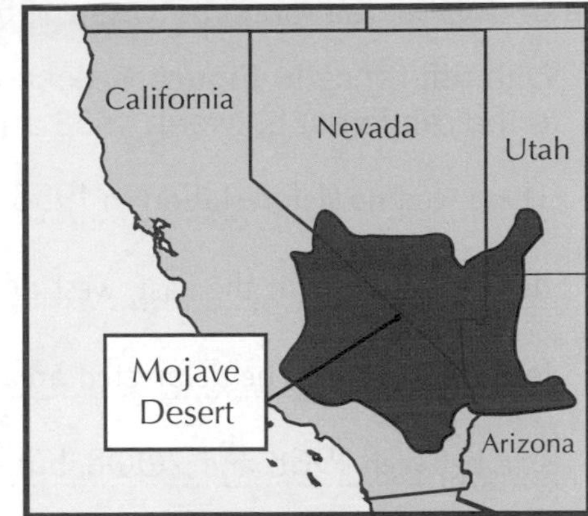

1) The Mojave Desert in the USA covers over 57 000 km² and includes parts of California, Nevada, Utah and Arizona.
2) The region gets less than 250 mm of rain per year.
3) There's commercial farming in the area. For example, there have been cattle ranches in the region for over 100 years.
4) The area is sparsely populated but the population is increasing, e.g. Las Vegas in Nevada is the USA's fastest growing city. The area is popular with people retiring due to its year-round good weather, e.g. 80% of the people in Sun City in Arizona are over 65.
5) Water for farming and for people comes from groundwater, the Mojave River and the Colorado River.
6) The region has many tourist destinations including Las Vegas, Death Valley and the Grand Canyon. The Death Valley National Park gets around 1 million visitors per year. Tourists are attracted by the wildlife and geology, and activities like camping, hiking, horse riding and off-road driving.

7) In the past, gold, silver, copper, lead and salts were mined, although most mines have now closed. There are a few borax mines still working in California.
8) Some uses of the Mojave have negative impacts:
   1) Rapid population growth (including retirement migrants) has depleted water resources.
   2) Farming uses a lot of water, and it can also cause soil erosion.
   3) Tourists deplete water resources, drop litter, damage plants and cause soil erosion (e.g. by using off road vehicles).
9) Here are a few of the management strategies being carried out in the Mojave:
   1) There are water conservation schemes in the area, e.g. the Mojave Water Agency gives people vouchers to buy water efficient toilets and washing machines. They also pay people to remove grass lawns (which need a lot of water) and replace them with plants that don't use as much water. These things are more sustainable because they don't deplete water supplies as much, so there's more for future generations.
   2) The Mojave Desert has four National Parks (Death Valley, Joshua Tree, Zion and the Grand Canyon). Native species are protected and there are strict rules on land use, e.g. there are strict rules on mining to reduce environmental damage. This is sustainable because it conserves the area, so future generations can use it.
   3) There are designated roads for off-road vehicles, and sensitive areas are fenced off so they can't get in. This is sustainable because it helps conserve the plant life for future generations.
   4) Some hotels in Las Vegas are trying to conserve water, e.g. the MGM Mirage® Hotels use drip-irrigation to water lawns. This is more sustainable as it doesn't use as much water as other irrigation methods, so conserves more water for the future.

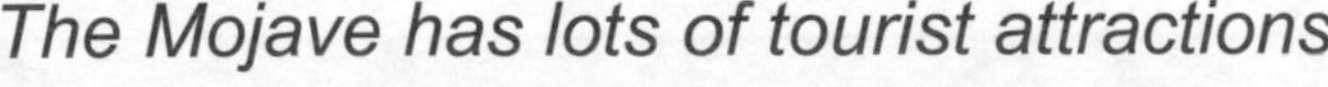

The Mojave has lots of tourist attractions

Mojave (said 'mo-har-ve') means 'the meadows', which is a bit weird as not much grows there. It's also a bit weird that something like water can run out, but hot deserts don't get a lot of it so if people use it up, it might not get replaced.

Worked Exam Questions

Another really useful worked exam question now, to help you answer them for yourself.
Read through this page carefully, then have a bash at the questions on the next page on your own.

1 Study **Figure 1**, a series of maps showing the extent of deforestation in an area of tropical rainforest between 1958 and 2008.

(a) With reference to **Figure 1**, describe the changes to the rainforest between 1958 and 2008.

Study the figure carefully before you start writing.

Figure 1

There was no deforestation in 1958 but there were deforested areas in the east, west and south of the forest by 1968. The deforested areas increased in size between 1968 and 2008, but they increased more rapidly after 1988. A new deforested area appeared in the forest in 1988.

(4 marks)

(b) Give two advantages of deforestation.

Logging, farming and mining in deforested areas can create jobs for the local population.

A lot of money can be made from selling timber produced when trees are felled.

(2 marks)

(c) Describe and explain the environmental impacts of rainforest deforestation.

Always re-read long answers to check they make sense and the spelling is correct.

Deforestation reduces biodiversity in the rainforest because removing trees destroys habitats and food sources for animals and birds, so they either move away or die. It causes soil erosion because heavy rain washes away the soil if there are no trees to hold the soil together. Deforestation can also cause flooding because the soil from deforested areas gets washed into the rivers by the rain, raising the riverbed so it can't hold as much water.

(6 marks)

(d) For a tropical rainforest you have studied describe the strategies being used to reduce deforestation.

The wording 'you have studied' tells you it's a case study question, so include loads of details.

Since 1970, 600 000 km^2 of the Amazon has been destroyed by deforestation. Some countries are trying to reduce the number of hardwood trees felled, e.g. Brazil banned mahogany logging in 2001. Some countries have national parks where trees are protected, e.g. one park in Brazil is over 25 000 km^2. Some deforested areas are also being replanted, e.g. Peru plans to replant more than 100 000 km^2 of forest before 2018.

(4 marks)

Exam Questions

1 Study **Figure 1**, part of a newspaper article on the Amazon Education Project in Brazil.

Figure 1

Education Scheme Offers Hope for Amazon Rainforest

Brazilian environmentalists have set up an Education Project that aims to educate the local population about the devastating impacts of deforestation.

The project manager Silverado Arboles said: "The local population is reliant on the rainforest, but the problem is that they can make a lot of money from illegal logging. Hardwoods such as mahogany fetch high prices so it is hard to find alternative sources of income that pay as much".

The project also aims to help locals to sustainably manage the forest — it runs schemes to teach locals selective logging techniques, and it provides discounted tree saplings for replanting schemes.

(a) What is meant by 'the sustainable management of tropical rainforests'?

....

....

(2 marks)

(b) Use evidence from **Figure 1** to describe how forests can be sustainably managed.

....

....

....

....

(4 marks)

2 Study **Figure 2**, which shows the global distribution of hot deserts and some of their main uses.

Use evidence from **Figure 2** to describe and compare the main uses of hot deserts in rich and poor countries.

Figure 2

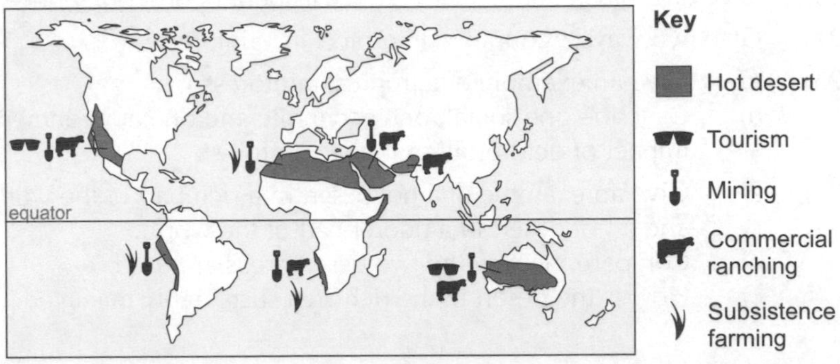

....

....

....

....

....

....

....

(6 marks)

Revision Summary for Section 4

So now you know absolutely everything there is to know about ecosystems. Or at least you know everything you need to for the exam. But before you go rushing off to celebrate, best make sure you actually do know it. Now's as good a time as any, so give these questions a go.

1) Define the term ecosystem.
2) What is a consumer?
3) What is a food web?
4) Describe how nutrients are transferred to the soil in an ecosystem.
5) Describe the global distribution of tropical rainforests.
6) How many layers of vegetation does a tropical rainforest have?
7) What is an emergent tree?
8) Give three ways rainforest plants are adapted to their environment.
9) Describe the soil in a rainforest.
10) Give two ways plants are adapted to the hot desert environment.
11) Describe the climate of a temperate deciduous forest.
12) How tall is the top tree layer in a temperate deciduous forest?
13) What is controlled felling?
14) a) Give an example of a temperate deciduous forest.
    b) Describe how the forest is used for recreation.
    c) Describe how the forest is managed to make sure the way it's used is sustainable.
15) What are the five main causes of rainforest deforestation?
16) Give two economic impacts of rainforest deforestation.
17) Give two social impacts of rainforest deforestation.
18) What is selective logging?
19) What is replanting?
20) How does reducing demand for hardwood help to conserve rainforests?
21) How can education be used to reduce rainforest deforestation?
22) What is ecotourism?
23) Give one way a country can reduce its debt in order to reduce deforestation.
24) Give two ways a country can protect its rainforest.
25) a) Give an example of a tropical rainforest.
    b) Describe one social, one economic and one environmental impact of deforestation in that rainforest.
26) a) Give an example of a hot desert in a rich part of the world and a hot desert in a poorer part of the world.
    b) Compare the way the two desert areas are used.
    c) How is the desert in the rich area sustainably managed?

The Hydrological Cycle

Since this is the first page of a shiny new section I'm going to treat you to something special — the hydrological cycle (a.k.a. the water cycle in non-geography lingo).

The Hydrological Cycle Shows How Water Moves Around

1) The hydrological cycle has different parts — the sea, the land and the atmosphere.
2) Water flows between the different parts in various ways, and is also stored on the land (see below).
3) The hydrological cycle is a closed system. This means there are no inputs (water going in) or outputs (water going out) — the water just flows round and round the cycle:

1 Water evaporates from the sea and the land — evaporation is when water is heated by the sun and turns into water vapour. Transpiration is the evaporation of water from plants. Evapotranspiration is both evaporation and transpiration happening together.

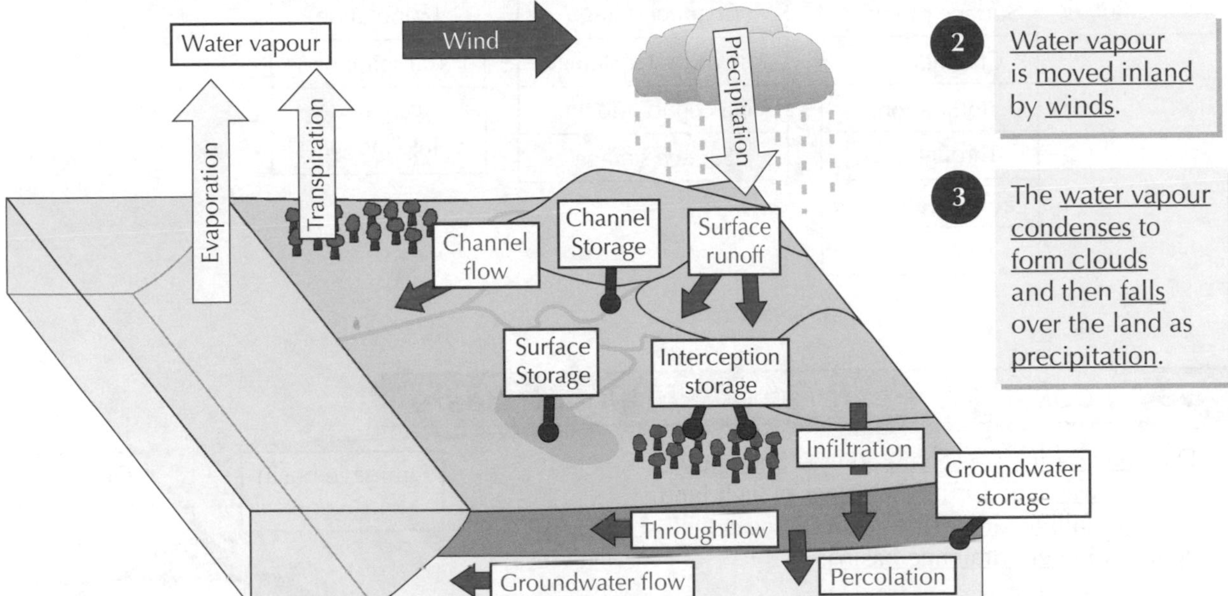

2 Water vapour is moved inland by winds.

3 The water vapour condenses to form clouds and then falls over the land as precipitation.

4 Water moves from one place to another in many ways (called flows or transfers):

- Infiltration is when water soaks into the soil.
- Percolation is when water moves vertically down through soil and rock.
- Throughflow is when water in the soil flows downhill.
- Groundwater flow is when water in rock flows downhill.
- Surface runoff is when water flows overground.
- Channel flow is the flow of water in a river.

The movement of water vapour by wind is also a flow.

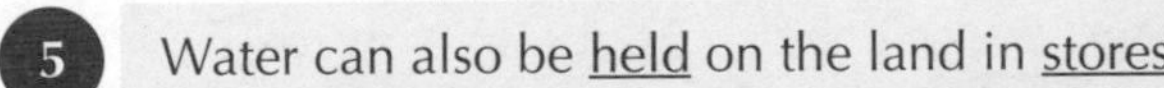

5 Water can also be held on the land in stores:

- Channel storage is when water is held in a river.
- Groundwater storage is when water is stored underground in soil and rock. A rock that stores water is called an aquifer, e.g. chalk.
- Interception storage is when water lands on things like plant leaves and doesn't hit the ground.
- Surface storage is when water is held in things like lakes, reservoirs and puddles.

6 The water eventually ends up in the sea, where it evaporates and goes round the cycle again...

The hydrological cycle is made up of flows and stores

There are a lot of geography terms to get your head round on this page — make sure you understand what each one means. To check, shut the book and scribble out as many definitions as you can remember (no sneaky peeking either).

Drainage Basins

If you've had a crack at the hydrological cycle then drainage basins should be a doddle — they're just a part of the hydrological cycle. But you might want to know a little bit more than that, so have a read...

*A **Drainage Basin** is the Area of Land **Drained by a River***

1) The part of the hydrological cycle that happens on land goes on in drainage basins.
2) Drainage basins are open systems:
   - There are inputs of water to drainage basins.
   - Water flows through them and is stored in them.
   - There are outputs of water from drainage basins.

The movement of water through a drainage basin is the same as in the hydrological cycle (see previous page), but without the sea and wind bit.

Here's a handy table to show you what's going on:

INPUTS	FLOWS	STORES	OUTPUTS
Precipitation	Surface runoff	Channel storage	Evaporation
	Channel flow	Groundwater storage	Transpiration
	Infiltration	Interception storage	River flow into the sea
	Throughflow	Surface storage	
	Groundwater flow		
	Percolation		

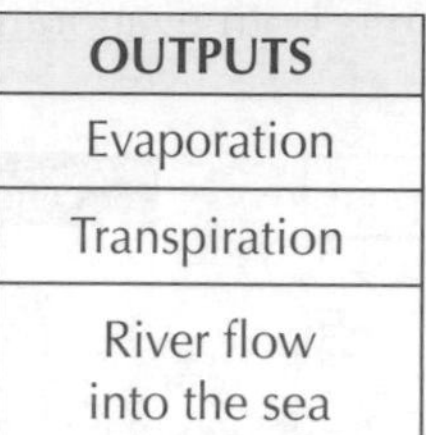

*Have a Look at the **Features** of a **Drainage Basin***

1) Drainage basins are separated by a boundary called a watershed. They're ridges of high land — water falling either side of these ridges will go into different drainage basins.

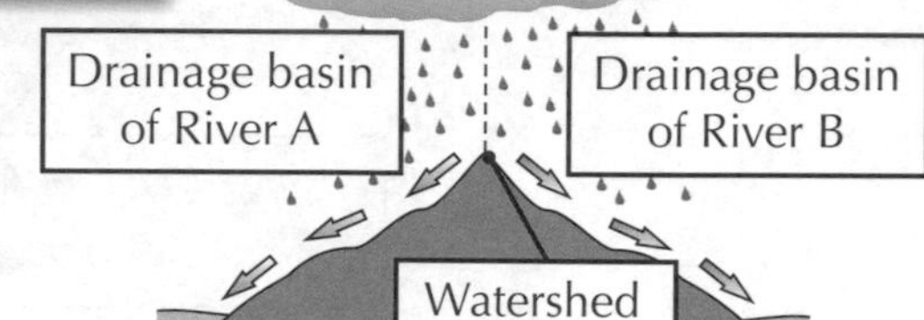

2) These are a few of the key features of a drainage basin:

- A tributary is a smaller river (e.g. a stream) that joins a main river.
- The source is where a river starts, usually in an upland area (e.g. mountains).
- A confluence is a point where two rivers join.
- The mouth is where a river flows into the sea or a lake.

Some drainage basins are massive, e.g. the drainage basin of the Amazon River is more than 6 million km^2.

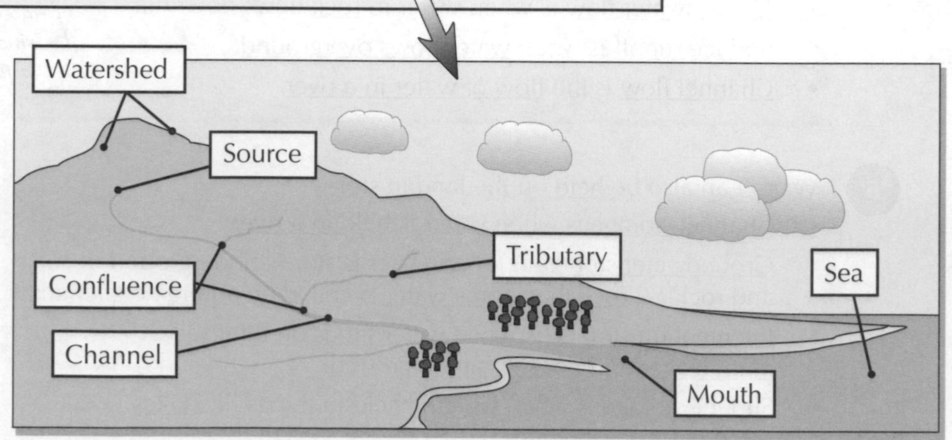

Drainage basins are open systems — they have inputs and outputs

A lot of what you've just learned about the hydrological cycle also applies to drainage basins — they both have the same flows and stores. As well as flows and stores, it's worth learning the different inputs and outputs of a drainage basin.

Weathering and the River Valley

Right, time to get into the details of what goes on in an individual drainage basin.

Rocks in a Drainage Basin are Broken Down by Weathering

Weathering happens in drainage basins — it's the breakdown of rocks where they are (the material created doesn't get taken away like with erosion). There are three main types of weathering:

1) Mechanical weathering is the breakdown of rock without changing its chemical composition. Freeze-thaw weathering is a type of mechanical weathering that happens in drainage basins:

    1) It happens when the temperature alternates above and below 0 °C (the freezing point of water).
    2) Water gets into rock that has cracks, e.g. granite.
    3) When the water freezes it expands, which puts pressure on the rock.
    4) When the water thaws it contracts, which releases the pressure on the rock.
    5) Repeated freezing and thawing widens the cracks and causes the rock to break up.

2) Chemical weathering is the breakdown of rock by changing its chemical composition. Carbonation weathering is a type of chemical weathering that happens in warm and wet conditions:

    1) Rainwater has carbon dioxide dissolved in it, which makes it a weak carbonic acid.
    2) Carbonic acid reacts with rock that contains calcium carbonate, e.g. limestone, so the rocks are dissolved by the rainwater.

3) Biological weathering is the breakdown of rocks by living things, e.g. plant roots break down rocks by growing into cracks on their surfaces and pushing them apart.

A River's Long Profile and Cross Profile Vary Over its Course

1) The path of a river as it flows downhill is called its course.
2) Rivers have an upper course (closest to the source of the river), a middle course and a lower course (closest to the mouth of the river).
3) Rivers flow in channels in valleys.
4) They erode the landscape — wear it down, then transport the material to somewhere else where it's deposited.
5) The shape of the valley and channel changes along the river depending on whether erosion or deposition is having the most impact (is the dominant process).
6) The long profile of a river shows you how the gradient (steepness) changes over the different courses.
7) The cross profile shows you what a cross-section of the river looks like.

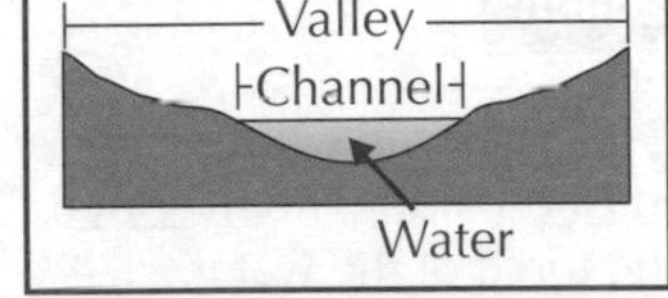

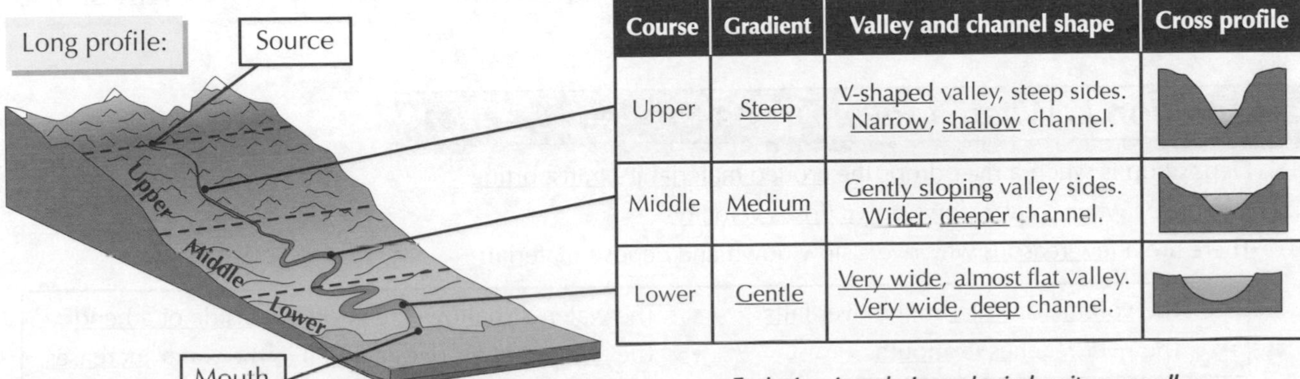

Course	Gradient	Valley and channel shape	Cross profile
Upper	Steep	V-shaped valley, steep sides. Narrow, shallow channel.	
Middle	Medium	Gently sloping valley sides. Wider, deeper channel.	
Lower	Gentle	Very wide, almost flat valley. Very wide, deep channel.	

Each river in a drainage basin has its own valley.

Long profile = gradient, cross profile = a cross-section of the river

Weathering breaks rocks down, and annoyingly there are quite a few ways it happens that you need to learn. Try drawing the cross profile diagrams and describing the shape of the valley and channel, just to check that you remember it.

Erosion, Transportation and Deposition

As rivers flow, they erode material, transport it and then deposit it further downstream.

Vertical and Lateral Erosion Change the Cross Profile of a River

Erosion can be vertical or lateral — both types happen at the same time, but one is usually dominant over the other at different points along the river:

The faster a river's flowing, the more erosion happens.

Vertical erosion

This deepens the river valley (and channel), making it V-shaped. It's dominant in the upper course of the river.

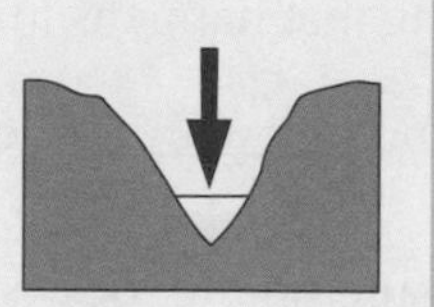

Lateral erosion

This widens the river valley (and channel). It's dominant in the middle and lower courses.

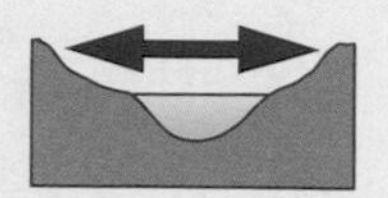

There are Four Processes of Erosion

1) Hydraulic action — The force of the water breaks rock particles away from the river channel.
2) Abrasion — Eroded rocks picked up by the river scrape and rub against the channel, wearing it away. Most erosion happens by abrasion.
3) Attrition — Eroded rocks picked up by the river smash into each other and break into smaller fragments. Their edges also get rounded off as they rub together.
4) Solution — River water dissolves some types of rock, e.g. chalk and limestone.

Abrasion is sometimes called corrasion.

Transportation is the Movement of Eroded Material

The material a river has eroded is transported downstream.
There are four processes of transportation:

1 Traction

Large particles like boulders are pushed along the river bed by the force of the water.

2 Saltation

Pebble-sized particles are bounced along the river bed by the force of the water.

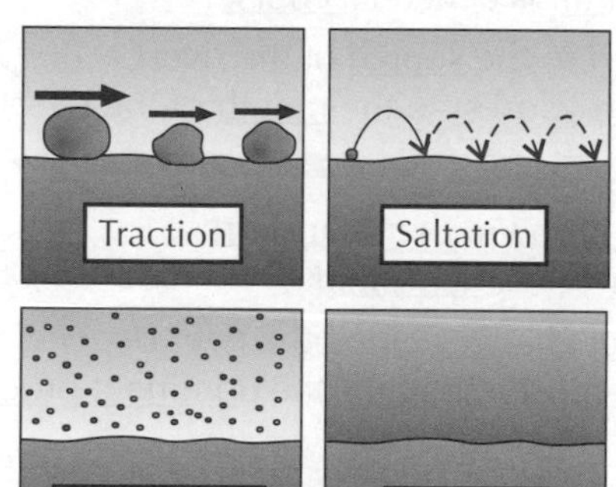

3 Suspension

Small particles like silt and clay are carried along by the water.

4 Solution

Soluble materials dissolve in the water and are carried along.

Deposition is When a River Drops Eroded Material

1) Deposition is when a river drops the eroded material it's transporting.
2) It happens when a river slows down (loses velocity).
3) There are a few reasons why rivers slow down and deposit material:

- The volume of water in the river falls.
- The river reaches its mouth.
- The water is shallower, e.g. on the inside of a bend.
- The amount of eroded material in the water increases.

Learn the four processes of erosion and the four processes of transportation

There are loads of amazingly similar names to remember here — try not to confuse saltation, solution and suspension. And yes, solution is a process of erosion and transportation. Learn them now and you'll be sorted come exam time.

Erosional River Landforms

So you now know how rock is eroded — it must be time to find out all about the landforms the erosion creates.

Waterfalls and Gorges are Found in the Upper Course of a River

1) Waterfalls (e.g. High Force waterfall on the River Tees) form where a river flows over an area of hard rock followed by an area of softer rock.
2) The softer rock is eroded more than the hard rock, creating a 'step' in the river.
3) As water goes over the step it erodes more and more of the softer rock.
4) A steep drop is eventually created, which is called a waterfall.

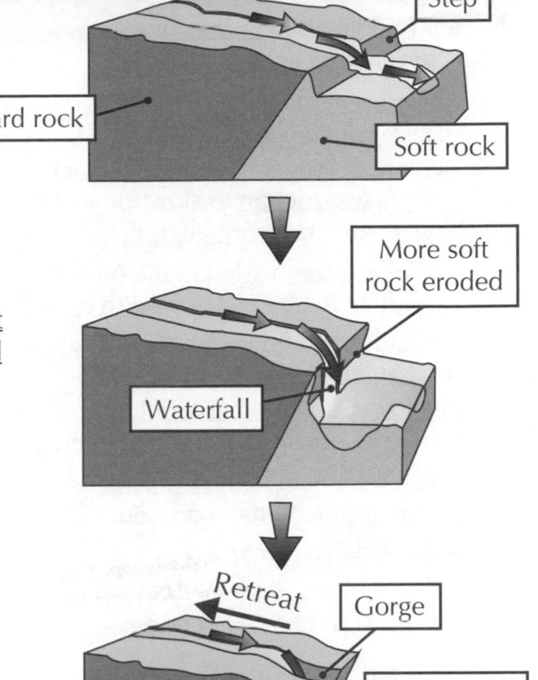

5) The hard rock is eventually undercut by erosion. It becomes unsupported and collapses.
6) The collapsed rocks are swirled around at the foot of the waterfall where they erode the softer rock by abrasion (see previous page). This creates a deep plunge pool.
7) Over time, more undercutting causes more collapses. The waterfall will retreat (move back up the channel), leaving behind a steep-sided gorge.

Interlocking Spurs Form when Rivers Wind Around Hills

1) In the upper course of a river most of the erosion is vertically downwards. This creates steep-sided, V-shaped valleys.
2) The rivers aren't powerful enough to erode laterally (sideways) — they have to wind around the high hillsides that stick out into their paths on either side.
3) The hillsides that interlock with each other (like a zip if you were looking from above) as the river winds around them are called interlocking spurs.

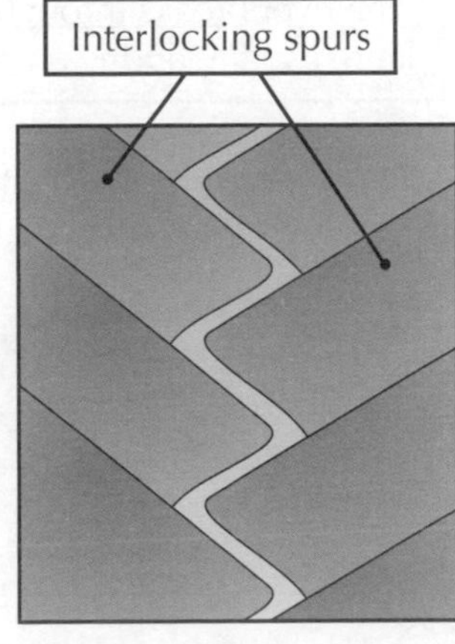

Interlocking spurs along a river in Georgia

Waterfalls form where there are bands of hard and soft rock

Step over the hard rock and plunge into the pool — that's how I remember how waterfalls are formed.
Geography examiners love river landforms so if you want top marks in the exam it's worth knowing how they form.

Erosional and Depositional River Landforms

When a river's eroding and depositing material, meanders and ox-bow lakes can form. Australians have a different name for ox-bow lakes — billabongs. Stay tuned for more incredible facts.

Meanders are Large Bends in a River

In their middle and lower courses, rivers develop meanders:

1) The current (the flow of the water) is faster on the outside of the bend because the river channel is deeper (there's less friction to slow the water down, so it has more energy).
2) So more erosion takes place on the outside of the bend, forming river cliffs.
3) The current is slower on the inside of the bend because the river channel is shallower (there's more friction to slow the water down, so it has less energy).
4) So eroded material is deposited on the inside of the bend, forming slip-off slopes.

The Mississippi River in the USA has lots of meanders.

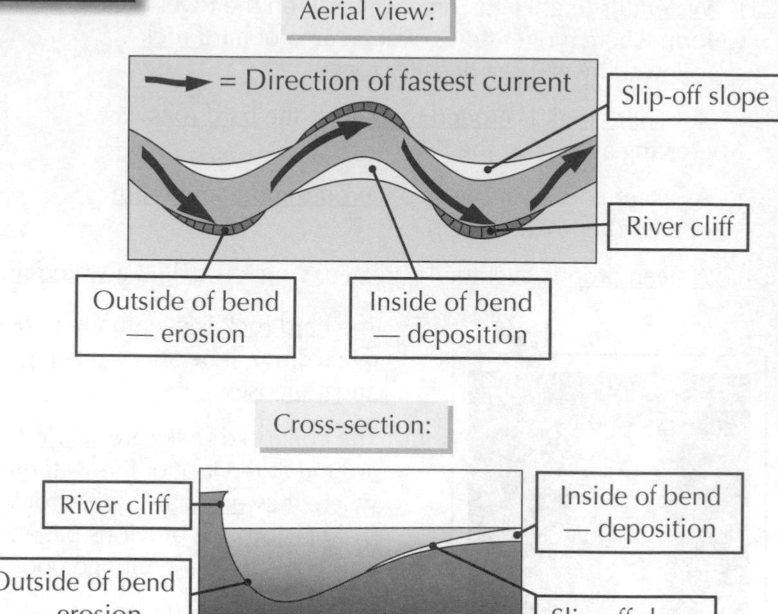

Ox-Bow Lakes are Formed from Meanders

Meanders get larger over time — they can eventually turn into an ox-bow lake:

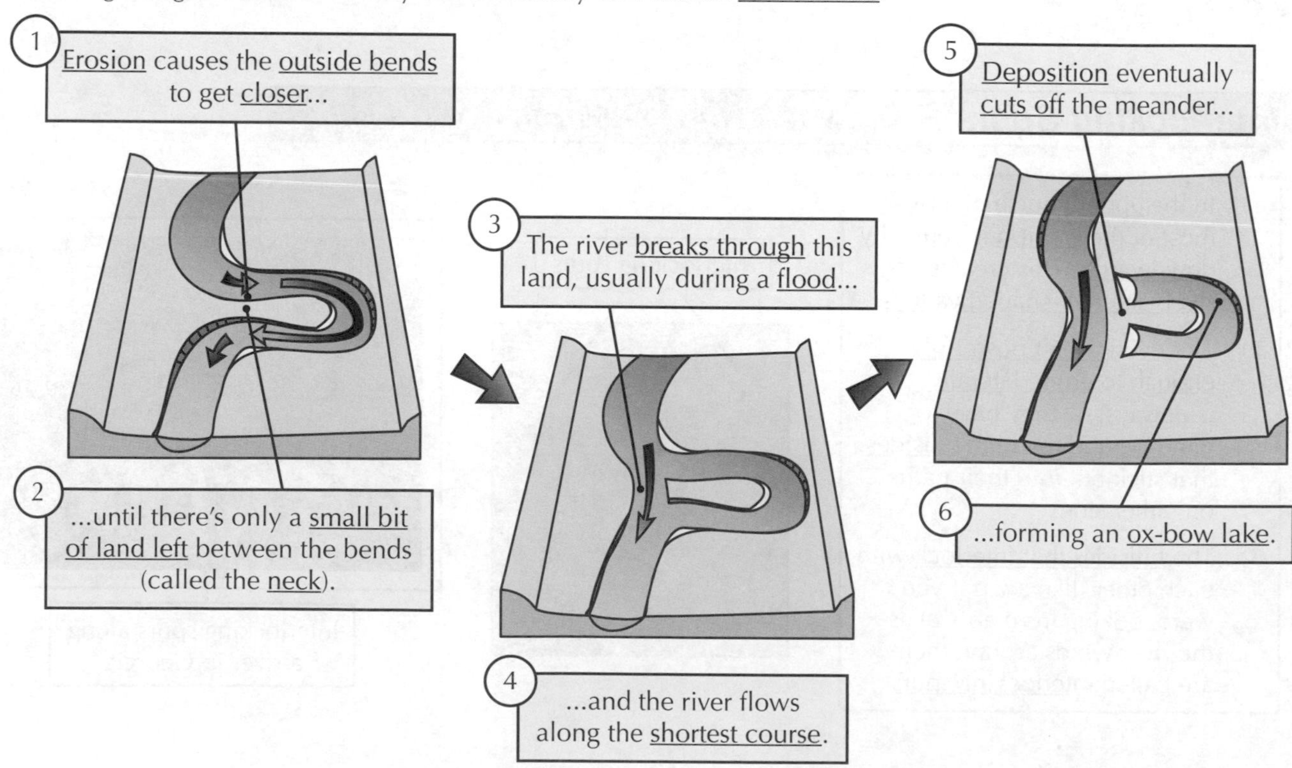

1
Erosion causes the outside bends to get closer...
2
...until there's only a small bit of land left between the bends (called the neck).
3
The river breaks through this land, usually during a flood...
4
...and the river flows along the shortest course.
5
Deposition eventually cuts off the meander...
6
...forming an ox-bow lake.

Learn how the features of meanders are formed by erosion and deposition

In the exam, don't be afraid to draw diagrams of river landforms — examiners love a good diagram. Don't worry about it being a pretty picture though, it's just there to make your answer clearer. Now, meander over to the next page...

Depositional River Landforms

As rivers slow down they lose power and deposit the material they're carrying, making a few more landforms.

Flood Plains are Flat Areas of Land that Flood

1) The flood plain is the wide valley floor on either side of a river which occasionally gets flooded.
2) When a river floods onto the flood plain, the water slows down and deposits the eroded material that it's transporting. This builds up the flood plain (makes it higher).
3) Meanders migrate (move) across the flood plain, making it wider.
4) The deposition that happens on the slip-off slopes of meanders also builds up the flood plain.

All these landforms are found in the lower course of a river.

Levees are Natural Embankments

Levees are natural embankments (raised bits) along the edges of a river channel. During a flood, eroded material is deposited over the whole flood plain. The heaviest material is deposited closest to the river channel, because it gets dropped first when the river slows down. Over time, the deposited material builds up, creating levees along the edges of the channel, e.g. along the Yellow River in China.

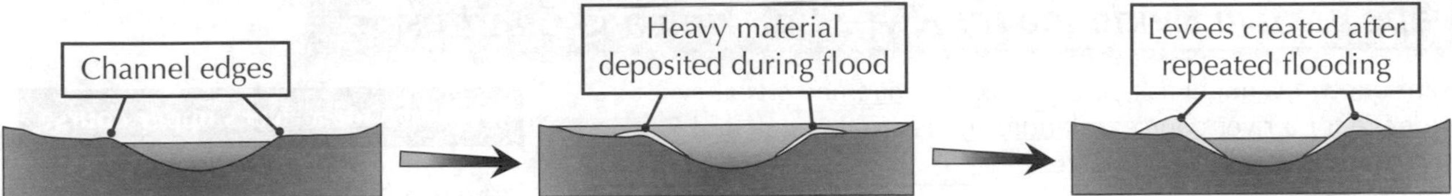

Deltas are Low-Lying Areas Where a River Meets the Sea or a Lake

1) Rivers are forced to slow down when they meet the sea or a lake. This causes them to deposit the material that they're carrying.
2) If the sea doesn't wash away the material it builds up and the channel gets blocked. This forces the channel to split up into lots of smaller rivers called distributaries.
3) Eventually the material builds up so much that low-lying areas of land called deltas are formed.
4) There are three types of delta:

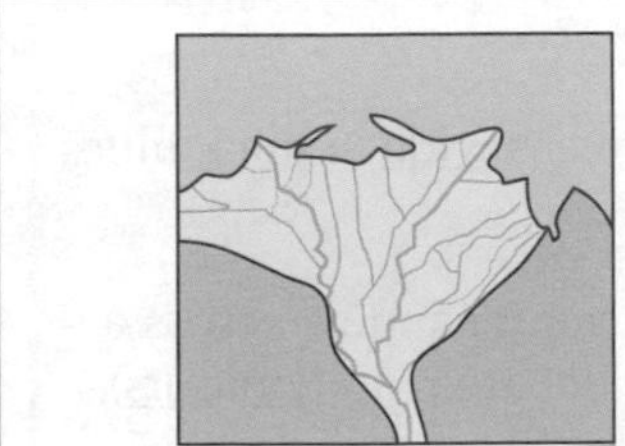

Arcuate — have a rounded shape and lots of distributaries, e.g. the Nile delta.

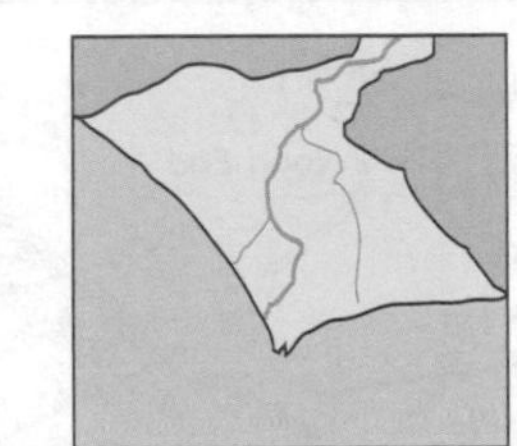

Cuspate — have a triangular shape and few distributaries, e.g. the Tiber delta.

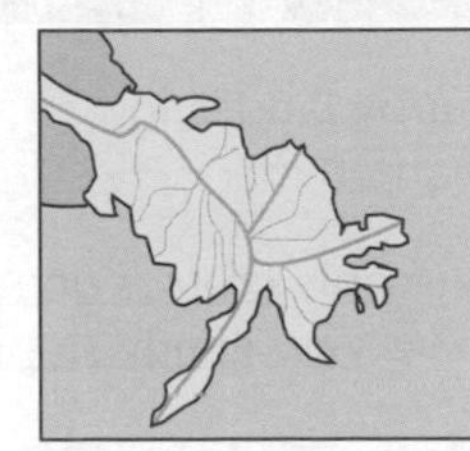

Bird's foot — wait for it... are shaped like a bird's foot, e.g. the Mississippi delta.

Deposition is common in the lower course of a river

I'll be the first person to admit that these depositional landforms aren't as exciting as waterfalls, but it's still worth knowing about them. The only tricky bits on this page are the names of the types of delta — the rest is a piece of cake.

Rivers on Maps

You can know all the facts about rivers, but if you don't know what their features look like on maps then some of the exam questions could be a wee bit tricky. Here's something I prepared earlier...

Contour Lines Tell you the Direction a River Flows

Contour lines are the orange lines drawn all over maps. They tell you about the height of the land (in metres) by the numbers marked on them, and the steepness of the land by how close together they are (the closer they are, the steeper the slope).

It sounds obvious, but rivers can't flow uphill. Unless gravity's gone screwy, a river flows from higher contour lines to lower ones. Have a look at this map of Cawfell Beck:

Take a peek at pages 230-231 for more on reading maps.

1 The height values get smaller towards the west (left), so west is downhill.

2 Cawfell Beck is flowing from east to west (right to left).

*
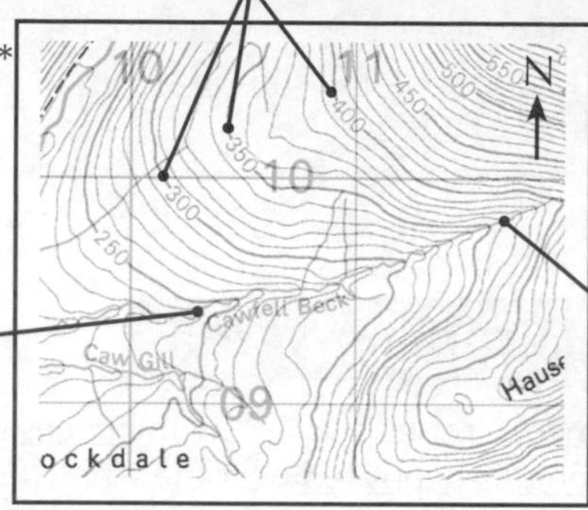

3 A V-shape is formed where the contour lines cross the river. The V-shape is pointing uphill to where the river came from.

Maps contain Evidence for River Courses and Landforms

Exam questions might ask you to look at a map and give the evidence for a river course or landform. Learn this stuff and those questions will be a breeze:

Evidence for a waterfall

Waterfalls are marked on maps, but the symbol for a cliff (black, blocky lines) and the close contour lines are evidence for a waterfall.

*
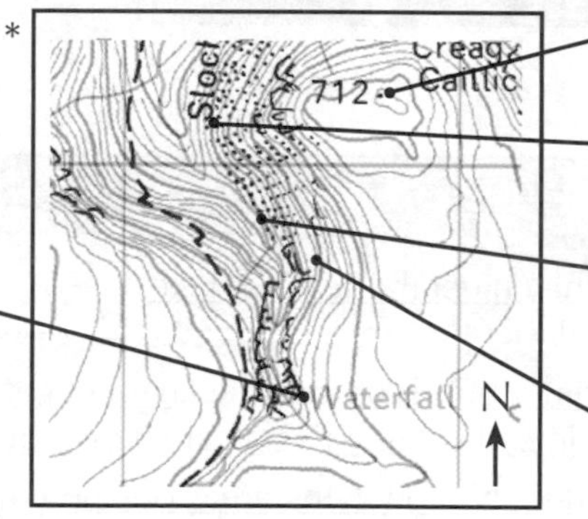

Evidence for a river's upper course

The nearby land is high (712 m).

The river crosses lots of contour lines in a short distance, which means it's steep.

The river's narrow (a thin blue line).

The contour lines are very close together and the valley floor is narrow. This means the river is in a steep-sided V-shaped valley.

Evidence for a river's lower course

The nearby land is low (less than 20 m).

The river only crosses one contour line so it's very gently sloping.

Another piece of evidence would be the river joining a sea or lake.

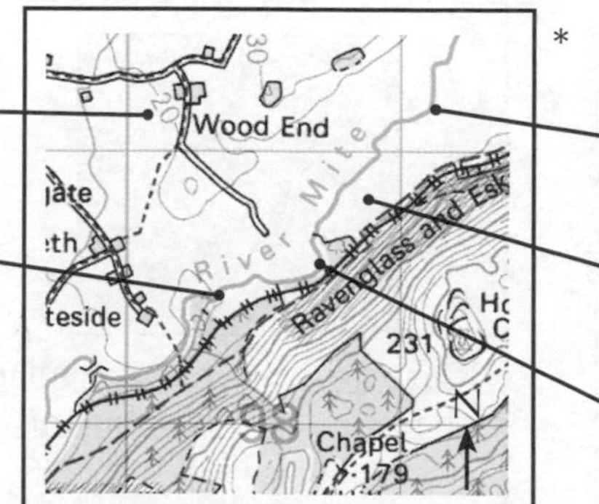

*

The river's wide (a thick blue line).

The river meanders across a large flat area (no contours), which is the flood plain.

The river has large meanders.

Pay close attention to contour lines, height values and symbols

Map questions can be a goldmine of easy marks — all you have to do is say what you see. You just need to understand what the maps are showing, so read this page like there's no tomorrow, then see if you can remember it all.

River Valley — Case Study

Yep, it's case study time, and I've got a real treat lined up for you — we're off to Glasgow...

*The **River Clyde** Flows Through **Scotland***

1) The River Clyde is about 160 km long.
2) Its source is in the Southern Uplands region of Scotland and the river flows north-west through Motherwell and Glasgow.
3) The mouth of the River Clyde is an estuary on the west coast of Scotland.
4) Here are some of the features and landforms in the valley that the River Clyde flows through:

Glasgow

River Clyde

Drainage basin of River Clyde

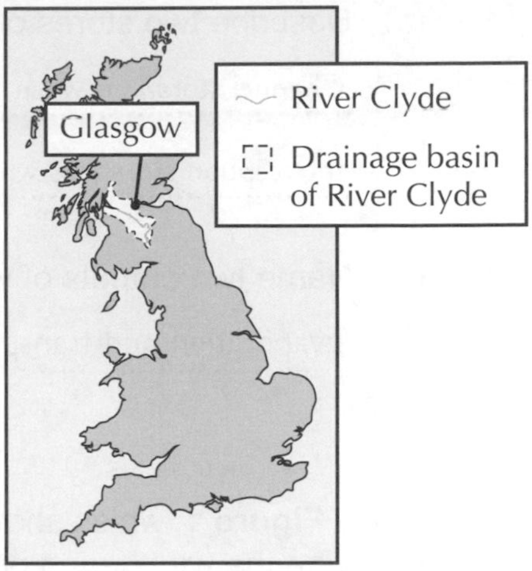

An estuary is the mouth of a river that joins the sea.

The River Clyde's flood plain

©iStockphoto.com/Martin McCarthy

The river's estuary is about 34 km west of Glasgow — the estuary is about 3 km wide. The river joins the Firth of Clyde, which eventually becomes the Irish Sea.

Glasgow is built on the flood plain of the River Clyde. The land is about 5 m above sea level on either side of the river.

There's an ox-bow lake forming near the village of Uddingston.

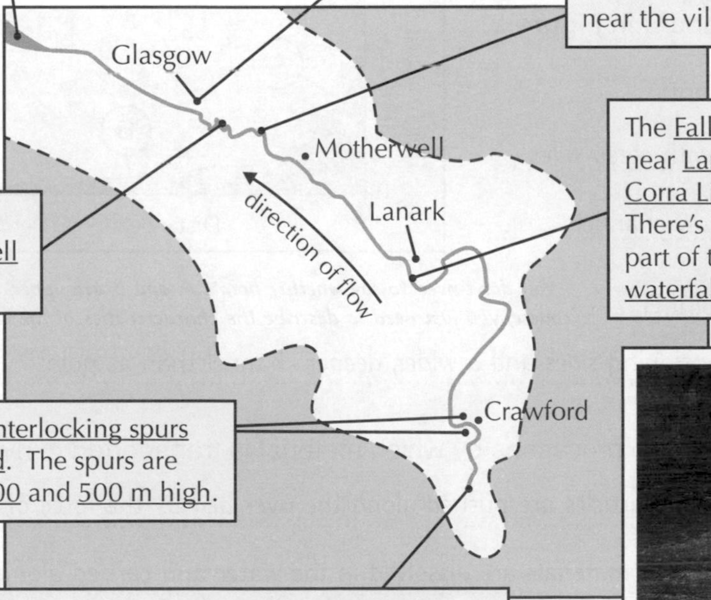

Glasgow

Motherwell

Lanark

direction of flow

Crawford

The Falls of Clyde are four waterfalls near Lanark. The highest fall is Corra Linn — it's about 27 m high. There's also a gorge along this part of the river, formed by the waterfalls retreating.

The river meanders between Motherwell and Glasgow.

There are interlocking spurs at Crawford. The spurs are between 300 and 500 m high.

Corra Linn

©iStockphoto.com

The source of the river is in the Lowther Hills — two tributaries (Daer Water and Portail Water) come together to form the River Clyde.

The River Clyde's got it all...

Almost all of the landforms you've learned about in this section are found somewhere along the River Clyde. The important bits of this case study are the landforms, place names and measurements, so get learning.

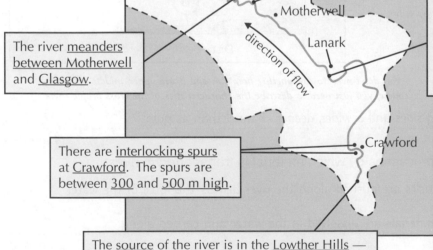

Worked Exam Questions

Sadly, the answers won't be written in for you in your exam, so make the most of these worked examples.

1 (a) Describe two stores of water in the hydrological cycle.

If you've learned the diagram on page 69, questions like this should be a doddle.

Channel storage is when water is held in a river.

Interception storage is when water lands on things like plant leaves and doesn't hit the ground.

(2 marks)

(b) Name two outputs of water from a drainage basin.

Evaporation and transpiration. *(Or river flow into the sea.)*

(2 marks)

2 Study **Figure 1**, which shows a rock in a drainage basin being weathered. Describe the weathering process shown in **Figure 1**.

Figure 1

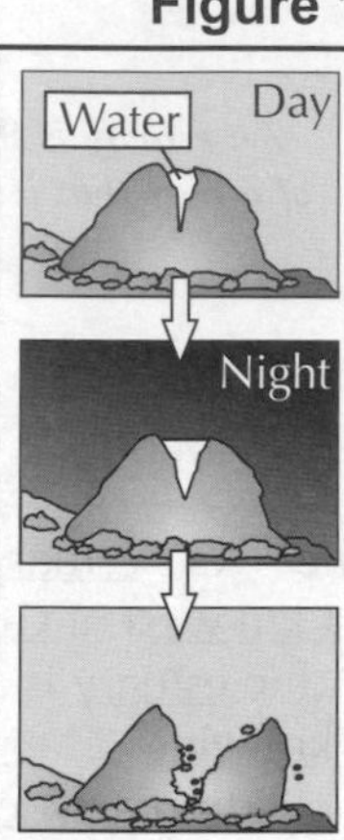

Water gets into rock that has cracks, e.g. granite. The water freezes at night and expands, which puts pressure on the rock. The water then thaws during the day and contracts, which releases the pressure on the rock. Repeated freezing and thawing widens the cracks and causes the rock to break up.

(4 marks)

3 Study **Figure 2**, which shows the long profile of a river.

(a) Describe the cross profile at the points labelled A and B in **Figure 2**.

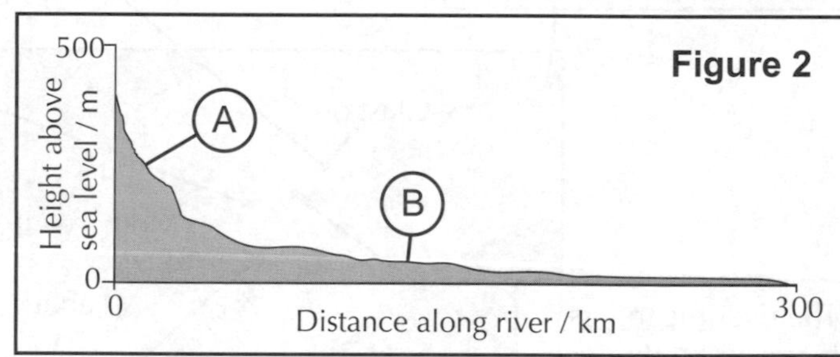

Figure 2

Cross profile at point A

A V-shaped valley with steep sides and a narrow, shallow channel.

Cross profile at point B

You don't need to say whether points A and B are upper, middle or lower course, you just need to describe the characteristics of the cross profile there.

A valley with gently sloping sides and a wider, deeper channel than at point A.

(4 marks)

(b) Name and describe two processes by which material is transported in rivers.

Traction is when large particles are pushed along the river bed by the force of the water.

Solution is when soluble materials are dissolved in the water and carried along.

(4 marks)

(c) Deposition occurs when rivers slow down. Describe two reasons why rivers slow down.

Rivers slow down when the volume of water in the river falls, or when the amount of eroded material in the water increases.

You could also say that rivers slow down when the water is shallower, e.g. on the inside of a bend, and when they reach their mouths.

(2 marks)

Exam Questions

1 Study **Figure 1**, which is an Ordnance Survey® map showing part of Snowdonia, Wales.

(a) Use evidence from **Figure 1** to show that the Afon Merch is an upper course stream.

....

....

....

....

....

....

....

....

(4 marks)

Figure 1

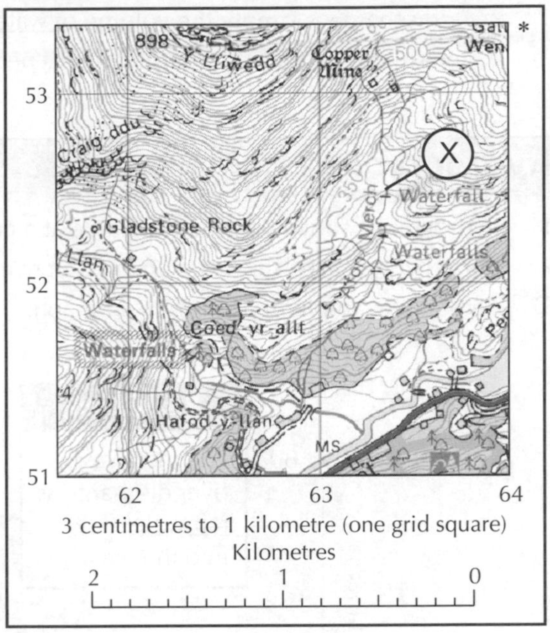

3 centimetres to 1 kilometre (one grid square)

Kilometres

2 1 0

(b) A waterfall is located at point X on **Figure 1**. Describe how waterfalls are formed.

....

....

....

(4 marks)

2 Explain how ox-bow lakes are formed.

....

....

....

....

....

(6 marks)

3 (a) What is a flood plain?

....

(1 mark)

(b) Explain how flood plains are built up.

....

....

....

(3 marks)

River Discharge

We've not really talked much about the actual water in a river. Well, all that's about to change.

River Discharge is the Volume of Water Flowing in a River

1) River discharge is simply the volume of water that flows in a river per second.
2) It's measured in cumecs — cubic metres per second (m^3/s).

Hydrographs Show River Discharge (and Rainfall)

1) Hydrographs show how the discharge at a certain point in a river changes over time.
2) Storm hydrographs show the changes in river discharge around the time of a storm.
3) Here's an example of a storm hydrograph:

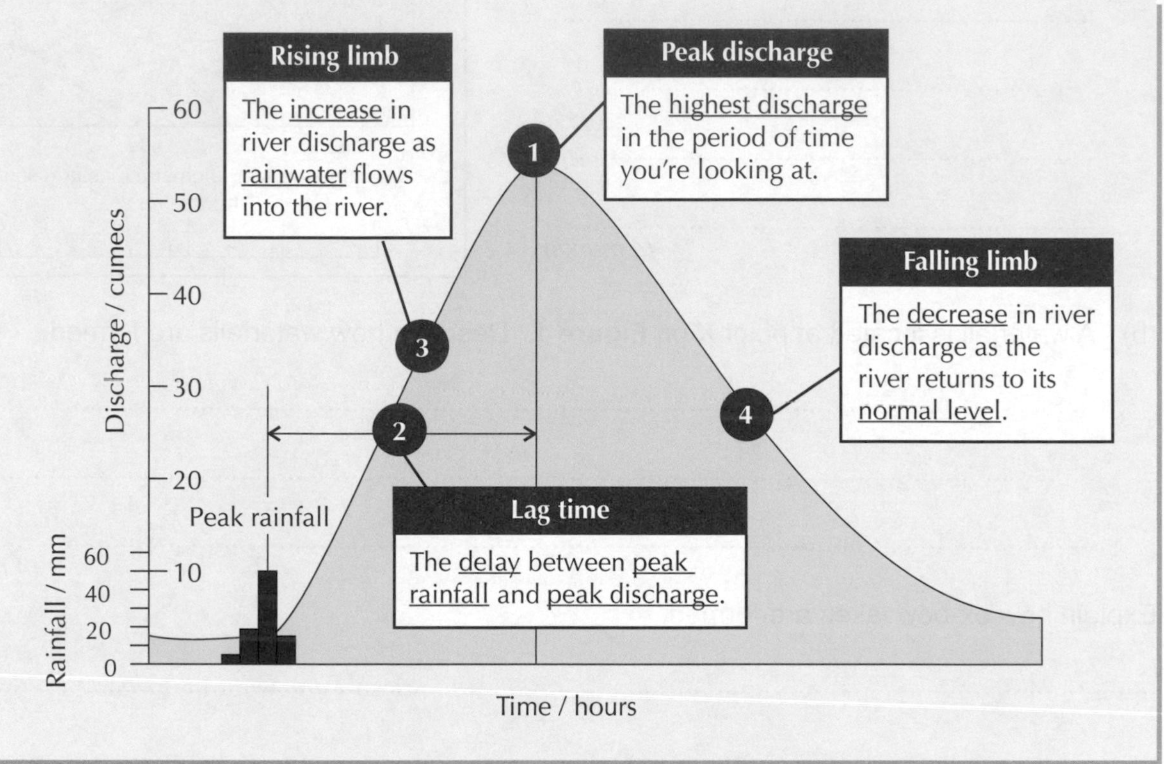

Rising limb
The increase in river discharge as rainwater flows into the river.
Peak discharge
The highest discharge in the period of time you're looking at.
Falling limb
The decrease in river discharge as the river returns to its normal level.
Lag time
The delay between peak rainfall and peak discharge.
Peak rainfall
Discharge / cumecs
60
50
40
30
20
10
Rainfall / mm
60
40
20
0
Time / hours
1
2
3
4

Lag time happens because most rainwater doesn't land directly in the river channel — there's a delay as rainwater gets to the channel. It gets there by flowing quickly overland (called surface runoff, or just runoff), or by soaking into the ground (called infiltration) and flowing slowly underground.

Some Factors Increase Discharge and Make the Hydrograph Steeper

If more water flows as runoff the lag time will be shorter.
This means discharge will increase and the hydrograph will be steeper because more water gets to the river in a shorter space of time.

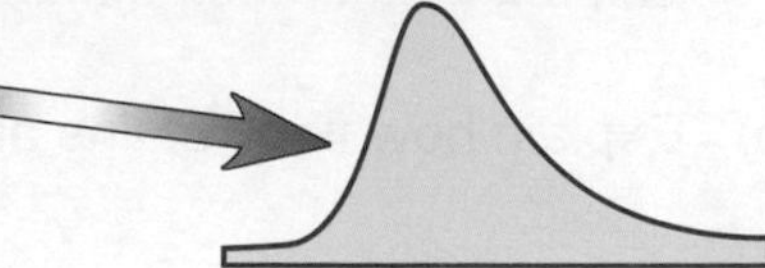

Here are a few factors that increase discharge by increasing runoff:

- High rainfall causes more runoff and a shorter lag time.
- Intense rainfall causes more runoff and a shorter lag time.

River Discharge

- Impermeable rock — water can't infiltrate into the rock so there's more runoff and a shorter lag time.
- Hot, dry conditions and freezing conditions both result in hard ground, so there's more runoff and a shorter lag time.
- Previously wet conditions — water can't infiltrate into saturated soil so there's more runoff and a shorter lag time.
- Steep slopes cause more runoff and a shorter lag time.

Another factor that affects discharge is the amount of vegetation — less vegetation means less water is intercepted and evaporates so more water reaches the channel. Throughflow isn't slowed down by roots, so there's a shorter lag time.

URBAN AREAS have drainage systems and they're covered with impermeable materials — these increase discharge so hydrographs for rivers in urban areas are steep.

Other Factors ***Decrease Discharge*** *and Make the* ***Hydrograph Gentler***

If less water flows as runoff the lag time will be longer. This means discharge will increase more slowly and the peak discharge will be lower. The hydrograph will be less steep because the water is reaching the river over a longer period of time.

Here are a few factors that decrease discharge by decreasing runoff:

- Low rainfall causes less runoff and a longer lag time.
- Light rainfall causes less runoff and a longer lag time.
- Permeable rock — water infiltrates through pore spaces in permeable rock, so there's less runoff and a longer lag time.
- Mild conditions result in soft ground so water can infiltrate. There's less runoff and a longer lag time.
- Previously dry conditions — water can infiltrate into dry soil so there's less runoff and a longer lag time.
- Gentle slopes cause less runoff and a shorter lag time.

More vegetation decreases discharge because more water is intercepted and evaporates, so less water reaches the channel. Also, throughflow is also slowed down by roots, so there's a longer lag time.

RURAL AREAS have more vegetation, which decreases discharge. There are also more reservoirs in rural areas — they store water and release it slowly, decreasing discharge in the river below. This means hydrographs for rivers in rural areas are more gently sloping.

Remember, high runoff = steep hydrograph, low runoff = gentle hydrograph

There are loads of different factors that can affect the discharge of a river and hydrographs are a helpful way of working out what's going on, so make sure you understand what they're showing. It's all quite logical, so even if your mind goes blank in the exam and you can't remember all the different factors, you can probably figure some of them out.

Flooding

Flooding happens when the level of a river gets so high that it spills over its banks.

Rivers Flood due to Physical Factors

The river level increases when the discharge increases because a high discharge means there's more water in the channel. This means the factors that increase discharge can also cause flooding:

Prolonged rainfall

After a long period of rain, the soil becomes saturated. Any further rainfall can't infiltrate, which increases runoff into rivers. This increases discharge quickly, which can cause a flood.

Heavy rainfall

Heavy rainfall means there's a lot of runoff. This increases discharge quickly, which can cause a flood.

Relief (how the height of the land changes)

If a river is in a steep-sided valley, water will reach the river channel much faster because water flows more quickly on steeper slopes. This increases discharge quickly, which can cause a flood.

Snowmelt

When a lot of snow or ice melts it means that a lot of water goes into a river in a short space of time. This increases discharge quickly, which can cause a flood.

Geology

When a river is in an area of permeable rock (e.g. limestone), more water percolates into the rock instead of flowing on the surface. This means there's less runoff, so the risk of flooding is lower. When a river is in an area of impermeable rock (e.g. clay), water doesn't percolate into the rock but flows on the surface. This means there's more runoff, so the risk of flooding is higher.

Rivers also Flood because of Human Factors

Here are a couple of examples of how human actions can make flooding more frequent and more severe:

Deforestation

Trees intercept rainwater on their leaves, which then evaporates. Trees also take up water from the ground and store it. This means cutting down trees increases the volume of water that reaches the river channel, which increases discharge and makes flooding more likely.

Building Construction

Buildings are often made from impermeable materials, e.g. concrete, and they're surrounded by roads made from tarmac (also impermeable). Impermeable surfaces increase runoff and drains quickly take runoff to rivers. This increases discharge quickly, which can cause a flood.

River Flooding in the UK Appears to be Happening More Often

Some rivers in the UK have been flooding more frequently over the last 20 years.
For example, the River Ouse in Yorkshire reached a high water level 29 times between 1966 and 1986. But between 1987 and 2007 it reached the same level 80 times.

The table shows the locations and dates of some of the big floods that have happened in the UK since 1988.

Year	Rivers	Places affected
1988	Kenwyn	Cornwall
1990	Severn	Gloucestershire
1994	Lavant, Clyde	West Sussex, Glasgow
1998	Severn, Trent, Wye	The Midlands, Mid and South Wales
2000	Ouse, Alyn	Yorkshire, North Wales
2004	Valency	Cornwall
2005	Eden	Cumbria and North Yorkshire
2007	Many	Many parts of the UK
2008	Severn	South Midlands

Remember the seven main factors that cause flooding

If you're having a bath and you leave the taps on the water will eventually go over the sides. It's the same with rivers — they've got a limit to the volume of water they can hold. Learn the physical and human factors that can cause them to overflow.

Flood Management

Floods can be devastating, but there are a number of different strategies to stop them or lessen the blow.

Floods have Some Serious Impacts

1) Floods have many impacts, but the most serious ones are that people are killed by flood waters, buildings are damaged or destroyed and jobs are lost because of damage to premises and equipment.
2) The effects of flooding are worse in poorer countries than richer countries because there's less money to spend on flood protection and to help people after a flood. Also, more people live and work in areas that are likely to flood and poorer transport links mean it's more difficult to get help to places that have been affected.

Strategies can be classed as Hard Engineering or Soft Engineering

Hard Engineering Strategies can Reduce the Risk of Flooding Occurring

Hard engineering strategies are man-made structures built to control the flow of rivers and reduce flooding.

Have a look at page 84 for information about soft engineering.

Strategy	What it is	Benefits	Disadvantages
Channel straightening	The river's course is straightened — meanders are cut out by building artificial straight channels.	Water moves out of the area more quickly because it doesn't travel as far — reducing the risk of flooding.	Flooding may happen downstream of the straightened channel instead, as flood water is carried there faster.
Man-made levees	Man-made embankments along both sides of the river.	The embankments mean that the river channel can hold more water, which reduces the risk of flooding. They're also quite cheap.	If the levees fail (break) it can cause catastrophic flooding.
Dams and reservoirs	Dams (huge walls) are built across the rivers, usually in the upper course. A reservoir (artificial lake) is formed behind the dam.	Reservoirs store water and release it slowly, which reduces the risk of flooding. The water in the reservoir is used as drinking water and can be used to generate hydroelectric power (HEP). Reservoirs are also attractive and can be used for recreation.	Dams are very expensive to build. Creating a reservoir can flood existing settlements. Eroded material is deposited in the reservoir and not along the river's natural course making farmland downstream less fertile.

Make sure you know the disadvantages as well as the benefits of each strategy

Flooding can be a nightmare, especially if you live in a poorer country. But, as luck would have it, there are plenty of strategies to reduce the impacts. What's less lucky is the fact that they might come up in the exam, so get learning.

Flood Management

The table on the previous page gives some of the disadvantages of hard engineering strategies. Because of these drawbacks, soft engineering strategies can sometimes be a better solution.

Soft Engineering Strategies can Reduce the Effects of Flooding

Soft engineering strategies are schemes set up using knowledge of a river and its processes to reduce the effects of flooding.

Strategy	What it is	Benefits	Disadvantages
Flood warnings	People are warned about possible flooding through TV, radio, newspapers and the internet.	The impact of flooding is reduced — warnings give people time to move possessions upstairs, put sandbags in position and to evacuate.	Warnings don't stop a flood from happening. People may not hear or have access to warnings (especially in poorer countries where communications are less developed).
Preparation	Buildings are modified to reduce the amount of damage a flood could cause. People make plans for what to do in a flood, e.g. keep a blanket and torch in a handy place.	The impact of flooding is reduced — buildings are less damaged and people know what to do when a flood happens.	Preparation doesn't guarantee safety from a flood and it could give people a false sense of security. It's expensive to modify homes and businesses.
Flood plain zoning	Restrictions prevent building on parts of a flood plain that are likely to be affected by a flood.	The risk of flooding is reduced — impermeable surfaces aren't created, e.g. roads. The impact of flooding is reduced — there aren't any houses or roads to damage.	The expansion of an urban area is limited if there aren't any other suitable building sites. It's no help in areas that have already been built on.
'Do nothing'	No money is spent on new engineering methods or maintaining existing ones. Flooding is a natural process and people should accept the risks of living in an area that's likely to flood.	The river floods, eroded material is deposited on the flood plain, making farmland more fertile.	The risk of flooding and the impacts of flooding aren't reduced. A flood will probably cause a lot of damage.

Some strategies for flood management are more sustainable than others. Sustainable strategies meet the needs of people today (i.e. they reduce flooding), without stopping people in the future getting the things they need. This means not using up resources (e.g. money) or damaging the environment.

Hard engineering strategies are usually less sustainable than soft engineering strategies because they generally cost more to build and maintain, and they damage the environment more.

Soft engineering strategies are generally more sustainable

Soft engineering strategies work with the river's natural processes, so they tend to be more environmentally friendly than hard engineering strategies. They have drawbacks too though — a big one is that they don't prevent flooding.

Flooding — Case Studies

It's time for the inevitable case studies...

Rich and Poor parts of the World are Affected Differently by Flooding

The effects of floods and the responses to them are different in different parts of the world. A lot depends on how wealthy the part of the world is. Learn the following case studies — you might have to compare two floods like these in your exam:

Flood in a rich part of the world:

Place: Carlise, England
Date: 8th January, 2005
River: Eden

Flood in a poor part of the world:

Place: South Asia (Bangladesh and India)
Date: July and August, 2007
Rivers: Brahmaputra and Ganges

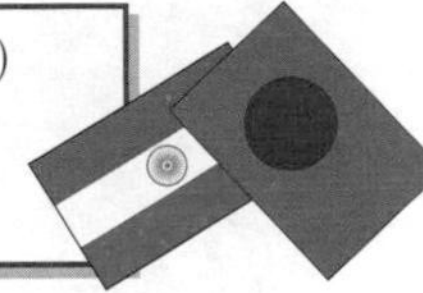

	Carlisle (rich)	South Asia (poor)
Causes	• Heavy rainfall — 200 mm of rain fell in 36 hours. The continuous rainfall saturated the soil, increasing runoff into the River Eden. • Carlisle is a large urban area — impermeable materials like concrete increased runoff. • This caused the discharge of the River Eden to reach 1520 cumecs (its average is 52 cumecs).	• Heavy rainfall — in one region, 900 mm of rain fell in July. • The continuous rainfall saturated the soil, increasing runoff into rivers. • Melting snow from glaciers in the Himalayan mountains increased the discharge of the Brahmaputra river. • The peak discharge of both rivers happened at the same time, which increased discharge downstream.
Primary effects	• 3 deaths. • Around 3000 people were made homeless. • 350 businesses were shut down. • Some roads and bridges were damaged. • Rivers were polluted with rubbish and sewage.	• Over 2000 deaths. • Around 25 million people were made homeless. • Many factories closed and lots of livestock were killed. • 112 000 houses were destroyed in India. • Rivers were polluted with rubbish and sewage.
Secondary effects	• Children lost out on education — one school was closed for months. • Stress-related illnesses increased after the floods. • Around 3000 jobs were at risk in businesses affected by floods.	• Children lost out on education — around 4000 schools were affected by the floods. • Around 100 000 people caught water-borne diseases like dysentery and diarrhoea. • Flooded fields reduced basmati rice yields — prices rose 10%. • Many farmers and factory workers became unemployed.
Flood management	• The Environment Agency monitors river levels and issues flood warnings to the public, local authorities and the media. • The local council distributes sandbags when flood warnings have been issued. • There are man-made levees along the river to help prevent flooding.	• Bangladesh has a Flood Forecasting and Warning System (FFWS) with 85 flood monitoring stations. Flood warnings can be issued up to 72 hours before a flood occurs, but the warnings don't reach many rural communities. • There are around 6000 km of man-made levees to prevent flooding in Bangladesh, but they're easily eroded and aren't properly maintained so are often breached by flood waters.
Immediate response	• People were evacuated from areas that flooded. • Reception centres were opened around Carlisle to provide food and drinks for evacuees. • Temporary accommodation was set up for the people made homeless.	• Many people didn't evacuate from areas that flooded, and blocked transport links slowed down any evacuations that were attempted. • Other governments and international charities distributed food, water and medical aid. Technical equipment like rescue boats were also sent to help people who were stranded.
Long-term response	• Community groups were set up to provide emotional support and to give practical help to people who were affected by the floods. • The Eden and Petteril Flood Alleviation Scheme was completed in 2008 — this involved things like building up flood defence walls and levees on the rivers to prevent flooding.	• International charities have funded the rebuilding of homes and the agriculture and fishing industries. • Some homes have been rebuilt on stilts, so they're less likely to be damaged by future floods.

The South Asia flood had a much larger impact than the Carlisle flood

Well, it's pretty clear that floods have different impacts and the responses to them are different when you compare a rich and a poor part of the world. You might be asked to write about a couple of examples in the exam, so why not learn these two...

Managing the UK's Water

It might not feel like there's any shortage of water in the UK, but in some places demand outstrips natural supply.

The Demand for Water is Different Across the UK

In the UK, the places with a good supply of water aren't the same as the places with the highest demand:

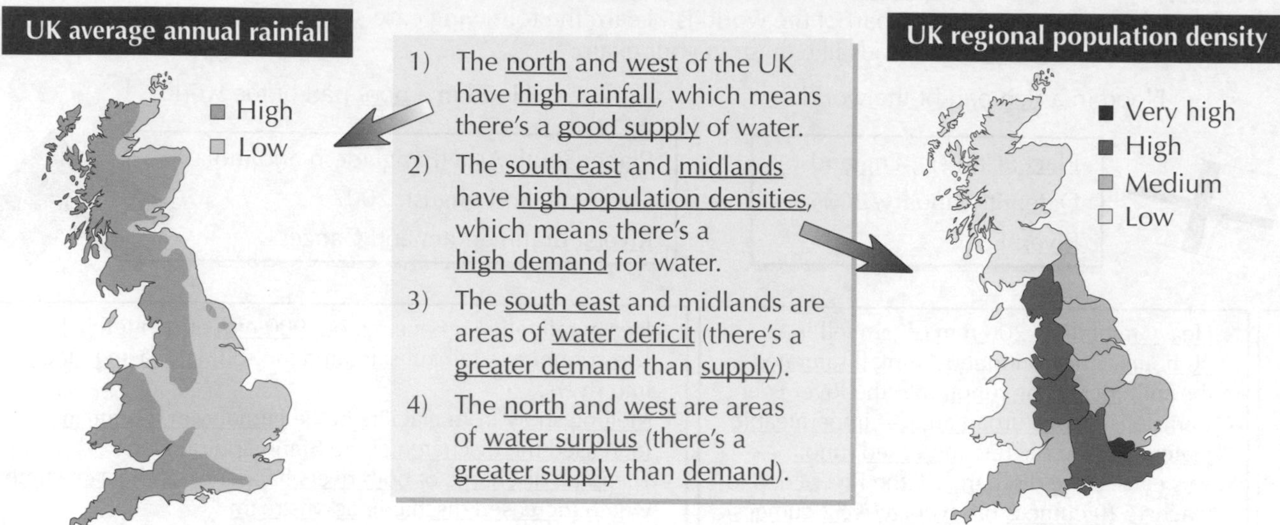

1) The north and west of the UK have high rainfall, which means there's a good supply of water.
2) The south east and midlands have high population densities, which means there's a high demand for water.
3) The south east and midlands are areas of water deficit (there's a greater demand than supply).
4) The north and west are areas of water surplus (there's a greater supply than demand).

The demand for water in the UK is increasing:

1) Over the past 25 years, the amount of water used by people in the UK has gone up by about 50%.
2) The UK population is predicted to increase by around 10 million people over the next 20 years.

The UK needs to Manage its Supply of Water...

1) One way to deal with the supply and demand problem is to transfer water from areas of surplus to areas of deficit. For example, Birmingham (an area of deficit) is supplied with water from the middle of Wales (an area of surplus).
2) Water transfer can cause a variety of issues:
   - The dams and aqueducts (bridges used to transport water) that are needed are expensive.
   - It could affect the wildlife that lives in the rivers, e.g. fish migration patterns could be disrupted by dam building.
   - There might be political issues, e.g. people may not want their water given to another country.
3) Another way to increase water supplies in deficit areas is to build more reservoirs to store more water. However, building a reservoir can involve flooding settlements and relocating people.
4) Fixing leaky pipes would mean less water is lost during transfer. For example, millions of litres of water are lost everyday through leaky pipes around London — fixing leaky pipes would save some of this.

...and Reduce its Demands for Water

1) People can reduce the amount of water that they use at home, e.g. by taking showers instead of baths, running washing machines only when they're full and by using hosepipes less.
2) Water companies want people to have water meters installed — meters are used to charge people for the exact volume of water that they use. People with water meters are more likely to be careful with the amount of water they use — they're paying for every drop.

Some areas have a water surplus, other areas have a water deficit

The UK isn't a desert by any means, but there's an increasing demand for water, which means that supplies have to be managed. Make sure you understand how they are managed, and some of the problems that this can cause.

UK Reservoir — Case Study

There's just time for one last case study. This one's about a UK reservoir that supplies water to a lot of people.

Rutland Water is a Reservoir in the East Midlands

1) The dam was built and Rutland Water was created during the 1970s.
2) The reservoir covers a 12 km² area and it's filled with water from two rivers — the River Welland and the River Nene.
3) Rutland Water was designed to supply the East Midlands with more water — enough to cope with rapid population growth in places like Peterborough.
4) Areas around the reservoir are also used as a nature reserve and for recreation.
5) Here are some of the economic, social and environmental impacts of Rutland Water:

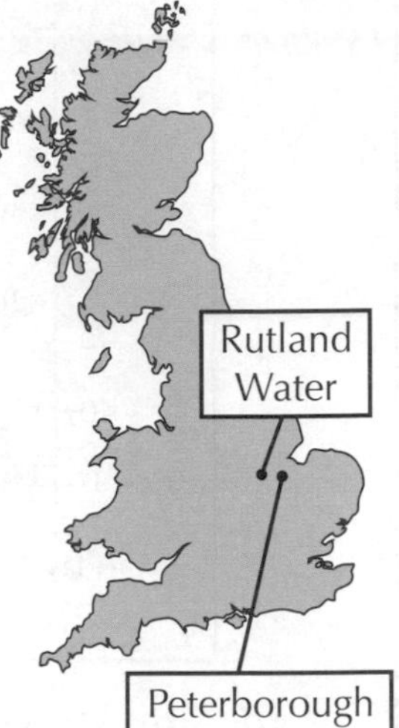

Economic

- The reservoir boosts the local economy — it's a popular tourist attraction because of the wildlife and recreation facilities.
- Around 6 km² of land was flooded to create the reservoir. This included farmland, so some farmers lost their livelihoods.

Social

- Lots of recreational activities take place on and around the reservoir, e.g. sailing, windsurfing, birdwatching and cycling.
- Many jobs have been created to build and maintain the reservoir, and to run the nature reserve and recreational activities.
- Schools use the reservoir for educational visits.
- Two villages were demolished to make way for the reservoir.

Environmental

- Rutland Water is a Site of Special Scientific Interest (SSSI) — an area where wildlife is protected.
- Hundreds of species of birds live around the reservoir and tens of thousands of waterfowl (birds that live on or near water) come to Rutland Water over the winter.
- A variety of habitats are found around the reservoir, e.g. marshes, mudflats and lagoons. This means lots of different organisms live in or around the reservoir.
- Ospreys (fish-eating birds of prey that were extinct in Britain) have been reintroduced to central England by the Rutland Osprey Project at the reservoir.
- A large area of land was flooded to create the reservoir, which destroyed some habitats.

Rutland Water has to be Managed Sustainably

The supply of water from the reservoir has to be sustainable. This means that people should be able to get all the water they need today, without stopping people in the future from having enough water.

Basically, people today can't deplete the water supply or damage the environment too much, or the supply won't be the same in the future. To use the reservoir in a sustainable way, people can only take out as much water as is replaced by the rivers that supply it. That way, the supply will stay the same for the future.

Rutland Water has had positive and negative impacts — learn them

Learning facts for case study questions is a great way of earning loads of marks in the exam. Once you've had a good read of this page, have a go at the questions on the next few pages to see how much of this section you can remember.

Worked Exam Questions

Have a good read of these worked examples to get an idea of the kind of things you should write in the exam.

1 Study **Figure 1**, which shows storm hydrographs for two rivers.

Figure 1

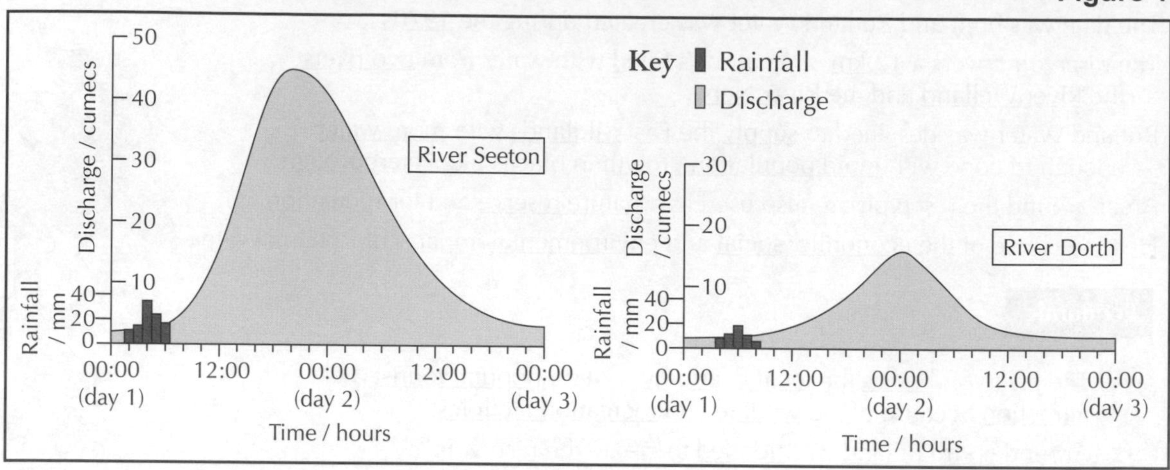

(a) (i) What is meant by the term 'peak discharge'?

The highest discharge in the period of time you're looking at.

You might well be asked to interpret a hydrograph in the exam, so make sure you understand how to read them.

(1 mark)

(ii) At what time was the River Seeton at peak discharge? 20:00 on day 1.

(1 mark)

(b) Suggest reasons why the storm hydrographs in **Figure 1** are different shapes.

Use info from the graphs as well as your own knowledge to answer questions like this.

There was about 20 mm more rainfall around the River Seeton than around the River Dorth. This may have caused more runoff into the river channel, so a higher discharge and a shorter lag time. The rainfall around the River Seeton may have been more intense than around the River Dorth. This would have caused more runoff into the river channel, so a higher discharge and a shorter lag time. There may be more urban areas around the River Seeton than the River Dorth which are covered with impermeable materials like concrete. This increases runoff into the river channel, which increases discharge and shortens the lag time.

(6 marks)

2 (a) What is meant by a water deficit?

The demand for water is greater than the supply.

(1 mark)

(b) The supply of water can be managed by transferring water from areas of surplus to areas of deficit. Describe two issues that this strategy could cause.

It could affect the wildlife that lives in rivers, e.g. fish migration patterns could be affected by dam building. The dams and reservoirs that are needed are expensive.

(2 marks)

(c) Give two other ways in which the supply of water in the UK can be managed.

More reservoirs could be built in water deficit areas to store more water.

Leaky pipes could be fixed so less water is lost during water transfer.

It's only worth 2 marks, so you don't need to go into too much detail.

(2 marks)

Exam Questions

1 Study **Figure 1**, which shows the frequency of flooding of the River Turb.

Figure 1

Year	1997 - 1998	1998 - 1999	1999 - 2000	2000 - 2001	2001 - 2002	2002 - 2003	2003 - 2004	2004 - 2005	2005 - 2006	2006 - 2007	2007 - 2008
Number of floods	0	1	1	0	0	2	2	3	2	4	3

(a) Describe the trend shown in **Figure 1**.

....

....

(2 marks)

(b) Explain how being in an area of permeable rock would affect the risk of a river flooding.

....

....

....

(3 marks)

2 Study **Figure 2**, which shows the engineering strategies used to combat flooding along a river.

(a) (i) What engineering strategy has been used to protect Moritt?

....

....

(1 mark)

Figure 2

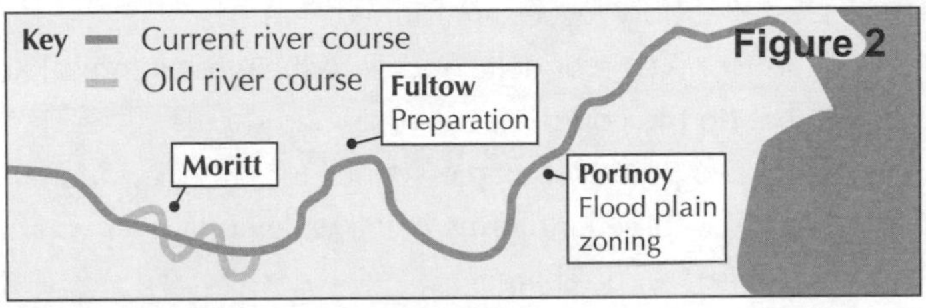

(ii) Suggest why it could cause problems in Fultow.

....

(1 mark)

(b) Describe the benefits of the engineering strategy being used at Portnoy.

....

....

....

(3 marks)

3 Describe and explain the human factors that can increase the risk of flooding.

....

....

....

....

....

(6 marks)

Revision Summary for Section 5

Now it's time to see how much information your brain has soaked up. Have a go at the questions below and then go back over the section to check your answers. If something's not quite right, have another read of the page. Once you can answer everything correctly you're ready to move on to the next section.

1) What does the hydrological cycle show?
2) Describe three flows in the hydrological cycle.
3) What is a drainage basin?
4) Name an input to a drainage basin system.
5) What happens at a confluence?
6) Describe carbonation weathering.
7) What does a river's long profile show?
8) Describe the cross profile of a river's lower course.
9) Name the river course where vertical erosion is dominant.
10) What's the difference between abrasion and attrition?
11) Describe how material is moved by saltation.
12) Where do waterfalls form? Name an example.
13) How is a gorge formed?
14) Why do rivers have to wind around interlocking spurs?
15) Where is the current fastest on a meander?
16) Name the landform created when a meander is cut off by deposition.
17) What is a levee?
18) Describe how levees are formed.
19) Name one type of delta and describe what it looks like.
20) What do the contour lines on a map show?
21) Give two pieces of map evidence for either a waterfall or a river's lower course.
22) Describe three landforms in the valley of a river you have studied.
23) What is river discharge?
24) How does impermeable rock affect river discharge?
25) Describe two physical factors that can increase the risk of floods.
26) Name a hard engineering strategy and describe its benefits.
27) Name a soft engineering strategy and describe its disadvantages.
28) Why are hard engineering strategies usually less sustainable than soft engineering strategies?
29) a) Name a flood that you have studied and state when it occurred.
    b) Describe the causes of the flood and the long-term responses to it.
30) Which areas of the UK have a water deficit?
31) Describe one way that the demand for water in the UK can be reduced.
32) a) Name a reservoir in the UK.
    b) Describe two social impacts and two environmental impacts that the reservoir has had.
33) How can water be taken from a reservoir in a sustainable way?

Ice Levels Over Time

It's time to put your hat, scarf and jumper on, you've arrived at the section that's all about ice...

The Earth has Glacial Periods and Interglacial Periods

1) The Earth goes through cold periods which last for millions of years called ice ages. During ice ages, large masses of ice cover parts of the Earth's surface.
2) The last ice age was the Pleistocene that began around 2.6 million years ago.
3) During ice ages there are cooler periods called glacial periods when the ice advances to cover more of the Earth's surface. Each one lasts for about 100 000 years.
4) In between the glacial periods are warmer periods called interglacial periods when the ice retreats to cover less of the Earth's surface. Each one lasts around 10 000 years.
5) The last glacial period began around 100 000 years ago and ended around 10 000 years ago.

Ice Covered Much More of the Earth's Surface 20 000 Years Ago

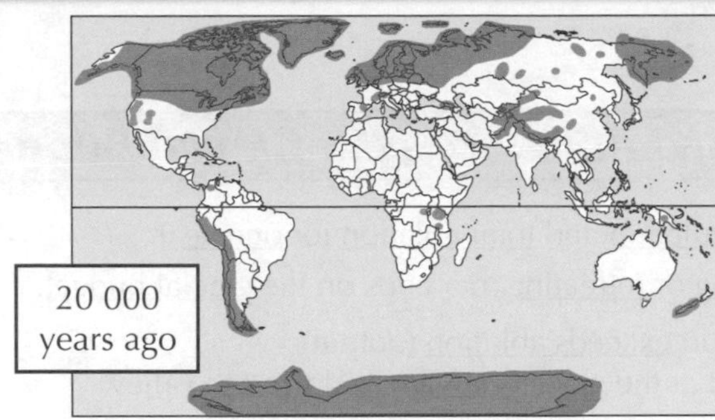

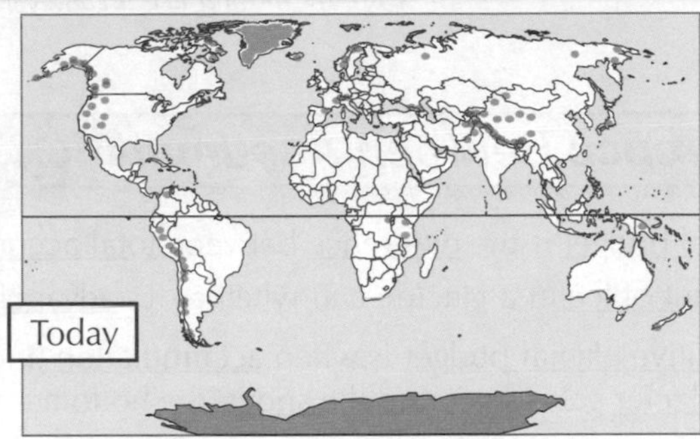

= Ice

1) Since the beginning of the Pleistocene there have been permanent ice sheets on Greenland and Antarctica. Ice has also covered other parts of the world during the colder glacial periods.
2) Ice covered a lot more of the land around 20 000 years ago (during the last glacial period) — over 30% of the Earth's land surface was covered by ice, including nearly all of the UK.
3) We're currently in an interglacial period that began around 10 000 years ago. Today about 10% of the Earth's land surface is covered by ice — the only ice sheets are the ones on Greenland and Antarctica.

Ice sheets are huge masses of ice that cover whole continents. Glaciers are masses of ice that fill valleys and hollows.

Evidence of Changing Temperature Comes From Three Main Sources

CHEMICAL EVIDENCE

The chemical composition of ice and marine sediments change as temperature changes, so they can be used to work out how global temperature has changed in the past. Ice and sediments build up over thousands of years so samples taken at different depths show the temperature over thousands of years.
The records show a pattern of increasing and decreasing temperature, which caused the ice to advance and retreat.

GEOLOGICAL EVIDENCE

Some landforms we can see today were created by glaciers in the past (see p. 95). This shows that some areas that aren't covered in ice today were covered in the past, which means temperatures were lower.

FOSSIL EVIDENCE

The remains of some organisms are preserved when they die, creating fossils. Fossils show the distribution of plants and animals that are adapted to warm or cold climates at different times in the past. From this we can tell which areas were warmer or colder in the past.

The last ice age was called the Pleistocene

Don't take your warm clothes off yet — there's lots more ice to come. For now, see if you can remember what an ice age is, what a glacial period is, when the last glacial period was, and how far the ice sheets spread in that period.

Glacial Budget

Glaciers are masses of ice that fill valleys and hollows. They move downhill under the force of gravity.

A Glacier has a Zone of Accumulation and a Zone of Ablation

1) Accumulation is the input of snow and ice into the glacier.
2) Ablation is the output of water from a glacier as the ice melts.
3) You get more accumulation than ablation in the upper part of a glacier — so it's called the zone of accumulation.
4) You get more ablation than accumulation in the lower part of a glacier — so it's called the zone of ablation.

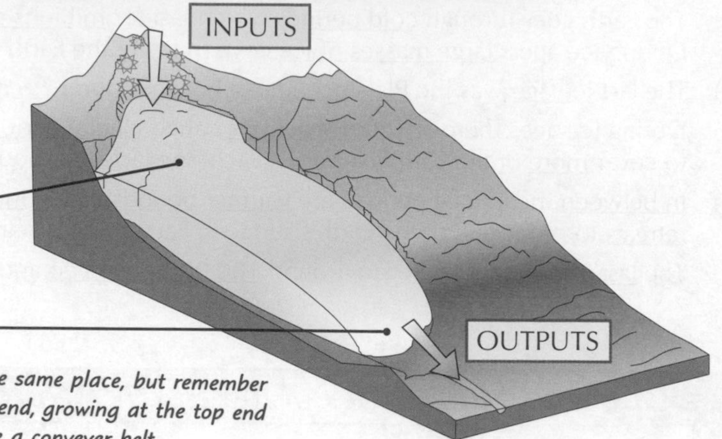

It can look like glaciers stay in the same place, but remember — they're melting at the bottom end, growing at the top end and always moving like a conveyer belt.

The Difference Between Accumulation and Ablation is the Glacial Budget

1) The glacial budget is the difference between total accumulation and total ablation for one year.
2) The amount of ice in a glacier, and whether it's advancing or retreating, depends on the glacial budget:
   - A positive glacial budget is when accumulation (input) exceeds ablation (output). The glacier gets larger and the snout (the bottom end of the glacier) advances down the valley.
   - A negative glacial budget is when ablation (output) exceeds accumulation (input). The glacier gets smaller and the snout retreats up the valley.
   - If there's the same amount of accumulation and ablation over a year, the glacier stays the same size and the position of the snout doesn't change.

The Glacial Budget Changes in the Short-Term and the Long-Term

Temperature changes throughout each year and over the years. Both these things affect the glacial budget:

1) Glaciers advance and retreat seasonally:
   - In the summer there's more ablation than accumulation because more ice melts when it's warm. This means there's a negative glacial budget so glaciers retreat.
   - In the winter there's more accumulation than ablation because there's more snowfall and less melting. This means there's a positive glacial budget, so glaciers advance.
2) Since 1950 most glaciers have had a negative glacial budget, so they've been retreating. This is because the earth's temperature has been increasing (global warming).

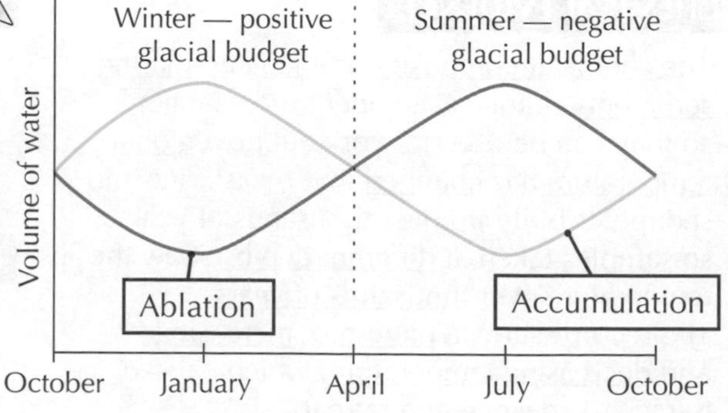

A glacial budget can be positive or negative over one year

This page has lots of technical terms on it — positive glacial budget, negative glacial budget, advance, retreat, ablation and accumulation. Examiners will expect you to use them in your exam answers about glaciers so get learning them.

Glacier — Case Study

Most glaciers are getting smaller, some by up to a few metres each year — and some are in serious danger of disappearing completely. This case study is about a retreating glacier in Switzerland.

The *Rhône Glacier* is *Retreating*

1) The Rhône Glacier is in the Swiss Alps.
2) It's currently about 7.8 km long.
3) Like most of the glaciers in the world, it's been retreating since the 19th century.

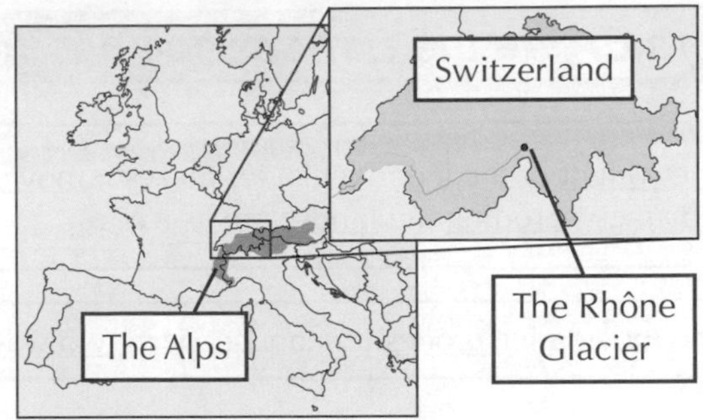

Evidence of *Glacial Retreat* comes from *Various Sources*

Postcard showing the glacier around 1900

Photo of the glacier in 2008

1 PICTURES

These pictures show the different size and position of the glacier in 1900 and 2008 — you can see that the glacier has retreated.

2 MONITORING DATA

The length of the Rhône Glacier has been measured since 1879. This graph shows the decrease in length since 1879.

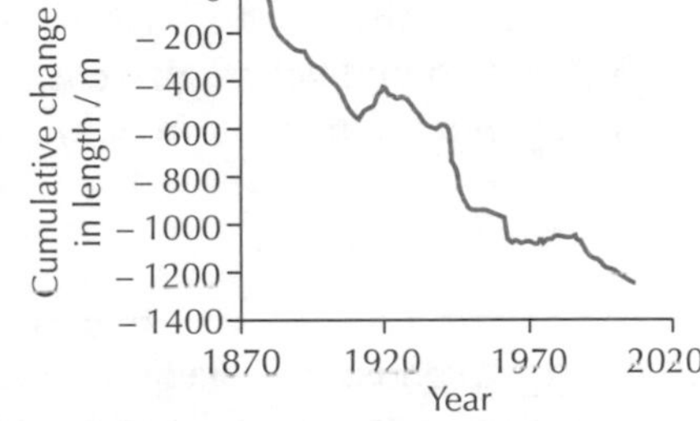

3 AMOUNT OF MELTWATER

As the glacier retreats it produces more meltwater. The meltwater has formed a new lake in front of the glacier which has been increasing in size. This shows the glacier has been melting more rapidly.

Global Warming is the Main Cause of *Glacial Retreat*

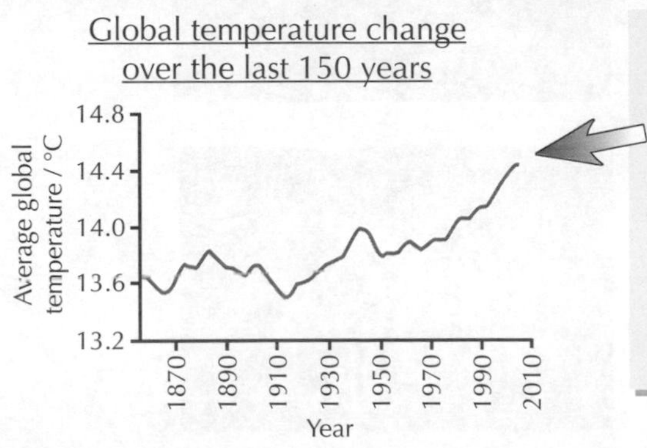

1) There's a consensus (general agreement) among scientists that glacial retreat is caused by global warming. The graph shows an increase in average global temperature of about 0.9 °C in the last 150 years.
2) In recent decades, parts of Switzerland have had above average temperature rises — a weather station near the Rhône Glacier recorded an increase of 1.8 °C between 1937 and 2005. This is thought to be because Switzerland has no coastline — the sea has a cooling effect on the land.

Most glaciers are getting smaller because of global warming

It might sound like a fairly obvious answer, but the evidence for glacial retreat is that the glaciers are getting smaller. However, you'll need to give more detail than that in the exam so cover the page and check what you know.

Glacial Erosion

It might not seem like glaciers do much — after all they're just large blocks of ice sitting around — but they actually cause rather a lot of erosion and have a massive effect on the landscape around us.

*Glaciers **Erode** the **Landscape** as They **Move***

1) The weight of the ice in a glacier makes it move downhill (advance), eroding the landscape as it goes.

2) The moving ice erodes the landscape in two ways:

1 PLUCKING

This occurs when meltwater at the base, back or sides of a glacier freezes onto the rock. As the glacier moves forward it pulls pieces of rock out.

2 ABRASION

This occurs where bits of rock stuck in the ice grind against the rock below the glacier, wearing it away (it's a bit like the glacier's got sandpaper on the bottom of it).

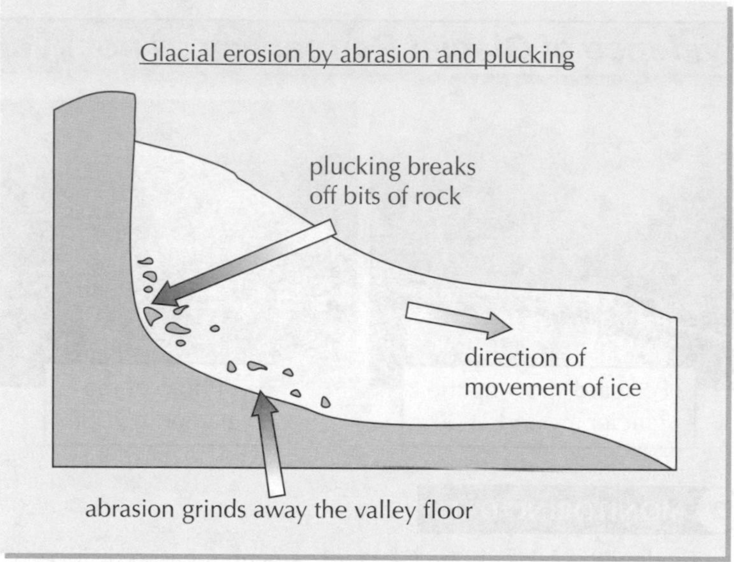
Glacial erosion by abrasion and plucking
plucking breaks off bits of rock
direction of movement of ice
abrasion grinds away the valley floor

3) At the top end of the glacier the ice doesn't move in a straight line — it moves in a circular motion called rotational slip. This can erode hollows in the landscape and deepen them into bowl shapes.

4) The rock above glaciers is also weathered (broken down where it is) by the conditions around glaciers. Freeze-thaw weathering is where water gets into cracks in rocks:

- The water freezes and expands, putting pressure on the rock.
- The ice then thaws, releasing the pressure.
- If this process is repeated it can make bits of the rock fall off.

Glaciers erode valleys in two ways — by plucking and abrasion

Make sure you know the difference between erosion and weathering so that you don't get them mixed up in the exam. Erosion happens where ice touches the valley sides or bottom, and weathering happens above the ice surface.

Glacial Erosion

All that erosion creates some attractive features...

Glacial Erosion Produces Seven Different Landforms

An arête is a steep-sided ridge formed when two glaciers flow in parallel valleys. The glaciers erode the sides of the valleys, which sharpens the ridge between them.

(E.g. Striding Edge, Lake District)

A pyramidal peak is a pointed mountain peak with at least three sides. It's formed when three or more back-to-back glaciers erode a mountain.

(E.g. Snowdon, Wales)

Corries begin as hollows containing a small glacier. As the ice moves by rotational slip, it erodes the hollow into a steep-sided, armchair shape with a lip at the bottom end. When the ice melts it can leave a small circular lake called a tarn.

(E.g. Red Tarn, Lake District)

Truncated spurs are cliff-like edges on the valley side formed when ridges of land (spurs) that stick out into the main valley are cut off as the glacier moves past.

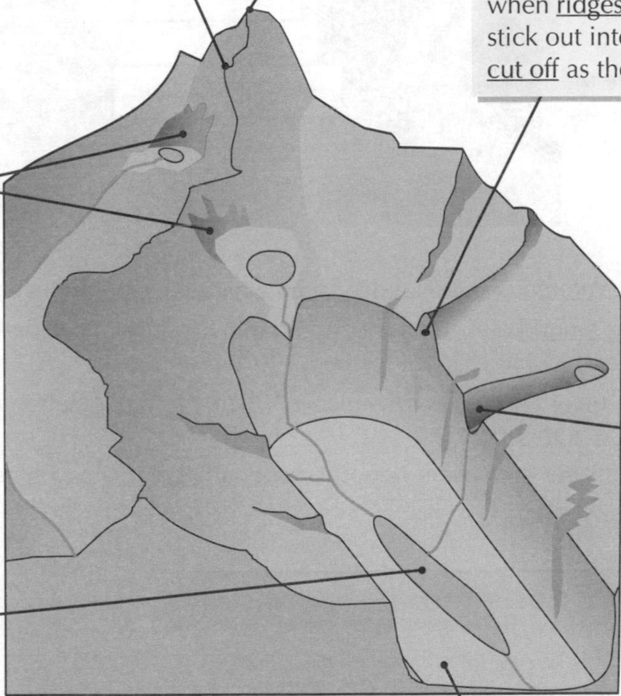

Hanging valleys are valleys formed by smaller glaciers (called tributary glaciers) that flow into the main glacier. The glacial trough is eroded much more deeply by the larger glacier, so when the glaciers melt the valleys are left at a higher level.

Ribbon lakes are long, thin lakes that form after a glacier retreats. They form in hollows where softer rock was eroded more than the surrounding hard rock.

(E.g. Windermere, Lake District)

Glacial troughs are steep-sided valleys with flat bottoms. They start off as a V-shaped river valley but change to a U-shape as the glacier erodes the sides and bottom, making it deeper and wider.

(E.g. Nant Ffrancon, Snowdonia)

Learn how ice produces these seven landforms

Make sure you know what each of the landforms looks like — and also make sure you know why they look the way they do. You might also need to spot them on a map in the exam — turn to page 97 if you need some help with that.

Glacial Transport and Deposition

Glaciers transport a lot of material — and that material has to end up somewhere.

Glaciers Transport and Deposit Material

1) Glaciers can move material (such as rocks and earth) over very large distances — this is called transportation.
2) The material is frozen in the glacier, carried on its surface, or pushed in front of it. It's called bulldozing when the ice pushes loose material in front of it.
3) When the ice carrying the material melts, the material is dropped on the valley floor — this is called deposition. It also occurs when the ice is overloaded with material.
4) The dropped material makes landforms such as moraines and drumlins (see below).
5) Glacial deposits aren't sorted by weight like river deposits — rocks of all shapes and sizes are mixed up together.

Glaciers Deposit Material as Different Types of Moraine

Moraines are landforms made out of material dropped by a glacier as it melts. There are four different types, depending on their position:

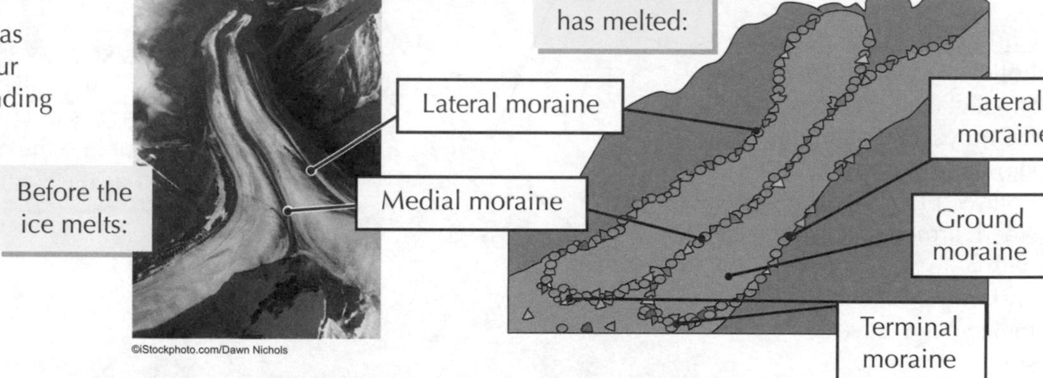

1) Lateral moraine is a long mound of material deposited where the side of the glacier was.
2) Medial moraine is a long mound of material deposited in the centre of a valley where two glaciers met (the two lateral moraines join together).
3) Terminal moraine builds up at the snout of the glacier when it remains stationary. It's deposited as semicircular mounds.
4) Ground moraine is a thin layer of material deposited over a large area as a glacier melts.

Material can also be Deposited as Drumlins

1) Drumlins are elongated hills of glacial deposits — the largest ones can be over 1000 m long, 500 m wide and 50 m high.
2) They're round, blunt and steep at the upstream end, and tapered, pointed and gently sloping at the downstream end.
3) An example of where drumlins can be found is the Ribble Valley, Lancashire.

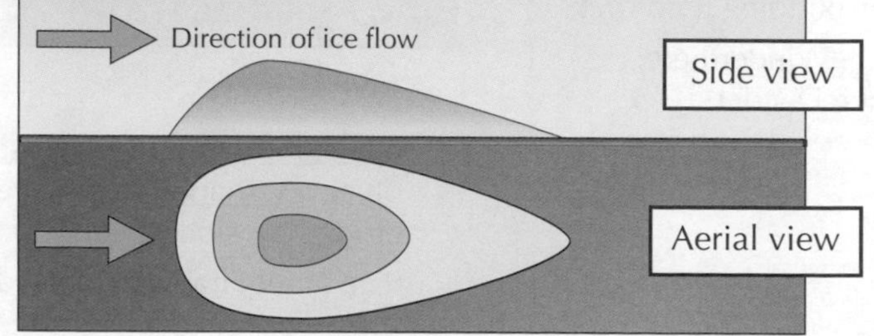

Glaciers deposit material when the ice melts

Moraines and drumlins are evidence that there used to be glaciers in the area, so remember what they look like. Check you know the difference between the four types of moraine too by drawing a simple version of the diagram.

Glacial Landforms on Maps

You might get asked to spot glacial landforms on OS®maps in the exam, so it's a good idea to practise now.

Use Contour Lines to Spot Pyramidal Peaks, Corries and Arêtes on a Map

Contour lines are the orange lines drawn all over maps. They tell you about the height of the land by the numbers marked on them, and the steepness of the land by how close together the lines are (the closer they are, the steeper the slope). Here are a few tips on how to spot pyramidal peaks, arêtes and corries on a map:

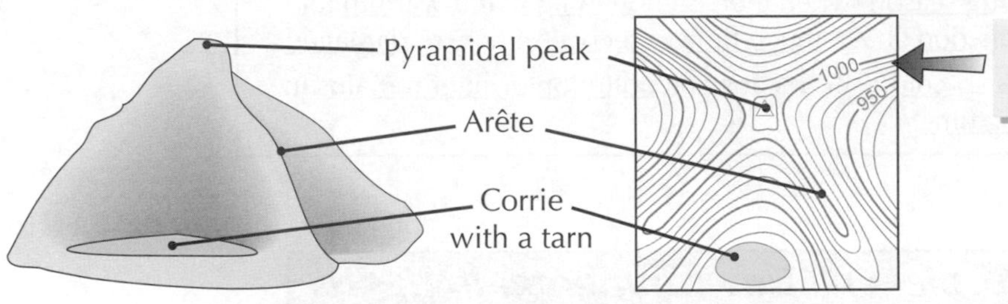

This is the sort of thing you're looking for on a map.

But on a real map, like this one of Snowdon in Wales, it's not as obvious.

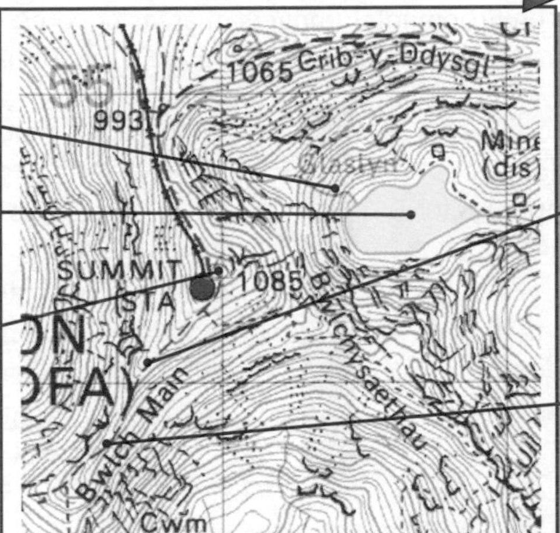

*

Corries have tightly packed contours in a U-shape around them.

Some corries have a tarn in them.

A pyramidal peak has tightly packed contour lines that curve away from a central high point. If you find this you'll find the arêtes and corries around it.

Arêtes are quite hard to see. Look for a really thin hill with tightly packed, parallel contours on either side.

Arêtes often have corries or tarns on either side, and footpaths on them with names like 'Something Edge', e.g. 'Striding Edge'.

You can also use Maps to Spot Glacial Troughs and Ribbon Lakes

This map of Nant Ffrancon (a glacial trough) and Llyn Ogwen (a ribbon lake) in Wales shows the classic things to look out for if you're ever asked to spot a glacial trough or a ribbon lake on a map extract:

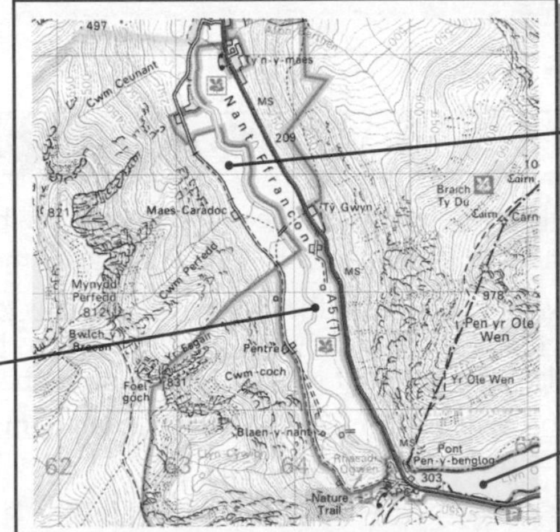

*

Look for a wide, straight valley in a mountainous area with a river that looks too small to have formed the valley.

Glacial troughs are flat valleys with very steep sides. There are no contour lines on the bottom of the valley but they're tightly packed on the sides.

Many glacial troughs have ribbon lakes in them. Look for a flat valley with steep sides surrounding a long straight lake.

Contour lines are the key to spotting glacial landforms on maps

Answering a question using a map shouldn't be too tricky, just study the map carefully and say what you see. Make sure you refer to the map in your answer though — for help with this, e.g. using grid references, see page 230.

Impacts and Management of Tourism On Ice

Tourists can have many impacts on glacial areas, but not to worry, these impacts can be reduced.

*Areas Covered in **Snow and Ice** are **Fragile Environments***

Areas that are covered in snow and ice attract lots of tourists for things like winter sports and sightseeing of glaciers. The environments are fragile though — they're easily damaged and difficult to manage:

- There's only a short growing season (when there's enough light and warmth for plants to grow) — so plants don't have much time to recover if they're damaged.
- Decay is slow because it's so cold. This means any pollution or litter remains in the environment for a long time.

Tourism** has **Economic**, **Social** and **Environmental Impacts

Tourists have economic, social and environmental impacts in areas covered in snow and ice, so there's conflict over how these areas should be used. Here are a few of the impacts:

ECONOMIC

1) Lots of new businesses are set up for the tourists, e.g. restaurants, hotels and guiding companies for the sports activities. This boosts the local economy.
2) New businesses means there are job opportunities for people in these remote areas.

SOCIAL

1) Increased numbers of people and businesses mean the infrastructure (roads and railways) becomes congested. This makes it more difficult for local people and tourists to get around.
2) More job opportunities mean that more young people will stay in the area instead of leaving to find work in cities.
3) Tourists can trigger avalanches on ski slopes which can cause injuries and deaths.

ENVIRONMENTAL

1) The fragile glacial environment is damaged by people trampling on the snow and the soil beneath, which causes soil erosion.
2) Glacial landforms like moraines are eroded by people walking on them.
3) There's increased noise, pollution and litter from all the people and traffic in the area.
4) The developments in the area, e.g. buildings and ski lifts, have a visual impact on the environment.

*There are **Management Strategies** to **Manage** the **Different Impacts***

There's a need to conserve the fragile environment, but people also have the right to see and experience it. There are different strategies to manage the environment so the impacts of tourism are reduced:

1) Tourists are kept informed of avalanche risks, so they know which areas to avoid. Resorts can build structures to slow and divert the moving snow, plant trees to act as barriers, and set off controlled avalanches to dislodge snow before tourists arrive on the slopes in the morning.
2) Improvements to public transport systems can reduce the amount of traffic and so reduce damage to the environment from pollution.
3) Areas can be set aside as nature reserves. Tourist activity in these areas is limited, so their environmental impact is reduced.

Glacial environments are fragile and easily damaged

Lots more impacts to get through here. Repeat after me... economic, social and environmental. At least there aren't any political ones for you to remember. Once you know the impacts, check you know how they're managed.

Tourism On Ice — Case Study

Chamonix is a good example of a glacial area used for tourism.

*People go to **Chamonix** for **Winter Sports** and **Sightseeing***

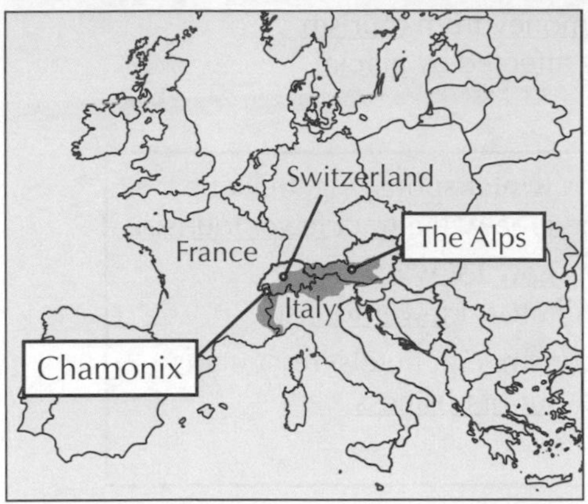

1) The Chamonix Valley is in eastern France at the foot of Mont Blanc (the highest mountain in the Alps). It's close to the border with Italy and Switzerland.
2) It's one of the most popular tourist destinations in the world with around 5 million visitors a year.
3) The region has lots of glaciers, including the Mer de Glace. The Mer de Glace is the longest glacier in France — it's 7 km long and 200 m deep.
4) There are also many other tourist attractions such as 6 ski areas, 350 km of hiking trails, 40 km of mountain bike tracks, an Alpine museum and an exhibition centre.

*Tourism has **Economic**, **Social** and **Environmental Impacts** on the Region*

ECONOMIC

1) The tourism industry in Chamonix creates a lot of jobs, e.g. 2500 people work as seasonal workers every year.
2) Companies make a lot of money from tourism in Chamonix, e.g. Compagnie du Mont Blanc is a company that runs ski lifts and rail transport — it has a turnover of €50 million.

SOCIAL

1) The types of jobs available in Chamonix have changed from farm labouring to jobs in restaurants and hotels etc.
2) Tourist developments, e.g. ski slopes, have increased the risk of avalanches. This means there are more deaths from avalanches, e.g. in 1999 an avalanche killed 12 people.

ENVIRONMENTAL

1) Large numbers of tourists cause a lot of traffic, which increases pollution. E.g. a study from 2002 to 2004 showed that traffic pollution was worse in the Chamonix region than in the centre of Paris.
2) A huge amount of energy is used to run the facilities for tourists, e.g. the hotels, ski lifts and snow-making machines. This increases CO_2 emissions, which increases global warming.

*Tourism in the Resort has to be **Carefully Managed***

Management of the Chamonix Valley has to balance the need to conserve the environment with the right of people to see and experience it. Here are a few of the strategies used:

1) A system of avalanche barriers is maintained around the resorts, e.g. there's a barrier at Taconnaz. There are also avalanche awareness courses and daily bulletins to keep tourists aware of the risks. This means tourists are less likely to be hurt or killed by an avalanche.
2) The amount of traffic in Chamonix is managed by providing free public transport for tourists. The amount of pollution from public transport is reduced by using low emission buses.
3) Some hotels are reducing their energy use, e.g. by installing solar panels to heat water and systems to automatically turn lights off. This means CO_2 emissions are reduced.

Learn facts and figures for case study questions

Another case study, another day — but at least this one makes you think of holidays. Maybe not the most exciting thing to learn but examiners love to read about 'real world' examples — so the more detail you can shove in the better.

Impacts of Glacial Retreat

This is the last revision page of the section and once it's done you'll be an expert on all things glacial.

Glacial Retreat and Unreliable Snowfall Affects Tourism

The economies of many areas that are covered in snow and ice rely on money from tourism (e.g. for winter sports and sightseeing of glaciers). These areas are being affected by glacial retreat (see p. 92) and unreliable snowfall:

1) Glacial retreat means the ice will no longer be available for winter sports, e.g. trekking and ice climbing, or sightseeing of glaciers. This means the area will attract fewer tourists.
2) Unreliable snowfall means that there might not be enough snow for winter sports, e.g. skiing and snowboarding. This also means the area will attract fewer tourists.
3) Fewer tourists will mean that the businesses that rely on tourism, e.g. hotels, restaurants and guiding companies, will make less money and may go out of business.
4) This would lead to increased unemployment in these areas.

Glacial Retreat has other Impacts

ECONOMIC

Once a glacier has completely melted, the amount of meltwater decreases. This means industries that rely on the supply of meltwater, e.g. agriculture for irrigation and hydroelectric power (HEP) for electricity production, will make less money and could shut down.

SOCIAL

1) Glacial retreat will mean the water supply to some settlements is reduced (see above).
2) Disruptions to power supplies from HEP could leave some people with an unreliable power supply.
3) If businesses shut down, local people will have to move away to find work. Young people in particular will move away, so older family members might be left behind.
4) If an area's population declines, local services and recreational facilities will also shut down.
5) The ice will no longer be available for recreational use for local people, e.g. for trekking and ice climbing.

ENVIRONMENTAL

1) Glacial retreat is linked to an increase in natural hazards — rapid melting can cause flooding, rockslides and avalanches. These hazards destroy habitats and disrupt food chains.
2) Meltwater from retreating glaciers contributes to rising sea level — water is no longer stored as ice on land and returns to the sea. Rising sea level destroys coastal habitats by causing flooding and erosion.
3) Lots of fish species are adapted to live in the cold meltwater that comes from glaciers. When glaciers have completely melted, there's no cold meltwater so these fish species may die out.
4) Harmful pollutants can be trapped in glacial ice, e.g. the pesticide DDT that was used from the 1940s to 1980s. Rapid melting releases them back into the environment, polluting streams and lakes.

Glacial retreat has economic, social and environmental impacts

Although glacial retreat has a big effect on the tourist industry, it's not the only thing it impacts on. Make sure you can write out at least five impacts of glacial retreat, then if you get a question on it in the exam, you'll have plenty to say.

Worked Exam Questions

With the answers written in, it's very easy to skim this worked example and think you've understood. But that's not going to help you, so take the time to make sure you've really understood it.

1 Study **Figure 1**, a diagram of a mountainous area where glaciers used to flow.

(a) (i) Label the glacial landforms shown in **Figure 1**.

(3 marks)

Figure 1

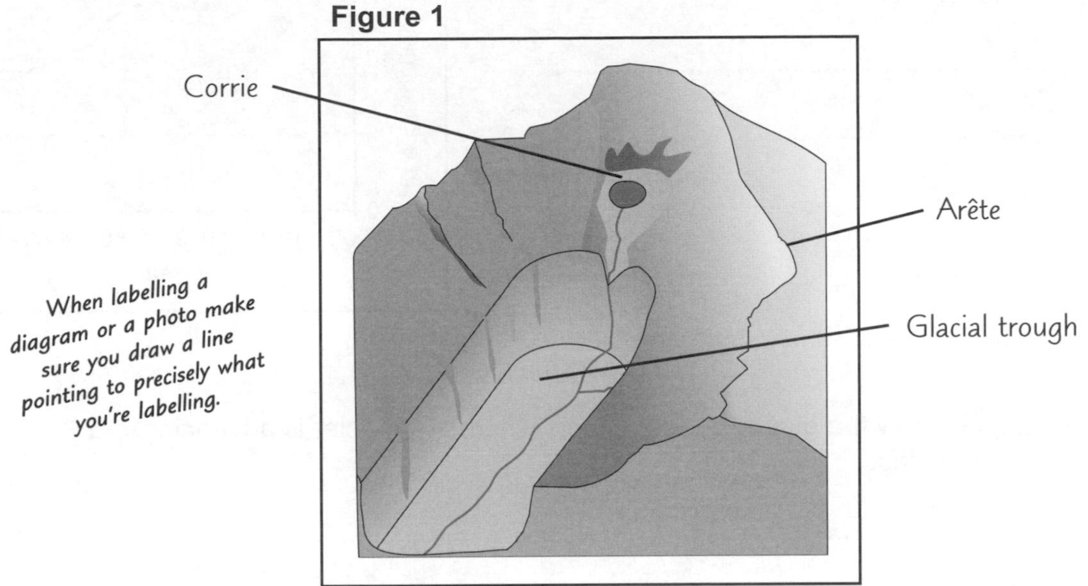

When labelling a diagram or a photo make sure you draw a line pointing to precisely what you're labelling.

(ii) Describe two ways in which moving ice erodes the landscape.

Plucking occurs when meltwater at the base, back or sides of a glacier freezes onto the rock. As the glacier moves forward it pulls pieces of rock out. Abrasion is where bits of rock stuck in the ice grind against the rock below the glacier, wearing it away.

(4 marks)

(b) Describe a ribbon lake and explain how it is formed.

A ribbon lake is a long, thin lake that formed after a glacier retreated. It is formed in a hollow where softer rock was eroded more than the surrounding harder rock.

(2 marks)

(c) Lateral and terminal moraines are often found in areas where glaciers used to flow.

Read the questions carefully so that you write about the right types of moraine for each part.

(i) Explain the formation of these two types of moraine.

Lateral moraine is a long mound of material deposited at the side of a glacier.

Terminal moraine builds up at the snout of a glacier when it remains stationary.

(2 marks)

(ii) Name two other types of moraine and explain their formation.

Ground moraine is a thin layer of material deposited over a large area as a glacier melts.

Medial moraine is material deposited at the centre of a valley where two glaciers meet — the two lateral moraines join together.

(4 marks)

Exam Questions

1 Study **Figure 1**, a graph showing how the length of a glacier changed between 1900 and 2000.

Figure 1

(a) (i) Explain the term 'ablation'.
On which part of a glacier does most ablation occur?

....

....

....

....

....

(2 marks)

(ii) Explain how the glacial budget affects whether a glacier is advancing or retreating.

....

....

....

....

....

....

(6 marks)

(iii) By how much did the glacier shown in **Figure 1** decrease in length between 1900 and 2000?

....

(1 mark)

(b) Unreliable snowfall can result in glacial retreat. Describe the social and environmental impacts of unreliable snowfall and glacial retreat.

....

....

....

....

....

....

(6 marks)

Revision Summary for Section 6

Now you've reached the end of the section it's a good idea to find out just how much information you've taken in. Have a look at the questions below and see how many of them you can answer. If you get stuck on any, go back and check the answer — don't move on until you're confident you know them all.

1) What's the name of the last ice age?
2) How long ago did the last glacial period end?
3) How much of the Earth's land surface is currently covered by ice?
4) What three types of evidence are used to identify past temperature changes?
5) Define the term accumulation.
6) What is the zone of accumulation?
7) Why does a glacier retreat in summer?
8) a) Give an example of a retreating glacier.
   b) What evidence is there that the glacier you named has retreated since the 19th century?
   c) Explain why this has happened.
9) What is rotational slip?
10) Explain what freeze-thaw weathering is.
11) What is a corrie?
12) How does a pyramidal peak form?
13) Give an example of a pyramidal peak.
14) Explain how a hanging valley forms.
15) What is bulldozing?
16) When does a glacier deposit material?
17) Describe what a drumlin looks like.
18) How would you identify a pyramidal peak on a map?
19) Describe what a glacial trough looks like on a map.
20) Give an example of a glacial trough.
21) What does a ribbon lake look like on a map?
22) Give one reason why areas covered in snow and ice are fragile environments.
23) Give two social impacts of tourism on areas covered in snow and ice.
24) Describe two environmental impacts of tourism on areas covered in snow and ice.
25) a) Give an example of an area in the Alps used for winter sports and sightseeing of glaciers.
   b) Give one economic, one social and one environmental impact of tourism in the area you named.
   c) Give three management strategies used in the area you named.
26) Name an industry affected by glacial retreat.
27) Give one economic impact of glacial retreat.

Coastal Weathering and Erosion

Weathering is the breakdown of rocks where they are, erosion is when the rocks are broken down and carried away by something, e.g. by seawater.

Rock is Broken Down by Mechanical and Chemical Weathering

1) Mechanical weathering is the breakdown of rock without changing its chemical composition. There's one main type of mechanical weathering that affects coasts — freeze-thaw weathering:

   1) It happens when the temperature alternates above and below 0 °C (the freezing point of water).
   2) Water gets into rock that has cracks, e.g. granite.
   3) When the water freezes it expands, which puts pressure on the rock.
   4) When the water thaws it contracts, which releases the pressure on the rock.
   5) Repeated freezing and thawing widens the cracks and causes the rock to break up.

2) Chemical weathering is the breakdown of rock by changing its chemical composition. Carbonation weathering is a type of chemical weathering that happens in warm and wet conditions:

   1) Rainwater has carbon dioxide dissolved in it, which makes it a weak carbonic acid.
   2) Carbonic acid reacts with rock that contains calcium carbonate, e.g. carboniferous limestone, so the rocks are dissolved by the rainwater.

Waves Wear Away the Coast using Four Processes of Erosion

1) Hydraulic power — waves crash against rock and compress the air in the cracks. This puts pressure on the rock. Repeated compression widens the cracks and makes bits of rock break off.
2) Abrasion (corrasion) — eroded particles in the water scrape against rock, removing small pieces.
3) Attrition — eroded particles in the water smash into each other and break into smaller fragments. Their edges also get rounded off as they rub together.
4) Solution (corrosion) — weak carbonic acid in seawater dissolves rock like chalk and limestone.

Destructive Waves Erode the Coastline

Coastlines that are being eroded by destructive waves are called destructive coastlines.

The waves that carry out erosional processes are called destructive waves:

1) Destructive waves have a high frequency (10-14 waves per minute).
2) They're high and steep.
3) Their backwash (the movement of the water back down the beach) is more powerful than their swash (the movement of the water up the beach). This means material is removed from the coast.
4) There are two main factors that affect the size and power of destructive waves, and so how much they erode the coast:
   - Wind — the force of the wind on the water's surface is what creates waves. A strong wind gives large, powerful waves.
   - Fetch — is the distance of water over which the wind has blown to produce a wave. The greater the fetch, the bigger and more powerful the wave.

Learn the four processes of coastal erosion

This page is packed full of information, but it's really only about how the coast is worn away and rocks are broken down into smaller pieces. Break your revision down into smaller pieces by learning the processes one at a time.

Coastal Landforms Caused by Erosion

Erosion by waves forms many coastal landforms over long periods of time.

Cliffs Retreat as a Result of *Erosion*, *Weathering* and *Mass Movements*

1) Waves cause most erosion at the foot of a cliff.

2) A wave-cut notch forms, which is enlarged as erosion continues, making the cliff above the notch unstable. The part of the cliff above sea level is also affected by mechanical and chemical weathering processes.

3) This makes the cliff more unstable and it eventually collapses.

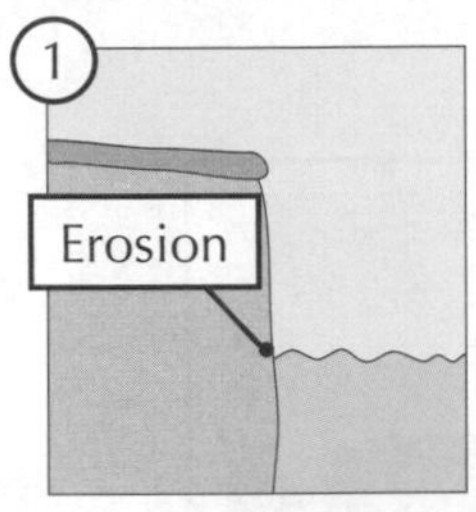

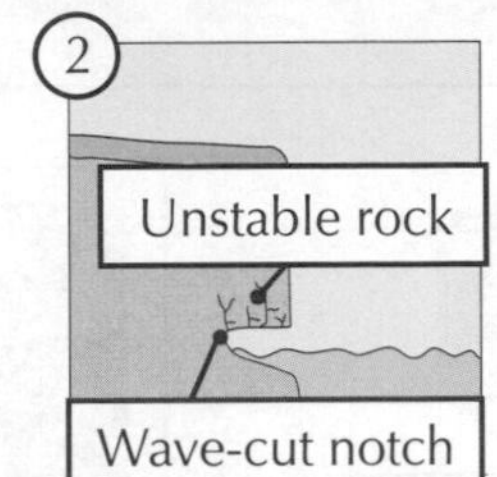

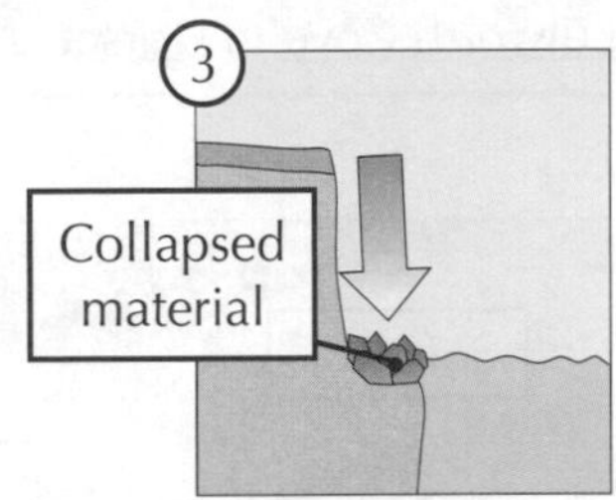

4) The collapsed material is washed away and a new wave-cut notch starts to form.

5) Repeated collapsing results in the cliff retreating. A wave-cut platform is the platform that's left behind as the cliff retreats.

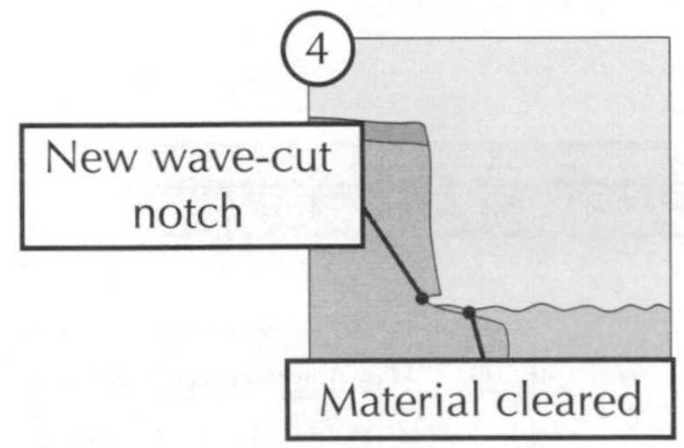

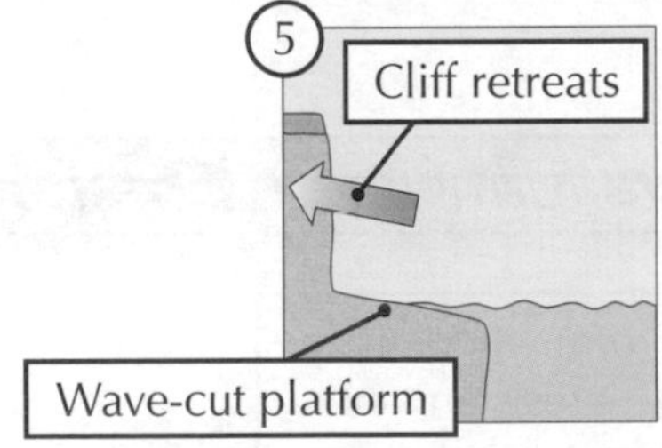

There are cliffs and wave-cut platforms at Beachy Head in Sussex.

1) The rate of retreat depends on lots of things. For example:
   - The geology of the cliff — cliffs formed from soft rock or loose material can retreat very quickly (e.g. several metres a year). Cliffs formed only from hard rock can be eroded over thousands of years.
   - Vegetation — cliffs covered in vegetation are more stable, so they're eroded less easily and retreat more slowly.
2) Cliff collapses are mass movements (the shifting of rock and loose material down a slope). They happen when the force of gravity acting on a slope is greater than the force supporting it, e.g. when the notch has made the cliff above unstable.
3) There are three types of mass movement that can affect cliffs — slides, slumps and rockfalls.

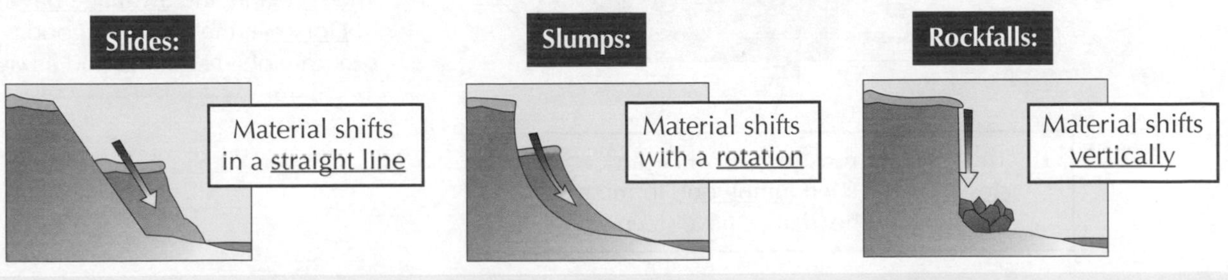

Remember the five steps of how erosion leads to cliff retreat

The process of cliff retreat looks a bit complicated, but if you learn each step one at a time it's not too bad. Don't forget to learn the rest of the stuff on the page too — any of it could come up in the exam.

Coastal Landforms Caused by Erosion

Some coastal landforms only form where there are bands of rock that are more resistant to erosion than others.

Coves Form where there are Parallel Bands of Hard and Soft Rock

1) A cove is a wide, circular bay with a narrow entrance.
2) They form where there's a band of hard rock (e.g. limestone) along a coast with a band of softer rock behind it (e.g. clay).
3) Where there's a weakness in the band of hard rock a narrow gap will be eroded. The softer rock behind will then be eroded much more to form the cove.
4) Lulworth Cove in Dorset is a good example.

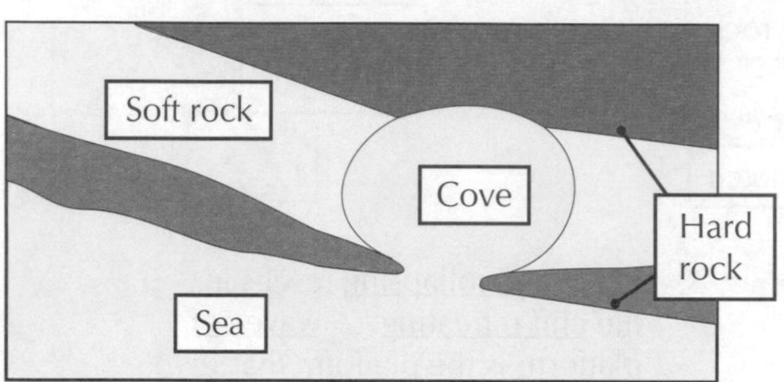

Lulworth Cove

Headlands and Bays form where Erosion Resistance is Different

1) Headlands and bays form where there are alternating bands of resistant and less resistant rock along a coast.

2) The less resistant rock (e.g. clay) is eroded quickly and this forms a bay — bays have a gentle slope.

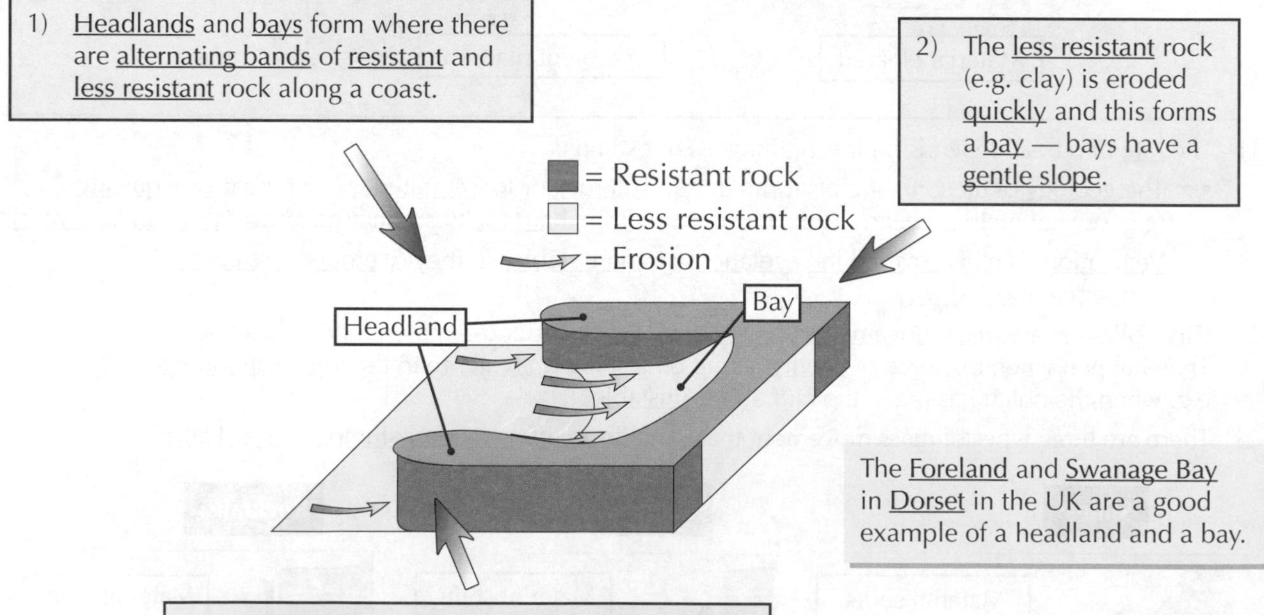

The Foreland and Swanage Bay in Dorset in the UK are a good example of a headland and a bay.

3) The resistant rock (e.g. chalk) is eroded more slowly and it's left jutting out, forming a headland — headlands have steep sides.

Which way the bands of hard and soft rock go determines the type of landform

It's always worth learning simple diagrams to show how landforms form. Things that are tricky to explain in the exam become much easier if you draw them — just make sure your sketches are neat and clearly labelled.

Coastal Landforms Caused by Erosion

You're not quite done with coastal erosion yet — it's got a few more tricks up its sleeve...

Headlands are Eroded to form Caves, Arches, Stacks and Stumps

1) Headlands are usually made of resistant rocks (see previous page) that have weaknesses like cracks.

2) Waves crash into the headlands and enlarge the cracks — mainly by hydraulic power and abrasion. Repeated erosion and enlargement of the cracks causes a cave to form.

3) Continued erosion deepens the cave until it breaks through the headland — forming an arch, e.g. Durdle Door in Dorset.

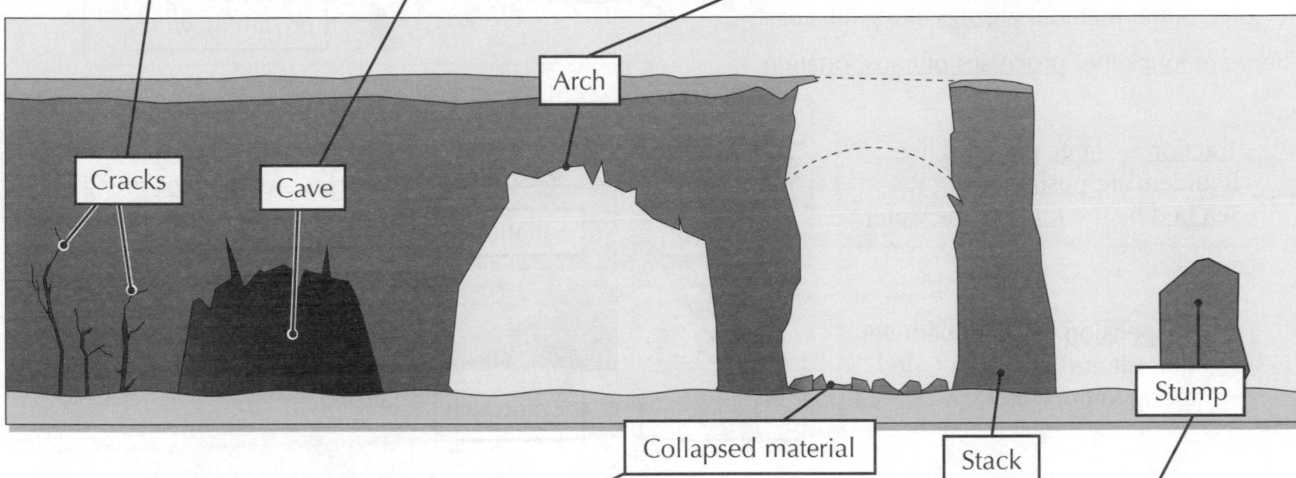

4) Erosion continues to wear away the rock supporting the arch, until it eventually collapses.

5) This forms a stack — an isolated rock that's separate from the headland, e.g. Old Harry in Dorset.

6) The stack is eventually worn away to give a stump, which can be covered by the water at high tide, e.g. Old Harry's Wife in Dorset.

Durdle Door

Old Harry and his Wife

©iStockphoto.com/Glen Rodgers

Caves are eroded to arches, which are eroded to stacks, then stumps

This might seem a bit of a complicated page to begin with but take your time to learn how each landform is created. You could be asked about any individual landform in the exam, or about the whole process.

Coastal Transportation and Deposition

The material that's been eroded is moved around the coast and deposited by waves.

Transportation is the Movement of Material

Material is transported along coasts by a process called longshore drift:

1) Waves follow the direction of the prevailing (most common) wind.
2) They usually hit the coast at an oblique angle (any angle that isn't a right angle).
3) The swash carries material up the beach, in the same direction as the waves.
4) The backwash then carries material down the beach at right angles, back towards the sea.
5) Over time, material zigzags along the coast.

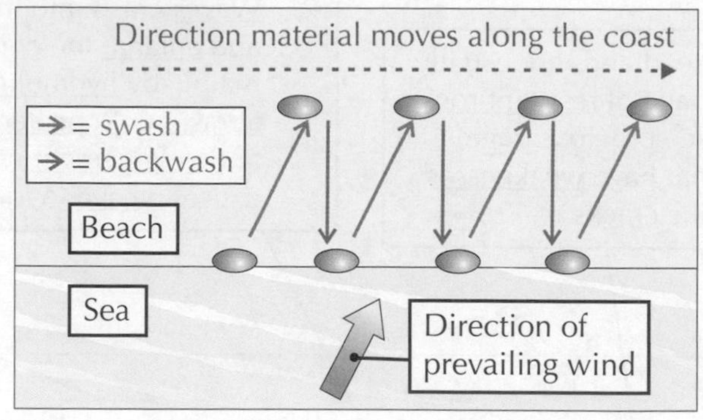

There are four other processes of transportation:

Traction — large particles like boulders are pushed along the sea bed by the force of the water.

Saltation — pebble-sized particles are bounced along the sea bed by the force of the water.

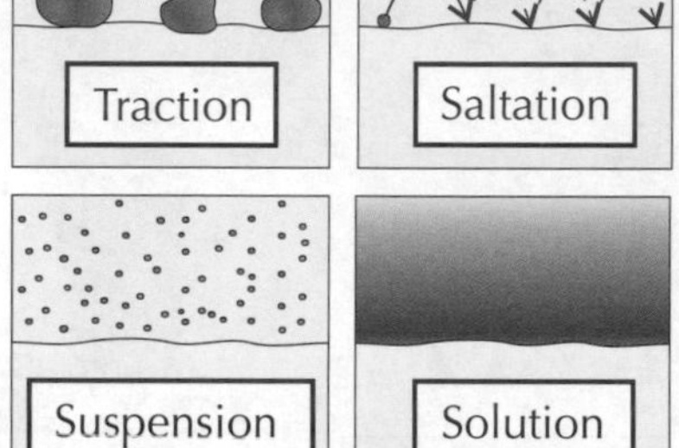

Suspension — small particles like silt and clay are carried along in the water.

Solution — soluble materials dissolve in the water and are carried along.

Deposition is the Dropping of Material

1) Deposition is when material being carried by the sea water is dropped on the coast.
2) Coasts are built up when the amount of deposition is greater than the amount of erosion.
3) The amount of material that's deposited on an area of coast is increased when:
   - There's lots of erosion elsewhere on the coast, so there's lots of material available.
   - There's lots of transportation of material into the area.
4) Low energy waves (i.e. slow waves) carry material to the coast but they're not strong enough to take a lot of material away — this means there's lots of deposition and very little erosion.

Constructive Waves Build Up the Coastline

Coastlines being built up by constructive waves are called constructive coastlines.

Waves that deposit more material than they erode and build up the coast are called constructive waves.

1) Constructive waves have a low frequency (6-8 waves per minute).
2) They're low and long.
3) The swash is powerful and it carries material up the coast.
4) The backwash is weaker and it doesn't take a lot of material back down the coast. This means material is deposited on the coast.
5) Constructive waves are made by weaker winds and have a shorter fetch than destructive waves.

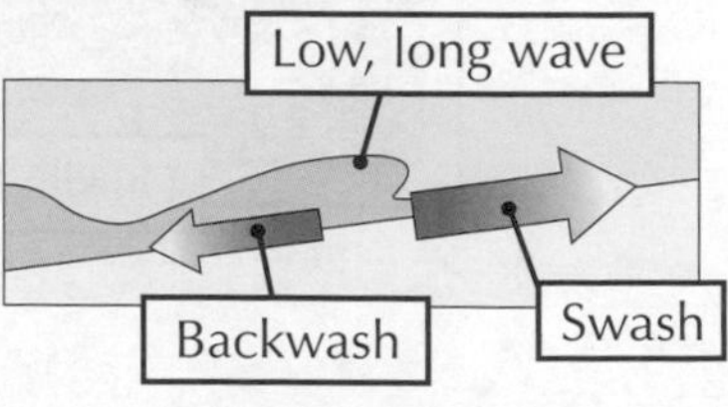

The amount of erosion affects the amount of deposition elsewhere

More processes for you to learn here but none of them are tricky. You might find it useful to draw yourself a diagram of how longshore drift works — you'll get a feel for how the material is moved along the coast in a zigzag pattern.

Coastal Landforms Caused by Deposition

Here are some more landforms for you to read about — this time they're all caused by deposition.

Beaches are formed by Deposition

1) Beaches are found on coasts between the high water mark (the highest point on the land the sea level gets to) and the low water mark (the lowest point on the land the sea level gets to).
2) They're formed by constructive waves (see previous page) depositing material like sand and shingle.
3) Sand and shingle beaches have different characteristics:
   - Sand beaches are flat and wide — sand particles are small and the weak backwash can move them back down the beach, creating a long, gentle slope.
   - Shingle beaches are steep and narrow — shingle particles are large and the weak backwash can't move them back down the beach. The shingle particles build up and create a steep slope.

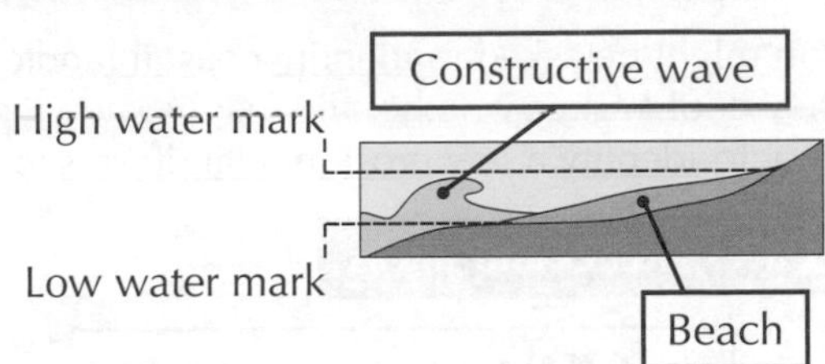

Spits and Bars are formed by Longshore Drift

Spits are just beaches that stick out into the sea — they're joined to the coast at one end. If a spit sticks out so far that it connects with another bit of the mainland, it'll form a bar. Spits and bars are formed by the process of longshore drift (see previous page).

SPITS

1) Spits form at sharp bends in the coastline, e.g. at a river mouth.
2) Longshore drift transports sand and shingle past the bend and deposits it in the sea.
3) Strong winds and waves can curve the end of the spit (forming a recurved end).
4) The sheltered area behind the spit is protected from waves — lots of material accumulates in this area, which means plants can grow there.
5) Over time, the sheltered area can become a mud flat or a salt marsh.

An example of a spit is Spurn Head in Yorkshire.

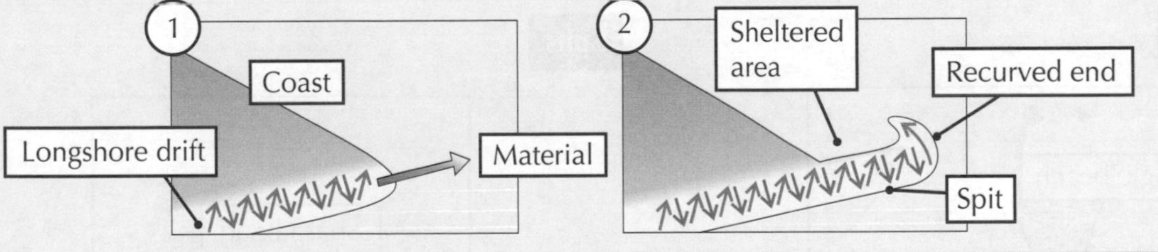

BARS

1) A bar is formed when a spit joins two headlands together, e.g. there's a bar at Slapton in Devon.
2) The bar cuts off the bay between the headlands from the sea.
3) This means a lagoon can form behind the bar.
4) A bar that connects the shore to an island (often a stack) is called a tombolo. For example, Chesil Beach in Dorset joins to the Isle of Portland.

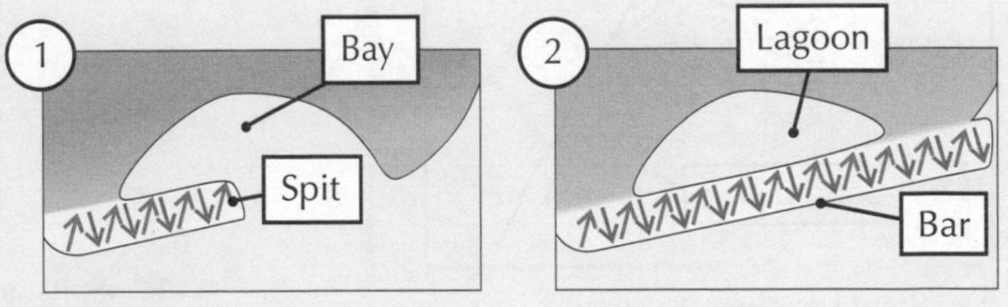

Bars are just spits that join two headlands together

In the exam, you might have to identify coastal landforms caused by deposition on photographs or diagrams. You could also be asked to spot them on a map. You'll find some help with that on the next page.

Coastal Landforms on Maps

Map skills will come in very useful in your exam so it's worth practising them now.

Identifying Landforms Caused by Erosion

You might be asked to identify coastal landforms on a map in the exam. The simplest thing they could ask is whether the map is showing erosional or depositional landforms, so here's how to identify a few erosional landforms to get you started:

Have a gander at pages 230-231 for more on reading maps.

Caves, arches and stacks

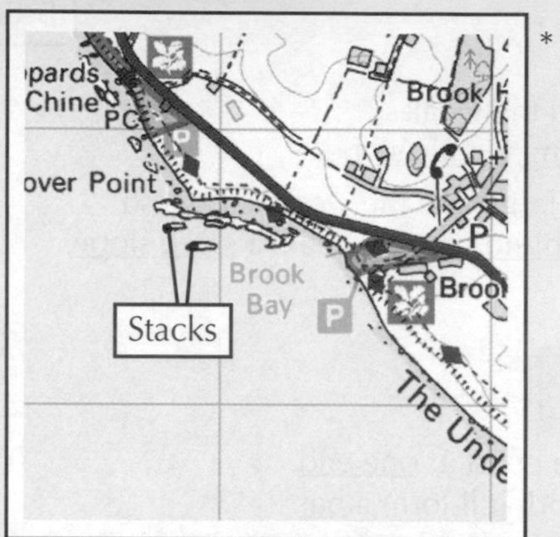

1) Caves and arches can't be seen on a map because of the rock above them.
2) Stacks look like little blobs in the sea.

Cliffs and wave-cut platforms

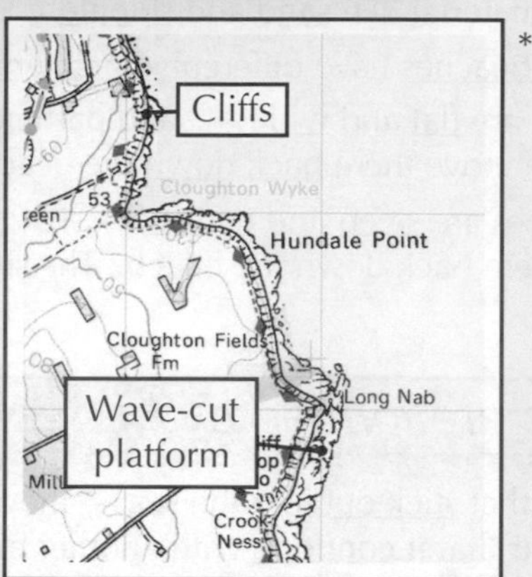

1) Cliffs (and other steep slopes) are shown on maps as little black lines.
2) Wave-cut platforms are shown as bumpy edges along the coast.

Identifying Landforms Caused by Deposition

Identifying depositional landforms is easy once you know that beaches are shown in yellow on maps. Here's how to identify a couple of depositional landforms:

Beaches

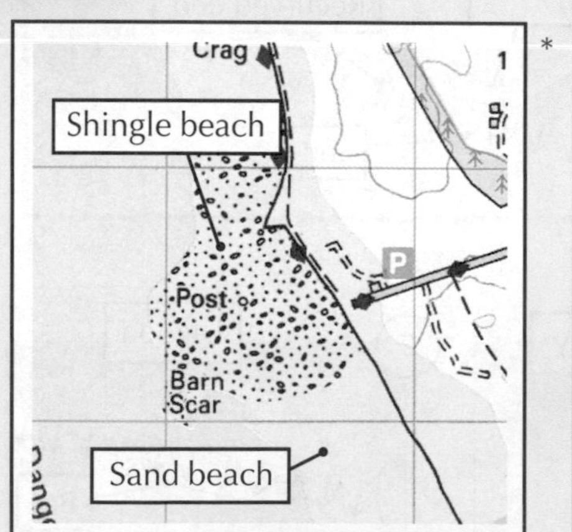

1) Sand beaches are shown on maps as pale yellow.
2) Shingle beaches are shown as white or yellow with speckles.

Spits

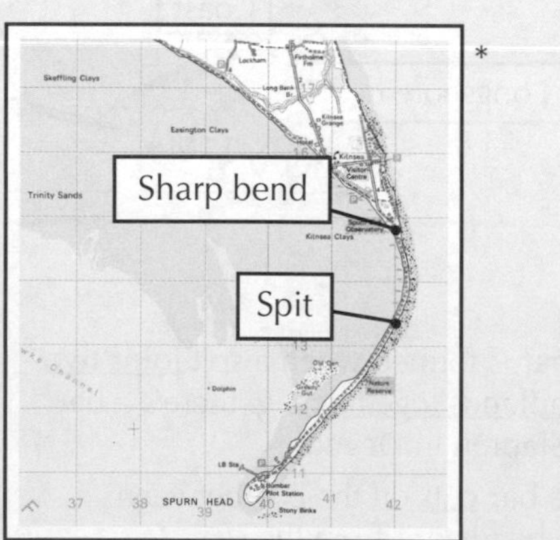

1) Spits are shown by a beach that carries on out to sea, but is still attached to the land at one end.
2) There might also be a sharp bend in the coast that caused it to form (see page 109).

Make sure you can identify each landform on a map

There are some seriously easy marks up for grabs with map questions so this is a really useful page. You could practise looking for landforms on any maps you can get a hold of. Don't forget though, caves and arches can't be seen.

Coastal Area — Case Study

The Dorset coast has lots of landforms — headlands, bays, arches, stacks, coves, tombolos, lagoons...

The Dorset Coast has Erosional and Depositional Coastal Landforms

The Dorset coast is made from bands of hard rock (like limestone and chalk) and soft rock (like clay). The rocks have been eroded at different rates giving headlands and bays and lots of other coastal landforms.

Durdle Door

Durdle Door is a great example of an arch. Erosion by waves opened up a crack in the limestone headland, which became a cave and then developed into an arch.

Lulworth Cove

Lulworth Cove is a cove formed after a gap was eroded in a band of limestone. Behind the limestone is a band of clay, which has been eroded away to form the cove. The same is now starting to happen at Stair Hole further west along the coast.

©iStockphoto.com/Leslie Budzynski

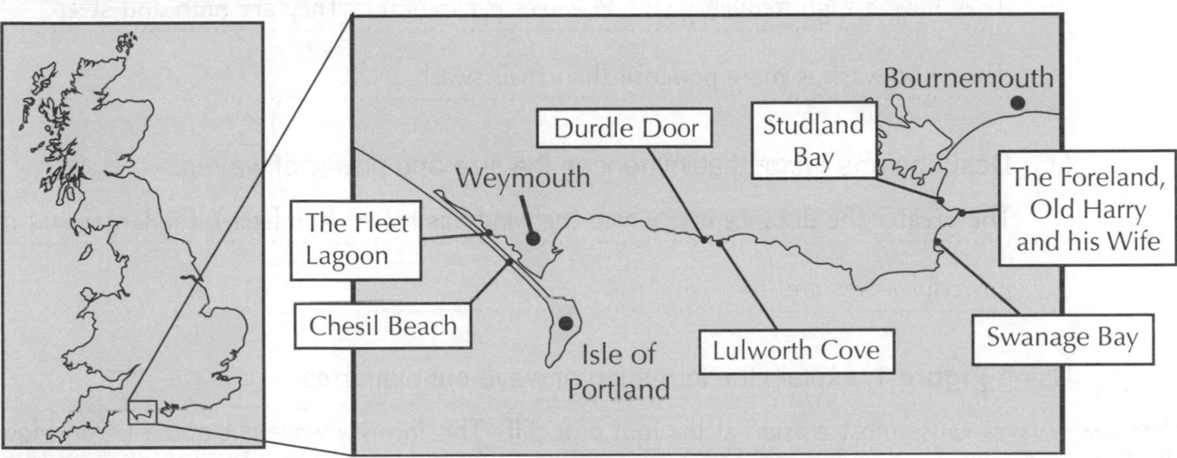

Chesil Beach

Chesil Beach is a tombolo formed by longshore drift. It joins the Isle of Portland to the mainland. Behind Chesil Beach is a shallow lagoon called The Fleet Lagoon.

©iStockphoto.com/IAN WATT

Swanage Bay and Studland Bay

There are two bays with beaches called Swanage Bay and Studland Bay. They're areas of softer rock (sandstone and clay). In between them is a headland called The Foreland made from a band of harder rock (chalk). The end of the headland has been eroded to become a stack called Old Harry and a stump called Old Harry's Wife.

©iStockphoto.com/Glen Rodgers

You'll need to give specific names of landforms for a case study question

That's actually Old Harry's second wife. His first wife collapsed into the sea in 1896. It was sad, but she would've wanted him to move on. Before you move on, check that you know the names of the landforms of the Dorset coast.

Worked Exam Questions

There's a knack to using what you've learned to get loads of lovely marks in the exam.
Have a good read of this worked example to get an idea of how it's done...

1 Wave-cut platforms are coastal landforms created by erosion. Study **Figure 1**, which shows one step in the formation of a wave-cut platform.

Figure 1

Y
X
Wave direction

(a) Name the features indicated by labels X and Y. *Check that you've got the labels the right way around.*

X: Wave-cut notch

Y: Unstable rock

(2 marks)

(b) (i) Name the type of waves shown in **Figure 1**.

Destructive waves

(1 mark)

(ii) Describe the characteristics of these waves.

They have a high frequency (10-14 waves per minute). They are high and steep. Their backwash is more powerful than their swash.

(3 marks)

(iii) Describe one factor that influences the size and power of waves.

The greater the distance over which the wind has blown (the fetch), the larger and more powerful waves are.

(1 mark)

(c) Using **Figure 1**, explain the formation of wave-cut platforms.

Make sure you refer to the figure in your answer.

Waves cause most erosion at the foot of a cliff. This forms a wave-cut notch (X on Figure 1), which is enlarged as erosion continues. As the notch grows, the rock above it becomes unstable (Y on Figure 1) and eventually collapses. The collapsed material is washed away and a new wave-cut notch starts to form. Repeated collapsing results in the cliff retreating. A wave-cut platform is left behind as the cliff retreats.

(6 marks)

(d) Arches and stacks are also coastal landforms created by erosion.

This is only worth 2 marks so you don't need to go into much detail.

(i) Explain how an arch is formed.

An arch forms from a cave. Continued erosion deepens the cave until it breaks through the rock and forms an arch.

(2 marks)

(ii) Describe the characteristics of a stack.

A stack is an isolated rock that's separate from the headland.

(1 mark)

Exam Questions

1 Study **Figure 1**, a graph showing how the width of a beach varied along its length in the years 2000 and 2005.

(a) Compare the width of the beach in 2000 with the width in 2005.

Figure 1

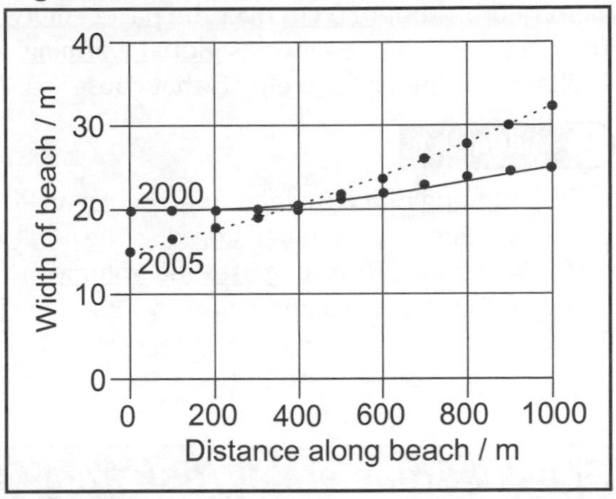

....

....

....

....

....

....

(3 marks)

(b) The changes in the width of the beach were caused by longshore drift.

(i) Describe the process of longshore drift.

....

....

....

....

....

....

(4 marks)

(ii) Spits and bars are coastal landforms caused by longshore drift.
Compare the characteristics of spits and bars.

....

....

....

(3 marks)

(iii) Name and describe two processes of transportation, apart from longshore drift, that take place in the sea.

....

....

....

....

(4 marks)

Rising Sea Level, Coastal Flooding and Erosion

Rising sea level is increasing the risk of coastal flooding. Coasts are also under threat from erosion.

Sea Level is Rising because of Global Warming

Global sea level is rising at a rate of about 2 mm per year. That might not sound like a lot, but sea level has increased by about 20 cm over the past century. It's predicted to rise by between 18 and 59 cm by 2100. The cause of rising sea level is global warming — the rapid rise in global temperature over the last 100 years. Global warming has two effects that cause sea level to rise:

1 Melting ice

The melting of ice on land (e.g. the Antarctic ice sheet) causes water that's stored as ice to return to the oceans. This increases the volume of water in the oceans and causes sea level to rise.

2 Heating oceans

Increased global temperature causes the oceans to get warmer and expand (thermal expansion). This increases the volume of water, causing sea level to rise.

Coastal Areas are at Risk from Flooding and Erosion

Rising sea level will mean coastal flooding will happen more often and will cause more damage, especially in low-lying parts of the world like Bangladesh and the Maldives. Coastal erosion (see page 104) also causes lots of damage along coastlines. Here are some of the impacts of flooding and erosion:

Economic

1) Loss of tourism — many coastal areas are popular tourist destinations. Flooding and erosion can put people off visiting. Fewer tourists means businesses that rely on tourism may close.
2) Damage repair — repairing flood damage can be extremely expensive.
3) Loss of agricultural land — seawater has a high salt content. Salt reduces soil fertility, so crop production can be affected for years after a flood. Farmland is also lost to coastal erosion, which has a huge effect on farmers' livelihoods.

Social

1) Deaths — coastal floods have killed thousands of people in the past.
2) Water supplies affected — floodwater can pollute drinking water with salt or sewage.
3) Loss of housing — homes near cliffs affected by erosion are at risk of collapsing into the sea. Over time whole villages can be lost due to erosion. Many people are also made homeless because of floods.
4) Loss of jobs — coastal industries may be shut down because of damage to equipment and buildings by floods, e.g. fishing boats can be destroyed.

Political

The government has to make policies to reduce the impacts of future flooding and erosion. They can do things like building more or better coastal defences, or they can manage the use of areas that might be flooded or eroded, e.g. by stopping people living there.

Environmental

1) Ecosystems affected by flooding — seawater has a high salt content. Increased salt levels can damage or kill organisms in an ecosystem. The force of floodwater also uproots trees and plants, and standing flood water also drowns some trees and plants.
2) Loss of habitats — wildlife habitats can be destroyed when coastlines are eroded, e.g. when cliffs collapse (see page 105).

Learn the impacts of coastal flooding and erosion

As you've just discovered, coastal flooding and erosion can have enormous impacts on coastal areas. But don't go thinking that all the impacts are just 'in theory' — there are some case studies coming up that show you the reality.

Coastal Flooding — Case Study

This case study is all about the impacts of coastal flooding on the Maldives.

The Maldives is a *Group of Islands* in the *Indian Ocean*

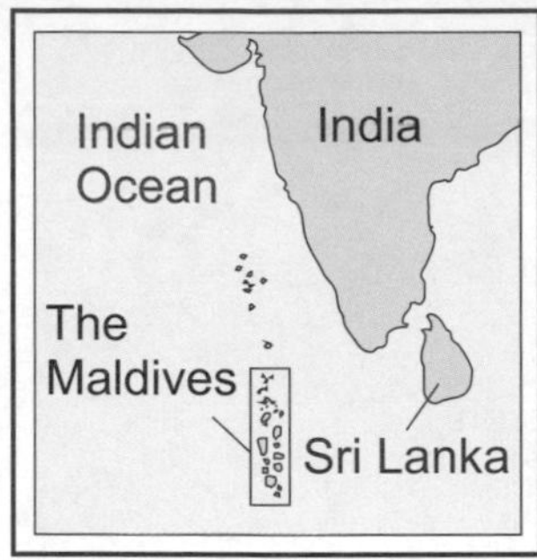

Population: About 300 000 people.

Number of islands: 1190, of which 199 are inhabited.

Average island height: 1.5 m above sea level — 80% of the land is below 1 m. Because of rising sea levels, scientists think the islands will be completely submerged within 50 to 100 years.

Coastal Flooding has a *Variety* of *Impacts* on the Maldives

Economic

1) Loss of tourism — tourism is the largest industry in the Maldives. If the main airport can't work properly because of coastal flooding the country will be cut off from international tourists. This will massively reduce the country's income.
2) Disrupted fishing industry — fish are the Maldives' largest export. Coastal flooding may damage fish processing plants, reducing the fish exports and the country's income.

Social

1) Houses damaged or destroyed — a severe flood could make entire communities homeless.
2) Less freshwater available — supplies of freshwater are already low on many of the islands. If supplies are polluted with salty seawater during floods, then some islands will have to rely on rainwater or build expensive desalination plants to meet their water demands.

Environmental

1) Loss of beaches — coastal flooding wears away beaches on the islands at a rapid rate. This destroys habitats and exposes the land behind the beach to the effects of flooding.
2) Loss of soil — the soil on most of the islands is shallow (about 20 cm deep or less). Coastal floods could easily wash away the soil layer, which would mean most plants won't be able to grow.

Political

1) The Maldivian Government had to ask the Japanese Government to give them $60 million to build the 3 m high sea wall that protects the capital city, Malé.
2) Changes to environmental policies — increased flooding is caused by rising sea level, which is caused by global warming (see page 114). The Maldives has pledged to become carbon neutral so it doesn't contribute to global warming. The Maldivian Government is encouraging other governments to do the same.
3) Changes to long-term plans — the government is thinking about buying land in countries like India and Australia and moving Maldivians there, before the islands become uninhabitable.

Carbon neutral means not adding carbon dioxide (CO_2) to the atmosphere — increasing CO_2 is causing global warming.

The Maldives are at serious risk of being submerged by the sea

The Maldives are as flat as a pancake and that's not ideal when you're surrounded by the sea. Now you've read this page you'll know about the impacts that coastal flooding is having on the country. In short, it's not looking good...

Coastal Erosion — Case Study

Holderness in East Yorkshire has one of the fastest eroding coastlines in Europe.

The Average Rate of Erosion at Holderness is About 1.8 Metres per Year

1) The Holderness coastline is 61 km long — it stretches from Flamborough Head (a headland) to Spurn Head (a spit).
2) Erosion is causing the cliffs to collapse along the coastline. The material then gets washed away, so the coastline is retreating.
3) About 1.8 m of land is lost to the sea every year — in some places, e.g. Great Cowden, the rate of erosion has been over 10 m per year in recent years.
4) Here are the main reasons for this rapid erosion at Holderness and the impact it has on people's lives and the environment:

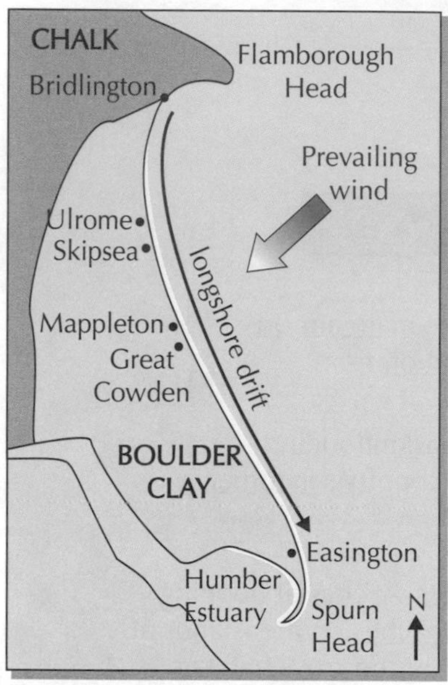

Main reasons for rapid erosion

1) Easily eroded rock type — the cliffs are mostly made of boulder clay which is easily eroded. It's likely to slump (see page 105) when it's wet, causing the cliffs to collapse.
2) Naturally narrow beaches — beaches slow waves down, reducing their erosive power so narrow beaches give less protection.
3) People worsening the situation — coastal defences called groynes (see page 117) have been built at Mappleton. Groynes stop material from being moved further down the coast. This means the beaches are narrower and more easily eroded in some other places.
4) Powerful waves — Holderness faces the prevailing wind direction, which brings waves from the north east (all the way from the Arctic Ocean). Waves increase in power over this long distance, so the coast is battered by highly erosive waves.

Impacts on people's lives

1) Homes near the cliffs (e.g. in Skipsea) are at risk of collapsing into the sea.
2) Property prices along the coast have fallen sharply for those houses at risk from erosion.
3) Accessibility to some settlements has been affected because roads near the cliff tops are at risk of collapsing into the sea, e.g. Southfield Lane which runs between Skipsea and Ulrome has been closed.
4) Businesses are at risk from erosion so people will lose their jobs, e.g. Seaside Caravan Park at Ulrome is losing an average of 10 pitches a year.
5) The gas terminal at Easington is at risk (it's only 25 m from the cliff edge). This terminal accounts for 25% of Britain's gas supply.
6) 80 000 m^2 of farmland is lost each year. This has a huge effect on farmers' livelihoods.

Environmental impacts

Some SSSIs (Sites of Special Scientific Interest) are threatened — e.g. the Lagoons near Easington are part of an SSSI. The Lagoons are separated from the sea by a narrow strip of sand and shingle (a bar). If this is eroded it will connect the Lagoons to the sea and they would be destroyed.

There are four main reasons for the rapid erosion at Holderness

Holderness really is taking a battering from the sea. See if you can remember the causes and the impacts of the rapid erosion — cover the page and write down three of each to find out what you know. To the next page...

Coastal Management Strategies

The aim of coastal management is to protect people and the environment from the impacts of erosion and flooding. This page covers hard engineering strategies — soft engineering strategies are on the next page.

Coastal Defences Include Hard Engineering

Hard engineering strategies are man-made structures built to control the flow of the sea and reduce flooding and erosion.

Here are some examples of hard engineering strategies:

1 Sea walls

These are walls made out of a hard material like concrete that reflects waves back to sea.

Benefits They prevent erosion of the coast. They also act as a barrier to prevent flooding.

Disadvantages They create a strong backwash, which erodes under the wall. Sea walls are very expensive to build and maintain.

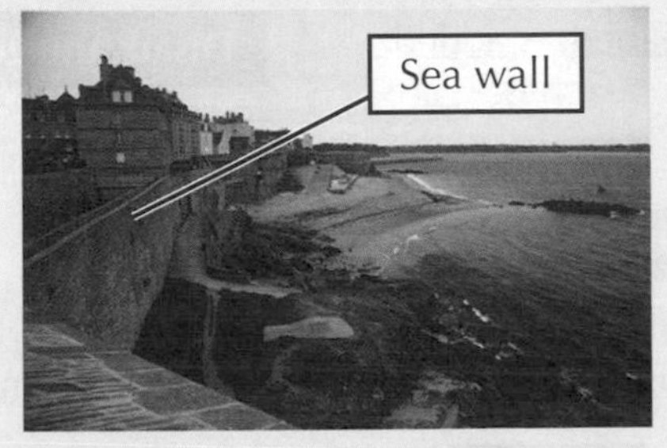

2 Rock armour

This is where boulders are piled up along the coast.

Benefit The boulders absorb wave energy and so reduce erosion and flooding. It's fairly cheap.

Disadvantage Boulders can be moved around by strong waves, so they need to be replaced.

3 Breakwaters

These are concrete blocks or boulders deposited on the sea bed off the coast.

Benefit They force waves to break offshore so their erosive power is reduced before they reach the shore.

Disadvantages They're expensive and can be damaged by storms.

4 Groynes

These are wooden or stone fences that are built at right angles to the coast. They trap material transported by longshore drift.

Benefits Groynes create wider beaches which slow the waves. This gives greater protection from flooding and erosion.

Disadvantages They starve beaches further down the coast of sand, making them narrower. Narrower beaches don't protect the coast as well, leading to greater erosion and floods.

Some strategies for coastal management are more sustainable than others.
Sustainable strategies meet the needs of people today (i.e. they reduce flooding and erosion), without stopping people in the future getting the things they need.
This means not using up too many resources (e.g. money) or damaging the environment.

Hard engineering strategies aren't usually very sustainable because they generally cost a lot of money to build and maintain, and they damage the environment.

Soft engineering can be used instead of hard engineering and these strategies are generally more sustainable (see next page).

Coastal Management Strategies

Coastal Defences also Include Soft Engineering

Soft engineering strategies are schemes set up using knowledge of the sea and its processes to reduce the effects of flooding and erosion.

Here are some examples of soft engineering strategies:

1 Beach nourishment

This is when sand and shingle from elsewhere (e.g. the offshore seabed) is added to beaches.

Benefit It creates wider beaches that slow the waves. This gives greater protection from flooding and erosion.

Disadvantages Taking material from the seabed can kill organisms like sponges and corals. It's a very expensive defence. It has to be repeated.

2 Dune regeneration

This involves creating or restoring sand dunes by either nourishment, or by planting vegetation to stabilise the sand.

Benefits Sand dunes provide a barrier between the land and the sea. Wave energy is absorbed which prevents flooding and erosion. Stabilisation is cheap.

Disadvantages The protection is limited to a small area. Nourishment is very expensive.

3 Marsh creation

This involves planting vegetation in mudflats along the coast.

Benefits The vegetation stabilises the mudflats and helps to reduce the speed of the waves. This prevents flooding and erosion. It also creates new habitats for organisms.

Disadvantages Marsh creation isn't useful where erosion rates are high because the marsh can't establish itself. It's a fairly expensive defence.

4 Managed retreat

This means removing an existing defence and allowing the land behind it to flood.

Benefits Over time the land will become marshland — creating new habitats. Flooding and erosion are reduced behind the marshland. It's a fairly cheap defence.

Disadvantage People may disagree over what land is allowed to flood, e.g. flooding farmland would affect the livelihood of farmers.

Soft engineering strategies are usually more sustainable than hard engineering strategies (see page 117) because they generally cost less money to build and maintain, and they damage the environment less.

Soft engineering schemes involve creating or strengthening natural defences

It's worth comparing these soft engineering strategies with the hard engineering strategies on the previous page. Make sure you learn at least two of each so you can compare the benefits and disadvantages if you're asked in the exam.

Coastal Management — Case Study

We're going back to Holderness to find out what management strategies are being used there.

Hard Engineering Strategies have been used Along Holderness

Page 116 outlines the main reasons for the rapid erosion along Holderness and the impacts it's having.
To try to reduce the effects of erosion, 11.4 km of Holderness coastline has been protected by hard engineering:

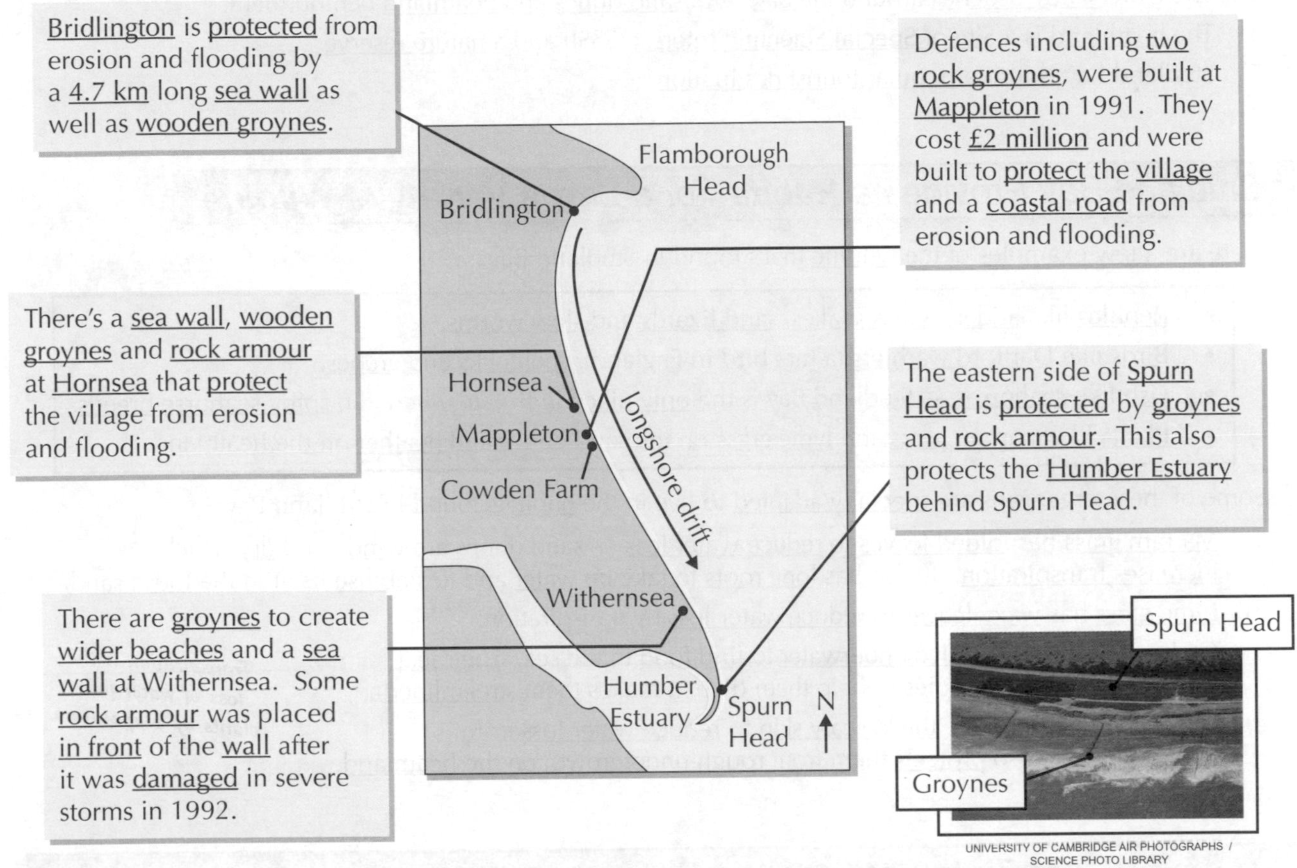

Bridlington is protected from erosion and flooding by a 4.7 km long sea wall as well as wooden groynes.
Defences including two rock groynes, were built at Mappleton in 1991. They cost £2 million and were built to protect the village and a coastal road from erosion and flooding.
There's a sea wall, wooden groynes and rock armour at Hornsea that protect the village from erosion and flooding.
The eastern side of Spurn Head is protected by groynes and rock armour. This also protects the Humber Estuary behind Spurn Head.
There are groynes to create wider beaches and a sea wall at Withernsea. Some rock armour was placed in front of the wall after it was damaged in severe storms in 1992.
Flamborough Head
Bridlington
Hornsea
Mappleton
Cowden Farm
longshore drift
Withernsea
Humber Estuary
Spurn Head
N
Spurn Head
Groynes

UNIVERSITY OF CAMBRIDGE AIR PHOTOGRAPHS / SCIENCE PHOTO LIBRARY

The Strategies are Locally Successful but Cause Problems Elsewhere

1) Groynes protect local areas but cause narrow beaches to form further down the Holderness coast. This increases erosion down the coast, e.g. Cowden Farm (south of Mappleton) is now at risk of falling into the sea.
2) The material produced from the erosion of Holderness is normally transported south into the Humber Estuary and down the Lincolnshire coast. Reducing the amount of material that's eroded and transported south increases the risk of flooding in the Humber Estuary, because there's less material to slow the floodwater down.
3) The rate of coastal retreat along the Lincolnshire coast is also increased, because less new material is being added.
4) Spurn Head is at risk of being eroded away because less material is being added to it.
5) Bays are forming between the protected areas, and the protected areas are becoming headlands which are being eroded more heavily. This means maintaining the defences in the protected areas is becoming more expensive.

The hard engineering strategies are moving the problems elsewhere

This follows on from the case study on page 116, so hopefully most of the place names will seem familiar to you. You'll probably be able to use information from both pages to answer a question on coastal management.

Coastal Habitat — Case Study

Coastal areas get pretty heavily used by people, but they're important for wildlife too...

Studland Bay *is a* ***Coastal Area*** *with* ***Beaches***, ***Dunes*** *and* ***Heathland***

1) Studland Bay is a bay in Dorset, in the south west of England.
2) It's mostly sheltered from highly erosive waves, but the southern end of the bay is being eroded.
3) There are sandy beaches around the bay, with sand dunes and heathland behind them.
4) The heathland is a Site of Special Scientific Interest (SSSI) and a nature reserve.
5) Studland Bay is also a popular tourist destination.

Studland Bay Provides a ***Habitat*** *for a* ***Large Variety*** *of* ***Wildlife***

Here are a few examples of the wildlife that's found in Studland Bay:

- Reptiles like adders, grass snakes, sand lizards and slow worms.
- Birds like Dartford warblers (a rare bird in England), shelducks and grebes.
- Fish like seahorses — Studland Bay is the only place in Britain where the spiny seahorse breeds.
- Plants like marram grass and lyme grass on the sand dunes and heather on the heathland.

Some of these organisms are specially adapted to live in the habitats found in Studland Bay:

1) Marram grass has folded leaves to reduce water loss — sand dunes are windy and dry which increases transpiration. It also has long roots to take up water and to stabilise itself in the loose sand.
2) Lyme grass has waxy leaves to reduce water loss by transpiration.
3) Grebes — these birds dive underwater to find food in the sea. Their feet are far back on their bodies to help them dive (it makes them streamlined).
4) Snakes and lizards have thick, scaly skin to reduce water loss from their bodies. It also protects them from rough undergrowth on the heathland.

Transpiration is the loss of water from plants by evaporation.

There are ***Conflicts*** *Between* ***Land Use*** *and the* ***Need for Conservation***

Some human activities (e.g. recreation) don't use the environment in a sustainable way (they use up resources or damage the environment). The environment is managed to make sure it's conserved, but can also be used for other activities:

1) Lots of people walk across the sand dunes which has caused lots of erosion. The National Trust manages the area so people can use the sand dunes without damaging them too much:

   - Boardwalks are used to guide people over the dunes so the sand beneath them is protected.
   - Some sand dunes have been fenced off and marram grass has been planted in them. This gives the dunes a chance to recover and the marram grass stabilises the sand.
   - Information signs have been put up to let visitors know why the sand dune habitat is important, and how they can enjoy the environment without damaging it.

2) Hundreds of boats use Studland Bay and their anchors are destroying the seagrass where seahorses live. Seahorses are protected by law, so boat owners are being told to not damage the seagrass.
3) The heathland behind the sand dunes is an important habitat, but it can be damaged by fires caused by things like cigarettes, e.g. in 2008 a fire destroyed six acres of heathland. The National Trust is educating visitors on the dangers of causing fires and has provided fire beaters to extinguish flames.

Not all recreation activities in Studland Bay are sustainable

Plenty of words here and no pretty pictures I'm afraid. It'll just be a case of cramming all these facts into your head so you can recall them in the exam if you need to — don't skimp on the details.

Worked Exam Questions

The answers might already have been done but don't just turn the page — they're there to help you.

1 Study **Figure 1**, a sketch map of the Sparkington coastal area.

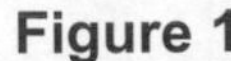

Figure 1

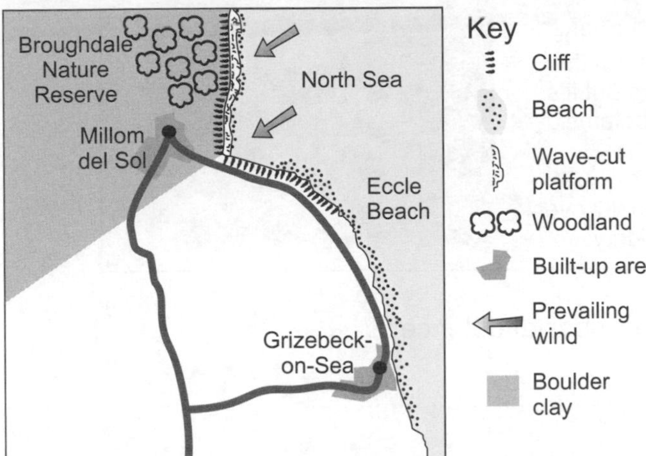

(a) Using **Figure 1**, explain why some parts of the Sparkington coastline are being rapidly eroded.

There is a band of boulder clay running inland through the Broughdale Nature Reserve. This rock is not very resistant so is easily eroded by the waves. The coastline faces the prevailing wind direction, which brings waves across the North Sea. The waves are likely to have travelled a long distance, which will increase their power and make them highly erosive. Also, the beaches around the coast are fairly narrow. Beaches slow waves down, reducing their erosive power, so the narrow beaches will give the coastline less protection.

It's a six mark question so make sure you write about at least three things from the figure and explain each of them.

(6 marks)

(b) Suggest how the actions of humans could increase coastal erosion in Sparkington.

If coastal defences such as groynes are built along Eccle Beach they would stop material from being moved further down the coast, making the beaches narrower and more easily eroded near Grizebeck-on-Sea.

This question is a tricky one because it's secretly asking you about the impacts of management strategies.

(2 marks)

(c) Describe the impacts of coastal erosion on a coastal area you have studied.

Don't forget to introduce the area before you launch into the facts.

Erosion of the Holderness coastline in North East England is causing cliffs to collapse. About 1.8 m of land is lost to the sea every year. Homes near the cliffs, e.g. in Skipsea, are at risk of collapsing into the sea. Accessibility to some settlements has been affected, e.g. Southfield Lane between Skipsea and Ulrome has been closed as it's at risk of collapsing into the sea. 80 000 m^2 of farmland is lost each year, which has a huge effect on farmers' livelihoods. The gas terminal at Easington is at risk because it's only 25 m from the cliff edge. The terminal accounts for 25% of Britain's gas supply. Some SSSIs, e.g. the Lagoons near Easington, could be destroyed if the bar that separates them from the sea is eroded away.

(8 marks)

Exam Questions

1 Study **Figure 1**, a news article about coastal defences in Cliffall, a UK coastal town.

Figure 1

Hope for Cliffall's coastline

Work is due to start next week on new defences for the Cliffall coastline. The town has been suffering from the effects of coastal erosion over the last few years but it's hoped the new defences will prevent further problems. The scheme will use a combination of defences, including groynes, dune regeneration and beach nourishment. The work will be completed gradually over the next four years, with the groynes the top priority.

(a) (i) What is meant by a 'soft engineering' coastal defence?

....

(1 mark)

(ii) Name one soft engineering strategy mentioned in **Figure 1**.

....

(1 mark)

(b) (i) Name and describe one hard engineering strategy not mentioned in **Figure 1** that could be used to protect the coastline.

....

....

(2 marks)

(ii) Explain the advantages of using this strategy as a coastal defence.

....

....

(2 marks)

2 Rising sea level is caused by global warming.

(a) Explain two ways that global warming causes sea level to rise.

....

....

....

....

(4 marks)

(b) As the sea level rises it will increase the risk of coastal flooding. Suggest two ways that coastal flooding can impact on the environment.

....

....

(2 marks)

Revision Summary for Section 7

So, you've reached the end of another section — that means it's time to find out just how much information you've remembered. Have a go at the questions below. If you're finding it tough, just look back at the pages in the section and then have another go. You'll be ready to move on when you can answer all of these questions without breaking sweat.

1) Describe the process of chemical weathering.
2) How do waves erode the coast by hydraulic power?
3) Give an example of one type of mass movement.
4) Are headlands made of more or less resistant rock?
5) Describe how erosion can turn a crack in a cliff into a cave.
6) Explain how a stack is formed. Name an example.
7) What is a cove?
8) By what process is material transported along coasts?
9) What is deposition?
10) What waves are associated with coastal deposition?
11) Where is a beach formed on a coast?
12) Why is a sand beach flatter and wider than a shingle beach?
13) Where do spits form? Name an example.
14) Why can't cracks, caves and arches be seen on a map?
15) How are cliffs shown on a map?
16) On maps, what do speckles on top of yellow shading tell you?
17) a) Name a coastal area you have studied which has erosional and depositional landforms.
    b) Name one erosional landform and one depositional landform in that area.
18) Give two economic impacts of coastal flooding and erosion.
19) Give two social impacts of coastal flooding and erosion.
20) a) For a coastal area you have studied, explain why the risk of coastal flooding is becoming greater.
    b) Describe a political impact of coastal flooding in that area.
21) Give two main reasons for rapid erosion along a named coastline.
22) Describe the difference between hard engineering and soft engineering coastal management strategies.
23) Explain a disadvantage of using groynes as a coastal defence.
24) a) Name two soft engineering strategies.
    b) Give one benefit of each strategy.
25) a) Give two examples of hard engineering strategies used along a named coastline.
    b) Describe two problems caused by the use of hard engineering strategies along the same coastline.
26) a) Describe how two organisms are adapted to living in a named coastal habitat.
    b) Describe two strategies for dealing with conflicts between land use and conservation in this coastal habitat.

Population Growth

This section is all about population change — how it's changing, why it's changing, the problems that this causes and what's being done to reduce these problems.

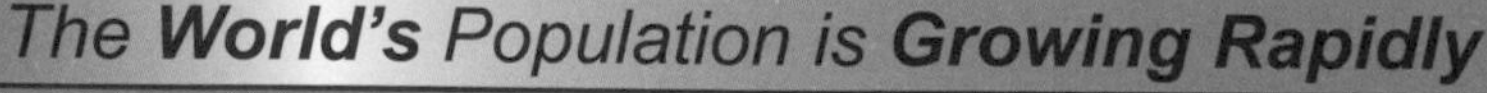

The World's Population is Growing Rapidly

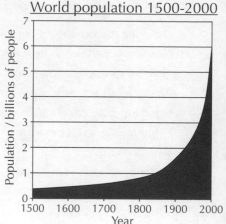

1) The graph shows world population for the years 1500-2000 — it's been increasing and is still increasing today.
2) The population of the world is increasing at an exponential rate — it's growing faster and faster.
3) There are two things that affect the population size of the world:

> Birth rate — the number of live babies born per thousand of the population per year.
>
> Death rate — the number of deaths per thousand of the population per year.

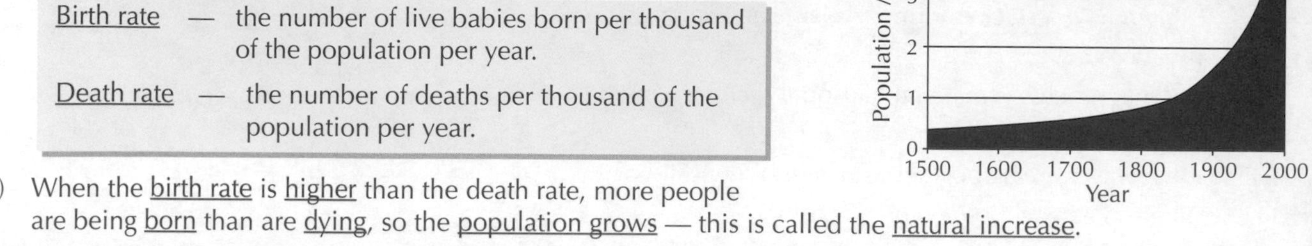

4) When the birth rate is higher than the death rate, more people are being born than are dying, so the population grows — this is called the natural increase.
5) It's called the natural decrease when the death rate's higher than the birth rate.
6) The population size of a country is also affected by migration — the movement of people from one area to another area (see page 135).

Countries go Through Five Stages of Population Growth

1) Birth rates and death rates differ from country to country. This means that population growth is faster in some countries than others.
2) Population growth also changes within a country over time (it can get faster or slower).
3) Countries go through five different stages of population growth.
4) These stages are shown by the Demographic Transition Model (DTM):

birth rate
Natural population increase
death rate
population size
Natural population decrease

	Stage 1	Stage 2	Stage 3	Stage 4	Stage 5
Birth rate	High and fluctuating	High and steady	Rapidly falling	Low and fluctuating	Slowly falling
Death rate	High and fluctuating	Rapidly falling	Slowly falling	Low and fluctuating	Low and steady
Population growth rate	Zero	Very high	High	Zero	Negative
Population size	Low and steady	Rapidly increasing	Increasing	High and steady	Slowly falling
Example countries	No countries, some tribes in Brazil	Gambia	Egypt	UK, USA	Japan

Learn the five stages of the Demographic Transition Model

The DTM may look complicated, but it's a pretty useful thing to know about when you're studying population change. You don't need to be able to draw it precisely, but you should learn what the population's doing during each stage.

Population Growth and Structure

As a country becomes more developed, its population growth rate and population structure both change.

Population Growth is Linked to How Developed a Country is

1) As countries become more developed, birth and death rates change, which affects the population growth. E.g. as a country develops healthcare improves, which leads to a drop in death rate and faster population growth.
2) So as countries become more developed the population changes and the country moves through the stages of the DTM.
3) This means poorer, less developed countries are in the earlier stages of the DTM (2-3) — population growth rate is high because birth rates are high and death rates are beginning to fall.
4) Richer, more developed countries are in the later stages of the DTM (4-5) — they usually have low or negative population growth because birth rates and death rates are low.

Why birth and death rates change as a country becomes more developed is covered on the next page.

A Country's Population Structure Changes as it Develops

The population structure of a country is how many people there are of each age group in the population, and how many there are of each sex. Population structure is shown using population pyramids. Population structure differs from country to country and it changes as countries become more developed. But before you get into the details, you should understand population pyramids. You can learn a lot about a country from its population pyramid. For example:

1. The higher the top bar on the pyramid, the better the life expectancy (the average age in years a person can expect to live). E.g. in the country shown in the pyramid some people are living to 100, so life expectancy will be quite high.

2. You can see if there are an equal number of men and women, and if they live to a similar age — the gender balance of the country. E.g. in the country shown in the pyramid, women are living longer than men.

If you have to sketch a pyramid just draw the outline shape, not the individual bars.

Population pyramid

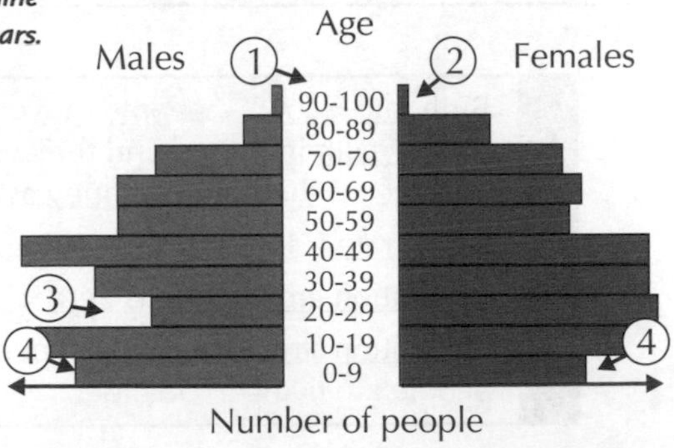

Age

Males ① ② Females

90-100
80-89
70-79
60-69
50-59
40-49
30-39
20-29 ③
10-19 ④ ④
0-9

Number of people

3. Sometimes pyramids have bulges or dips in them. This happens when lots of a particular age group move into or out of the country, or are killed in a war.

4. The 0-9 age group tells you about birth rate. E.g. there are fewer people aged 0-9 because the birth rate has decreased over the last 10 years.

Pyramids can have different age categories, e.g. 5 year intervals instead of 10 year intervals. Pyramids with 5 year intervals can be used to work out the dependency ratio (how many people are supported by the working population) — it's the number of people aged 0-15 plus the number of people aged 65 and over, divided by the number of people aged 16-64.

Population data comes from lots of sources, e.g. censuses and birth certificates.

Population pyramids show age and gender distributions of a country's population

And age distribution changes as a country becomes more developed. This means that countries at different stages of the DTM have very different population pyramids — turn over to the next page to find out all about it.

Population Growth and Structure

Population pyramids look very different depending on what stage of the DTM the country is at.

There are Many **Reasons** Why **Population Growth** and **Structure Change**

As a country develops and moves through the stages of the DTM its birth and death rates change. This causes the population growth rate, structure and pyramid to change too:

DEVELOPMENT

Stage 1

Birth rate is high because there's no use of contraception, and people have lots of children because many infants die.

Death rate is high due to poor healthcare or famine.

Population growth rate is zero.

Population structure — life expectancy is low (few people reach old age), so the population is made up of mostly young people.

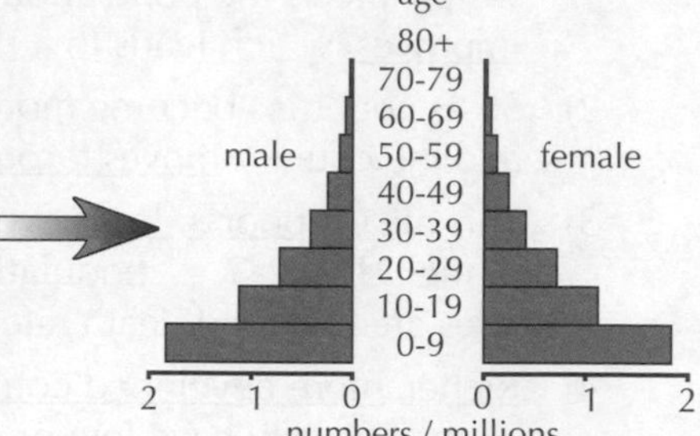

Stage 2

Birth rate is high because there's no use of contraception. Also, the economy is based on agriculture so people have lots of children to work on farms.

Death rate falls due to improved healthcare and diet.

Population growth rate is very high.

Population structure — life expectancy has increased, but there are still more young people than older people.

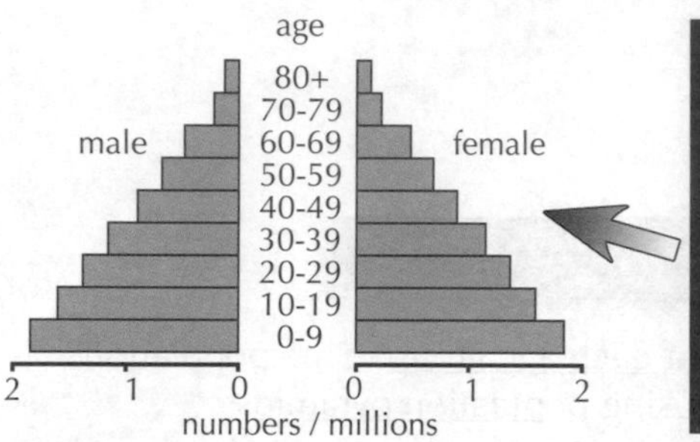

Stage 3

Birth rate is rapidly falling due to the emancipation of women (where they have a more equal place in society) and better education. The use of contraception increases and more women work instead of having children. The economy also changes to manufacturing, so fewer children are needed to work on farms.

Death rate falls due to more medical advances.

Population growth rate is high.

Population structure — more people are living to be older.

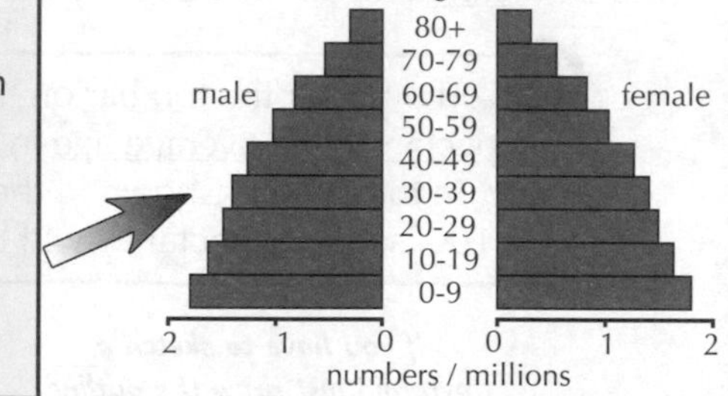

Stage 4

Birth rate is low — people move to urban areas (urbanisation), their wealth improves and they want more possessions. This means there's less money available for having children.

Death rate is low and fluctuating.

Population growth rate is zero.

Population structure — life expectancy is high, so even more people are living to be older.

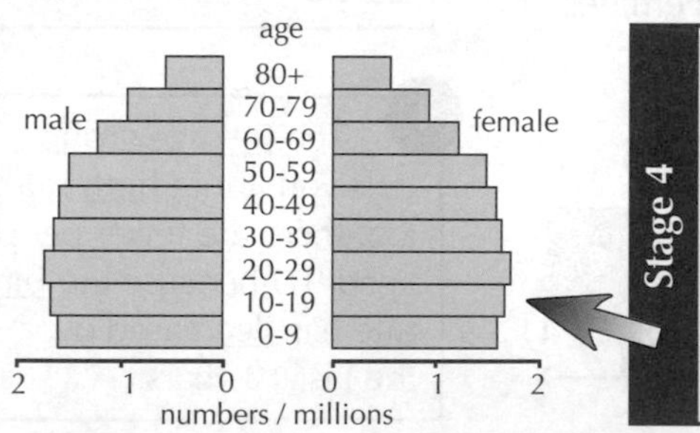

Stage 5

Birth rate is slowly falling — there's less money available to raise children because people have dependent elderly relatives.

Death rate is low and fluctuating.

Population growth rate is negative.

Population structure — more older people than young people.

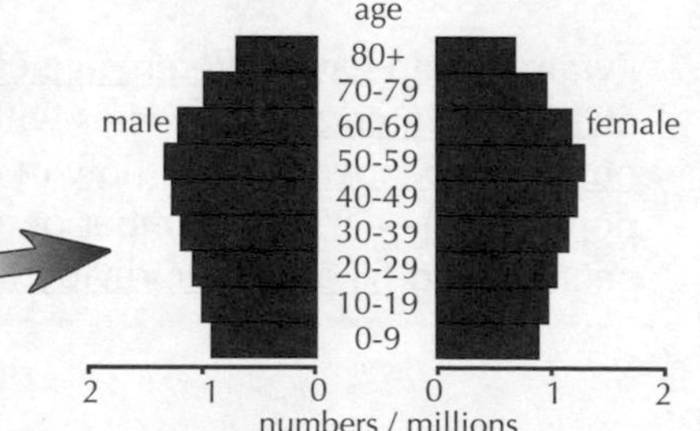

Population pyramids become more top heavy as countries develop

There are a fair few words on this page but they're all important. Check you know the reasons why birth rate, death rate, population growth and population structure change as countries become more developed.

Rapid Population Growth

If birth rate is high and death rate decreases, population growth can get a bit out of hand and cause problems.

Rapid Population Growth has many Negative Impacts

1) Rapid population growth is most likely to happen in poorer countries (such as Gambia) in Stages 2 and 3 of the DTM. They have a high birth rate and a falling death rate, causing a high population growth rate.
2) Rapid population growth can cause overpopulation (when there are too many people for the resources).
3) It can also lead to a youthful population. A youthful population has a high dependency ratio (see page 125) — there are lots of people under 15 that are dependent on the working population (aged 15–64).
4) Here are some social, economic, environmental and political impacts of rapid population growth:

SOCIAL

1) Services like healthcare and education can't cope with the large, young population, so not everybody has access to them.
2) Children have to work to help support their large families, so they miss out on education.
3) There aren't enough houses for everyone, so people are forced to live in makeshift houses in overcrowded settlements. This leads to health problems because the houses aren't always connected to sewers or they don't have access to clean water.

ECONOMIC

1) There aren't enough jobs for the number of people in the country, so unemployment increases.
2) There's increased poverty because more people are born into families that are already poor.

ENVIRONMENTAL

1) Increased waste and pollution, e.g. more cars will release more greenhouse gases, and more waste will need to go to landfill sites.
2) More natural resources are used up, e.g. more trees are chopped down for firewood.

POLITICAL

Most of the population is made up of young people so the government focuses on policies that are important to young people, e.g. education and provision of things like childcare, rather than policies that are important to older people, e.g. pensions.

Overpopulation causes problems. Makes sense.

It's not always a case of 'the more the merrier' — overpopulation and rapid population growth can cause problems. That's where strategies to control population growth come in — these are covered on the next page, so read on.

Managing Rapid Population Growth

If you haven't just come from page 127, then have a look at it now to learn about some of the problems caused by having too many people in a country. Now have a read of this page, which is all about solving these problems.

There are Different Strategies to Control Rapid Population Growth

Countries need to control rapid population growth so they don't become overpopulated. They also need to develop in a way that's sustainable.

Sustainable development means developing in a way that allows people today to get the things they need, but without stopping people in the future from getting what they need.

Here are a couple of examples of population policies and how they help to achieve sustainable development:

Birth control programmes

1) Birth control programmes aim to reduce the birth rate.

2) Some governments do this by having laws about how many children couples are allowed to have (see next page).

3) Governments also help couples to plan (and limit) how many children they have by offering free contraception and sex education.

4) This helps towards sustainable development because it means the population won't get much bigger. There won't be many more people using up resources today, so there will be some left for future generations.

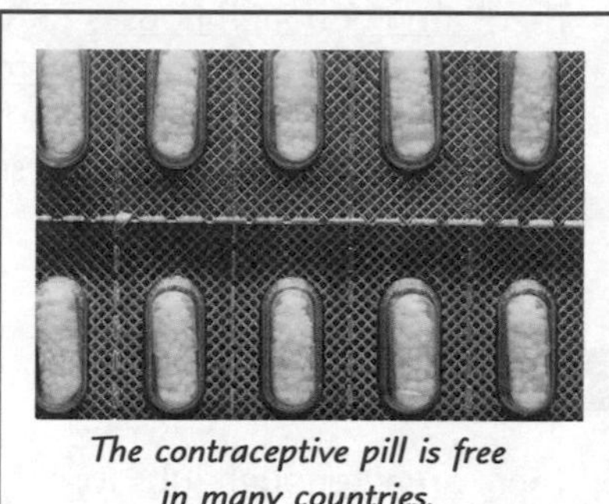

The contraceptive pill is free in many countries.

Immigration laws

1) Immigration laws aim to control immigration (people moving to a country to live there permanently).

2) Governments can limit the number of people that are allowed to immigrate (see page 137).

3) They can also be selective about who they let in, e.g. letting in fewer people of child-bearing age means there will be fewer immigrants having children.

4) This helps towards sustainable development because it slows down population growth rate.

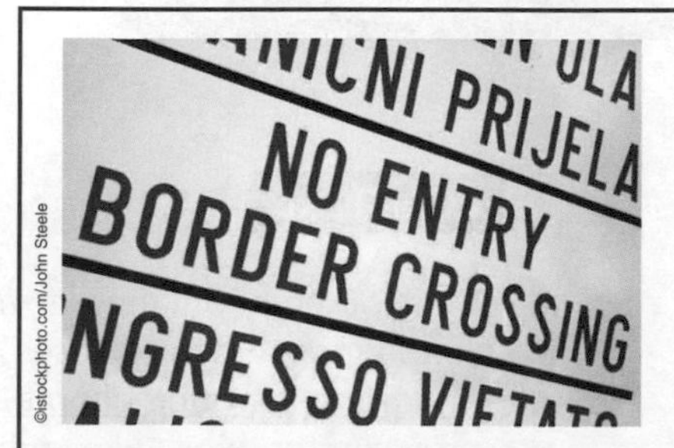

Reducing rapid population growth helps sustainable development

Birth control programmes help to control world population, whereas immigration laws control the population of an individual country. Check that you know the facts about each strategy and how they relate to sustainable development.

Managing Rapid Population Growth — Case Study

You've learned the principles behind some of the strategies for managing population growth, so it's time to have a look at a couple of case studies and find out how effective different strategies have been in the real world.

China has a Strict Birth Control Programme

1) China has the largest population of any country in the world — over 1.3 billion.

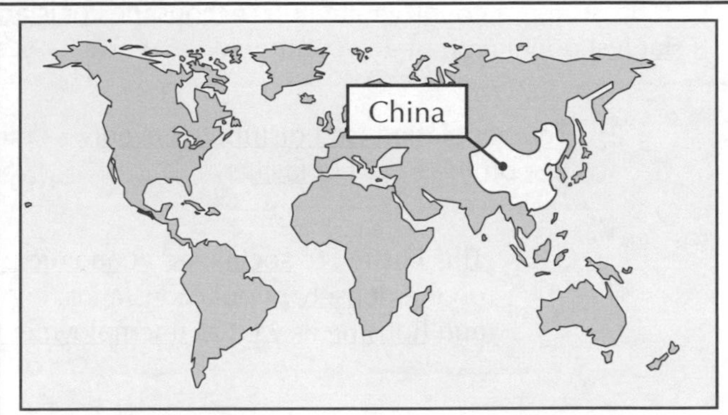

2) Different policies have been used to control rapid population growth — the most important is the 'one-child policy' introduced in 1979. This means that all couples are very strongly encouraged to have only one child.

3) Couples that only have one child are given benefits like longer maternity leave, better housing and free education for the child. Couples that have more than one child don't get any benefits and are also fined part of their income.

4) Over the years, the policy has changed so there are some exceptions:

- In some rural areas, couples are allowed to have a second child if the first is a girl, or has a physical disability. This is because more children are still needed to work on farms in rural areas.
- If one of the parents has a disability or if both parents are only children, then couples are allowed to have a second child. This is so there are enough people to look after the parents.

Effectiveness

1) The policy has prevented up to 400 million births. The fertility rate (the average number of children a woman will have in her life) has dropped from 5.7 in 1970 to around 1.8 today.

2) Some people think that it wasn't just the one-child policy that slowed population growth. They say older policies about leaving longer gaps between children were more effective, and that Chinese people want fewer children anyway as they've become more wealthy.

China's one-child policy helps towards sustainable development — the population hasn't grown as fast (and got as big) as it would have done without the policy, so fewer resources have been used.

The one-child policy has slowed down China's population growth

You know the drill when it comes to case study pages — examiners love those details, so shut the book and write down what you can remember. If you can't remember much then give this page another read through.

Managing Rapid Population Growth — Case Study

Rather than controlling the number of children being born, some countries rely on moving people from overpopulated to underpopulated regions. One place where this has been tried is Indonesia.

Indonesia has Tried to Tackle the Problems of Rapid Population Growth

1) Indonesia is a country made up of thousands of islands. It has the fourth largest population of any country in the world — over 240 million.

2) The population isn't distributed evenly — most people (around 130 million) live on the island of Java.

3) This has led to social and economic problems (see page 127) on the densely populated islands, e.g. a lack of adequate services and housing as well as unemployment and poverty.

4) The Indonesian Government started a policy in the 1960s called the transmigration policy, which aims to reduce the impacts of population growth.

5) Millions of people have been moved from the densely populated islands like Java, to the less densely populated islands like Sumatra.

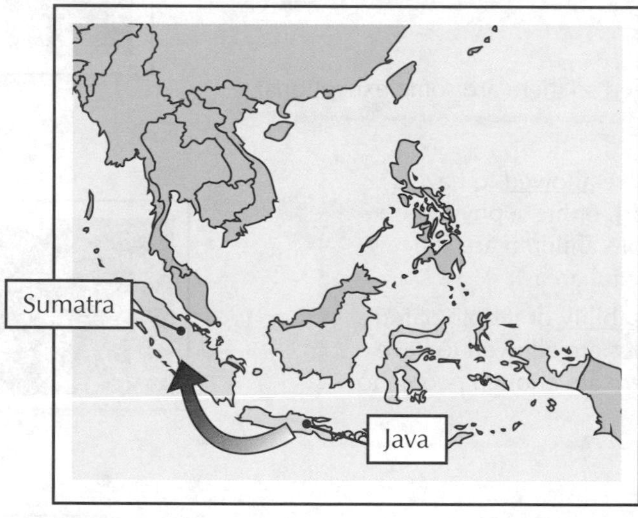

Effectiveness

1) Millions of people have been moved, but the population still isn't much more evenly distributed.

2) Not all the people who were moved escaped poverty — either they didn't have the skills to farm the land, or the land was too poor to be farmed on their new island.

3) Lots of people were moved to land that was already occupied by native people. This created a new problem — conflict between the natives and the migrants.

Indonesia's transmigration policy hasn't helped towards sustainable development because it only reduces the impacts of population growth — the population is still getting much bigger.

Moving people doesn't reduce the population, it just redistributes it

The Indonesian Government took pretty drastic action to deal with rapid population growth. Just try and imagine what you'd say if your local MP knocked on your door and told you to move to another island...

Worked Exam Questions

Exams can be pretty scary, but the best preparation you can do is to practise answering exam questions. Read this page to get an idea of how to answer exam questions, then turn over and have a go at the next lot yourself.

1 Study **Figure 1**, which shows the Demographic Transition Model (DTM).

Figure 1

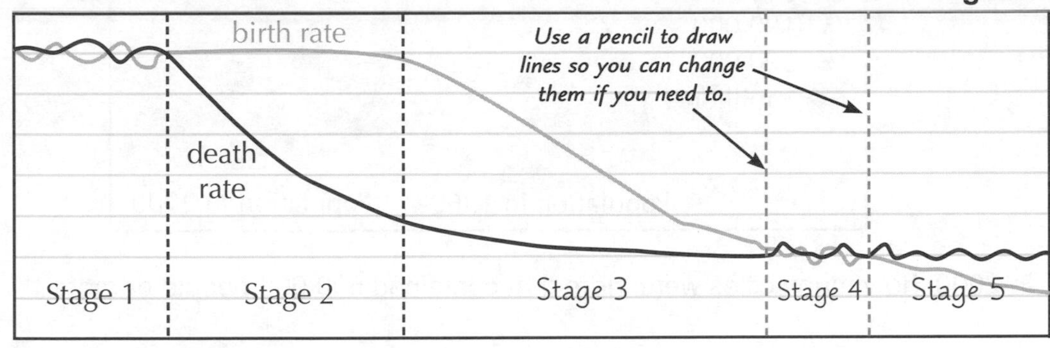

(a) Add dotted lines and labels to show when Stages 3, 4 and 5 occur. *(1 mark)*

(b) Using **Figure 1**, compare the death rate and birth rate of a country in Stage 1 with a country in Stage 2.

Birth rate in Stage 1 is high and fluctuating but in Stage 2 it is high and steady.

Death rate in Stage 1 is high and fluctuating but it is falling rapidly in Stage 2.

(2 marks)

(c) How does the rate of population growth change between Stages 3 and 5?

Population growth rate changes from being high in Stage 3 to zero in Stage 4.

Population growth rate is negative in Stage 5.

Even if you can't remember what population growth rate does at each stage, you can work it out from the graph.

(2 marks)

2 Study **Figure 2**, which shows a population pyramid for a richer country.

(a) Describe the population structure of the country in **Figure 2**.

Figure 2

Age

Males | Females

80-89
70-79
60-69
50-59
40-49
30-39
20-29
10-19
0-9

Number of people

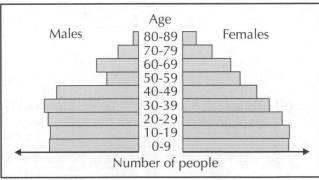

Some people are living to between 80 and 89 years. There are more females than males and more females are living to an older age. There is a big dip in the number of males aged 50-59.

There are loads of other things you could say here — basically just say what you see. E.g. there are about the same number of people aged 0-9, 10-19 and 20-29, most people are under the age of 49 etc.

(3 marks)

(b) Describe and explain how a sudden decrease in birth rate would affect the shape of a population pyramid.

Don't forget to explain (i.e. give reasons) if the question asks you to.

The bottom of the pyramid would become undercut with a shorter bar for the 0-9 age group.

This is because fewer people are being born than in the previous generation.

(2 marks)

Exam Questions

1 Study **Figure 1**, which shows how the population has changed in the region of Thirton.

Figure 1

(a) In 2000, how many cities were there that contained 500 000 people or more?

....

(1 mark)

(b) Use **Figure 1** to describe how the population of Thirton changed between 1960 and 2000.

....

....

(2 marks)

(c) Rapid population growth has many impacts on a country.
Describe two social and two economic impacts of rapid population growth.

....

....

....

....

....

....

(4 marks)

(d) Describe a population policy that could help control rapid population growth and explain whether or not the policy helps to achieve sustainable development.

....

....

....

....

....

....

(4 marks)

Ageing Populations

An ageing population is one that has a high proportion of older people. Ageing populations can face economic and social problems, so governments have had to come up with some strategies to reduce these problems.

An Ageing Population Impacts on Future Development

The population structure of an ageing population has more older people than younger people because few people are being born, and more people are surviving to old age.

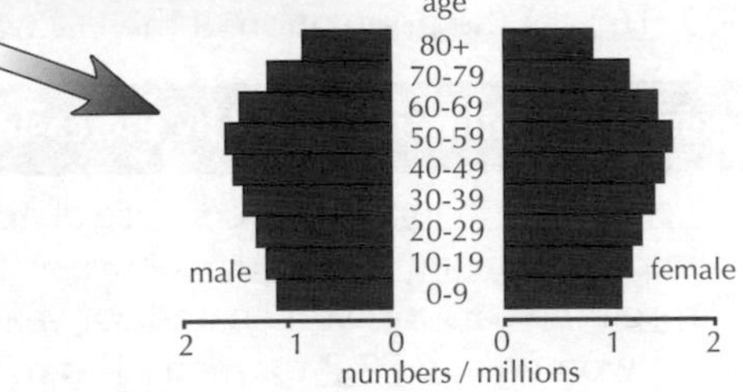

Countries with an ageing population are usually the richer countries in Stage 5 of the DTM (see pages 124 and 126).

Older people (over 65) are supported by the working population (aged 16-64) — they're dependent on them. So in a country with an ageing population there's a higher proportion of people who are dependent. This has economic and social impacts, which can affect a country's future development:

ECONOMIC

1) The working population pay taxes, some of which the government use to pay the state pensions of older people, and to pay for services like retirement homes and healthcare. Taxes would need to go up because there are more pensions to pay for, and older people need more healthcare.
2) The economy of the country would grow more slowly — less money is being spent on things that help the economy to grow, e.g. education and business, and more money is being spent on things that don't help the economy to grow, e.g. retirement homes.

SOCIAL

1) Healthcare services are stretched more because older people need more medical care.
2) People will need to spend more time working as unpaid carers for older family members. This means that the working population have less leisure time and are more stressed and worried.
3) People may have fewer children because they can't afford lots of children when they have dependent older relatives. This leads to a drop in birth rate.
4) The more old people there are, the lower the pension provided by the government will be. People will have to retire later because they can't afford to get by on a state pension.

There are Different Strategies to Cope with an Ageing Population

1) Encouraging larger families, e.g. in Italy women are offered cash rewards to have more children. This increases the number of young people — when they start work there will be a larger working population to pay taxes and support the ageing population.
2) Encouraging the immigration of young people from other countries. This increases the working population so there are more people paying taxes to support the ageing population.

These strategies don't help towards sustainable development because they increase the population size.

3) Raising the retirement age — people stay in work longer and contribute to state pensions and personal pensions for longer. They will also claim the state pension for less time.
4) Raising taxes for the working population — this would increase the amount of money available to support the ageing population.

These strategies help towards sustainable development because they help to reduce the impacts of an ageing population, without increasing the population size.

More developed countries often have ageing populations

'Live long enough to be a burden on your children' — I thought it was just a phrase... Learn about the social and economic impacts an ageing population can have, and the strategies governments have come up with to deal with them.

Ageing Populations — Case Study

Like most wealthy and developed countries around the world, the UK has an ageing population.
This case study's got lots of juicy statistics for you to read about, so get swotting.

The UK's Population is Ageing

In 2005, 16% of the population of the UK was over 65. By 2041 this could be 25%.

The Ageing Population is Caused by Increasing Life Expectancy and Dropping Birth Rate

1) People are living longer because of advances in medicine and improved living standards. Between 1980 and 2006 life expectancy rose 2.6 years for women and 6.4 years for men — it's currently 81.5 for women and 77.2 for men. This means the proportion of older people in the population is going up.
2) Lots of babies were born in the 1940s and 1960s — periods called 'baby booms'. Those born in the 1940s are retiring now, creating a 'pensioner boom'.
3) Since the 1970s, the number of babies born has fallen. With fewer young people in the population the proportion of older people goes up.

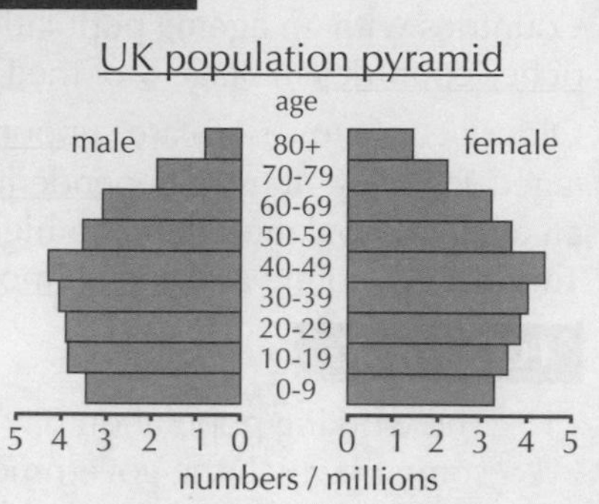

The UK's Ageing Population Causes a few Problems

1) More elderly people are living in poverty — the working population isn't large enough to pay for a decent pension, and many people don't have other savings.
2) Even though the state pension is low the government is struggling to pay it. The taxes paid by people in work aren't enough to cover the cost of pensions and as the population ages the situation is getting worse.
3) The health service is under pressure because older people need more medical care than younger people. For example, in 2005 the average stay in hospital for people over 75 was 13 nights, but for the whole of the UK the average stay was only 8 nights.

The UK Government has Strategies to Cope with the Ageing Population

1) Raise the retirement age — the retirement age in the UK is currently 65 for men and 60 for women. This is going to change in stages, so that by 2046 it will be 68 for everyone. People will have to work for longer, so there will be more people paying tax and fewer claiming a pension.
2) Encourage immigration of young people to the UK — the UK has allowed immigration of people from countries that joined the EU in 2004. Around 80% of immigrants from new EU countries in 2004 were 34 or under. This increases the number of people paying taxes, which helps to pay for the state pension and services.
3) Encourage women to have children — working family tax credits support women (and men) who go back to work after their children are born. This makes it more affordable for couples to have children.
4) Encourage people to take out private pensions — the government gives tax breaks for some types of private pension. With private pensions, people won't be so dependent on the state pension.

We Don't Know if the Strategies have Worked Yet

It's too early to tell if government strategies are working. Even if they do have some effect it's likely that future generations will have to work longer and rely on their families to support them in old age.

Learn the causes, problems and strategies

This case study is perfect exam fodder. Nothing makes an examiner's eyes light up as much as real-life examples. Memorise the facts and figures from this page and you'll be all set up to get top marks in your exam.

Migration

Migration is the movement of people from one area to another area. However, they don't just do it for the fun of it — this page is all about the reasons why people move, as well as some good old impacts.

People Migrate **Within Countries** and To **Different Countries**

1) When people move into an area, it's called immigration. The people are called immigrants.
2) When people exit an area, it's called emigration. The people are called emigrants.
3) People can move to different countries — this is known as international migration. It might be across the world, or just a few miles over a border.
4) People can move between different regions within countries, e.g. from the countryside to a city (called rural-urban migration). This is known as internal migration.

There are two main types of migrant:

Refugees are people who've been forced to leave their country due to things like war, persecution or a natural disaster, e.g. thousands of refugees migrated to escape the war in Kosovo in 1999.

Economic migrants are people who move voluntarily from poorer places to richer places looking for jobs or higher wages, e.g. from Mexico to the USA. They often migrate so they can earn more money and then send some back to family in their country of origin.

Migration Happens Because of **Push** and **Pull Factors**

The reasons a person migrates can be classified as either push or pull factors:

Push Factors

Push factors are negative things about a person's place of origin (where they originally lived) that make them want to leave. They're usually things like not being able to find a job, poor living conditions, war or a natural disaster in their country of origin.

Pull Factors

Pull factors are positive things about a person's destination that attract them to the destination. They're usually things such as job opportunities or a better standard of living.

Migration Has **Positive** and **Negative Impacts**

Migration has impacts on both the source country (where they come from) and the receiving country (where they're going to):

	Positive impacts	Negative impacts
Source country	Reduced demand on services, e.g. schools and hospitals. Money is sent back to the source country by emigrants.	Labour shortage — it's mostly people of working age that emigrate. Skills shortage — sometimes it's the more highly educated people that emigrate. Ageing population — there's a high proportion of older people left.
Receiving country	Increased labour force — young people immigrate to find work. Migrant workers pay taxes that help to fund services.	Locals and immigrants compete for jobs — this can lead to tension and even conflict. Increased demand for services, e.g. overcrowding in schools and hospitals. Not all the money earnt by immigrants is spent in the destination country — some is sent back to their country of origin.

People move between different regions and countries for lots of reasons

Migration sounds like a rough business, people being pushed and pulled all over the place. Remember that migration affects both the place the people leave, and the place they go to, and that the effects can be positive or negative.

International Migration

It seems that an awful lot of people are on the move. Here are a couple of examples to spice up your life...

Case Study 1 — There are **Economic** Migrations **From Poland To the UK**

People who come from a country in the EU can live and work in any other EU country. In 2004, ten eastern European countries joined the EU. Since then, people from these countries have been moving to other EU countries. More than half a million people from Poland came to the UK between 2004 and 2007.

There were push and pull factors for why people left Poland and came to the UK:

Push factors from Poland (in 2004):

1) High unemployment — around 19%.
2) Low average wages — about one third of the average EU wage.
3) Housing shortages — just over 300 dwellings for every 1000 people.

Pull factors to the UK:

1) Ease of migration — the UK allowed unlimited migration in 2004 (it was restricted in some other EU countries).
2) More work and higher wages — wages in the UK were higher and there was a big demand for tradesmen, e.g. plumbers.
3) Good exchange rate — the pound was worth a lot of Polish currency, so sending a few pounds back to Poland made a big difference to family at home.

Impacts in Poland

1) Poland's population fell (by 0.3% between 2003 and 2007), and the birth rate fell as most people who left were young.
2) There was a shortage of workers in Poland, slowing the growth of the economy.
3) The Polish economy was boosted by the money sent home from emigrants — around €3 billion was sent to Poland from abroad in 2006.

Impacts in the UK

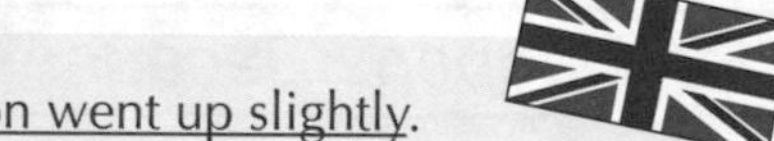

1) The UK population went up slightly.
2) Immigration boosted the UK economy, but a lot of the money earned in the UK was sent home.
3) New shops selling Polish products opened to serve new Polish communities.
4) Many Poles are Catholic so attendance at Catholic churches went up.

Case Study 2 — **Refugees** Migrate **To the EU**

Huge numbers of people migrate from Africa to the EU. For example, by crossing the Mediterranean sea to Spain — in 2001, 45 000 emigrants from Africa were caught and refused entry to Spain.

Many of these migrants are refugees (see the previous page) from wars in central and western African countries. For example, more than 2 million people were forced from their homes because of the civil war in Sierra Leone (in West Africa) between 1991 and 2002.

There are only push factors for African refugees of war — people flee the countries because of the threat of violence or death during the wars.

Here are some of the impacts:

Impacts in African Countries

1) The working population is reduced so there are fewer people contributing to the economy.
2) Families become separated when fleeing from wars.

Impacts in Spain

1) Social tension between immigrants and Spaniards.
2) More unskilled workers in Spain, which has filled gaps in the labour market.
3) Average wages for unskilled jobs have fallen because there are so many people who want the jobs.
4) The birth rate has increased because there are so many young immigrants.

Migration has impacts for the source country and for the receiving country

Migration within the EU tends to be for economic reasons — people move so that they can get better jobs and earn more money. Migration to the EU is often for political reasons — people are forced to move for their own safety.

Managing International Migration

International migration causes population change in a country, which leads to problems. Receiving countries have different ways of managing international migration — read on to find out what they are.

There are Different Ways to Manage International Migration

Different countries manage international migration in different ways. Here are a few examples:

Points-based Systems

1) Points-based systems let countries choose who they want to let in.
2) People who want to move are given points for things like age, education, work experience and whether they speak the language.
3) Only those with enough points are allowed in, so in theory only the most skilled immigrants who'll adapt well are allowed to enter.
   Australia, New Zealand and Canada use systems like this.

Limits and Targets

1) Limits and targets are set by some countries to make sure they don't let in too many or too few immigrants (although having too few is less likely to be a problem for most countries).
2) The limits are set by looking at things like how many jobs are available and public opinion.
3) If the limit has already been reached that year, no one else is allowed in.

Controlling Illegal Immigration

1) Lots of countries, especially richer countries, have problems with people entering illegally or staying after they should have left (e.g. at the end of a holiday).
2) In many countries illegal immigrants can be arrested and forced to leave the country, e.g. Italy fines and deports illegal immigrants, and people can go to jail for knowingly housing an illegal immigrant.

Case Study — The UK has now Changed How it Manages Immigration

Economic migration from Poland to the UK has many impacts (see Case Study 1 on page 136). As a result, the UK has had to change how it manages immigration.

1) Immigrants from Poland entering the UK aren't limited in number, but they do have to register under the Worker Registration Scheme if they want to work in the UK.
2) This lets the UK Border Agency monitor how many people are coming into the country, what type of work they're doing and the effect this is having on the UK economy.
3) The large number of Polish immigrants entering the UK led to some complaints — some people thought the resources in the UK wouldn't be able to cope with all the new people, e.g. there wouldn't be enough jobs or housing to go around.
4) In response to this, the Government tightened the control of migration from some of the newer EU states. For example, immigrants from the two newest EU states, Bulgaria and Romania, have to get permission from the Home Office to work in the UK (and this is only granted for certain types of jobs).

Learn the different strategies for managing migration

Managing immigration is a tricky issue. There are lots of ways to do it and none of them pleases everybody — think how long politicians spend arguing about it. Don't argue about learning this page though — just get it in your noggin.

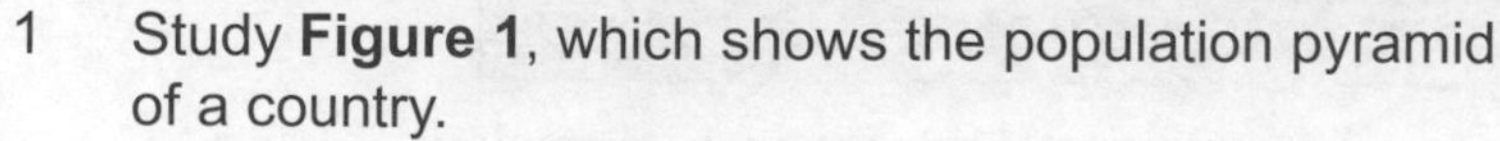

Worked Exam Questions

I'm afraid this helpful blue writing won't be there in the exam, so if I were you I'd make the most of it and make sure you fully understand it now.

1 Study **Figure 1**, which shows the population pyramid of a country.

Figure 1

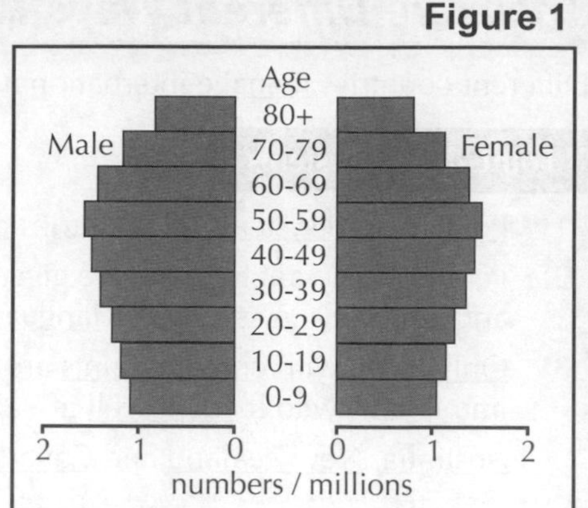

(a) Give evidence from **Figure 1** to show that the country has an ageing population.

There are about 6-7 million people over the age of 60 compared to about 4-5 million people below the age of 20.

It's always good to throw in some figures from the graph to back up your answer.

(1 mark)

(b) (i) Suggest which stage of the Demographic Transition Model a country with a population structure like that shown in **Figure 1** would be in.

Countries with ageing populations are usually in Stage 5 of the DTM.

(1 mark)

(ii) Name a country with a population structure similar to that shown in **Figure 1**.

Japan.

Ideally you should name a Stage 5 country, but any country with an ageing population (e.g. UK, Italy, Sweden) would get you the mark.

(1 mark)

(c) Describe the social and economic impacts of an ageing population.

People may need to spend more time working as unpaid carers for older family members. This means that the working population would have less leisure time, making them more stressed and worried. Healthcare services would be stretched because older people need more medical care. Taxes may need to increase because there are more pensions to pay for. The economy of the country may grow more slowly because more money would be spent on things that don't help the economy to grow, e.g. retirement homes.

Make sure you include a mixture of social and economic impacts.

(6 marks)

2 For a country with an ageing population you have studied, explain why this country has an ageing population and describe the strategies that are being used to cope with the ageing population.

In the UK, people are living longer because of advances in medicine and improved living standards. Life expectancy rose between 1980 and 2006 by 2.6 years for women and 6.4 years for men. Since the 1970s, birth rate in the UK has declined. This means the proportion of older people in the population is rising. The government is gradually going to increase retirement age from 60 for women and 65 for men to 68 for everyone by 2046. This means that more people will be paying taxes for longer, and fewer people will be claiming a pension. The government is also encouraging women to have children by giving them tax credits if they go back to work, and is encouraging people to take out private pensions, so they won't be so dependent on the state pension. However, it's too early to tell whether these strategies are working.

(8 marks)

Exam Questions

1 Study **Figure 1**, an extract from a report about migration from Poland to the UK.

(a) What is immigration?

....

....

....

(1 mark)

Figure 1

Between 2004 and 2007 it's estimated that more than half a million Poles migrated to the UK. The reasons for migration vary from person to person, but most Polish immigrants are thought to be economic migrants who wanted to work to support their family in Poland. Unlike most EU countries, the UK doesn't have a limit to the number of immigrants it will accept from Poland.

(b) (i) Using **Figure 1**, suggest two push factors that might have caused Polish people to migrate to the UK.

....

....

(2 marks)

(ii) Using **Figure 1**, suggest two pull factors that might have caused Polish people to migrate to the UK.

....

....

(2 marks)

(c) Suggest two impacts that migration to the UK might have on the UK.

....

....

....

(2 marks)

2 For an international migration you have studied, describe the impacts of the migration and explain how it is being managed.

....

....

....

....

....

....

....

....

....

(8 marks)

Revision Summary for Section 8

That's another smashing section under your belt — congratulations. And here's a delightful array of questions so you can check you've taken it all in. If you'd care to begin...

1) What are the two things that affect the population size of the world?
2) Under what circumstances does natural increase happen to a population?
3) What happens to death rate at Stage 2 of the DTM?
4) What happens to birth rate at Stage 3 of the DTM?
5) Are richer countries or poorer countries more likely to be in the early stages of the DTM?
6) What is the population structure of a country?
7) Give one reason why birth rate is high during Stage 1 of the DTM.
8) Describe how changes in the economy affect the population growth rate.
9) Give one reason why the birth rate rapidly falls during Stage 3 of the DTM.
10) Briefly describe the population structure of a country in Stage 5 of the DTM.
11) Give a political impact of rapid population growth.
12) Describe what it means for a country to develop in a way that's sustainable.
13) Give an example of a strategy a country could use to control rapid population growth.
14) What is an ageing population?
15) Give two causes of an ageing population.
16) Describe one strategy to cope with an ageing population.
17) Define 'migration'.
18) What's it called when a person leaves an area?
19) What is a refugee?
20) a) Explain what 'pull factors' are.
    b) Give an example of a pull factor.
21) Give one negative impact of migration on a receiving country.
22) Give one positive impact of migration on a source country.
23) a) Describe an example of international migration.
    b) Describe the push and pull factors.
    c) Give one impact on the source country, and one impact on the receiving country.
24) Describe one way in which international migration can be managed.

Urbanisation

Lots of people around the world are upping sticks and moving to urban areas (towns and cities).

Urbanisation is Happening Fastest in Poorer Countries

Urbanisation is the growth in the proportion of a country's population living in urban areas. It's happening in countries all over the world — more than 50% of the world's population currently live in urban areas (3.4 billion people) and this is increasing every day. But urbanisation differs between richer and poorer countries:

1) Most of the population in richer countries already live in urban areas, e.g. more than 80% of the UK's population live in urban areas.
2) Not many of the population in poorer countries currently live in urban areas, e.g. around 25% of the population of Bangladesh live in urban areas.
3) Most urbanisation that's happening in the world today is going on in poorer countries and it's happening at a fast pace.

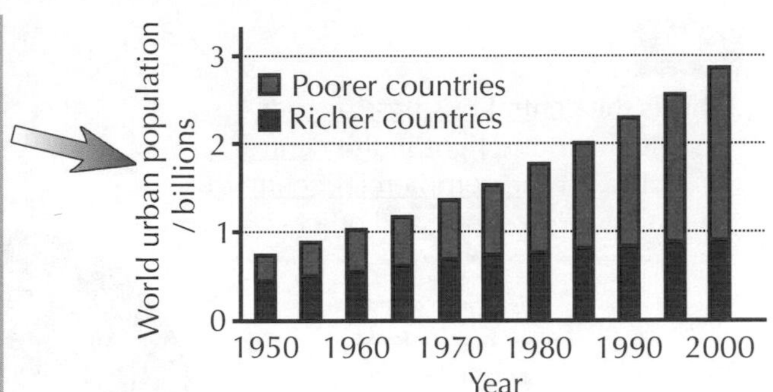

Urbanisation is Caused By Rural-urban Migration...

Rural-urban migration is the movement of people from the countryside to the cities.
Rural-urban migration causes urbanisation in richer and poorer countries.
The reasons why people move are different in poorer and richer countries though.

Here are a few reasons why people in poorer countries move from rural areas to cities:

1) There's often a shortage of services (e.g. education, access to water and power) in rural areas. Also, people from rural areas sometimes believe that the standard of living is better in cities (even though this often turns out not to be the case).
2) There are more jobs in urban areas. Industry is attracted to cities because there's a larger workforce and better infrastructure than in rural areas.
3) In rural areas some people are subsistence farmers. This means they grow food to feed their family and sell any extra to make a small income. Poor harvests and crop failures can mean they make no income and even risk starvation.

Here are a couple of reasons why people in richer countries move from rural areas to cities:

1) Most urbanisation in rich countries occurred during the Industrial and the Agricultural Revolutions (18th and 19th centuries) — machinery began to replace farm labour in rural areas, and jobs were created in new factories in urban areas. People moved from farms to towns for work.
2) In the late 20th century, people left run-down inner city areas and moved to the country. But people are now being encouraged back by the redevelopment of these areas.

... And Good Healthcare and a High Birth Rate in Cities

It's normally young people that move to cities to find work. These people have children in the cities, which increases the proportion of the population living in urban areas. Also, better healthcare in urban areas means people live longer, again increasing the proportion of people in urban areas.

People usually move to cities to look for better jobs and services

Nothing too difficult on this page — richer countries have a high percentage of their population in urban areas, but urbanisation in poorer countries is happening fast. Try scribbling down the reasons for the migration to check you know them.

Urban Land Use

Different areas of a city are used for different things — but the pattern of use is the same in many cities.

A City can be Split into Four Main Parts

Cities are usually made up of four parts — each part has a different land use (e.g. housing or industrial).
The land use of each part stays fairly similar from city to city, but it can differ a bit (see below).
The diagram below is a view from above of a typical city — it shows roughly where the four parts are:

CBD

This is the central business district. It's usually found right in the centre of a city. It's the commercial centre of the city with shops and offices.

The inner city

This part is found around the CBD. It has a mix of poorer quality housing (like high-rise tower blocks) and older industrial buildings.

This is just a model — no city looks exactly like this.

The rural-urban fringe

This is the part right at the edge of a city, where there are both urban land uses (e.g. factories) and rural land uses (e.g. farming).

The suburbs

These are housing areas found towards the edge of the city.

Land Use is decided by Social, Economic and Cultural Factors

Part of city	Land use	Social factors	Economic factors	Cultural factors
CBD	Businesses, e.g. shops and offices	It's busy and very accessible.	Land is expensive (only businesses can afford it).	It's a centre point for entertainment, e.g. cinemas.
Inner city	Low-class housing and industry	Traditionally small houses were built here near to factories to house workers.	Poorer people who can't afford to commute and can only afford small houses live here.	Ethnic groups live here so they're near to important services, e.g. places of worship.
Suburbs	Medium-class housing	It's less crowded and more pleasant, with less traffic and pollution.	Richer people who can afford to commute and to have big houses live here.	People with families live here due to the space for leisure activities, e.g. BBQs.
Rural-urban fringe	Business parks and high-class housing	It's still accessible for commuters and there's lots of space.	The land is often cheaper here so bigger houses can be built for richer people.	Richer people who like a rural lifestyle and being in reach of the city live here.

The Land Use of the Parts can Differ from City to City

1) Sometimes the land use of each part doesn't match the model above — real cities are all slightly different. For example, in cities in poorer countries, e.g. Rio de Janeiro, there's usually low-cost housing and squatter settlements on the outskirts of cities, but high-class housing in the CBD.
2) The land use of each part of a city can also change over time, for example:
   - In recent years a lot of shopping centres have been built in out-of-town locations in the UK, e.g. Meadowhall Shopping Centre was built on the outskirts of Sheffield in 1990.
   - Inner city tower blocks have been removed and replaced with housing estates on the rural-urban fringe, e.g. this has happened in Birmingham.

Most cities have a CBD, an inner city, suburbs and a rural-urban fringe

Check that you know the four main parts of a city and the land use in each bit, but remember that the land use isn't the same everywhere — I'm sure city planners do this on purpose, just to make your revision awkward.

Urban Issues

Urbanisation can lead to problems — urban areas often have social and environmental issues.

Many Urban Areas Have the Same Problems

Cities in richer countries all have the same kind of problems:

1. A shortage of good quality housing.
2. Run down CBDs.
3. Traffic congestion and pollution from cars.
4. Ethnic segregation (people from different races and religions not mixing).

Over the next couple of pages you'll look at each problem and the solutions for them in a bit more detail.

Growing Populations Need More Housing

Some richer countries (e.g. the UK) have housing shortages in urban areas because the urban population has grown quickly. Here are a few ways the shortages are being tackled:

1) Urban renewal schemes

- These are government strategies first widely used in the 1990s. They encourage investment in new housing, services and employment in derelict inner city areas.
- A successful example is the dockland development in Liverpool — the derelict docks (a brownfield site) were converted into high quality housing with good local services.

2) New towns

- Brand new towns have been built to house the overspill populations from existing towns and cities where there was a shortage of housing. Milton Keynes the one of the most well-known examples of a new town — building started in 1970.

3) Relocation incentives

- These are used to encourage people living in large council houses (who don't really need a big house or to live in the city) to move out of urban areas. This frees up houses in urban areas for other people, e.g. working families.
- For example, a scheme that's run by a London council encourages older people who live in big houses in the city to move to the seaside or the countryside. The council helps people who volunteer to move out and it also gives them money.

Efforts are being Made to Revitalise CBDs

The CBDs in some cities are run down. One reason for this is competition from out-of-town shopping centres and business parks, which have cheaper rent (so lure shops to move there) and are easier to drive to. But steps are being taken to revitalise some CBDs and attract people back to them. For example:

1) Pedestrianising areas (stopping car access) to make them safer and nicer for shoppers.
2) Improving access with better public transport links and better car parking.
3) Converting derelict warehouses and docks into smart new shops, restaurants and museums.
4) Improving public areas, e.g. parks and squares, to make them more attractive.

Initial government investment encourages businesses to return, attracting more customers, which attracts more businesses and so on. The London docklands development is a good example of this.

Learn the four main issues in urban areas in richer countries

Not all cities have a lack of housing and run down CBDs, but plenty do. Luckily, city planners have some good ideas about how to deal with housing shortages and revitalise CBDs — check how many of them you remember.

Urban Issues

Another page of urban problems (and solutions to them) — this time it's car use and ethnic segregation.

Increased Car Use has an *Impact* on *Urban Environments*

There are more and more cars on the roads of cities in richer countries. This causes a variety of problems, which can discourage people from visiting and shopping in the city:

1 More air pollution, which damages health
2 More road accidents
3 Air pollution also damages buildings
4 More traffic jams and congestion

There are a variety of solutions to help reduce traffic and its impacts:

1) Improving public transport. This encourages people to use public transport instead of cars, which reduces traffic congestion, air pollution, traffic jams and accidents.
2) Increasing car parking charges in city centres. This discourages car use, so people are more likely to use public transport instead.
3) Bus priority lanes — these speed up bus services so people are more likely to use them.
4) Pedestrianisation of central areas. This removes traffic from the main shopping streets, which reduces the number of accidents and pollution levels. It also makes these areas more attractive to shoppers.

Many Urban Areas *Have a* Variety *of* Cultures

Cities usually have a variety of people from different ethnic backgrounds (people from different races and religions). But there's often ethnic segregation in urban areas, i.e. people of different ethnicities not mixing. There are several reasons for this:

1) People prefer to live close to others with the same background and religion, and who speak the same language.
2) People live near to services that are important to their culture, e.g. places of worship. This means people of the same ethnic background tend to live in the same area.
3) People from the same ethnic background are often restricted in where they can live in the same way, e.g. because of a lack of money, so they all end up in the same place.

Strategies to support the multicultural nature of urban areas aren't aimed at forcing people to mix. The strategies make sure that everyone has equal access to services, like healthcare and education. Some of the ways to do this include:

1) Making sure everyone can access information about the different services, e.g. by printing leaflets in a variety of languages.
2) Improving communication between all parts of the community, e.g. by involving the leaders of different ethnic communities when making decisions.
3) Providing interpreters at places like hospitals and police stations.
4) Making sure there are suitable services for the different cultures. For example, in some cultures it's unacceptable to be seen by a doctor of the opposite sex, so alternatives should be provided.

Cities are trying to reduce car use to cut pollution and congestion

All this stuff seems pretty straightforward but keep going over it until it's all lodged in your brain. Cover the page and try to remember the problems and the solutions. Don't move on until you can remember them all.

Squatter Settlements

Squatter settlements are found in lots of big cities — people live there if they have nowhere else to go.

Squatter Settlements are Common in Cities in Poorer Countries

1) Squatter settlements are settlements that are built illegally in and around the city, by people who can't afford proper housing.
2) Squatter settlements are a problem in many growing cities in poorer countries, e.g. São Paulo (Brazil) and Mumbai (India).
3) Most of the inhabitants have moved to the city from the countryside — they're rural–urban migrants.
4) The settlements are badly built and overcrowded. They often don't have basic services like electricity or sewers.
5) They're called favelas in Brazil and shanty towns or slums in some other places.

Life in a squatter settlement can be hard and dangerous — the people living there don't have access to basic services like clean running water, proper sewers or electricity. They may also lack policing, medical services and fire fighting. Because of these problems, life expectancy is often lower than in the main city. Many inhabitants work within the settlements, e.g. in factories and shops. The jobs aren't taxed or monitored by the government — they're referred to as the informal sector of the economy. People often work long hours for little pay in the informal sector. But squatter settlements often govern themselves more successfully than you might expect and have a strong community spirit.

There are Ways to Improve Squatter Settlements

Squatter settlements aren't great places to live, but there's often nowhere else for poor migrants to go. People living in squatter settlements usually try to improve the settlements themselves. For example, neighbours help each other with building and some have even built small schools. But the residents have little money and can achieve much more with a bit of help:

SELF-HELP SCHEMES

These involve the government and local people working together to improve life in the settlement. The government supplies building materials and local people use them to build their own homes. This helps to provide better housing and the money saved on labour can be used to provide basic services like electricity and sewers.

SITE AND SERVICE SCHEMES

People pay a small amount of rent for a site, and they can borrow money to buy building materials to build or improve a house on their plot. The rent money is then used to provide basic services for the area. An example is the Dandora scheme in Nairobi, Kenya.

LOCAL AUTHORITY SCHEMES

These are funded by the local government and are about improving the temporary accommodation built by residents. For example, the City of Rio (Brazil) spent $120 million on the Favela-Bairro project, which aimed to improve life for the inhabitants of Rio de Janeiro's favelas (see next page).

Squatter settlements are sometimes called slums, shanty towns or favelas

Life in a squatter settlement is pretty tough. It's not all doom and gloom though — people who live in them try to improve the conditions themselves, and there are usually government schemes to help them too.

Squatter Settlements — Case Study

This case study is about a Brazilian project to help thousands of people living in squatter settlements.

The **Favela-Bairro Project** Helps People in **Rio de Janeiro's** Favelas

1) Rio de Janeiro is in south east Brazil. It has 600 squatter settlements (favelas), housing one-fifth of the city's population (more than one million people).
2) The Favela-Bairro project started in 1995 and is so successful it's been suggested as a model for redeveloping other squatter settlements.
3) The project involves 253 000 people in 73 favelas, and is being extended to help even more people.
4) 40% of the $300 million funding for the project came from the local authority. The rest was provided by an international organisation called the Inter-American Development Bank.

The Project Includes **Social**, **Economic** and **Environmental Improvements**

1) Social improvements:
   - Daycare centres and after school schemes to look after children while their parents work.
   - Adult education classes to improve adult literacy.
   - Services to help people affected by drug addiction, alcohol addiction and domestic violence.
2) Economic improvements:
   - Residents can now apply to legally own their properties.
   - Training schemes to help people learn new skills so they can find better jobs and earn more.
3) Environmental improvements:
   - Replacement of wooden buildings with brick buildings and the removal of homes on dangerously steep slopes.
   - Widening and paving of streets to allow easier access (especially for emergency services).
   - Provision of basic services such as clean water, electricity and weekly rubbish collection.

Community involvement is one of the most important parts of the project:

- Residents choose which improvements they want in their own favela, so they feel involved.
- Neighbourhood associations are formed to communicate with the residents and make decisions.
- The new services are staffed by residents, providing income and helping them to learn new skills.

The **Favela-Bairro Project** has been **Very Successful**

1) The standard of living and health of residents have improved.
2) The property values in favelas that are part of the programme have increased by 80–120%.
3) The number of local businesses within the favelas has almost doubled.

The Favela-Bairro project is helping over a quarter of a million people

If you get a squatter settlement case study question in the exam, you need to impress the examiner with lots of facts and figures. It's no good just saying that favelas aren't very nice. It might be true but it won't get you any marks.

Urbanisation — Environmental Issues

Rapid urbanisation in poorer countries brings a whole host of environmental problems...

Rapid Urbanisation** and **Industrialisation** Affect the **Environment

Rapid urbanisation and industrialisation (where the economy of a country changes from being based on agriculture to manufacturing) can cause a number of environmental problems:

1) Waste disposal problems — people in cities create a lot of waste. This can damage people's health and the environment, especially if it's toxic and not disposed of properly.
2) More air pollution — this comes from burning fuel, vehicle exhaust fumes and factories.
3) More water pollution — water carries pollutants from cities into rivers and streams. For example, sewage and toxic chemicals from industry can get into rivers which causes serious health problems. Wildlife can also be harmed.

***Waste Disposal** is a **Serious Problem** in Poorer Countries*

In richer countries, waste is disposed of by burying it in landfill sites, or by burning it. The amount of waste is also reduced by recycling schemes. Poorer countries struggle to dispose of the large amount of waste that's created by rapid urbanisation for many reasons:

1) Money — poorer countries often can't afford to dispose of waste safely, e.g. toxic waste has to be treated and this can be expensive. There are often more urgent problems to spend limited funds on, e.g. healthcare.
2) Infrastructure — poorer countries don't have the infrastructure needed, e.g. poor roads in squatter settlements mean waste disposal lorries can't get in to collect rubbish.
3) Scale — the problem is huge. A large city will generate thousands of tonnes of waste every day.

Air** and **Water Pollution** Have **Many Effects

Air pollution

Effects:

- Air pollution can lead to acid rain, which damages buildings and vegetation.
- It can cause health problems like headaches and bronchitis.
- Some pollutants destroy the ozone layer, which protects us from the sun's harmful rays.

Management of the pollution:

This can involve setting air quality standards for industries and constantly monitoring levels of pollutants to check they're safe.

Water pollution

Effects:

- Water pollution kills fish and other aquatic animals, which disrupts food chains.
- Harmful chemicals can build up in the food chain and poison humans who eat fish from the polluted water.
- Contamination of water supplies with sewage can spread diseases like typhoid.

Management of the pollution:

This can involve building sewage treatment plants and passing laws forcing factories to remove pollutants from their waste water.

Managing air and water pollution costs a lot of money and requires lots of different resources, e.g. skilled workers and good infrastructure. This makes it harder for poorer countries to manage pollution.

Poorer countries can't afford to dispose of all their waste properly

The UK has laws that help to stop air and water pollution reaching dangerous levels, but many poorer countries have no regulations or regulations that aren't enforced — either way, it leads to environmental problems.

Urbanisation — Case Study

China's population is 1.3 billion and the proportion who are living in urban areas is increasing all the time.

Push and Pull Factors have Caused Urbanisation in China

Urbanisation in China is being caused by the internal migration of people from rural areas to urban areas (rural-urban migration). In 1990 around 26% of the population lived in urban areas, but by 2006 a whopping 44% did (over 550 million people).
Urbanisation is happening because of push and pull factors.

PUSH factors from rural areas:

1) Fewer jobs — more machinery has made farming more efficient, so fewer workers are needed. This has created high unemployment, e.g. 150 million rural people were unemployed in 2004.
2) Lower wages and higher poverty — wages are normally lower in rural areas in China, leading to more poverty. E.g. in 2004 there were 26.1 million people in rural areas in poverty.
3) Shortage of services — services like education and healthcare are funded by taxes collected within the local area. This means poor rural areas don't have the money to improve their services.

PULL factors to urban areas:

1) More jobs — there are more industries and jobs in urban areas.
2) Higher wages and lower poverty — the average income is three times higher in urban areas than in rural areas.
3) Better services — there are more (and better) education and healthcare services in urban areas because there's more money to pay for them. For example, lack of funding in rural areas meant that in 2002, 1.1 million children couldn't go to primary school.

Urbanisation in China has had Lots of Impacts

There are impacts of urbanisation in the urban areas, e.g. Beijing:

1) Positive — more workers and an increase in the demand for services in the urban areas helps to increase trade and industry. This is good for the economy.
2) Negative — the increasing population causes more pollution and environmental damage. Over 270 cities in China have no water treatment plants so sewage is dumped straight into local rivers.

And there are impacts for the rural areas too:

1) Positive — about 130 million people who've left rural areas to work in towns send money home to their families. This increases their income and helps them to avoid poverty.
2) Negative — it's usually the young people who migrate, leaving an ageing population behind. About half of all Chinese people aged over 60 now live without any younger relatives to help look after them.

Urbanisation is Being Managed in China

China is trying to manage the problems of urbanisation in both rural and urban areas. For example:

1) Urban — in 2001, China changed its water supply system so it could cope with the increased sewage and pollution in urban areas. This helped to improve both water quality and supply.
2) Rural — in 2009, a pilot pension scheme was set up to give retired farmers a pension every month. This will help to raise income and reduce poverty in rural areas.

People in China move to urban areas for jobs, better wages and better services

The number of people in urban areas in China is growing very rapidly — and it's likely to continue to grow as the country's population increases in size. Cover the page and check you know the impacts of the rural-urban migration.

Worked Exam Questions

Imagine if you opened up the exam paper and all the answers were already written in for you. Hmm, well I'm afraid that's not going to happen, the only way you'll do well is hard work now.

1 Study **Figure 1**, which shows the population growth of Pieville, a city in a rich country.

Figure 1

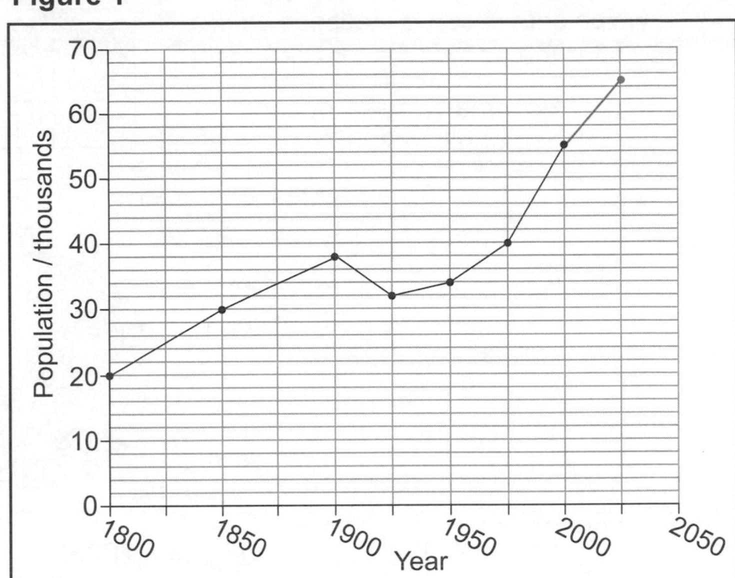

(a) (i) The population of Pieville is predicted to reach 65 000 in 2025. Complete the graph by plotting this figure.

(1 mark)

When you're completing a graph, keep it neat and readable — use a ruler, mark points with a sharp pencil, join the dots and then check it's right.

(ii) Use **Figure 1** to describe how the population of Pieville changed between 1800 and 2000.

The population steadily increased from 20 000 in 1800 to 38 000 in 1900.

The population then decreased to 32 000 in 1925, and then increased again to about 55 000 in 2000.

This answer is worth three marks, so you need to include plenty of detail and give data points from the graph.

(3 marks)

(iii) The population of Pieville has been affected by rural-urban migration. Suggest two reasons why people migrate to urban areas.

People migrate to urban areas to find jobs, as there are more available in towns and cities.

They also move because there are more services in urban areas, e.g. better healthcare.

(2 marks)

(b) Describe how you would expect the following parts of Pieville to be used:

the inner city a mix of poor quality housing and older industrial buildings. It can be quite run-down and deprived, but there can also be newer housing and redevelopment.

Remember that Pieville is in a rich country.

the rural-urban fringe there are both urban land uses, e.g. factories, and rural land uses, e.g. farming. There are also some larger houses.

(4 marks)

(c) The increase in population in Pieville has led to increased traffic congestion. Describe two strategies that could help reduce car use in Pieville.

The city could have bus priority lanes, which speed up bus services so people are more likely to use them instead of their car. They could also increase car parking charges in the centre of Pieville, to discourage people from using their cars and encourage them to use public transport.

(2 marks)

Exam Questions

1 In 2000, Sharky City Council introduced a policy to reduce the impacts of urbanisation. Study **Figure 1**, which shows some statistics before and after the policy was introduced.

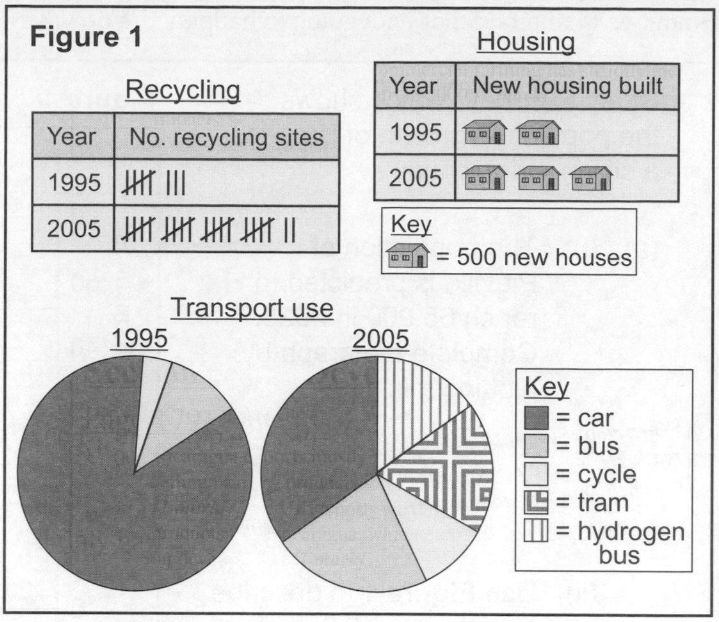

Figure 1

Recycling

Year	No. recycling sites
1995	𝍸 |||
2005	𝍸 𝍸 𝍸 𝍸 ||

Housing

Year	New housing built
1995	🏠 🏠
2005	🏠 🏠 🏠

Key
🏠 = 500 new houses

Transport use

1995

2005

Key
= car
= bus
= cycle
= tram
= hydrogen bus

(a) (i) How many new houses were built in 2005?

....

(1 mark)

(ii) How many extra recycling sites were created between 1995 and 2005?

....

(1 mark)

(iii) Describe the change in transport use between 1995 and 2005.

....

....

(2 marks)

(b) Use **Figure 1** to suggest how the council is trying to reduce the impacts of urbanisation.

....

....

....

....

....

(4 marks)

2 (a) What is meant by the term 'squatter settlement'?

....

(1 mark)

(b) Explain why squatter settlements develop in some cities in poorer countries.

....

....

(2 marks)

(c) Describe one type of scheme that aims to improve conditions in squatter settlements.

....

....

....

(2 marks)

Counter-urbanisation

Not everyone in richer countries is moving to urban areas — some are moving away from them.

Counter-urbanisation is Happening in Richer Countries

Counter-urbanisation is the opposite of urbanisation — it's people moving out of cities and into rural areas. It's happening more in richer countries and here's why:

Counter-urbanisation is also called deurbanisation.

PUSH factors

1) Pollution and traffic congestion are higher in cities.
2) Crime rates are also often higher.
3) Houses in cities can cost more.

PULL factors

1) Better transport links and increased car ownership mean people can easily commute to work in cities.
2) The growth of IT (e.g. e-mail, internet) means more people can work from home.
3) New out-of-town business parks mean more jobs are available outside cities.

Counter-urbanisation has Lots of Impacts

Rural impacts

1) Increased demand for houses drives up house prices. Young people can't afford to buy homes, so have to move away, which can lead to resentment.
2) Many commuters prefer to use shops and services closer to work. This means local ones may shut down due to lack of demand. As a result, local people who don't have transport have no access to services and become isolated.
3) People leave commuter villages (villages where most people commute to the city) during the day, so the village is largely empty then. This can cause a decline in community spirit.

Urban impacts

1) Inner city areas with high crime and pollution become more empty and disused as people move away. This makes them more unpopular, so they get more and more run-down.
2) Commuters prefer to shop and work on the outskirts of the city. So services and shops in the centre lose customers and close.

Governments try to Manage the Impacts of Counter-urbanisation

Governments try to manage the problems caused by counter-urbanisation in...

When people move back into cities it's called re-urbanisation.

...urban areas by:

1) Redeveloping urban areas — this makes them more attractive places, which slows down counter-urbanisation and encourages people to move back, e.g. the Albert Dock development in Liverpool.
2) Regenerating shopping areas, e.g. by pedestrianising them (stopping car access), having better public transport links and better car parking. This makes them more attractive.

...rural areas by:

1) Making policies to provide more housing for local people — these can stop commuters and second home buyers from getting houses. E.g. in the Yorkshire Dales, new housing is only available for people who work locally.
2) Investing in services — governments can provide extra money for services in commuter villages, so they don't close down.

Governments are improving urban areas to reduce counter-urbanisation

You might find all this urbanisation and counter-urbanisation a bit confusing. Just remember that urbanisation is happening fastest in poorer countries while counter-urbanisation is mainly happening in richer countries.

Sustainable Cities

You can't get away from sustainability in geography — this page is about the sustainability of cities.

Urban Areas Need to Become More Sustainable

1) Sustainable living means doing things in a way that lets the people living now have the things they need, but without reducing the ability of people in the future to meet their needs.
2) Basically, it means behaving in a way that doesn't irreversibly damage the environment or use up resources faster than they can be replaced.
3) For example, using only fossil fuels for power will add to climate change and eventually use them all up. This means the people in the future won't have any and the environment will be damaged — it's unsustainable.
4) Big cities need so many resources that it's unlikely they'd ever be truly sustainable. But things can be done to make a city (and the way people live there) more sustainable:

Schemes to reduce waste and safely dispose of it

More recycling means fewer resources are used, e.g. metal cans can be melted down and used to make more cans. Less waste is produced, which reduces the amount that goes to landfill. Landfill is unsustainable as it wastes resources that could be recycled and eventually there'll be nowhere left to bury the waste.

Safely disposing of toxic waste helps to prevent air and water pollution.

Conserving natural environments and historic buildings

Historic buildings, natural environments and open spaces are resources. If they get used up by people today (i.e. built on, or knocked down), they won't be available for people in the future to use. Historic buildings can be restored and natural environments can be protected. Existing areas of green space, like parks, should be left alone.

Building on brownfield sites

Brownfield sites are derelict areas that have been used, but aren't being used anymore. Using brownfield sites for new buildings stops green space being used up. So the space will still be available for people in the future. Developing brownfield sites also makes the city look nicer.

Building carbon-neutral homes

Carbon-neutral homes are buildings that generate as much energy as they use, e.g. by using solar panels to produce energy. For example, BedZED is a carbon-neutral housing development in London. More homes can be provided, without damaging the environment too much or causing much more pollution.

Creating an efficient public transport system

Good public transport systems mean fewer cars on the road, so pollution is reduced. Bus, train and tram systems that use less fuel and give out less pollution can also be used, e.g. some buses in London are powered by hydrogen and only emit water vapour.

5) People are much more likely to support sustainability initiatives like increased recycling or new public transport systems if they're involved in making the decisions about them. Including local people makes the schemes much more likely to succeed.

It's unlikely that big cities will ever be sustainable, but they can improve

Sustainability's a tough one to get your head around. Make sure you're clear on what it means before you memorise all the attempts to make it happen. Cover the page and check you can write down the definition of sustainability.

Sustainable Cities — Case Study

The key points to remember for this case study are: where the sustainable city is, its size, how the city is trying to be sustainable, what it costs, and how successful it is in being sustainable.

*Curitiba is Aiming to be a **Sustainable City***

Brazil
Curitiba

1) Curitiba is a city in southern Brazil with a population of 1.8 million people.
2) The overall aims of its planners are to improve the environment, reduce pollution and waste, and improve the quality of life of residents.
3) The city has a budget of $600 million to spend every year.
4) Curitiba is working towards sustainability in different ways:

1 Reducing car use

- There's a good bus system, used by more than 1.4 million passengers per day.
- It's an 'express' bus system — they have special pre-pay boarding stations that reduce boarding times, and bus-only lanes on the roads that speed up journeys.
- The same cheap fare is paid for all journeys, which benefits poorer residents who tend to live on the outskirts of the city.
- There are over 200 km of bike paths in the city.
- The bus system and bike paths are so popular that car use is 25% lower than the national average and Curitiba has one of the lowest levels of air pollution in Brazil.

2 Plenty of open spaces and conserved natural environments

- Green space increased from 0.5 m^2 per person in 1970 to 52 m^2 per person in 1990.
- It has over 1000 parks and natural areas. Many of these were created in areas prone to flooding, so that the land is useful but no serious damage would be done if it flooded.
- Residents have planted 1.5 million trees along the city's streets.
- Builders in Curitiba are given tax breaks if their building projects include green space.

3 Good recycling schemes

- 70% of rubbish is recycled. Paper recycling saves the equivalent of 1200 trees per day.
- Residents in poorer areas where the streets are too narrow for a weekly rubbish collection are given food and bus tickets for bringing their recycling in to local collection centres.

*Curitiba has been Very **Successful** in its Aim to be Sustainable*

1) The reduction in car use means that there's less pollution and use of fossil fuels. This means the environment won't be damaged so much for people in the future.
2) Leaving green, open spaces and conserving the natural environment means that people in the future will still be able to use the open spaces.
3) The high level of recycling means that fewer resources are used and less waste has to go to landfill. This means more resources will be available in the future.
4) Curitiba is also a nice place to live — 99% of its residents said in a recent survey that they were happy with their town.

Making Curitiba more sustainable has made it a great place to live

I wish I lived in Curitiba. No traffic jams, buses that run on time, plenty of places to ride my bike and lots of lovely green parks. They even have a flock of sheep that goes around the parks to eat the grass instead of using lawnmowers.

Urban Development

Urban development isn't easy to get right — it takes a lot of planning...

Planners Look at Social, Economic and Environmental Needs

Planners look at the needs of the population when designing new developments. For example:

Social needs

1) More housing — this can be built on old industrial sites (brownfield sites) near the city centre, or on the rural-urban fringe for commuters.
2) More room for social activities — e.g. parks replace brownfield sites in cities and places for activities like golf are set up in the rural-urban fringe.

3) Better transport systems and routes — more roads can be built in the rural-urban fringe to cope with increased traffic. Also, more and better public transport systems need to be planned.

Economic needs

More jobs — business parks and out-of-town shopping centres can be built on undeveloped land (greenfield sites) in the rural-urban fringe where land is cheap and it's easily accessible.

Environmental needs

1) More waste disposal systems — landfill sites can be built on the rural-urban fringe to cope with the increase in waste.
2) More green spaces — derelict land in cities can be turned back into open spaces.

It's important for developments to meet the needs of local people

Designing developments that take into account the social, economic and environmental needs of the local population isn't easy, but it can be done — have a look at the case study on the next page about the redevelopment of Glasgow.

Urban Development — Case Study

This case study shows how the theory on page 154 is being put into practice.

Glasgow is being *Developed*

Glasgow has a population of over 580 000 people. The decline in traditional industries, such as shipbuilding, has led to changes to Glasgow's social, economic and environmental needs. For example:

1) Some areas have poor quality, high-rise housing that was built in the 1960s and needs replacing.
2) More jobs are needed as there's high unemployment in Glasgow. In 2008, 7.1% of working age people in Glasgow were unemployed, compared to 4.9% for the whole of Scotland.

But recently the city has been benefiting from major redevelopments. For example:

Clyde Waterfront Regeneration Project

This project is helping to change old inner city industrial land, e.g. land that had shipbuilding yards on it. The land will now be used for business, recreational and residential developments. Over 200 projects costing over £5 billion are ongoing including the Glasgow Science Centre, new offices, shops, parks and improved transport services (e.g. new buses).

Glasgow Science Centre

Regeneration in the Gorbals

£170 million is being invested in this declining neighbourhood. There's an ongoing project to build a new 'urban village' with over 1500 new homes, a shopping centre, a library, a community centre and a good quality bus service.

The Developments Aim *to* Meet *the* Needs *of the* Local Population

1) Social needs — the projects will improve transport and leisure facilities, and provide new homes.
2) Economic needs — new businesses are being attracted into the area, bringing jobs. E.g. over 50 000 new jobs are being created by the Waterfront Project.
3) Environmental needs — the areas will be more attractive and have more green spaces. E.g. the Waterfront Project will have various parks and natural areas.

The Planners have Tried to make the Developments Sustainable

Clyde Waterfront Regeneration Project

1) The Clyde Waterfront Regeneration Project has bus links, and walking and cycling routes to encourage lower car use. This means less pollution and fewer greenhouse gases will be emitted. Also, less fossil fuel will be used, which saves resources for future use.
2) The development is on derelict, brownfield sites, which saves land.
3) A lot of material from old buildings has been reused, so fewer resources have been used up.

Regeneration in the Gorbals

The development projects use derelict, brownfield sites to create new green spaces such as Gorbals Park. This reuses land and makes space for future generations to use.

Make sure you know what the developments are and why they're needed

To pick up lots of marks in case study questions you need to refer to specific examples. This case study has lots of nice facts for you — the types of developments, where they are, how much they cost, why they're important and so on.

Retail Services

And now for a page about shopping — you get to think about retail therapy and call it revision.

Start by Learning These Terms

1) There are two types of consumer goods (things people buy):
   - High order goods — these are goods that are only bought occasionally and are usually more expensive, e.g. clothes, furniture and cars. They're also called comparison goods.
   - Low order goods — these are goods that are bought frequently and are usually quite cheap, e.g. milk, bread and newspapers. They're also called convenience goods.
2) The threshold population — the minimum population needed to support a shop. Shops that sell high order goods have a high threshold population.
3) The sphere of influence — the area that people come from to visit a shop or an area. Shops that sell high order goods have a large sphere of influence because people will travel a long way occasionally to buy expensive items. People won't travel a long way to buy things they need regularly, so shops that sell low order goods will have a small sphere of influence. The distance people will travel for a particular good or service is called its range.

Different Shopping Areas have Different Characteristics

Here are some characteristics of retail services in urban and rural areas:

	SHOPPING AREA	LOCATION	GOODS SOLD	THRESHOLD POPULATION	SPHERE OF INFLUENCE
URBAN	City centre	CBD	High order, e.g. clothes and jewellery.	High — because they sell high order goods and the rent is expensive.	Large — they attract people from a wide area.
URBAN	Out-of-town shopping centre	Rural-urban fringe	High order, e.g. clothes and hardware.	Medium — they sell high order goods but the cost of rent is lower.	Large — they attract people from a wide area.
URBAN	Shopping parades (short rows of shops)	Suburbs	High and low order, e.g. newspapers and clothes.	Medium — they sell a mixture of goods and the cost of rent is lower than in the city centre.	Medium — they attract people from the nearby area.
URBAN	Corner shops	Inner city	Low order, e.g. newspapers and bread.	Low — because they sell goods that are bought often and rent is cheap.	Small — they only attract local customers.
RURAL	Village shops	Villages	Low order, e.g. newspapers and bread.	Low — because they sell goods that are bought often and rent is cheap.	Small — they only attract local customers.

The size of a settlement will also affect what shops can locate there — the bigger a settlement is, the greater its population, so shops will have more potential customers. So the larger a settlement, the more likely it is to have shops selling high order goods.

Some Rural Shops Sell High Order Goods

Shops in rural areas sell mainly low order goods (see above), but some specialist shops that have a large sphere of influence can be found there. People are willing to travel far to buy specialist, rural goods, e.g. caravans or walking equipment (they have a large range).

Learn the difference between high order and low order goods

Shut the book and see how much of the table you can write down. If you get stuck, have a think about the shops you visit — what they sell, whether they need a lot of people to support them and how far customers travel to shop at them.

Changing Retail Services — Case Study

We all know clothing fashions come and go, but it's the same for retail services — for example, corner shops are out and out-of-town shopping centres are in.

Retail Services **Change** Over Time

There have been major changes in the way we shop in the UK in the last 100 years. This is mainly due to two factors:

CHANGES TO TRANSPORT

Car ownership has increased so people can travel further for their shopping. This means there are fewer, smaller convenience stores in rural areas, but there are more out-of-town shopping centres. They're built out of town because land is cheaper, there's more available and it's accessible with on-site parking.

CHANGING MARKET FORCES

1) Changing market forces means changes in the supply and demand for goods and retail services.
2) Supply is how easy and cheap it is to get products.
3) Demand is what products people want and how much they are willing to pay for them.
4) Basically, people now want a larger range of goods at cheaper prices.
5) Smaller, specialist shops can't meet this demand, but larger chain stores and supermarkets can — they have lots of different products under one roof at much cheaper prices, so people shop there instead.

Social habits and work patterns have also changed — people have less time to shop for the things they really need (e.g. food) but want more leisure shopping time (e.g. to shop for clothes). This means it's convenient to use supermarkets, which stock all different types of food all together.

Retail Services have Changed in **South Yorkshire**

South Yorkshire has a mixture of rural and urban areas, e.g. Sheffield and part of the Peak District. In recent years the provision of retail services in this area has changed:

1) In 1990, a large out-of-town shopping centre called Meadowhall was built near Sheffield. The centre has 280 shops, is easily accessible by car and has 12 000 free parking spaces. Around 800 000 shoppers visit the centre every week.

2) The number of shops in Sheffield city centre has declined. Some, such as House of Fraser, have moved to Meadowhall where the rent is cheaper and they can have more space. Some have closed down, possibly because shoppers are going to Meadowhall instead. Early estimates suggested a 15% trade loss from the city centre due to the building of Meadowhall.
3) There are also fewer shops and Post Offices® in the surrounding rural villages, such as Hope. This is because more people own cars and travel to urban areas to do their shopping.

Sheffield city centre is now fighting back by redeveloping itself, improving parking and using a 'City Watch' scheme to reduce crime.

People are happy to travel out of town to shop these days

People may be willing to travel further to shop but they want everything in one place (and sometimes under one roof) once they get there. Unfortunately, that means that town and village centres just aren't the places to be these days.

Worked Exam Questions

Unfortunately the answers won't already be written in on your exam paper, so enjoy it while you can.

1 Study **Figure 1**, an extract from an article on Little Yeoton, a rural village close to the city of Hamslow.

Figure 1

Little Yeoton was once a thriving agricultural village, its inhabitants working mostly in farming or for local shops and amenities. Over the last 20 years, an influx of people from the nearby city of Hamslow has changed all this. Little Yeoton now buzzes into life each morning to the sound of commuters hurrying towards the train station or starting their cars ready for the daily commute. The village, with its convenient road and rail transport links to Hamslow, is an ideal location for those who want to work in the city but wish to avoid living amongst pollution and crime. However, the impact that this counter-urbanisation is having on Little Yeoton is a growing concern for those who've lived in the village for decades.

(a) What is meant by the term 'counter-urbanisation'?

The movement of people out of cities and into rural areas.

(1 mark)

(b) Describe two causes of counter-urbanisation not mentioned in **Figure 1.**

The growth of IT means more people can work at home, so don't need to live in the city.

New out-of-town business parks mean more jobs are available outside cities.

(2 marks)

Double check you haven't mentioned any causes covered in Figure 1.

(c) Suggest three impacts of counter-urbanisation on Little Yeoton.

The increased demand for houses may drive prices up. If young people can't afford to buy a house they'll have to move away, which can lead to resentment. Commuters may prefer to use shops and services closer to work, so local ones could shut down due to lack of demand, which isolates local people without transport. Commuter villages are empty during the day, which can cause a decline in community spirit.

(3 marks)

2 (a) Explain the difference between high order and low order goods.

Add examples of goods to illustrate your answer.

High order goods are bought occasionally and are usually more expensive, e.g. furniture and cars. Low order goods are bought frequently and are usually cheap, e.g. milk and newspapers.

(2 marks)

(b) Shops located in the CBD have a large sphere of influence.

(i) What is meant by the term 'sphere of influence'?

Definitions are an easy way to pick up marks in the exam — learn them.

The area that people come from to visit a shop or an area.

(1 mark)

(ii) Explain why shops in the CBD have a large sphere of influence.

They sell expensive goods that are only bought occasionally, so people are prepared to travel from a wide area.

(1 mark)

Exam Questions

1 Study **Figure 1**, which shows some statistics for Plum City in the years 1992, 2000 and 2008.

Figure 1

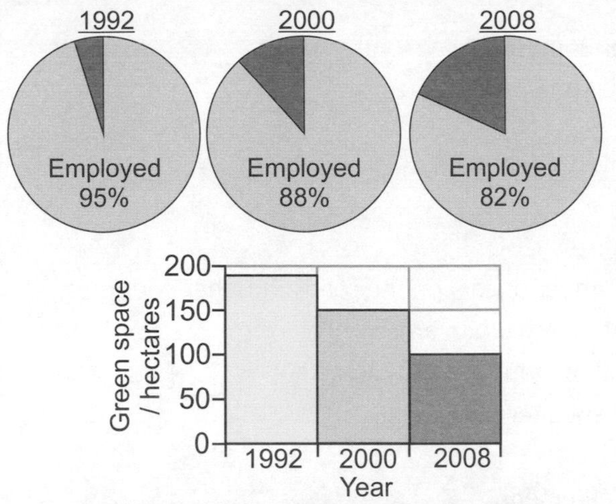

Year	Housing available	No. of people on housing list	Housing deficit
1992	9000	12 000	3000
2000	7500	23 000	15 500
2008	14 000	18 000	

(a) (i) What percentage of the population was unemployed in 2008?

....

(1 mark)

(ii) What happened to the amount of green space between 2000 and 2008?

....

....

(1 mark)

(iii) 'Housing deficit' is the shortfall of available housing compared to the number of people on the housing list. Fill in the table in **Figure 1** to show the housing deficit for 2008.

(1 mark)

(b) An area of Plum City is being redeveloped. Give one social, one economic and one environmental need of the Plum City population that the developers should consider.

....

....

....

(3 marks)

2 Using a named example, describe an attempt at sustainable urban living. How successful has this attempt been?

....

....

....

....

....

....

....

....

....

(8 marks)

Revision Summary for Section 9

There was an awful lot going on in that section but before you head off to do something else find out whether you've taken in all the details with these questions.

1) Is most urbanisation happening today in rich countries or poor countries?
2) What is rural-urban migration?
3) Give one cause of rural-urban migration in poorer countries.
4) Describe the land use of the following parts of a UK city:
   a) CBD, b) the suburbs.
5) Give two problems that cities in rich countries have to deal with.
6) Describe two solutions to one of these problems.
7) Give an example of a successful attempt to revitalise a CBD.
8) Name three problems caused by the increasing number of cars on the roads in richer countries.
9) Give one reason why there is ethnic segregation in many urban areas.
10) Give one strategy used to support the multicultural mixture of urban areas.
11) Describe what life is like for residents in a typical squatter settlement.
12) What is the informal sector of the economy?
13) a) Name a project that has improved a squatter settlement.
    b) Give one environmental improvement, one social improvement and one economic improvement that has happened. How successful has the project been?
14) Give one reason why waste disposal is such a problem in the cities of many poorer countries?
15) Give three effects of water pollution.
16) How can air pollution be managed?
17) a) Give an example of a country you have studied where urbanisation is taking place.
    b) Give two push factors and two pull factors that cause urbanisation in that country.
18) Give three ways the impacts of counter-urbanisation in rural areas can be managed.
19) What is meant by a sustainable city?
20) Explain how reducing waste can help a city to be more sustainable.
21) Explain how building on brownfield sites can help a city to become more sustainable.
22) a) Give one economic and one social aim of a development project you have studied.
    b) Describe how sustainable the development project is.
23) Describe the goods sold, threshold population, sphere of influence and accessibility for shops in the following areas:
    a) CBD, b) rural-urban fringe.
24) What are the two main factors that have changed the way we shop in the UK in the last 100 years?
25) Describe how retail services in a named area have changed and what effects this has had on the surrounding area.

Change in the Rural–Urban Fringe

The rural-urban fringe is the area right at the edge of a city, where there are both urban land uses (e.g. factories) and rural land uses (e.g. farming).

The Rural–Urban Fringe is a Popular Site for Development

As the population of an urban area increases the urban area gets bigger. This is called urban sprawl. One way it gets bigger is by development of the rural-urban fringe. Developments often include:

1) Out-of-town retail outlets.
2) Leisure facilities, e.g. golf courses, riding stables.
3) New transport links, e.g. new motorways connecting cities.
4) Housing — more housing is built in existing villages.

EXAMPLE: Golf courses, thousands of houses and the M5 motorway have been built in the rural area between Gloucester and Cheltenham.

The rural-urban fringe is popular for development because:

1) There's plenty of land available and it's cheaper than in urban areas. Some developments are huge so can only be built where there's lots of land, e.g. retail outlets need lots of space for car parking.
2) It's easy to reach from the urban areas, e.g. people can quickly drive out to retail outlets or golf courses and there's plenty of room to park.

Development of the Rural–Urban Fringe has Impacts

1) Traffic noise and pollution increase as there's more traffic.
2) People already living there may feel the extra housing and developments spoil the area.
3) Farmers may be forced to sell their land so it can be built on, meaning they can't earn a living.
4) Wildlife habitats are destroyed by building on them.

Some urban areas have 'greenbelts' around them though — a ring of land where development is restricted.

The Number and Size of Commuter Villages is Increasing

1) Some people live in villages and commute (travel) to work in urban areas. They choose to live there because it's a nicer environment and there's less crime, pollution and noise than in urban areas. Villages where there are a lot of commuters are called commuter villages.
2) Transport has become cheaper and faster in the 20th century. Road and rail links have improved too. This means more people can live further away from where they work and still commute to work easily. This has increased the number and size of commuter villages.
3) As a village becomes more popular it can cause property prices to increase. It can also cause an increase in traffic congestion.

Commuter villages are sometimes called suburbanised villages.

Growing Commuter Villages have Certain Characteristics

Lots of services, e.g. shops, schools and restaurants.

Lots of middle-aged couples with children, professionals and wealthy retired people who have moved there from the city as it's a nicer environment.

Lots of new detached houses, converted barns or cottages and expensive estates.

Good public transport links.

Some jobs, e.g. in local shops.

Learn the impacts of developing the rural-urban fringe

The rural-urban fringe is a pretty popular place to build, for plenty of good reasons. Make sure you can reel off the impacts of rural-urban fringe development. Try and remember at least three, but four would be even better.

Change in Rural Areas — Case Study

Rural areas are changing, and it's not always for the good. Read on and you'll soon see exactly what I mean.

*The **Population** of Some **Rural Villages** is **Decreasing***

There are two main reasons why:

1) Fewer jobs — the decline in agriculture and manufacturing in some rural areas means there are fewer jobs, so people have to move away to find work.
2) Growth in second home ownership — second homes are homes that people own as well as their main house. They usually use them at weekends or for holidays. The popularity of these properties increases house prices in the area so many young locals can't afford to live there and are forced to move away to somewhere they can afford a house.

*A **Decreasing Population** Causes a **Decrease** in **Services***

(1) A smaller population means there's less demand for services, e.g. shops, schools, pubs. → (2) Services like shops and schools close due to the lack of demand. → (3) This means that there are fewer jobs, so more people move away to find work. And so on...

Villages where the population is falling and services are decreasing are called declining villages.

Declining Villages** Have **Certain Characteristics

An elderly population — young people move away, leaving older people behind.

Few jobs (often badly paid) and relatively high unemployment.

Few services due to lack of demand. Often no school or shops.

Little or no public transport due to lack of demand.

Some poor quality housing, which may be quite basic. Some second homes.

Case Study — Cumbrian Villages

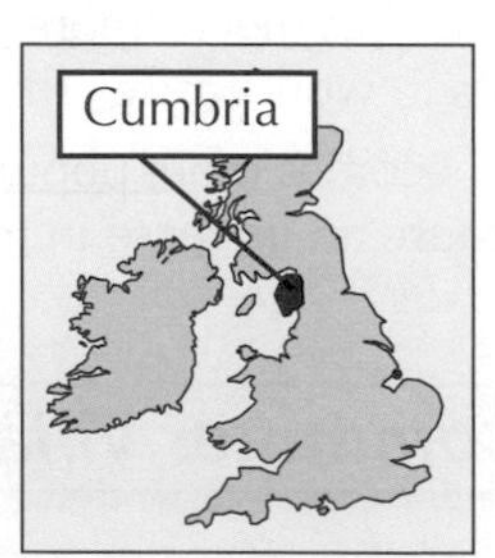

1) Cumbria is a rural area in north west England. It includes the Lake District National Park.
2) The population of some Cumbrian villages has decreased recently, especially in western Cumbria.
3) Here are the two main reasons why people are leaving the villages:
   - Fewer jobs — agriculture and manufacturing are big industries in Cumbria but they're both in decline. E.g. between 2000 and 2007 over 700 agricultural jobs were lost in Cumbria.
   - Lots of second homes as people are attracted by the beautiful scenery. In the Lake District National Park, 15% of houses are second homes or holiday lets, but it's much higher in some villages, e.g. in Chapel Stile it's 37%. This has pushed house prices right up, e.g. in 2009 the average house price in Ambleside was over £400 000.
4) As the population has dropped it's caused a decrease in services. Schools, shops and other businesses in some areas are closing, e.g. 35 Post Office® branches closed in Cumbria in 2008.
5) One in five people who live in Cumbria are over 65 compared to one in six for the UK overall.

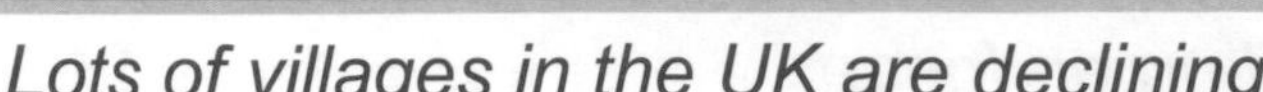

Lots of villages in the UK are declining

At this point I reckon you should check you know why people leave some rural villages, and why this makes it harder to buy a pint or post a parcel. Make sure you've a couple of case study facts stashed away too, to impress the examiner.

Change in UK Commercial Farming

Commercial farming (farming to make money) in some rural areas is changing.

Agri-business has Replaced Traditional Farming in Some Areas

1) In the UK, 60 years ago, there used to be lots of small family farms that sold a mixture of produce. Now there are lots of large companies that own large farms. They often produce a single product.
2) This kind of large-scale commercial farming is called agri-business.
3) Modern farming practices used by agri-businesses help to maximise production and profits. But the practices can take their toll on the environment:

- Monoculture (growing just one type of crop) reduces biodiversity as there are fewer habitats.
- Removing hedgerows to increase the area of farmland destroys habitats. It also increases soil erosion (hedgerows normally act as windbreaks).
- Herbicides are used to maximise crop production, but they can kill wildflowers.
- Pesticides are used to maximise crop production, but they can kill other insects as well as pests.
- Fertilisers are also used to maximise crop production, but they can pollute rivers, killing fish.
- Making fertilisers, pesticides and herbicides uses fossil fuels, which adds to global warming.

Biodiversity is the number and variety of organisms. A habitat is where an organism lives.

When fertilisers pollute rivers it's called eutrophication.

Organic Farming is Also Becoming More Common

1) Organic farming is basically farming without using artificial pesticides or fertilisers.
2) Methods used include crop rotation (changing the type of crop that's planted every year to stop pests building up), using manure as a fertiliser, manual weeding and using biological control (e.g. using ladybirds instead of pesticides to kill aphids). These methods can be less damaging to the environment than other methods.
3) Organic farming is becoming more common, e.g. in the UK in 1998, 100 000 hectares of land were organically farmed and in 2003 this had increased to 700 000 hectares.
4) This is because the demand for organic food has increased. Some people buy organic food because they're concerned that modern farming practices damage the environment or that eating food that contains pesticide residues might be harmful.

Government Policies Aim to Reduce Farming's Environmental Impact

Here are two examples:

Environmental Stewardship Scheme

This involves paying farmers money for every hectare of land they manage in a way that reduces the environmental impact. For example, by farming organically.

Single Payment Scheme

This involves paying farmers a subsidy (paying them money to help them earn a decent living). But they're only paid it if they keep their land in a good environmental condition, e.g. if they leave 2 m around the edge of crop fields uncut to provide habitats. This encourages farmers to reduce the environmental impact of their farming.

Both schemes involve things like using fewer chemicals or leaving some areas uncultivated, so less food can be produced from the same area of land.
This can mean that more land has to be used for farming and the food produced is more expensive.

Large-scale commercial farming is called agri-business

It turns out farming isn't as simple as throwing a few seeds around a field and making the world's best scarecrow. Nope it's a serious business. Agri-business in fact, so make sure you know the definition.

Change in UK Commercial Farming — Case Study

More exciting info on UK farming and a nice case study to get your teeth into.

The Prices Farmers can Charge May be Decided by Supermarkets

1) Four major supermarket chains now control 75% of grocery sales in the UK.
2) This means farmers often have no choice but to cut their prices when asked to by the supermarkets, as there's no-one else to sell to. If they don't cut their prices the supermarkets will find other suppliers.
3) Many foods need processing before supermarkets will buy them, so sometimes farm products are bought by a processing firm. That firm then sells the finished product on to the supermarket at a profit. This adds another step to the supply chain, which can further reduce prices paid to farmers.
4) Some farmers struggle to earn a living due to the low prices (and some go out of business).

UK Farmers Now Have to Compete with the Global Market

1) Before the 1960s most of the food people ate was grown in the UK, usually in the local area.
2) Since then there's been an increase in the global trading of food with more and more of our food being imported from other countries.
3) This has helped to provide enough food for the growing population and has meant people in the UK can get a wide range of food all year round.
4) Imported food is often cheaper if it's grown in poorer countries where farmers pay less for land and pay less for workers to harvest it. UK farmers have to compete with these lower prices.

Transporting food a long way produces lots of CO_2, which adds to global warming.

Case Study — East Anglia

1) East Anglia is an area that includes Norfolk, Suffolk, Cambridgeshire and Essex.
2) It's known as the UK's 'bread basket' because it produces more than a quarter of England's wheat and barley. Farms in the area also produce 2.2 million eggs every day.
3) Agri-business has increased in East Anglia, e.g. in Essex the number of farms over 100 hectares increased from 828 in 1990 to 849 in 2005.

East Anglia

4) Organic farming in East Anglia has increased, but it's still quite low in the area, e.g. in 2008 1.3% of farmland was farmed organically, compared to 3.7% for England overall.
5) Farmers in East Anglia are trying to reduce the environmental impact of farming — the area has more land covered by the Environmental Stewardship Scheme (see previous page) than any other area in the UK.
6) Farmers in East Anglia have been affected by supermarket prices and competition from overseas. E.g. in 1997 peas from East Anglia sold at 25p per kilo but by 2002 this had dropped to 17p.

Competition from foreign farmers drives down prices

Make sure you know a case study for all things farming — examiners are absolutely crazy about them. Just knowing the name of a farming area and where it is won't do either, you need to know the details.

Sustainable Rural Living

A lot of people live and work in rural areas — sometimes in an unsustainable way.

Rural Living Needs to be *Sustainable*

Sustainable living means living in a way that lets the people alive now get the things they need, but without stopping people in the future getting the things they need. Basically it means behaving in a way that doesn't irreversibly damage the environment or use up resources faster than they can be replaced. There are two main reasons why rural living can be unsustainable:

1) High car use — many rural areas have little public transport (often due to low demand) so lots of people travel by car. This uses up fossil fuel resources and releases carbon dioxide, which adds to global warming.
2) Use of some farming techniques:
   - Some farming techniques use up fossil fuels. For example, some farms use a lot of artificial fertilisers — making artificial fertilisers uses up fossil fuel.
   - Irrigation of farmland can also deplete water resources.
   - Some techniques damage the environment (see page 163 for a list).

There are ways to make rural living more sustainable:

1) Conserve resources such as water and fossil fuels. For example, by:
   - Using public transport more to reduce car use.
   - Using irrigation techniques that don't waste water, e.g. drip-irrigation.
2) Protect the environment. For example, by:
   - Reducing the use of herbicides, fertilisers and pesticides to reduce their impacts.
   - Maintaining hedgerows to provide wildlife habitats.

Drip-irrigation uses pipes to deliver drops of water directly to plant roots.

Any attempts to make rural living sustainable have to support the needs of the rural population, e.g. you can't just stop all farming to reduce its environmental impacts because local people need a source of income.

Government Initiatives Protect the *Rural Economy* and *Environment*

There are various government initiatives (schemes) to help protect the rural environment and the rural economy — they help towards sustainable living. Here are a couple of examples:

1 Community Rail Partnerships help increase local train use by improving bus links, developing cycle routes to stations and improving station buildings. This reduces car use and the environmental impacts it has.

2 The Rural Development Programme for England gives farmers financial support to diversify their farms, e.g. to provide bed and breakfast accommodation or set up a tourist attraction. This gives farmers an extra income, so they're not as dependent on farming. It can also reduce the environmental impact of farming as some farmers don't need to farm as much.

3 The Environmental Stewardship Scheme involves paying farmers money to manage their land in a way that reduces the environmental impact (see page 163).

Living sustainably involves conserving resources and protecting the environment

First get your head around why rural living can be unsustainable, then even if you can't remember how to make it more sustainable in the exam, you should be able to work it out. Don't forget, any changes have to support the needs of the locals.

Changes to Farming in Tropical Areas

A lot of farming goes on in tropical areas, and guess what... it's changing too.

Subsistence Farming is being Replaced by Commercial Farming

1) Subsistence farming is where farmers only produce enough food to feed their families. In tropical areas farmers usually clear an area of rainforest to make land for producing food. The soil quickly becomes infertile though, so the farmers move to another area and start again. This is called shifting cultivation.
2) Subsistence farming is being replaced in some tropical areas by commercial farming — where crops and animals are produced to be sold, e.g. coffee, cotton, sugar cane and cattle.
3) Sometimes subsistence farmers switch to commercial farming, and sometimes big companies set up farms (they often take over subsistence farmers' land).
4) Commercial farm products are usually sold to richer countries.
5) This has a few impacts:
    - Subsistence farmers who've had their land taken by big companies are forced onto poorer land where it's harder to grow food for themselves.
    - If farmers are dependent on a single crop or animal and prices drop they might not have enough money to buy food. It also means farmers will only have an income around harvest or slaughter time — if they can't make a lot of money, they'll struggle to buy food for the rest of the year.
    - There isn't as much food being produced locally, so food has to be brought in from further away. This increases food prices.

Commercial farming in tropical areas can also be called cash cultivation.

Irrigation has Changed Agriculture

Growing lots of crops to sell needs a lot of water, so farmers often have to irrigate their land (artificially apply water). Irrigation has physical and human impacts:

	Positive	Negative
Physical impacts	• More land can be farmed. • Crop yields are higher and fewer harvests are lost due to lack of water. • High yields mean farmers don't need to clear more land for farming, e.g. by deforestation.	• Irrigation can cause soil erosion. • Without proper drainage salt can build up (salinisation) causing crops to fail. • If the land isn't well drained it becomes waterlogged so nothing can grow.
Human impacts	• Higher yields mean more food. This decreases the risk of famine. • Higher yields mean farmers make more profit — giving them a better quality of life.	• Large-scale irrigation projects can be expensive and cause rural debt to increase. • Mosquitoes that spread malaria breed in irrigation ditches. • Waterborne diseases can also become more common.

Appropriate Technologies have also Changed Agriculture

Appropriate technologies are simple, low cost technologies that increase food production. They're made and maintained using local knowledge and resources, so they're not dependent on any outside support, expensive equipment or fuel. Here are two examples:

1) The treadle pump is a human-powered pump used in Bangladesh. It pumps water from below the ground to irrigate small areas of land. This is important in Bangladesh as the main crop (rice) needs lots of water to grow. It costs US $7 to buy and it's increased Bangladeshi farmers' average annual incomes by roughly $100 because of increased crop yields.
2) Lines of stones are used to trap water on sloping fields in Burkina Faso. It increases the amount of water that soaks into the soil so more is available for crops. It's increased crop yields by about 50%.

Commercial farming is on the increase

The idea of appropriate technology is pretty important. You could be asked whether an irrigation system would be appropriate technology for a tropical region. Think about how it's suited to the area and what problems it could cause.

Factors Affecting Farming in Tropical Areas

It's not always plain sailing if you're a farmer in a tropical area...

Soil Erosion can be a Big Problem for Tropical Farmers

Soil erosion happens naturally due to the action of wind and rain. Soil erosion is common in tropical areas because there's heavy rainfall, which washes away the soil. Overgrazing can cause erosion because plants that hold the soil together are removed. Soil erosion can cause serious problems:

1) Erosion of the nutrient-rich top layer of soil makes the soil unsuitable for farming — it doesn't have enough nutrients and it can't hold water as well.
2) When the land can't be farmed anymore, the farmers either have to move away (e.g. to urban areas, see below) or they have to clear more land and start again.
3) The eroded soil is washed into rivers, which raises riverbeds. This means the rivers can't hold as much water and are more likely to flood.

Mining and Forestry Affect Subsistence Farming

A lot of mining and forestry goes on in tropical rainforests, which affects subsistence farming there:

MINING

1) Mining companies can force local people off their land. This means the local farmers have no source of income.
2) Mining uses lots of water. This can reduce crop yields for local farmers because there's less water for irrigation.
3) After the resources have all been extracted the land is often left unusable (e.g. because of pollution). This means there's less land available for local farmers.

FORESTRY

1) Deforestation can make floods more common as there are fewer trees to intercept rainfall. Floods can waterlog soil, reducing crop yields. They can also wash away crops.
2) Without trees, less water is removed from the soil and evaporated into the atmosphere. This means fewer clouds form and rainfall in the area is reduced. Reduced rainfall means lower crop yields for local farmers.
3) It's not all bad though — deforestation means more land is available for farming, so farmers can increase their income.

Farming Difficulties Lead to Rural-Urban Migration

1) Factors such as soil erosion, mining and forestry can cause farms to fail.
2) This means farmers can't make a profit or grow enough to feed themselves and their families.
3) People are forced to abandon their land and look for other work. They leave the countryside and move to towns and cities (this is known as rural-urban migration).
4) However, there aren't enough jobs or houses in the cities for all the people that move there. This means things like squatter settlements spring up (poor quality houses built illegally).
5) As more land is abandoned, less food is produced by the country. This causes food prices to rise due to the cost of importing it from other countries.
6) Governments can reduce rural-urban migration by helping farmers, e.g. by encouraging the use of appropriate technology to decrease water shortages and educating farmers about sustainable farming methods.

Soil erosion, mining and deforestation can all be problematic for farmers

More impacts to learn again here, but I guess you're getting used to that by now. If not, I recommend a smidge more revision. Cover the page and write down as many impacts of mining and forestry on subsistence farming as you can.

Worked Exam Questions

There's no better preparation for exam questions than doing, err practice exam questions. Hold on, what's this I see...

1 Study **Figure 1**, which shows how the population of Bumbleside, a rural village, has changed between 1950 and 2000.

Figure 1

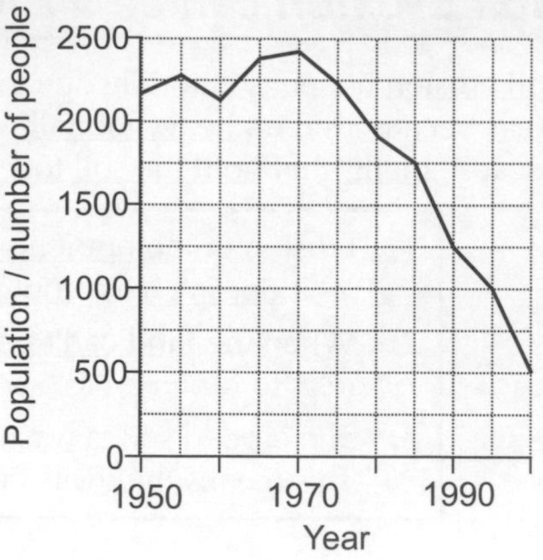

(a) What was the population of Bumbleside in 1985?

1750

Read the value off the vertical axis carefully, then double check it to avoid throwing away easy marks.

(1 mark)

(b) In 1970, a nearby mine closed. Explain how this may have caused the population decrease.

With fewer jobs in the area, people would have moved away to find work. This would have meant less demand for services like shops, and if they closed, there would have been even fewer jobs so more people would have moved away.

(3 marks)

(c) Describe the causes and impacts of depopulation of a named rural area in the UK.

The wording 'named rural area' tells you it's a case study question. Try to include plenty of relevant details in case study answers.

Cumbria is a rural area in north west England. The population of some Cumbrian villages has decreased recently, especially in western Cumbria. There are two main reasons why people are leaving the villages. Firstly, there are fewer jobs in agriculture and manufacturing. For example, between 2000 and 2007, over 700 agricultural jobs were lost. Secondly, an increase in second home ownership has driven up prices, so young locals can't afford to buy houses and have to move away. For example, in Ambleside an average house is £400 000. As the population has dropped, it has caused a decrease in services. Schools, shops and other businesses are closing. For example, 35 Post Office® branches closed in Cumbria in 2008.

(8 marks)

(d) Rural living needs to be sustainable. What does the term 'sustainable living' mean?

Living in a way that lets the people alive now get the things they need, but without stopping people in the future getting the things they need.

(2 marks)

(e) A lot of the residents of Bumbleside moved to the rural-urban fringe on the outskirts of the nearest city. This area has recently been developed to include more housing. Describe and explain the impacts these changes may have had on the rural-urban fringe.

Traffic noise and pollution may have increased due to more traffic. People already living there may feel that the changes spoil the area. Farmers may have been forced to sell their land, so they may not be able to earn a living. Wildlife habitats may have been destroyed by building on them.

This question is worth four marks, so try to give four impacts.

(4 marks)

Exam Questions

1 Study **Figure 1**, showing the use of an area of agricultural land in 1950 and in 2000.

Figure 1

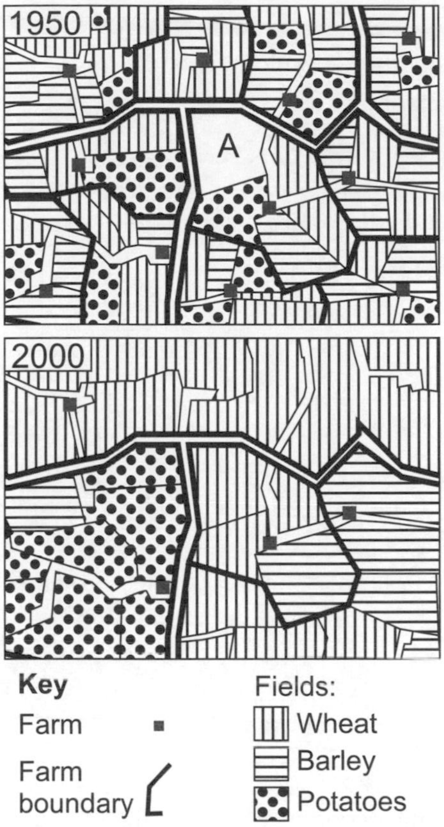

(a) Complete **Figure 1** to show that field A was used for growing wheat in 1950.

(1 mark)

(b) (i) Using the information shown in **Figure 1**, describe how farming has changed between 1950 and 2000.

....

....

....

....

(3 marks)

(ii) Explain how these changes could have a negative impact on the environment.

....

....

....

....

....

(2 marks)

2 Study **Figure 2** which shows the changing nature of farming in Lartua between 1960 and 2000. Lartua is a poor rural area in the tropics.

(a) What is commercial farming?

....

....

....

(1 mark)

Figure 2

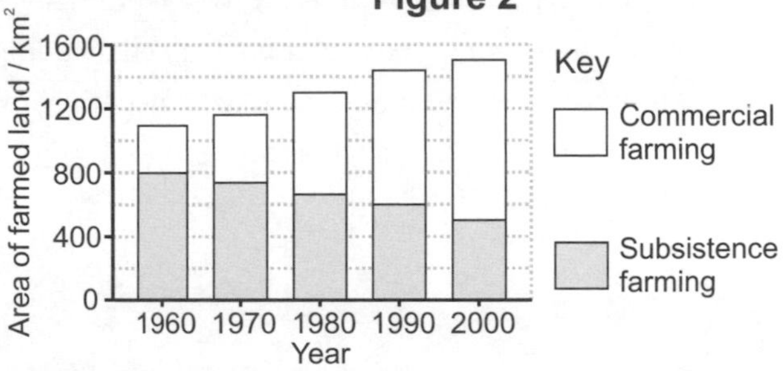

(b) How much land was used for commercial farming in Lartua in 2000?.................................

(1 mark)

(c) Using the information in **Figure 2**, describe how the nature of commercial farming in Lartua changed between 1960 and 2000, and give two likely impacts of this change.

....

....

....

....

(3 marks)

Revision Summary for Section 10

At last, the end of another tricky section — well nearly the end. Before you stop for a well-earned cup of tea, there's just the small matter of this list of questions. It's really in your best interests to have a look through them, because if there are any you can't answer then you can bet that that's exactly what will come up in the exam.

1) List four types of development often found in the rural-urban fringe.
2) Give two reasons why the rural-urban fringe is a popular place for these developments.
3) Give one way the rural-urban fringe can be protected from development.
4) Give two reasons why people live in commuter villages.
5) List four characteristics of commuter villages.
6) What are the two main reasons why the populations of some rural villages are decreasing?
7) Explain why a decrease in population in a village can cause a decrease in services.
8) Give four characteristics of declining villages.
9) Define the term agri-business.
10) What is monoculture?
11) Give two ways modern farming practices can affect the environment.
12) Explain what organic farming is.
13) Describe one government policy aimed at reducing the environmental impact of farming.
14) Explain how supermarkets may influence the prices farmers charge.
15) How does competition from the global market affect the prices UK farmers can get for their produce?
16) a) Give an example of a commercial farming area in the UK.
    b) Give two ways farming in the area has changed recently.
    c) Give one way the environmental impact of farming in the area has been reduced.
17) Give two ways that rural living can be unsustainable.
18) Describe two ways rural living can be made more sustainable.
19) Describe three government initiatives that are designed to boost the economy or protect the environment in rural areas.
20) Explain what is meant by subsistence farming.
21) Give two physical and two human impacts of irrigation.
22) What is meant by appropriate technology?
23) Explain why soil erosion is a problem for tropical farmers.
24) How can mining in an area have a negative impact on subsistence farming?
25) How can forestry in an area have a negative impact on subsistence farming?
26) Explain how factors such as soil erosion, mining and forestry can lead to rural-urban migration by farmers in tropical countries.

Development Basics

OK, this topic's a bit trickier than the other human ones, but fear not — I'll take it slowly.

Development is when a Country is Improving

1) When a country develops it basically gets better for the people living there — their quality of life improves (e.g. their wealth, health and safety). Some people think quality of life just includes wealth, but it doesn't. (When you're just on about wealth it's usually referred to as economic development.)
2) The level of development is different in different countries, e.g. France is more developed than Ethiopia.
3) Development is pretty hard to measure because it includes so many things. But you can compare the development of different countries using 'measures of development'. Here are a few:

Name	What it is	A Measure of...	As a Country Develops it gets...
Gross Domestic Product (GDP)	The total value of goods and services a country produces in a year. It's often given in US dollars (US$).	Wealth	Higher ↑
Gross National Income (GNI)	The total value of goods and services people of that nationality produce in a year (i.e. GDP + money from people living abroad). It's often given in US$. It's also called Gross National Product (GNP).	Wealth	Higher ↑
GNI per head	This is the GNI divided by the population of a country. It's sometimes called GNI per capita.	Wealth	Higher ↑
Birth rate	The number of live babies born per thousand of the population per year.	Women's rights	Lower ↓
Death rate	The number of deaths per thousand of the population per year.	Health	Lower ↓
Infant mortality rate	The number of babies who die under 1 year old, per thousand babies born.	Health	Lower ↓
People per doctor	The average number of people for each doctor.	Health	Lower ↓
Literacy rate	The percentage of adults who can read and write.	Education	Higher ↑
Access to safe water	The percentage of people who can get clean drinking water.	Health	Higher ↑
Life expectancy	The average age a person can expect to live to.	Health	Higher ↑
Human Development Index (HDI)	This is a number that's calculated using life expectancy, literacy rate, education level (e.g. degree) and income per head.	Lots of things	Higher ↑

Many of these measures are linked — there's a relationship between them (the posh name for this is a correlation). For example, countries with high GNI tend to have low death rates and high life expectancy because they have more money to spend on healthcare.

There are lots of ways of measuring level of development

These measures could come up in the exam, so it'll help if you know what each one means. There are a lot to remember, but at least you can work out if each one gets higher or lower as a country develops, rather than memorising it.

Development Basics

Development is very difficult to measure accurately — none of the measures described on the previous page are perfect. In the exam you might be asked about the difficulties of using measures of development, so get reading.

Measures of Development Have *Disadvantages*

1) Economic measures can be inaccurate for countries where trade (the exchange of goods and services) is informal (not taxed). They're also affected by exchange rate changes (they're often given in US$).

2) The measures can be misleading when used on their own because they're averages — they don't show up elite groups in the population or variations within the country. For example, if you looked at the GNI of Iran it might seem quite developed (because the GNI is quite high), but in reality there are some really wealthy people and some poor people.

3) They also shouldn't be used on their own because as a country develops, some aspects develop before others. So it might seem that a country's more developed than it actually is.

4) Using more than one measure or using the HDI (which uses lots of measures) avoids these problems.

Quality of Life Isn't the Same as *Standard of Living*

1) As a country develops the quality of life and standard of living of the people who live there improves.
2) Someone's standard of living is their material wealth, e.g. their income, whether they own a car.
3) Quality of life includes standard of living and other things that aren't easy to measure, e.g. how safe they are and how nice their environment is.
4) In general, the higher a person's standard of living the higher their quality of life. But just because they have a high standard of living doesn't mean they have a good quality of life. For example, a person might earn loads and have a flash car, but live somewhere where there's lots of crime and pollution.
5) Different people in different parts of the world have different ideas about what an acceptable quality of life is. For example, people in the UK might think it means having a nice house, owning a car, and having access to leisure facilities — people in Ethiopia might think it means having clean drinking water, plenty of food, somewhere to live and no threat of violence.

OR

Quality of life includes standard of living

Figuring out how developed a country is can be tricky because using measures like GDP or literacy rate has plenty of disadvantages — learn them. Also, make sure you know the difference between quality of life and standard of living.

Global Inequalities

'Global inequalities' means the level of development of different countries in the world is unequal.

Some Countries are More Developed than Others

1) Countries used to be classified into two categories based on how economically developed they were.
2) Richer countries were classed as More Economically Developed Countries (MEDCs) and poorer countries were classed as Less Economically Developed Countries (LEDCs).
3) MEDCs were generally found in the north. They included the USA, European countries, Australia and New Zealand.
4) LEDCs were generally found in the south. They included India, China, Mexico, Brazil and all the African countries.

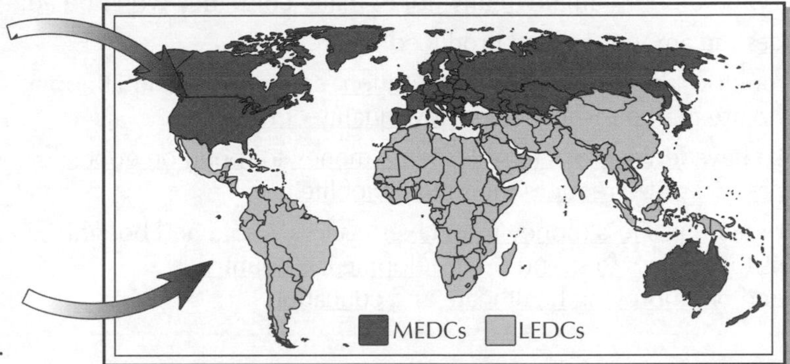

5) But using this simple classification you couldn't tell which countries were developing quickly and which weren't really developing at all.
6) Nowadays, countries are classified into more categories, for example:

Rich industrial countries

These are the most developed countries in the world. For example, the UK, Norway, USA, Canada, France.

Former communist countries

These countries aren't really poor, but aren't rich either (they're kind of in the middle). They're developing quickly, but not as quick as NICs are. For example, the Czech Republic, Bulgaria, Poland.

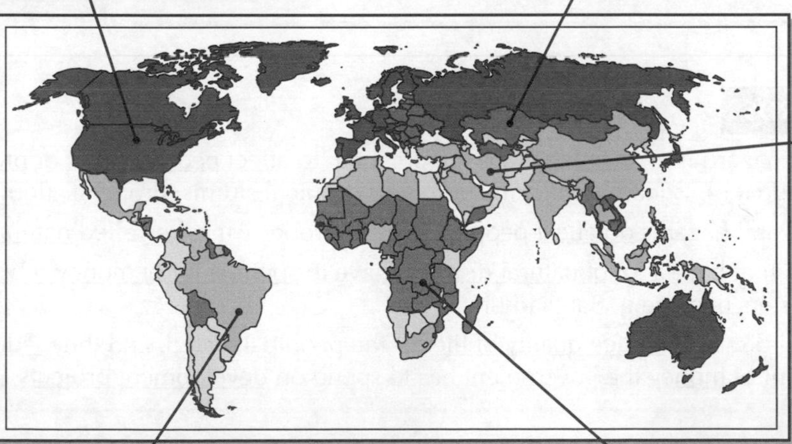

Oil-exporting countries

These are quite rich (they have a high GNI) but the wealth often belongs to a few people and the rest are quite poor. For example, Qatar, Kuwait, Saudi Arabia.

Newly Industrialising Countries (NICs)

These are rapidly getting richer as their economy is moving from being based on primary industry (e.g. agriculture) to secondary industry (manufacturing). For example, China, India, Brazil, Mexico, South Africa, Taiwan.

Heavily indebted poor countries

These are the poorest, least developed countries in the world. For example, Ethiopia, Chad, Angola.

These categories are based mainly on wealth...

...but they are a fairly good way of showing how developed different countries are relative to one another. Unfortunately, revising development categories is a teeny bit more difficult now that there are a few categories rather than just two.

Causes of Global Inequalities

There are plenty of reasons why global inequalities exist — i.e. why countries differ in how developed they are.

Environmental Factors *Affect How Developed* a Country Is

A country is more likely to be less developed if it has...

1 A POOR CLIMATE

1) If a country has a poor climate (really hot or really cold) they won't be able to grow much.
2) This reduces the amount of food produced.
3) In some countries this can lead to malnutrition, e.g. in Chad and Ethiopia. People who are malnourished have a low quality of life.
4) People also have fewer crops to sell, so less money to spend on goods and services. This also reduces their quality of life.
5) The government gets less money from taxes (as less is sold and bought). This means there's less to spend on developing the country, e.g. to spend on improving healthcare and education.

2 POOR FARMING LAND

If the land in a country is steep or has poor soil (or no soil) then they won't produce a lot of food. This has the same effect as a poor climate (see above).

3 LIMITED WATER SUPPLIES

Some countries don't have a lot of water, e.g. Egypt, Jordan. This makes it harder for them to produce a lot of food. This has the same effect as a poor climate (see above).

4 LOTS OF NATURAL HAZARDS

1) A natural hazard is an event that has the potential to affect people's lives or property, e.g. earthquakes, tsunamis, volcanic eruptions, tropical storms, droughts, floods.
2) When natural hazards do affect people's lives or property they're called natural disasters.
3) Countries that have a lot of natural disasters have to spend a lot of money rebuilding after disasters occur, e.g. Bangladesh.
4) So natural disasters reduce quality of life for the people affected, and they reduce the amount of money the government has to spend on development projects.

5 FEW RAW MATERIALS

1) Countries without many raw materials like coal, oil or metal ores tend to make less money because they've got fewer products to sell.
2) This means they have less money to spend on development.
3) Some countries do have a lot of raw materials but still aren't very developed because they don't have the money to develop the infrastructure to exploit them (e.g. roads and ports).

Learn these environmental reasons why some countries struggle to develop

Basically, if a country is rubbish for farming, or tropical storms keep wrecking the place, then it's going to be difficult for it to develop. There are a few exceptions though, e.g. Japan gets battered by natural hazards but is developed.

Causes of Global Inequalities

Countries really do have a tough time trying to develop. It's not just things like earthquakes and a shortage of water that hold them back — things like trade problems, debt and producing low profit goods are to blame too...

Economic Factors Affecting Development Include Trade and Debt

A country is more likely to be less developed if it has...

1 Poor Trade Links

1) Trade is the exchange of goods and services between countries.
2) World trade patterns (who trades with who) seriously influence a country's economy and so affect their level of development.
3) If a country has poor trade links (it trades a small amount with only a few countries) it won't make a lot of money, so there'll be less to spend on development.

2 Lots of Debt

1) Very poor countries borrow money from other countries and international organisations, e.g. to help cope with the aftermath of a natural disaster.
2) This money has to be paid back (sometimes with interest).
3) Any money a country makes is used to pay back the money, so isn't used to develop.

3 An Economy Based On Primary Products

1) Countries that mostly export primary products (raw materials like wood, metal and stone) tend to be less developed.
2) This is because you don't make much profit by selling primary products. Their prices also fluctuate — sometimes the price falls below the cost of production.

3) This means people don't make much money, so the government has less to spend on development.
4) Countries that export manufactured goods tend to be more developed.
5) This is because you usually make a decent profit by selling manufactured goods. Wealthy countries can also force down the price of raw materials that they buy from poorer countries.

Less money made = less to spend on development

Once countries are in debt, it's very hard for them to break the cycle and develop. Don't forget though, there are always exceptions to the rules above, e.g. countries that export oil (a primary product) are often quite rich.

Causes of Global Inequalities

Over the last couple of pages you've looked at some of the environmental and economic reasons why some countries struggle to develop, but social and political factors can be just as important. This page is all about them.

Social Factors Affect Development Too

1 Drinking Water

1) A country will be more developed if it has clean drinking water available.
2) If the only water people can drink is dirty then they'll get ill — waterborne diseases include typhoid and cholera. Being ill a lot reduces a person's quality of life.
3) Ill people can't work, so they don't add money to the economy, and they also cost money to treat.
4) So if a country has unsafe drinking water they'll have more ill people and so less money to develop.

2 The Place Of Women In Society

1) A country will be more developed if women have an equal place with men in society.
2) Women who have an equal place in society are more likely to be educated and to work.
3) Women who are educated and work have a better quality of life, and the country has more money to spend on development because there are more people contributing to the economy.

3 Child Education

1) The more children that go to school (rather than work) the more developed a country will be.
2) This is because they'll get a better education and so will get better jobs. Being educated and having a good job improves the person's quality of life and increases the money the country has to spend on development.

There are Three Main Political Factors that Slow Development

1) If a country has an unstable government it might not invest in things like healthcare, education and improving the economy. This leads to slow development (or no development at all).

2) Some governments are corrupt. This means that some people in the country get richer (by breaking the law) while the others stay poor and have a low quality of life.

3) If there's war in a country the country loses money that could be spent on development — equipment is expensive, buildings get destroyed and fewer people work (because they're fighting). War also directly reduces the quality of life of the people in the country.

The more people in work or in better jobs, the quicker the country develops

Reading this page makes you realise how nice the UK is — there's clean water, free schooling and women can work. Make sure you know some social, economic, environmental and political reasons for slow development (at least two for each).

Global Inequalities — Case Study

It's time for a case study about why there are global inequalities (why some countries are less developed than others).

Hurricane Mitch Hit Nicaragua and Honduras in October 1998

Hurricane Mitch hit a few countries in 1998, but Nicaragua and Honduras were the worst hit.
Here are some of the impacts in each country:

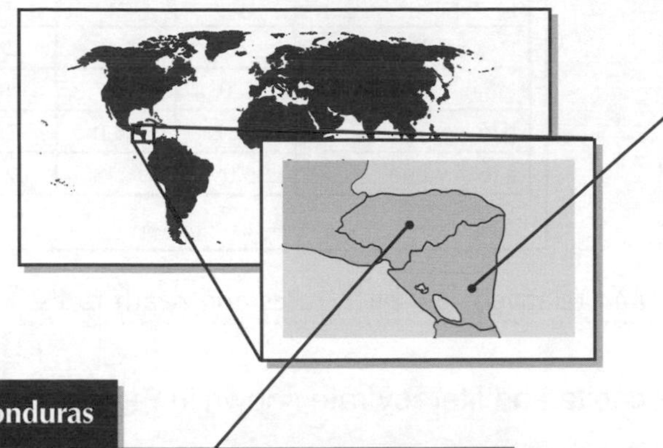

Nicaragua

1) Around 3000 people were killed.
2) The impact on agriculture was high — crops failed and 50 000 animals died.
3) 70% of roads were unusable and 71 bridges were damaged or destroyed.
4) 23 900 houses were destroyed and 17 600 more were damaged.
5) 340 schools and 90 health centres were damaged or destroyed.

Honduras

1) Around 7000 people were killed.
2) The hurricane destroyed 70% of the country's crops, e.g. bananas, rice, coffee beans.
3) Around 70-80% of the transport infrastructure (e.g. roads and bridges) was severely damaged.
4) 35 000 houses were destroyed and 50 000 more were damaged.
5) 20% of schools were damaged, as well as 117 health centres and six hospitals.

Hurricane Mitch Set Back Development in Nicaragua...

1) In 1998 the GDP grew by 4%, which was less than estimated. The rate of growth slowed in the later months of 1998 — after Hurricane Mitch hit.
2) Exports of rice and corn went down because crops were damaged by the hurricane. This meant people earnt less money, so were poorer, and the government had less to spend on development.
3) The total damage caused by the hurricane is estimated to be $1.2 billion. The cost of repairs took money away from development.
4) The education of children suffered — the number of children that worked (rather than went to school) increased by 8.1% after the hurricane. This meant the children had a lower quality of life and found it harder to get good jobs later in life.

...and In Honduras

1) In 1998 money from agriculture made up 27% of the country's GDP. In 2000 this had fallen to 18% because of the damage to crops caused by the hurricane. This reduced the quality of life for people who worked in agriculture because they made less money.
2) GDP was estimated to grow 5% in 1998, but it only grew 3% due to the hurricane. This meant there was less money available for development than there would have been if Mitch hadn't hit.
3) The cost of repairing and rebuilding houses, schools and hospitals was estimated to be $439 million — this money could have been used to develop the country.
4) All these things set back development — the Honduran President claimed the hurricane destroyed 50 years of progress.

This case study's full of facts and figures for you to impress the examiner with

There are tons of facts on this page for you to cram into your brain. If you already know a case study of how a natural disaster affected development that's fine, but if not, shut the book and scribble what you can remember till you get it all.

Worked Exam Questions

Here are some handy worked examples to get you in the exam mood. Use them wisely.

1 Study **Figure 1**, which shows measures of development for Canada, Taiwan and Angola.

Figure 1

	Canada	Taiwan	Angola
GNI per capita	$32 220	$22 900	$2210
Birth rate	10.3	9	43.7
Death rate	7.7	6.8	24.1
Infant mortality rate	5.0	5.4	180.2
Life expectancy	81.2	78.0	38.2
Literacy rate	99.0%	96.1%	67.4%

* GNI per capita information from Hutchinson Country Facts. © RM, 2009. All rights reserved. Helicon Publishing is a division of RM.

(a) Using **Figure 1**, explain which country is most developed.

Try to include all the measures given in Figure 1 in your answer.

Canada is the most developed because it has the highest GNI per capita, life expectancy rate and literacy rate. It also has the lowest infant mortality rate and relatively low birth rates and death rates.

(3 marks)

(b) Explain the correlation between GNI per capita and literacy rate shown in **Figure 1**.

You need to say what the correlation is before you explain it.

A country with a higher GNI per capita has a higher literacy rate. This is because a country that has a higher GNI per capita will have more money to spend on education.

(2 marks)

(c) Give one disadvantage of using measures of development to judge how developed a country is.

The measures can be misleading when used on their own because they are averages so they don't show up elite groups in the population or variations within the country.

(1 mark)

2 Study **Figure 2**, which shows the global distribution of MEDCs and LEDCs.

Figure 2

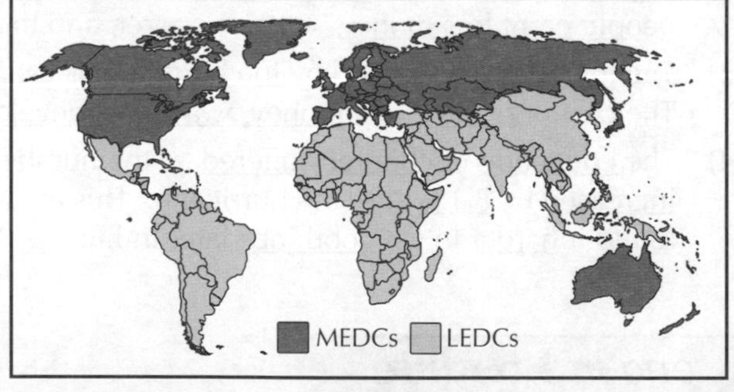

(a) Describe the global distribution of MEDCs and LEDCs.

MEDCs are generally found in the north, e.g. the USA, Canada and European countries. However, some MEDCs are found in the south, e.g. Australia and New Zealand. LEDCs are generally found in the south, e.g. Brazil and all the African countries.

(3 marks)

(b) Give one problem with classifying countries as MEDCs or LEDCs.

It doesn't show which countries are developing quickly. *You could also say that it doesn't show which countries aren't really developing at all*

(1 mark)

(c) Describe two development categories, other than MEDC and LEDC.

Try to give examples of countries in each category that you write about.

Newly Industrialising Countries (NICs) are rapidly getting richer as their economies move from being based on primary industry to secondary industry, e.g. China and Brazil. Former communist countries are not rich but not poor. They're also developing quite quickly, e.g. Bulgaria and Poland.

(2 marks)

Exam Questions

1 In 2007, Nicaragua had a 0.01% share of the world's total exports while the UK had a 3.04% share. Study **Figure 1**, which shows the types of goods exported by each country.

Figure 1

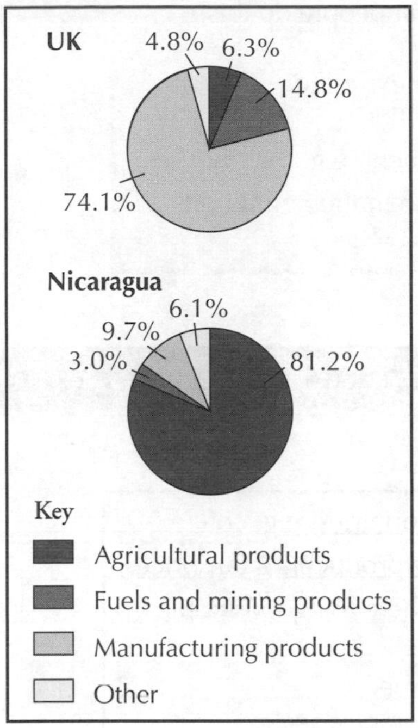

(a) Using **Figure 1**, explain why Nicaragua is less developed than the UK.

....

....

....

....

....

(2 marks)

(b) Explain how poor trade links affect a country's development.

....

....

....

(2 marks)

2 Study **Figure 2**, which shows the change in HDI for three countries between 1990 and 2005.

(a) Describe how the HDI for Botswana changed between 1990 and 2005.

....

....

....

....

....

(2 marks)

Figure 2

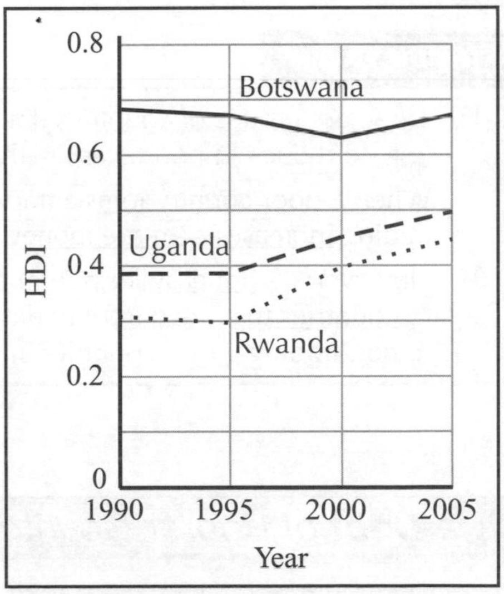

(b) The government of Uganda has been accused of corruption. Describe and explain how a corrupt or unstable government can affect a country's development.

....

....

....

....

....

(4 marks)

Reducing Global Inequality

As you might have gathered, global inequality is a bad thing. One way to reduce it is to help poorer countries develop.

Some People are Trying to *Improve Their Own Quality of Life*

Some people in poorer countries try to improve their quality of life on their own — rather than relying on help from others. This is called 'self-help'. Here are a few ways that people do this:

1) Moving from rural areas to urban areas often improves a person's quality of life. Things like water, food and jobs are often easier to get in towns and cities.
2) Some people improve their quality of life by improving their environment, e.g. their houses.
3) Communities can work together to improve quality of life for everyone in the community, e.g. some communities build and run services like schools.

Fair Trade and *Trading Groups* Help *Increase* the *Money Made* from *Trade*

Fair trade

1) Fair trade is all about getting a fair price for goods produced in poorer countries, e.g. coffee.
2) Companies who want to sell products labelled as 'fair trade' have to pay producers a fair price.
3) Buyers also pay extra on top of the fair price to help develop the area where the goods come from, e.g. to build schools or health centres.
4) Only producers that treat their employees well can take part in the scheme. E.g. producers aren't allowed to discriminate based on sex or race, and employees must have a safe working environment. This improves quality of life for the employees.
5) However, producers in a fair trade scheme often produce a lot because of the good prices — this can cause them to produce too much. An excess will make world prices fall and cause producers who aren't in a fair trade scheme to lose out.

A 'fair price' is a price that's high enough for the producer to make a profit.

Trading groups

1) These are groups of countries that make agreements to reduce barriers to trade (e.g. to reduce import taxes) — this increases trade between members of the group.
2) When a poor country joins a trading group, the amount of money the country gets from trading increases — more money means that more development can take place.
3) However, it's not easy for poorer countries that aren't part of trading groups to export goods to countries that are part of trading groups. This reduces the export income of non-trading group countries and slows down their development.

E.g. NAFTA is a trade group including the USA, Canada and Mexico.

The *Debt* of Poorer Countries can be *Reduced*

1) Debt abolition is when some or all of a country's debt is cancelled. This means they can use the money they make to develop rather than to pay back the debt. For example, Zambia (in southern Africa) had $4 billion of debt cancelled in 2005. In 2006, the country had enough money to start a free healthcare scheme for millions of people living in rural areas, which improved their quality of life.
2) Conservation swaps (debt-for-nature swaps) are when part of a country's debt is paid off by someone else in exchange for investment in conservation. For example, in 2008 the USA reduced Peru's debt by $25 million in exchange for conserving its rainforests.

There are lots of ways to help poor countries develop

Lots of people in poorer countries are keen to improve their own quality of life, so they set up self-help schemes. Richer countries are also trying to help by reducing debt and making trade more profitable for poor countries.

Reducing Global Inequality

One way less developed countries are given a helping hand is through international aid.

Some Types of International Aid Speed Up Development

1) Aid is given by one country to another country in the form of money or resources (e.g. food, doctors).
2) The country that gives the aid is called the donor — the one that gets the aid is called the recipient.
3) There are two main sources of aid from donor countries — governments (paid for by taxes) and Non-Governmental Organisations (NGOs, paid for by voluntary donations).
4) There are two different ways donor governments can give aid to recipient countries:

- Directly to the recipient — this is called bilateral aid.
- Indirectly through an international organisation that distributes the aid — this is called multilateral aid.

International organisations include the United Nations (UN) and the World Bank.

5) Bilateral aid can be tied — this means it's given with the condition that the recipient country has to buy the goods and services it needs from the donor country. This helps the economy of the donor country. However, if the goods and services are expensive in the donor country, the aid doesn't go as far as it would if the goods and services were bought elsewhere.
6) Aid can be classed as either short-term or long-term depending on what it's used for:

Short-Term Aid

1) This is money or resources that help recipient countries cope during emergencies, e.g. floods.
2) The aid has an immediate impact so more people will survive the emergency.
3) There are disadvantages though:
   - The stage of development of the recipient country remains unchanged overall.
   - If either country is slow to react, aid may not get to where it's most needed.
   - The aid may not reach those who need it because of things like theft and transport problems.

Long-Term Aid

1) This is money or resources that help recipient countries to develop, e.g:
   - It's used to build dams and wells to improve clean water supplies.
   - It's used to construct schools to improve literacy rates.
2) Over time, recipient countries become less reliant on foreign aid as they become more developed.
3) However, it can take a while before the aid benefits a country, e.g. hospitals take a long time to build.

7) For both types of aid the recipient may become dependent on the aid — they don't bother spending their own money developing themselves because they get it from someone else.
8) In some recipient countries aid is misused because they have corrupt governments — the government uses the money and resources to fund their lifestyle or to pay for political events.

International Aid may not be Sustainable

1) To be sustainable, aid must help development in ways that don't irreversibly damage the environment or use up resources (including money) faster than they can be replaced.
2) An example of a sustainable aid project would be a scheme that helps people switch from earning money by deforestation to earning money in a more environmentally friendly way. This reduces environmental damage and makes sure trees are still there for future generations.
3) An example of an unsustainable aid project would be investment in large, shallow water wells in areas with little rainfall. Use of the wells could use up water faster than it's replaced. This would mean that the amount of water available for future use would be reduced.

Long-term aid is spent on development projects

There's quite a bit to remember on this page — try drawing a simple diagram to show the different ways that aid goes from a donor country to a recipient country. Then check that you understand what makes aid sustainable.

Reducing Global Inequality — Case Study

There are loads of development projects going on around the world to reduce inequality. Much as I'd like to, I can't possibly tell you about all of them, so here's an example of one...

FARM-Africa helps the Development of Rural Africa

1) FARM-Africa is a non-governmental organisation (NGO) that provides aid to eastern Africa.
2) It's funded by voluntary donations.
3) It was founded in 1985 to reduce rural poverty.
4) FARM-Africa runs programmes in five African countries — Ethiopia, Sudan, Kenya, Uganda and Tanzania.
5) FARM-Africa has been operating in Ethiopia since 1988. Here are four of the projects it runs there:

Project	Region	Problem	What's being done	Helping...	Sustainability
Rural Women's Empowerment	Various	There are very few opportunities for Ethiopian women to make money. This means they have a low quality of life and struggle to afford things like healthcare.	Women are given training and livestock to start farming. Loan schemes have been set up to help women launch small businesses like bakeries and coffee shops. Women have been given legal training to advise other women of their rights.	Around 15 160 people.	Once the new businesses have been set up they'll continue to grow and make money. This means that money will be available as a future resource.
Prosopis Management	Afar	Prosopis, a plant introduced by the government to stabilise soils, has become a pest — it invades grazing land, making farming difficult.	Farmers are shown how to convert prosopis into animal feed. The animal feed is then sold, generating a new source of income.	Around 4400 households.	Once the farmers have been taught the new technique they'll be able to carry on using it. This means that money will be available as a future resource.
Community Development Project	Semu Robi	Frequent droughts make farming very difficult. This reduces the farmer's income and can lead to malnutrition. Semu Robi is a remote region, so getting veterinary care for livestock is difficult.	People are given loans to buy small water pumps to irrigate their farmland. This reduces the effects of drought. People are trained in basic veterinary care so they can help keep livestock healthy.	Around 4100 people.	The project means people are able to farm more crops and animals. This means they can earn more money. But if too much water is used there won't be any left for other people.
Sustainable Forest Management	Bale	Forests are cut down to make land for growing crops and grazing livestock. Trees are also cut down for firewood. This reduces resources for future generations.	Communities are taught how to produce honey and grow wild coffee. These are then sold, so people can make money without cutting down trees. Communities are also taught how to make fuel-efficient stoves that use less wood. This also reduces deforestation.	Around 7500 communities.	Less deforestation means there'll still be trees for future generations. Also, people can make money themselves by selling the coffee and honey.

FARM-Africa runs a whole range of projects to improve people's lives

Yes, it's another case study for you. I think this one's pretty interesting though, and it's not too difficult to get your head around. The more facts and figures you can remember in the exam, the more impressed the examiner will be...

Development Levels in the EU

Different countries in the EU have very different levels of development. And here's a lovely example...

Bulgaria is Less Developed than The UK

Bulgaria joined the EU in 2007 — it's less developed than the UK. For example:

- In 2007 Bulgaria had a GNI per head of $11 180 and the UK had a GNI per head of $33 800.
- Life expectancy in Bulgaria is six years lower (73 compared to 79).
- The HDI for Bulgaria is 0.824, whereas it's 0.947 for the UK.

Here are a few reasons why Bulgaria is less developed than the UK:

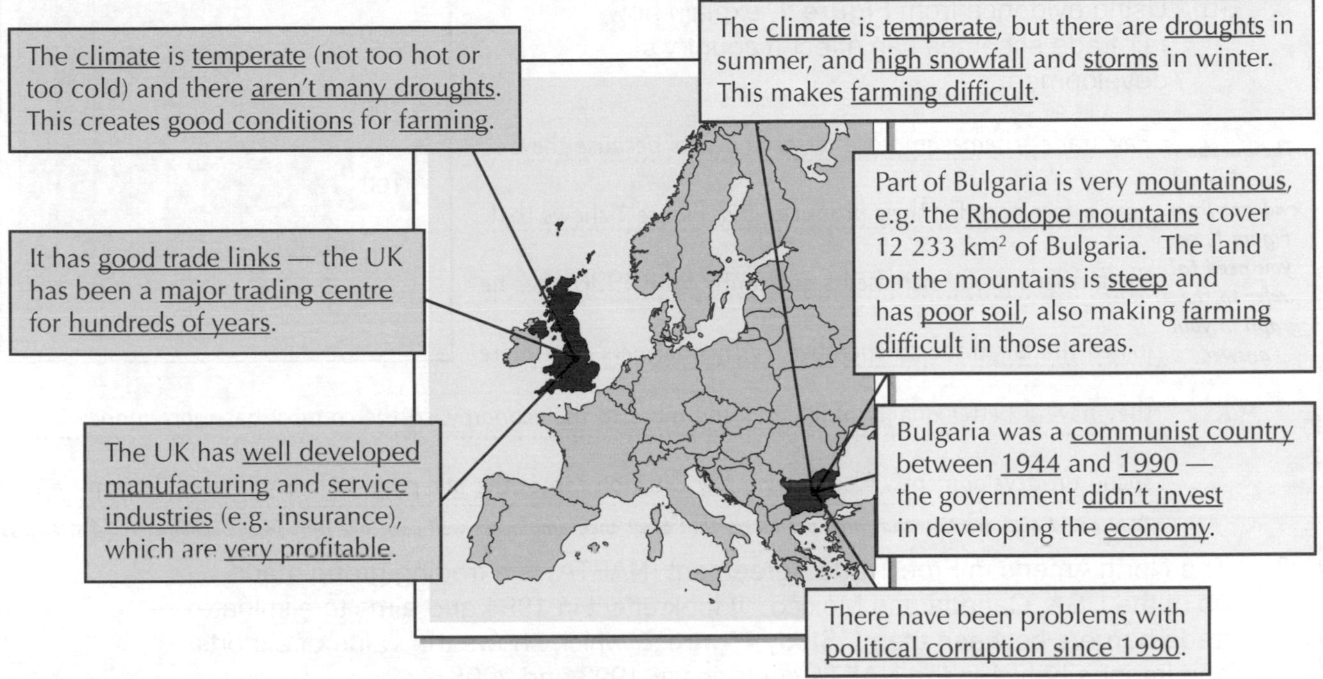

The climate is temperate (not too hot or too cold) and there aren't many droughts. This creates good conditions for farming.
It has good trade links — the UK has been a major trading centre for hundreds of years.
The UK has well developed manufacturing and service industries (e.g. insurance), which are very profitable.
The climate is temperate, but there are droughts in summer, and high snowfall and storms in winter. This makes farming difficult.
Part of Bulgaria is very mountainous, e.g. the Rhodope mountains cover 12 233 km² of Bulgaria. The land on the mountains is steep and has poor soil, also making farming difficult in those areas.
Bulgaria was a communist country between 1944 and 1990 — the government didn't invest in developing the economy.
There have been problems with political corruption since 1990.

The EU is Trying to Reduce Inequalities

Here are some of the ways that the EU is trying to reduce inequality in and between its member countries:

1) The URBAN Community Initiative — money is given to certain EU cities to create jobs, reduce crime and increase the area of green space (e.g. parks).
2) The Common Agricultural Policy (CAP) — farmers are subsidised (paid) to grow certain products. Also, when world food prices are low, the EU buys produce and guarantees farmers a reasonable income. The CAP also puts a high import tax on foreign produce so people in the EU are more likely to buy food produced in the EU. All these things improve the quality of life for farmers.
3) Structural Funds — these provide money for research and development, improving employment opportunities, reducing discrimination and improving transport links. The aim of the fund is to get all members of the EU to a similar level of development (reducing inequalities within Europe).

The EU is also trying to develop Bulgaria in some specific ways:

- SAPARD (Special Accession Programme for Agriculture and Rural Development) gives money to Bulgaria and two other countries to invest in agriculture.
- Funds earmarked for Bulgaria have been partially frozen until the government shows it's making progress in fighting corruption.

Learn why Bulgaria's less developed than the UK and what the EU's doing about it

Well, you've nearly made it to the end of this section. Most of the hard work is done — all that's left to do now is check how much of it you've taken in, so turn over and have a go at the exam questions and revision summary.

Worked Exam Questions

Another set of worked exam questions to look at here. It's tempting to skip over them without thinking, but it's worth taking time to look carefully — similar questions might just come up in your own exams...

1 Study **Figure 1**, which shows the annual income of a farmer in Mali between 1994 and 2002. He joined a fair trade co-operative in 1996.

Figure 1

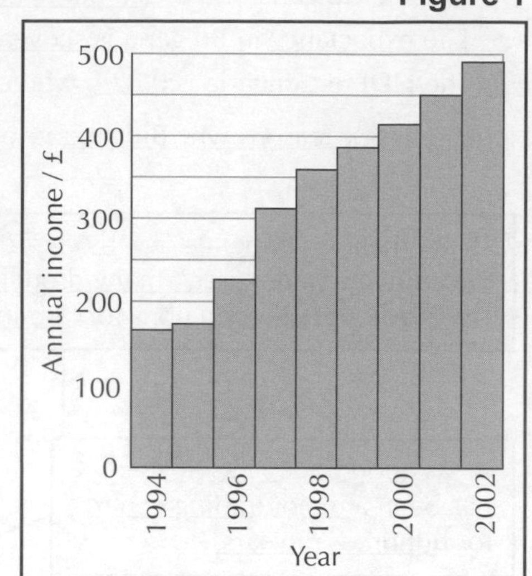

(a) What was the farmer's income in 1999?

£390

(1 mark)

(b) Using evidence from **Figure 1**, explain how fair trade schemes can affect a country's development.

The question says 'using evidence from Figure 1', so you need to refer to the graph in your answer.

Fair trade schemes improve farmers' profits because they're paid a fair price for their produce. E.g. Figure 1 shows that the farmer's profit increased significantly from 1996 after he joined the fair trade co-operative. When farmers earn more they have a better quality of life and add more to the economy, so the country has more money to spend on development. Also, buyers pay extra on top of the fair price to help the area develop.

You could also mention that only producers that treat their employees well can take part in the scheme.

(4 marks)

2 The North American Free Trade Agreement (NAFTA) is a trading group made up of the USA, Canada and Mexico. It took effect in 1994 and aims to eliminate trade barriers between them. Study **Figure 2**, which shows the value of exports and imports between the NAFTA countries in 1993 and 2008.

Figure 2

1993 2008

Value of exports and imports / US$ billion

0-100
101-200
201-300
301-400

(a) (i) What was the value of USA exports to Mexico in 2008?

With questions like this, make sure you read the key carefully and get the units right.

US$ 101-200 billion.

(1 mark)

(ii) How did the value of USA exports to Canada change between 1993 and 2008?

It increased from between 0 and US$100 billion to between 201 and US$300 billion.

(1 mark)

(b) With reference to **Figure 2**, suggest how joining NAFTA may have affected Mexico's development. Explain your answer.

You don't need to write about how trading groups work — just use the info in Figure 2 to work out how Mexico's trading has changed, then explain what effect this might have had on development.

It would have helped Mexico to develop. Figure 2 shows that between 1993 and 2008 exports from Mexico to the US increased. This means that the amount of money Mexico made from trading would have increased so the country would have had more money to spend on development.

(4 marks)

Exam Questions

1 Study **Figure 1**, a newspaper article about an aid project in Ghana.

Figure 1

UK Government Support for Ghana

The UK is the second largest aid donor to Ghana. The UK Government's Department for International Development (DFID) gave over £205 million between 2005 and 2007 towards Ghana's poverty reduction plans. This level of aid continues, with donations of around £85 million per year. The aid is used in several ways, including to improve healthcare, education and sanitation.

About 15% of the UK's funding in 2008 was used to support the healthcare system in Ghana — £42.5 million was pledged to support the Ghanaian Government's 2008-2012 health plan. On top of that, in 2008 the UK gave nearly £7 million to buy emergency equipment to reduce maternal deaths.

Thanks to a £105 million grant from the UK in 2006, Ghana has been able to set up a ten year education strategic plan. It was the first African country to do this. The UK pledged additional money to help 12 000 children in North Ghana to get a formal basic education.

(a) (i) Is the aid described in **Figure 1** an example of multilateral aid or bilateral aid?

....

(1 mark)

(ii) Suggest the potential advantages and disadvantages for the recipient country of long-term aid projects such as the one described in **Figure 1**.

....

....

....

....

(4 marks)

(b) Describe what is meant by sustainable aid and explain whether the aid described in **Figure 1** is sustainable.

....

....

....

(3 marks)

2 Bolivia was one of the first countries to make a conservation swap agreement. The agreement with Conservation International in 1987 led to the cancellation of $650 000 of debt.

(a) What is a conservation swap?

....

....

(1 mark)

(b) Suggest how the conservation swap agreement could have affected Bolivia's development.

....

....

(2 marks)

Revision Summary for Section 11

Time to find out if you've developed a memory of development facts. Try these questions and if there are any that you don't know immediately have a look back at the page to refresh your memory. I know it's hard work, but it'll be worth it come the exam...

1) What is Gross National Income (GNI)?
2) Define birth rate.
3) Does literacy rate get higher or lower as a country develops?
4) Does infant mortality rate get higher or lower as a country develops?
5) Give three things that are used to calculate the HDI for a country.
6) Explain the difference between standard of living and quality of life.
7) What does MEDC stand for?
8) Describe what a rich industrial country is and give one example.
9) Describe the general level of development of former communist countries.
10) Give one way a poor climate can lead to slow development.
11) Is a country likely to be more or less developed if it doesn't have a lot of water?
12) How do natural hazards slow down development?
13) Why does being in debt slow a country's development?
14) Why are countries with unsafe drinking water more likely to be less developed?
15) Describe a political factor that affects development.
16) a) Name a natural disaster that set back a country's development.
    b) Describe the effects that the disaster had on development.
17) Give two ways that people in poor countries are trying to improve their own quality of life.
18) What is fair trade?
19) Describe how trading groups can cause problems for poorer non-member countries.
20) Give two ways the debt of a poor country can be reduced.
21) What is multilateral aid?
22) a) What is tied aid?
    b) Give one disadvantage of tied aid.
23) What's the difference between short-term and long-term aid?
24) Give one advantage of short-term aid.
25) a) Name two countries in the EU that have contrasting levels of development.
    b) State three reasons why they have different levels of development.
    c) Give two ways in which the EU is trying to reduce the differences.

Types of Industry and Employment Structure

Right, it's the start of a brand new section. No need to go dashing ahead with excitement though — get your head around these basics first. Otherwise, you might find things get tricky later in the section.

There are Four Different Types of Industry

The four types are — primary, secondary, tertiary and quaternary. The employment structure of a country describes what proportion of its workforce is employed in each type of industry.

1) Primary industry involves collecting raw materials, e.g. farming, fishing, mining and forestry.
2) Secondary industry involves turning a product into another product (manufacturing), e.g. making textiles, furniture, chemicals, steel and cars.
3) Tertiary industry involves providing a service — anything from financial services, nursing and retail to the police force and transport.
4) Quaternary industry is high technology — where scientists and researchers investigate and develop new products, e.g. in the electronics and IT industry.

Quaternary industry is sometimes thought of as a part of tertiary industry.

A Country's Employment Structure Changes as it Develops

Less developed countries

1) Most of the workforce is employed in primary industry.
2) Few people work in secondary industry because there's not enough money to invest in the technology needed for this type of industry, e.g. to build large factories.
3) A small percentage of people work in tertiary industry — usually in cities where there are banks, hospitals and schools.
4) There's no quaternary industry because the country doesn't have enough educated or skilled workers, and it can't afford to invest in the technology needed, e.g telescopes.

Many workers in less developed countries don't appear in official statistics because they work in jobs that aren't taxed or monitored by the government, e.g. street traders. These jobs are referred to as the informal sector of the economy.

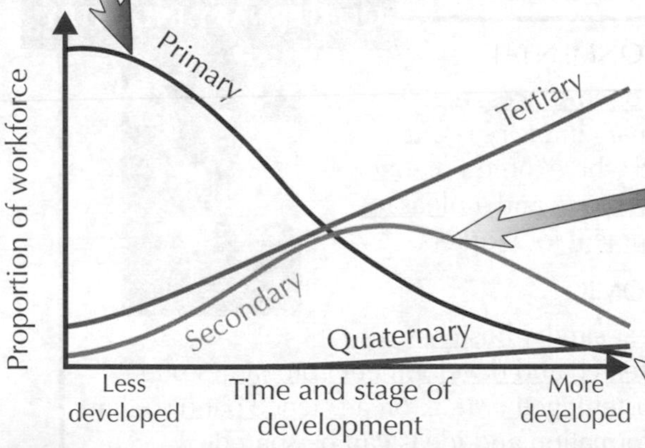

NICs are countries where the employment in secondary industry is increasing. As a country becomes more developed the percentage of people employed in secondary industry increases then decreases. This is because as infrastructure develops, businesses move their factories to less developed countries where labour is cheaper.

More developed countries

1) Few people work in primary industry because machines replace workers, and it's cheaper to import primary products from other countries, e.g. farm workers in poorer countries earn very little so the produce is cheap.
2) Fewer people work in secondary industry than in NICs (see above).
3) Most people work in tertiary industry because there's a skilled and educated workforce, and there's a high demand for services like banks and shops.
4) There's some quaternary industry because the country has lots of highly skilled labour and has money to invest in the technology needed.

Employment structure changes over time because countries become more wealthy, and education and infrastructure improve.

Learn the definition of each type of industry

There's a close link between a country's wealth and its employment structure. Primary industry doesn't make much profit whereas quaternary industry can make a lot. And more profit means a more developed country.

Location of Industry

Economic activity or industry doesn't just happen anywhere, you know. There are loads of factors that affect where things like farms, factories, shops and hospitals are located.

Many Factors *Influence the* ***Location of Industry***

PRIMARY INDUSTRY

ENVIRONMENTAL

1) Lots of raw materials, e.g. fisheries are by the coast.
2) A suitable climate — this affects the type of farming in an area, e.g. potatoes need a temperate climate and bananas need a tropical climate.
3) Good quality soil — farming will be most successful where there's nutrient-rich soil.

ECONOMIC

1) Cheap land, e.g. farming uses large areas of land so it's found where land is cheap.
2) Good transport routes, e.g. quarries need roads or railways to transport rock.

SECONDARY INDUSTRY

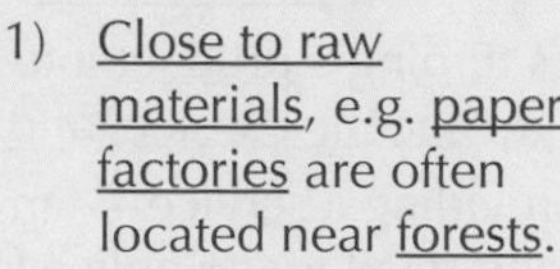

ENVIRONMENTAL

1) Close to raw materials, e.g. paper factories are often located near forests.
2) Plenty of flat land — it's easier to build a factory where the land is flat.
3) A local water supply — industries that use a lot of water are often located near rivers.

ECONOMIC

The 'market' means where the people are that buy the product.

1) A suitable local market, e.g. bakers are often based in residential areas.
2) Government grants, e.g. grants or loans may be provided to encourage industries to locate in particular areas.
3) Lots of workers, e.g. factories need lots of staff.
4) Good transport routes, e.g. factories are often near motorways, ports and railways.

TERTIARY INDUSTRY

ENVIRONMENTAL

Green open spaces, e.g. schools are often in areas that provide a pleasant environment for pupils.

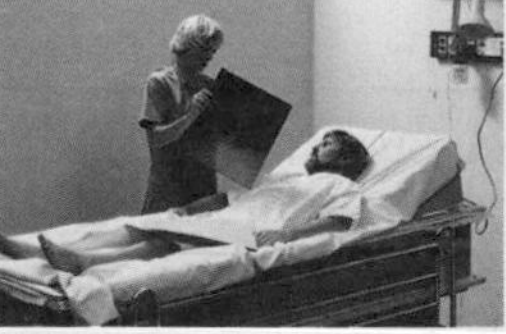

ECONOMIC

1) A suitable local market, e.g. you get lots of shops in cities as there are plenty of customers.
2) Good transport routes, e.g. shops are located near public transport routes so customers can get to them easily.
3) Skilled and educated workers, e.g. hospitals are often located near universities where there are skilled workers available.

SOCIAL

Enough local people to support the service, e.g. schools are found where there are lots of children.

QUATERNARY INDUSTRY

ENVIRONMENTAL

Green open spaces, e.g. quaternary industry is often located where there's plenty of open space and a pleasant environment for workers.

ECONOMIC

1) Near similar businesses — research and development companies often cluster together (e.g. on a science park) so that information and ideas can be shared.
2) Skilled and educated workers, e.g. scientific research companies are often near universities.

SOCIAL

Lots of nice quality housing, e.g. good houses nearby will encourage workers to move there.

Being near raw materials reduces transportation costs

Bit of a complicated page, this — industry is all about location, location, location. And because it's complicated you need to make extra sure you know it. Use the old drill — cover this page and scribble down as much as you can.

Location of Industry — Case Study

If you're not feeling very industrious, I think I can help you. A case study on why industry locates where it does should boost your enthusiasm — then you can turn this raw material into some exam fodder.

The Location of Industry in a Poorer Country — Kenya

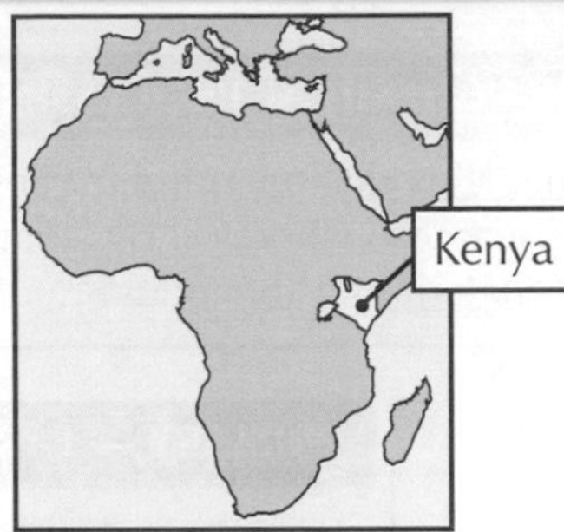

TERTIARY — TOURISM

There's a strong tourist industry in the Rift Valley. The area has several National Parks and lakes (e.g. Lake Turkana and Lake Magadi).

TERTIARY — TOURISM

There's a strong tourist industry near Mount Kenya because it's the second highest mountain in Africa and has a National Park.

SECONDARY — MANUFACTURING

There are lots of manufacturers in Nairobi that produce textiles, foods and drinks. The area has good transport links (including an airport) and a good labour supply — Nairobi's population is about 3 million people.

PRIMARY — FARMING

Livestock (e.g. camels and cattle) are reared on farms in the North Eastern Province because the climate is too dry for crops, but is suitable for grazing.

PRIMARY — FARMING

There are lots of farms in the Nyanza and Western Provinces that produce coffee, tea, tobacco and fruits — these are the areas that receive enough rainfall to grow crops.

TERTIARY — TOURISM

There's a strong tourist industry in the Coast Province because of its beaches, e.g. Diani Beach.

SECONDARY — MANUFACTURING

There are cement works in the Coast Province because they use limestone from the nearby deposits as a raw material.

PRIMARY — MINING

There's a large mine in Magadi that extracts trona (a mineral that's used to make glass). The mineral forms around Lake Magadi as the water evaporates.

Farming in Kenya is heavily influenced by the climate

This page is crammed with facts to learn. But, the good news is that Kenya is a less developed country so it doesn't have any quaternary industry. That means there are only three different types of industry to remember for this page.

Location of Industry — Case Study

Thought you could get away with just one case study on factors affecting the location of industry... think again.

The Location of Industry in a Richer Country — the UK

QUATERNARY — ELECTRONICS

Many electronics companies are based in the Central Lowlands of Scotland because of the local skilled labour supply — nearby universities such as Glasgow, Edinburgh and Heriot-Watt provide electronics and engineering graduates.

SECONDARY — CHEMICAL PROCESSING

There are chemicals works in North East England because they're near to offshore oil rigs that provide the raw material for the industry.

TERTIARY — TOURISM

There's a strong tourist industry in Cumbria because of the beautiful scenery.

PRIMARY — FARMING

There are lots of farms in Lincolnshire and East Anglia because of the good soil and mild climate. It's also very flat, which makes it easier to use large machinery such as tractors.

SECONDARY — MANUFACTURING

Government grants have encouraged car manufacturers to locate in Merseyside, e.g. in 1998 Jaguar cars began production at the Halewood plant after receiving a £50 million grant from the Government.

QUATERNARY — HIGH TECHNOLOGY

There are many high technology industries near Cambridge because the university provides educated and skilled workers.

PRIMARY — MINING

Coal mining has been a major industry in Nottinghamshire since the 13th century because of the coalfields in the area. Although most mines have now closed, a small amount of mining still goes on.

QUATERNARY — HIGH TECHNOLOGY

There are many high technology industries along the M4 corridor (the area near the M4 motorway). The area is close to universities (Bristol, Oxford and Reading) that provide skilled workers, and the motorway is good for communication.

TERTIARY — RETAIL

There are lots of shops in London because there are plenty of customers and good public transport. There are also excellent transport links for the delivery of products to shops.

Most of the quaternary industry is located near universities

So if you like a touch of farming, the east of England's the place to be. Industry within your local town will be based in suitable places for similar reasons. Try listing some local companies and working out why they might be based there.

Location of Industry Over Time

Time changes everything, honest. It even changes where industry locates — and not just from the revision chair to the exam room.

The Location of Industry Changes Over Time

The location of industry changes with time due to environmental, economic and social reasons:

	Primary Industry	Secondary Industry
ENVIRONMENTAL	• Raw materials become exhausted so industry moves elsewhere, e.g. quarries move once all the rock has been extracted. • Climate change means that some crops can be grown in new areas, e.g. increasing temperatures mean that vineyards have been set up in Kent.	New energy sources mean that industry doesn't have to be close to power sources, e.g. in the past many factories used coal for power so were near coalfields, but now they use electricity from the National Grid.
ECONOMIC	Lower costs make previously expensive areas cheaper, e.g. improvements in oil drilling technology mean that it's now economically viable (worth it) to reach much deeper oilfields.	• Changing capital (money) investment patterns encourage industry to locate to new areas, e.g. the UK Government and private investment in manufacturing in Scotland is encouraging industries to locate there.
SOCIAL	• Improved transport routes mean that primary industry can be located in more remote areas, e.g. better roads in Brazil mean forestry is possible in new parts of the Amazon rainforest. • Government policies change to allow industry in new areas, e.g. in 2008, Western Australia lifted its ban on uranium mining.	• Government policies change, which encourages industries to settle in different locations, e.g. the UK Government gives incentives to companies to open factories (and create jobs) in deprived areas. • Improved transport facilities mean more people have access to cars or public transport so can travel further to work, e.g. in the past many factories were located in city centres so workers could get there easily.

Social reasons are usually to do with changing transport or government policies

This isn't the most exciting page in the world, but it might come up in the exam, so unfortunately you need to know it. Cover up the page and see how much of this table you can scribble down. If you can't remember much, give it another read.

Location of Industry Over Time

You've covered the reasons why primary and secondary industry might change location, so now it's time to have a look at tertiary and quaternary industry.

The Location of Industry Changes Over Time

The location of industry changes with time due to environmental, economic and social reasons:

	Tertiary Industry	Quaternary Industry
ENVIRONMENTAL	• Workers increasingly want a nice working environment with pleasant surroundings, so industry moves in order to attract workers, e.g. offices move from the centre of a city to the outskirts. • Extreme environments are becoming more popular for tourists as travel gets cheaper and easier, e.g. the tourist industry is developing in Antarctica.	• Workers increasingly want to work in a nice environment with pleasant surroundings, so industry moves in order to attract them, e.g. research centres are often outside cities. • Some scientific research industries have environmental needs, e.g. research into GM crops needs land to grow experimental crops away from ordinary crops.
ECONOMIC	• Changing capital investment patterns encourage industry to locate to new areas, e.g. the UK Government has provided the money to build a new hospital development in Manchester and new mental health facilities in Merseyside.	• Changing capital investment patterns encourage industry to locate to new areas, e.g. increasing investment in digital telecommunications in rural areas encourages businesses to move there.
SOCIAL	• Improved transport facilities mean retailers don't have to be located in city centres for their customers to reach them, e.g. most people have access to cars now so there are more out-of-town shopping centres. • Shopping patterns have changed so people don't just shop on their local high street, e.g. many retailers sell products over the internet, so they don't need to be near their customers.	• The labour force moves as training and housing changes, e.g. electronics industries often locate near universities that have good electronics courses.

Workers in these industries want to work in nice environments

Make sure you know at least one example of each type of reason — environmental, economic and social for both types of industry on this page. That way you can tackle any exam question on it they can throw at you.

Environmental Impacts of Industry

Ah, impacts, impacts. As you might have guessed by now, geographers are obsessed by them.

Primary Industries Have a Huge Impact on the Environment

FARMING

1) Monoculture (growing just one type of crop) reduces biodiversity as there are fewer habitats.
2) Removing hedgerows to increase the area of farmland destroys habitats. It also increases soil erosion (hedgerows normally act as windbreaks).
3) Herbicides can kill wildflowers, pesticides can kill other insects (as well as pests) and fertilisers can pollute rivers, killing fish (this is called eutrophication).
4) Making fertilisers, pesticides and herbicides uses fossil fuels, which adds to global warming.
5) Cows produce methane, which also adds to global warming.

Biodiversity is the number and variety of organisms. A habitat is where an organism lives.

There's loads more about global warming on page 36.

MINING

1) Mining destroys large areas of land, so there are fewer habitats and food sources for animals and birds. This reduces biodiversity.
2) Mining uses lots of water, so it can deplete water sources.
3) Some kinds of mining can cause water pollution.

FISHING

1) Overfishing depletes resources and upsets food chains.
2) Fishing boats can leak oil and diesel, which kills aquatic animals.

FORESTRY

1) Fewer trees means fewer habitats and food sources for animals and birds. This reduces biodiversity.
2) Soil erosion is more common as there are fewer trees to hold the soil together.
3) Trees remove CO_2 from the atmosphere when they photosynthesise, so without them less CO_2 is removed. More forestry means more CO_2 in the atmosphere, which adds to global warming.
4) Without trees, less water is removed from the soil and evaporated into the atmosphere. So fewer clouds form and rainfall in the area is reduced. Reduced rainfall reduces plant growth.

Secondary Industries Cause Pollution

1) Factories can cause land, air and water pollution, e.g. dyes from textile factories can pollute rivers and sulfur dioxide emissions from metal works can cause acid rain.
2) Habitats are destroyed if factories are built in the countryside.
3) Some factories use a huge amount of energy, e.g. ice cream factories. This energy usually comes from burning fossil fuels, so adds to global warming.

Tertiary and Quaternary Industries Use a Lot of Energy

1) Tertiary and quaternary industries use a lot of energy, e.g. to run computers, shops or vehicles.
2) This energy usually comes from burning fossil fuels, so adds to global warming.
3) Also, all the resources these industries use cause an impact when they're manufactured. E.g. trees are cut down and made into paper in factories.

Maybe I'll turn my computer off standby then...

Crikey, industry has a lot of environmental impacts (especially primary and secondary industry). Check that you know them so you can trot them out in neat handwriting on demand (if it's illegible you won't get any marks).

Development and Environmental Impacts

Industry is good for a country's pocket (it helps its economy to develop), but it's not great for its back garden. There are things that can be done to make it better for the back garden though.

Economic Development often Damages the Environment

1) An increase in industry in an area helps it to develop economically — it creates more jobs, which increases the wealth of the area and the local people.
2) But some industries damage the environment a lot.
3) This means there's conflict between economic development (by increasing industry) and protecting the environment.
4) Economic development can aim to be sustainable though. To be sustainable it has to increase the wealth of an area in a way that doesn't stop people in the future getting what they need. Basically this means not depleting resources or damaging the environment irreversibly.

There are Ways to Make Economic Development More Sustainable

Economic development can be more sustainable if the industries that cause it reduce their environmental impacts. For example:

FARMING

1) Use fewer herbicides, pesticides and fertilisers (although this reduces crop yield).
2) Maintain hedgerows instead of removing them.

FORESTRY

Laws can be introduced that make logging companies plant one tree for each one cut down. This means that there will still be trees for the future.
It also reduces soil erosion.

FACTORIES

1) Laws to reduce water, air and land pollution can be introduced.
2) Building on brownfield sites (derelict areas that have been used, but aren't being used any more) stops habitat destruction.
3) Energy use can be reduced by using more energy efficient devices.

MINING

1) Laws can be introduced to help reduce water pollution.
2) The habitats in a quarry can be restored once it's disused, e.g. by planting trees and creating ponds.

FISHING

1) Quotas (limits on the number of fish caught) can be introduced to stop overfishing.
2) Fish can be raised on fish farms to prevent wild stocks from running out.

OFFICES, SHOPS and VEHICLES

1) Turning off computers instead of leaving them on standby reduces energy use.
2) Using more efficient vehicles reduces the amount of fossil fuel burnt.

Economic development's more sustainable if you reduce the environmental impacts

Economic development in a lot of countries isn't sustainable and the environment is suffering. The best way to make it more sustainable is to protect the environment by introducing things like environmental laws and energy efficient devices.

Development and Environmental Impacts — Case Study

Right — case study time.

Manufacturing is Helping Economic Development in South China

1) The Pearl River Delta (PRD) is an area in the Guangdong province of China that has lots of industry. There are lots of big companies like IBM®, Wal-Mart® and SAMSUNG.
2) The industries increase economic development by increasing the wealth of the area. In 1980 the area had a GDP of US$8 billion and by 2001 it had grown to about US$100 billion.
3) Industry has created lots of jobs in the area. E.g. Dongguan has over 25 000 factories and Honda employs over 6000 people in Guangzhou and Zhongshan.

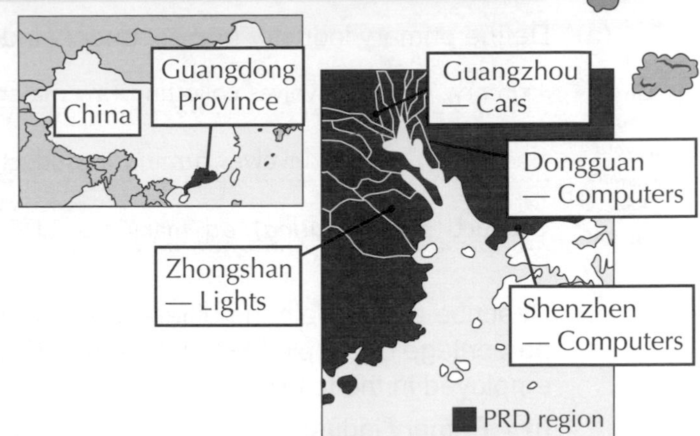

But There are Environmental Impacts

1) There's so much air pollution that the area's often covered in smog. Lots of it comes from power plants that burn coal. For example, the levels of sulfur dioxide and nitrogen dioxide in the air in the PRD area are around two to three times higher than in other areas of the Guangdong province. These gases cause acid rain.
2) Pollution from factory waste and untreated sewage also means that the water quality of the area is very poor. For example, Pearl River water in Guangzhou is only suitable for farm use (not for drinking or domestic use).
3) Humans aren't the only ones suffering from the pollution — it's affecting wildlife habitats too. The Pearl River drains into the South China Sea so this area is also affected. Local species such as the Chinese white dolphin are becoming endangered as a result.

Management Strategies Aim to Reduce the Impacts

The environmental impacts of industry in the PRD are being managed in several ways. For example:

> The Pearl River Delta Air Quality Management Plan aimed to reduce the amount of air pollution by 2010. They've tried to reduce the amount of sulfur dioxide emitted from power plants by 40% compared to 1997 levels. One way to do this is to reduce the dependence on coal for energy production by using natural gas instead, which produces fewer toxic emissions.

> The Government has pledged about US$7.1 billion to help clean up the Pearl River. It's being used to build around 30 sewage works and water treatment facilities — these will reduce the amount of untreated domestic sewage and industrial waste that goes into the river.

These management strategies are sustainable because they aim to reduce air and water pollution without stopping industry from expanding or closing down factories. This means that people will still be able to live and work in the PRD in the future as there will still be jobs and resources like water for them to use.

The Pearl River Delta is a hive of economic activity

The Pearl River Delta is a great example of how economic development can be unsustainable — learn what industry there is in the area, what the environmental impacts are and a couple of ways people are trying to reduce them.

Worked Exam Questions

Take your time to go through these worked exam answers — something similar might come up in the exam...

1 Study **Figure 1**, which shows the percentage of people employed in different industries in Country A (a developed country) and Country B (a developing country).

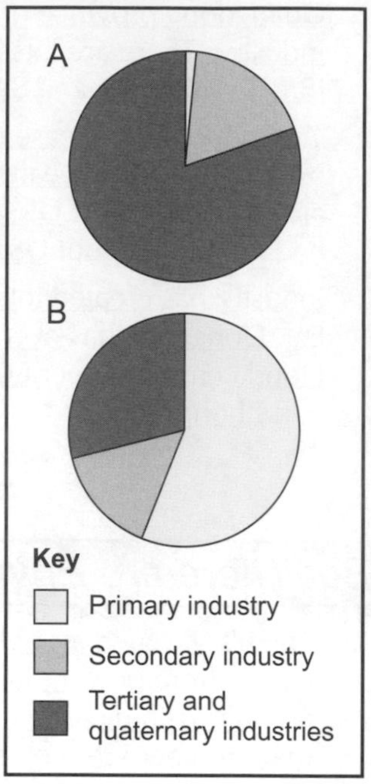

(a) Define primary industry and secondary industry.

Give examples in your answers whenever you can.

Primary industry involves collecting raw materials, e.g. farming.

Secondary industry involves turning a product into another product (manufacturing), e.g. making textiles.

(2 marks)

Figure 1

A

B

Key
Primary industry
Secondary industry
Tertiary and quaternary industries

(b) Describe and explain the difference between the percentage of people in Country A and Country B employed in the following industries:

(i) Primary industry

Many more people are employed in primary industry in Country B than in Country A. This is because in Country A machines have replaced workers and it's cheaper to import primary products from other countries.

(3 marks)

(ii) Tertiary and quaternary industries

Many more people are employed in tertiary and quaternary industries in Country A than in Country B. This is because Country A has a larger skilled and educated workforce, a higher demand for services like banks and shops and money to invest in the technology needed for quaternary industry.

Start by describing the difference, then give reasons for it.

(4 marks)

(c) 15% of people in Country B are employed in secondary industry.

(i) Describe and explain how this figure will change as Country B develops.

The percentage of people employed in secondary industry will initially increase. This is because as infrastructure improves, businesses will move their factories to Country B as labour will be cheap there. It will then decrease as Country B becomes more developed because it will be cheaper for businesses to move their factories to less developed countries.

(4 marks)

(ii) Describe two ways secondary industry can affect the environment.

Factories can cause land, air and water pollution, e.g. emissions from metal works can cause acid rain. Also, habitats are destroyed if factories are built in the countryside.

(2 marks)

Exam Questions

1 Study **Figure 1**, which shows the location of different industries in Friching in 1950 and in 2000.

Figure 1

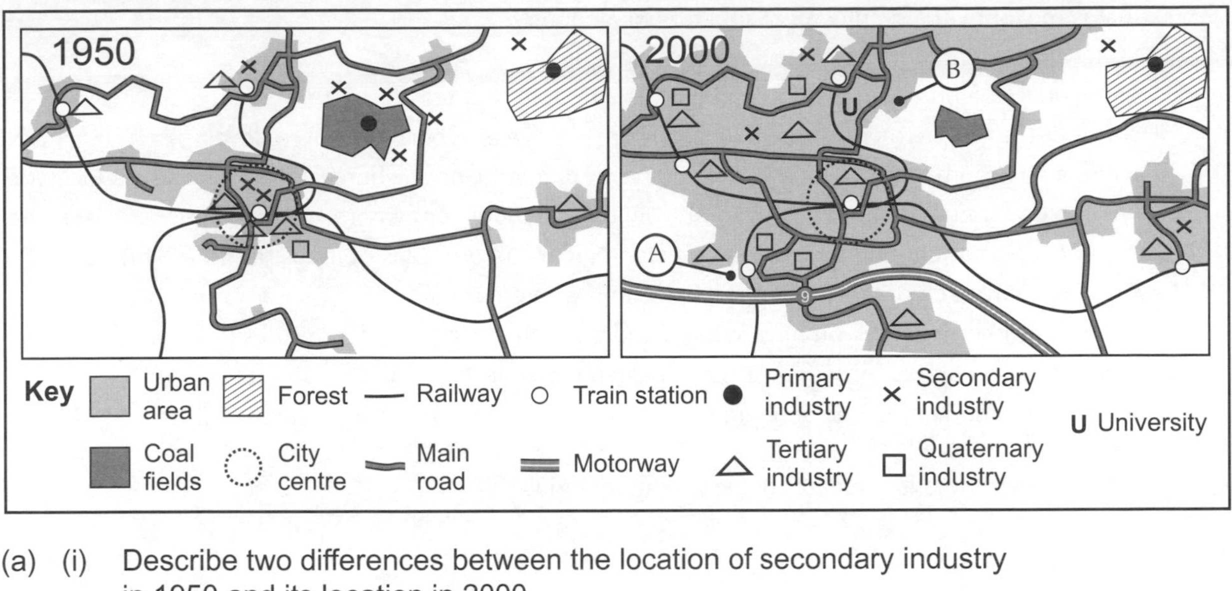

(a) (i) Describe two differences between the location of secondary industry in 1950 and its location in 2000.

....

....

(2 marks)

(ii) Suggest one environmental reason and one social reason for these changes.

....

....

....

(2 marks)

(b) Plans are being drawn up for a shopping centre at the site labelled A on **Figure 1**. Suggest three reasons why this is a good location for a shopping centre.

....

....

....

(3 marks)

(c) Himilton Computing, a company specialising in IT development, is relocating to Friching. It is considering basing itself at the site labelled B on **Figure 1**. Explain whether or not this is a good location for the company.

....

....

....

....

(3 marks)

Revision Summary for Section 12

So, you've reached the end of the industry section then. Try out these questions — you should be able to answer most, if not all, of them. If you do get stuck, don't be shy about going back and checking the answer.

1) What is meant by the employment structure of a country?
2) Define what tertiary industry is and give an example.
3) Define what quaternary industry is and give an example.
4) How does the employment structure of a country change as it becomes more developed?
5) Give one environmental and one economic factor that influences where primary industry is located.
6) Give one environmental and one economic factor that influences where secondary industry is located.
7) a) Name a poorer country you have studied and give four examples of industries found there.
   b) Explain why each of those industries is located where it is.
8) a) Name a richer country you have studied and give four examples of industries found there.
   b) Explain why each of those industries is located where it is.
9) Give one environmental, one economic and one social reason why the location of primary industry changes over time.
10) Give two environmental impacts of these primary industries:
    a) Farming
    b) Mining
    c) Fishing
    d) Forestry
11) How do tertiary and quaternary industries affect the environment?
12) Explain why there's often conflict between economic development and protecting the environment.
13) Give two ways to make primary industry more sustainable.
14) Give two ways to make secondary industry more sustainable.
15) Give two ways to make tertiary and quaternary industry more sustainable.
16) a) For an area you have studied describe how industry has contributed to economic development there.
    b) What have the environmental impacts of the industry been?
    c) What is being done in the area to reduce the impacts?

Globalisation Basics

Globalisation is a long word and a complicated subject. Better get started then...

Globalisation is the Process of Economies Becoming More Integrated

1) Globalisation is the process of all the world's economies becoming integrated — it's the whole world coming together like a single community.
2) It happens because of international trade, international investment and improvements in communications.
3) Countries have become interdependent as a result of globalisation — they rely on each other for resources or services.

Globalisation is also about cultures and political policies becoming more integrated.

Improvements in Communications have Increased Globalisation

Improvements in ICT (Information and Communication Technology) and transport have increased globalisation by increasing trade and investment:

ICT

1) Improvements in ICT include e-mail, the internet, mobile phones and phone lines that can carry more information and faster.
2) This has made it quicker and easier for businesses all over the world to communicate with each other. For example, a company can have its headquarters in one country and easily communicate with branches in other countries. No time is lost so it's really efficient.

Transport

1) Improvements in transport include more airports, high-speed trains and larger ships.
2) This has made it quicker and easier for people all over the world to communicate with each other face to face.
3) It's also made it easier for companies to get supplies from all over the world, and to distribute their product all over the world. They don't have to be located near to their suppliers or their product market anymore.

These improvements have allowed the development of call centres abroad and localised industrial regions:

Call centres abroad

1) Call centres are used by some companies to handle telephone enquiries about their business.
2) Improvements in ICT mean that it's just as easy for people to phone a faraway country as it is to phone people in their own country.
3) So a lot of call centres are now based abroad because the labour is cheaper, which reduces running costs.

EXAMPLE: In 2004 Aviva (an insurance company) moved 950 call centre jobs from the UK to India and Sri Lanka, as it costs less there (e.g. it costs 40% less in India).

Localised industrial regions

Improvements in ICT and transport have allowed some industries to develop around a specific region that's useful to them, but still have global connections to get all the other things they need.

EXAMPLE: A lot of motorsport companies have offices in Oxfordshire and Northamptonshire, e.g. the Renault Formula 1 team have their headquarters there. They're close to the Silverstone race circuit (so they can test their cars) and the area has lots of skilled workers. People like drivers and engineers can easily fly into the area. The manufacturers use the internet to easily send and receive information and data about their cars to people around the world.

Learn the definition of globalisation and why it's increased

Globalisation is a bit of a weird concept so don't panic if you don't get it straight away. This page has a lot of information on it so just take it slowly — make sure you understand it before moving on to the rest of the section.

Trans-National Corporations (TNCs)

You can't get too far into the topic of globalisation before stumbling across Trans-National Corporations.

TNCs also Increase Globalisation

1) TNCs are companies that produce products, sell products or are located in more than one country. For example, Sony is a TNC — it manufactures electronic products in China and Japan, and sells many of them in Europe and the USA.
2) TNCs are usually very rich companies that employ lots of people and have a large output (they make loads of products every year). For example:

   Ford is an American-owned TNC that makes cars. In 2008, it produced over 5 million cars worldwide. It also employs over 200 000 people at about 90 different sites around the world.

3) TNCs increase globalisation by linking together countries through the production and sale of goods.
4) They also bring the culture from their country of origin to many different countries, e.g. McDonald's brings Western-style fast food to other countries.

TNCs are also known as multinational companies (MNCs).

TNCs Affect Economic Development

1) TNCs create jobs in an area. This increases the wealth of the area (due to taxes) and the wealth of the local people (due to employment).
2) Taxes are used to improve infrastructure (e.g. roads) and services (e.g. schools, hospitals, etc.). People also have more money to spend. Both of these things attract more businesses to the area (including more TNCs), creating even more jobs, and so on...
3) This cycle (more jobs, leading to more services, leading to more jobs...) is called the multiplier effect.
4) TNC factories are often located in poorer countries because labour is cheaper, which means they make more profit. (See page 202 for more reasons why they're located in poorer countries.)
5) TNC headquarters and research centres are usually located in richer countries because there are more skilled and educated people (but there are some TNC factories in richer countries as well).

TNCs have Advantages and Disadvantages

Advantages	Disadvantages
TNCs create jobs in all the countries they're located in.	Employees in poorer countries may be paid lower wages than employees in richer countries.
Employees in poorer countries get a more reliable income compared to jobs like farming.	Employees in poorer countries may have to work long hours in poor conditions.
When they locate to poorer countries, TNCs create some skilled jobs, e.g. jobs in factory offices. This encourages more education and training in the area.	Most TNCs come from richer countries so the profits go back there — they aren't reinvested in the poorer countries they operate in.
TNCs spend money to improve the local infrastructure, e.g. airports and roads.	Large sites will attract lots of traffic, which increases pollution in the area.
New technology (e.g. computers) and skills are brought to poorer countries.	The jobs created in poorer countries aren't secure — the TNC could relocate the jobs to another country at any time.
Local companies supply the TNCs, increasing their income.	Other local companies may struggle to find business or workers, so shut down.

TNCs are everywhere — and I mean everywhere...

TNCs are companies that do business in more than one country — walk down your local high street and you'll see plenty of examples. Close the book and see if you can scribble down the advantages and disadvantages of TNCs.

TNCs — Case Study

You might need to know a TNC case study for the exam, so here's a lovely one for you.

Wal-Mart® is a Retail TNC with Headquarters in the USA

1) Wal-Mart began in 1962 when Sam Walton opened the first store in Arkansas, USA.
2) More stores opened across Arkansas, then across the USA, and more recently across the world, e.g. in Mexico, Argentina, China, Japan, Brazil, Canada and the UK (where it's called ASDA).
3) Wal-Mart sells a variety of products, e.g. food, clothes and electrical goods.
4) Wal-Mart is the biggest retailer in the world — it owns over 8000 stores and employs over 2 million people.

Wal-Mart has Positive Effects...

1 Wal-Mart creates lots of jobs in different countries, e.g. in construction, manufacturing and retail services. E.g. in Mexico, Wal-Mart employs over 150 000 people and in Argentina, three new stores opened in 2008, creating nearly 450 jobs.

2 Local companies and farmers supply goods to Wal-Mart, increasing their business. E.g. in Canada, Wal-Mart works with over 6000 Canadian suppliers, creating around US$11 billion of business for them each year.

■ = Location of Wal-Mart stores

3 Wal-Mart offers more skilled jobs in poorer countries. E.g. all the Wal-Mart stores in China, are managed by local people.

5 The company invests money in sustainable development. E.g. in Puerto Rico, 23 Wal-Mart stores are having solar panels fitted on their roofs to generate electricity.

4 Wal-Mart donates hundreds of millions of dollars to improve things like health and the environment in countries where it's based. E.g. in 2008 in Argentina, Wal-Mart donated US$77 000 to local projects and gave food and money to help feed nearly 12 000 poor people.

...and Negative Effects

1) Some companies that supply Wal-Mart have long working hours. E.g. Beximco in Bangladesh supplies clothing. Bangladesh has a maximum 60 hour working week, but some people claim employees at Beximco regularly work 80 hours a week.
2) Not all Wal-Mart workers are paid the same wages. E.g. factory workers in the USA earn around $6 an hour, but factory workers in China earn less than $1 an hour (although this is quite a lot in China).
3) Some studies have suggested that Wal-Mart stores can cause smaller shops in the area to shut — they can't compete with the low prices and range of products on sale.
4) The stores are often very large and out-of-town, which can cause environmental problems. Building them takes up large areas of land and people driving to them causes traffic and pollution. For example, the largest Wal-Mart store is in Hawaii and it covers over 27 000 m^2 — that's over three times the size of the football pitch at Wembley Stadium.

Wal-Mart has over 8000 stores

If you know squillions of details for another TNC case study then that's fine. If you don't then get your memorising hat on and get learning — you need to be able to jot down lots of facts and figures without looking at the page.

Change in Manufacturing Location

TNCs can put their factories anywhere in the world, but some countries are more attractive than others. This has meant some countries are now stuffed full of factories and others are waving bye bye to them.

The *Manufacturing Industry* is *Growing* in *Some Countries*...

1) Some countries that have traditionally relied on agriculture have seen a massive growth in their manufacturing industries recently — this process is called industrialisation.
2) These countries are called NICs (Newly Industrialising Countries). They include places like India, China and Brazil.
3) TNCs have increased manufacturing in NICs by basing factories there — here are five reasons why they do this:

An increase in manufacturing creates jobs.

1 Cheap labour

The minimum wage is the lowest amount a company is allowed to pay someone. It's set by governments. Some NICs don't have a minimum wage. In the ones that do it's much lower than in richer countries, e.g. the UK. This reduces the cost of manufacturing goods because factory workers are paid less.

2 Long working hours

The rules about working hours aren't as strict in NICs as in places like the EU. This means employees work longer hours so more product can be made in a day.

3 Laxer health and safety regulations

There are fewer health and safety regulations in NICs and they're often not enforced. This lowers the cost of manufacturing goods because less money is spent on increasing the safety of factories.

4 Prohibition of strikes

Some NICs don't allow employees to strike, e.g. to protest against low pay. This means money isn't lost due to employees stopping work.

5 Tax incentives and tax free zones

Some NICs offer TNCs a tax reduction if they move their manufacturing to the country. Some NICs have tax free zones — the TNCs don't have to pay taxes if they move their manufacturing to a specific area of the country. Both of these increase the profits of the TNC because they pay lower taxes.

...and *Declining* in *Other Countries*

1) Most rich countries have a history of manufacturing goods, e.g. cars have been manufactured in the UK for many years. In recent years manufacturing in some rich countries has decreased.
2) This process is called deindustrialisation.
3) Deindustrialisation can happen for a number of reasons, for example:
   - Manufacturers move factories abroad because they can produce goods more cheaply there.
   - Manufacturers close down because they can't compete with the price of goods manufactured abroad.
4) When deindustrialisation happens a lot of manual workers (e.g. factory and dock workers) lose their jobs. Also, as factories close some buildings become derelict. But, there's often an increase in service industries like banking and insurance. These industries pay people higher wages than manufacturing so deindustrialisation isn't all bad.

Producing goods more cheaply increases profits

The basic formula is 'more factories here = less factories there'. Get that fact fixed in your grey matter, then re-read the reasons why it's the height of fashion to put your factory in a NIC. Don't forget about deindustrialisation either.

Change in Manufacturing Location — Case Study

You're not getting away that easily — here's another case study for you. This page is about China's development into an economic giant and the reasons why manufacturing is moving to the country.

China is one of the World's Fastest Growing Industrial Economies

1) In 30 years China has gone from being a mainly agricultural economy to a strong manufacturing economy. It's now the third largest economy in the world after the US and Japan.
2) The percentage of China's GDP that came from agriculture fell between 1978 and 2004, from about 30% to less than 15%.
3) During the same time the number of products manufactured in China has increased rapidly, e.g. about 4000 colour TVs were made in China in 1978 compared to nearly 75 million in 2004.
4) China manufactures loads of different products like clothes, computers and toys.
5) Lots of TNCs have factories in China, for example NIKE, Hewlett-Packard and Disney.

GDP is the total value of goods and services a country produces in a year.

There are Lots of Reasons for the Growth in Manufacturing

1 Cheap labour

There's no single minimum wage in China — it's different all over the country. For example, in Shenzhen the minimum wage is about £90 per month and in Beijing it's about £70 per month. This makes labour in China much cheaper than other countries, e.g. in the UK the minimum wage is about £990 per month.

2 Long working hours

Chinese law says that people are only allowed to work 40 hours per week, with a maximum of 36 hours of overtime per month. This isn't always enforced though — for example, the manufacturing company foxconn® said that some of its Chinese factory workers have done about 80 hours of overtime per month to maximise the production of goods.

3 Laxer health and safety regulations

The health and safety laws in China are similar to other countries but they aren't heavily enforced, e.g. over the past decade, hundreds of factory workers have been treated for mercury poisoning despite strict laws on working with toxic materials.

4 Prohibition of strikes

Chinese workers can go on strike but the All-China Federation of Trade Unions (ACFTU) is required by law to get people back to work as quickly as possible so productivity is maximised. It's illegal for people to join any union other than the ACFTU.

5 Tax incentives and tax free zones

China has many Special Economic Zones (SEZs) that offer tax incentives to foreign businesses. Foreign manufacturers usually pay no tax for the first two years in the zone, 7.5% for the next three years and then 15% from then on (which is still half of the usual 30% tax elsewhere in China). Shenzhen is one of the most successful SEZs. There's been around $30 billion of investment by TNCs. Factories in Shenzhen make products for companies like Wal-Mart®, Dell™ and IBM®.

China's economy is growing rapidly due to a boom in manufacturing

Loads of TNCs have factories in China, so it's a safe bet that you're within about a metre of something that was made in China. Check that you can give all the reasons why manufacturing in China has gone through the roof.

Globalisation and Energy Demand

Globalisation has led to a huge increase in the demand for energy, and this has had some major impacts.

The Global Demand for Energy is Increasing

Globalisation has increased the wealth of some poorer countries so people are buying more things. A lot of these things use energy, e.g. cars, fridges and televisions. This increases the global demand for energy.

There are two other reasons why the global demand for energy is increasing:

1) Technological advances have created loads of new devices that all need energy, e.g. computers, mobile phones and MP3 players. These are becoming more popular so more energy is needed.
2) In 2000 the world population was just over 6 billion and it's projected to increase to just over 9 billion in 2050 — more people means more energy is needed.

Producing More Energy has Lots of Impacts

Most of the energy produced in the world comes from burning fossil fuels (i.e. oil, gas and coal). Nuclear power, wood and renewable sources (e.g. solar power) are also used to produce some energy. Increasing energy production to meet demand has social, economic and environmental impacts:

Social impacts

1) More power plants will have to be built to increase energy production. Power plants are extremely large — people may have to move out of an area so a power plant can be built.
2) The waste from nuclear power plants is radioactive. If it leaks out from where it's stored it can cause death and illness, and can contaminate large areas of land. If more nuclear power plants are built to increase energy production, there's a higher risk of radioactive waste leaking out.
3) Increasing energy production will create jobs — people will be needed to build more power stations, run them and maintain them.

Environmental impacts

1) Burning fossil fuels releases carbon dioxide (CO_2). This adds to global warming. Global warming will cause the sea level to rise, cause more severe weather and force species to move (to find better conditions) or make them extinct (if they can't move and it gets too hot). Using more fossil fuels will increase global warming.
2) Burning fossil fuels also releases other gases that dissolve in water in the atmosphere and cause acid rain. Acid rain can kill animals and plants. Using more fossil fuels will increase acid rainfall.
3) Gathering wood for fuel can cause deforestation (removing trees from forests). Removing trees destroys habitats for animals and other plants. Using more wood for fuel will increase deforestation.
4) Mining for coal causes air and water pollution. It also removes large areas of land, which destroys habitats. More coal mining will cause more pollution and destroy more habitats.
5) Transporting oil is a risky business — oil pipes and tankers can leak, spilling oil. Oil spills can kill birds and fish. Using more oil means more needs to be transported, increasing the risk of spills.

Economic impact

Countries with lots of energy resources, e.g. lots of coal, will become richer as energy demand increases — countries with few resources will need to buy energy from them.

Learn why energy demand is increasing, and the impacts it has

Producing energy has a lot of impacts and the impacts are bigger the more energy you produce. See how many of them you can remember — make sure you can jot down a mix of social, environmental and economic impacts.

Globalisation and Food Supply

If you've ever wondered how your local supermarket manages to stock strawberries in the middle of January, then this is the page for you. If not then I'm afraid you're going to have to read it anyway...

Food Production has become *Globalised*

1) Before the 1960s people mainly ate a small range of seasonal food that had been grown in their own country (often in their local area).

2) People now demand to have a range of foods all year round, regardless of growing seasons. This has led to globalisation of the food industry — food is produced in foreign countries and imported.

3) The increase in the world's population also means more food is needed — the demand has increased.

4) Countries are trying to increase food production to meet this demand, but some can't produce enough to feed their population so food has to be imported too.

Globalisation of *Food Supply* has *Social* and *Economic Impacts*

Social

1) Some farmers are switching from subsistence farming (where food is produced for their family) to commercial farming (where food is produced to sell).
2) This is because they can make more money due to the high demand for food.
3) This reduces the amount of food produced for local people so they have to import food (which is more expensive).
4) If food prices go down, then farmers might not earn enough money to buy food for themselves.

Crops sold to make money are called cash crops.

Economic

1) Using chemicals (e.g. fertilisers, pesticides and insecticides) helps to produce lots of food. These chemicals can be very expensive — farmers may have to borrow money to buy the chemicals and this gets farmers into debt.
2) Farmers can generate a steady income by producing food for export to other countries.

©iStockphoto.com/Federico Rostango

More food is needed and people want a greater variety of it

Switching from subsistence to commercial farming is mostly happening in poorer countries (in richer countries nearly all farming is commercial anyway). Some farmers benefit from this, but some get into poverty or debt.

Globalisation and Food Supply

As well as social and economic impacts, globalisation has some knock-on effects on the environment and politics.

Globalisation of Food Supply also has Environmental and Political Impacts

Environmental

1) Transporting food produces CO_2. The distance food is transported to the market is called food miles. The higher the food miles, the more CO_2 is produced. CO_2 adds to global warming.

2) The amount of CO_2 produced during growing and transporting a food is called its carbon footprint. A larger carbon footprint means more CO_2 and more global warming.

3) Imported foods have to be transported a long way so have high food miles and a large carbon footprint. A benefit of importing food is that a wide range of food is available all year round. Another benefit is it helps meet increasing demand in countries that can't produce a lot.

4) More food could be produced locally by energy intensive farming — pesticides, fertilisers and machinery are used to produce large quantities of food. Although food miles are low, loads of energy is needed to make chemicals and run the machinery. Energy production creates lots of CO_2 so local energy intensive farming can have a large carbon footprint.

5) To produce more food some farmers use marginal land (land that's not really suitable for farming), e.g. steep hillsides or the edges of deserts. The soil in marginal land is thin and it's quickly eroded by farming, degrading the environment.

Political

1) Lots of water is needed to produce lots of food.
2) Farmers in countries with low rainfall need to irrigate their land with water from rivers and lakes.
3) As the demand for water increases (due to the increased demand for food) there may be hostilities between countries that use the same water source for irrigation. For example, there's tension between Egypt, Sudan and Ethiopia because they all take water from the River Nile.

Globalisation of food supply has local and global impacts

Farming used to be a local business but nowadays our food comes flying in from all over the world (or trundling in on a lorry, train or ship). Check that you know all the effects — and don't forget the social and economic impacts on p. 205.

Reducing the Impacts of Globalisation

One impact of globalisation is that more people are gluttons for energy. Producing more energy using fossil fuels has plenty of impacts, but worry not, things can be done to make producing energy greener.

Using Renewable Energy Is a Sustainable Way to Meet Energy Demands

1) Energy production needs to be sustainable — it needs to allow people alive today to get what they need (energy), but without stopping people in the future getting what they need. This basically means not damaging the environment or using up resources faster than they can be replaced.
2) Producing energy using fossil fuels (i.e. coal, oil and gas) isn't sustainable.
3) This is because fossil fuels are non-renewable — this means they'll eventually run out so there won't be any for future generations.
4) Using fossil fuels also damages the environment, e.g. burning them produces CO_2, which causes global warming.
5) Energy produced from renewable sources is sustainable because it doesn't cause long-term environmental damage and the resource won't run out. Here are some renewable energy sources:

Have a look back at p. 204 for more on the impacts of producing energy.

- Wind — the wind turns blades on a wind turbine to generate electrical energy.
- Biomass — biomass is material that comes from organisms that are alive (e.g. animal waste) or were recently alive (e.g. plants). It can be burnt to release energy. It can also be processed to produce biofuels, which are then burnt to release energy.
- Solar power — energy from the sun can be used to heat water, cook food and generate electrical energy.
- Hydroelectric power — water is trapped behind a dam and forced through tunnels. The water turns turbines in the tunnels to generate electrical energy.

6) Producing energy from renewable sources contributes to sustainable development — it allows areas to develop (i.e. use more energy to improve the lives of the people there) in a sustainable way.

Case Study — Spain is Using Wind Energy to Meet Demand

1) Spain's energy consumption has increased 66% since 1990.
2) Some of the extra energy needed is being produced using wind turbines — the amount of energy produced from wind has increased 16-fold since 1995.
3) Spain is ideal for wind farms because it has large, windy areas where not many people live. This means wind farms can be built without annoying too many people.
4) Spain has over 400 wind farms and a total of over 12 000 turbines.
5) In 2008, 11.5% of Spain's energy was supplied by wind energy.
6) The wind farms have had positive and negative impacts:

Wind farms are groups of wind turbines.

Positive impacts

1) In 2008, using wind energy reduced Spain's CO_2 emissions by over 20 million tonnes.
2) In 2008, using wind energy saved Spain from importing about €1.2 billion of gas and oil.
3) Spain's wind energy industry has created around 40 000 jobs.

Negative impacts

1) Some conservationists say the wind farms are a danger to migrating birds.
2) Some people think wind farms are ugly — turbines can be seen from miles away.
3) Some people think the wind farms are too noisy.

Make sure you know the different types of renewable energy sources

You've already learned about the problems of producing more energy using fossil fuels, so it should come as a bit of a relief to find out that there are alternative sources of energy, and that some countries are putting them to use already.

Reducing the Impacts of Globalisation

This is the last page about globalisation you need to learn, then it's just a case of seeing how much you remember.

The Kyoto Protocol helps to Reduce Carbon Dioxide Emissions

1) Globalisation has increased the demand for energy (see p. 204) — more fossil fuels are being used to meet the demand, producing loads of CO_2 and adding to global warming.
2) The international community is working together to reduce the amount of CO_2 they produce because the problem of global warming affects everyone.
3) The Kyoto Protocol is an international agreement that has been signed by most countries in the world to cut emissions of CO_2 and other gases by 2012. Each country is set an emissions target, e.g. the UK has agreed to reduce emissions by 12.5% by 2012.
4) Another part of the protocol is the carbon credits trading scheme:

- Countries that come under their emissions target get carbon credits which they can sell to countries that aren't meeting their emissions target. This means there's a reward for having low emissions.
- Countries can also earn carbon credits by helping poorer countries to reduce their emissions. This means poorer countries will be able to reduce their emissions more quickly.

International agreements are also called international directives.

Other International Agreements help to Reduce Pollution

1) Globalisation has increased the emission of gases that cause pollution like acid rain (see p. 204).
2) There are international agreements that help to reduce pollution, e.g. the Gothenburg Protocol.
3) The Gothenburg Protocol sets emissions targets for European countries and the US. The protocol aims to cut harmful gas emissions to reduce acid rain and other pollution.

Recycling Reduces Waste Created by Globalisation

1) Globalisation means people have access to more products at low prices, so they can afford to be more wasteful, e.g. people throw away damaged clothes instead of repairing them.
2) Things that are thrown away get taken to landfill sites — the amount of waste going to landfill has increased as globalisation has increased.
3) One way to reduce this impact on a local scale is to recycle waste to make new products, e.g. recycling old drinks cans to make new ones.

Buying Local can Reduce the Impacts of a Globalised Food Supply

1) In recent years celebrity chefs, food writers and campaigners have encouraged people to eat more locally-produced food.
2) Buying local food helps to reduce food miles (see p. 206) because it hasn't been transported a long way. It also helps to support local farmers and businesses.
3) However, if people only buy locally it can put people in poorer countries who export food out of a job.

The impacts of globalisation can be reduced by everyone

As you've seen, globalisation can have some pretty serious impacts, but the good news is that we can all do our bit by recycling, buying locally-produced food and using less energy. Now, time for some lovely exam practice.

Worked Exam Questions

Exam questions tend to follow a pattern, so if you learn a few model answers now you'll have a really good idea of how to answer questions once you get into the exam. This page gives you a few model answers to have a look at.

1 Study **Figure 1**, which shows the distribution of Mega Lomania (a TNC) around the globe.

(a) What is meant by the term 'Trans-National Corporation' (TNC)?

TNCs are companies that produce products, sell products or are located in more than one country.

Make sure you know the definitions of things like TNCs.

(1 mark)

Figure 1

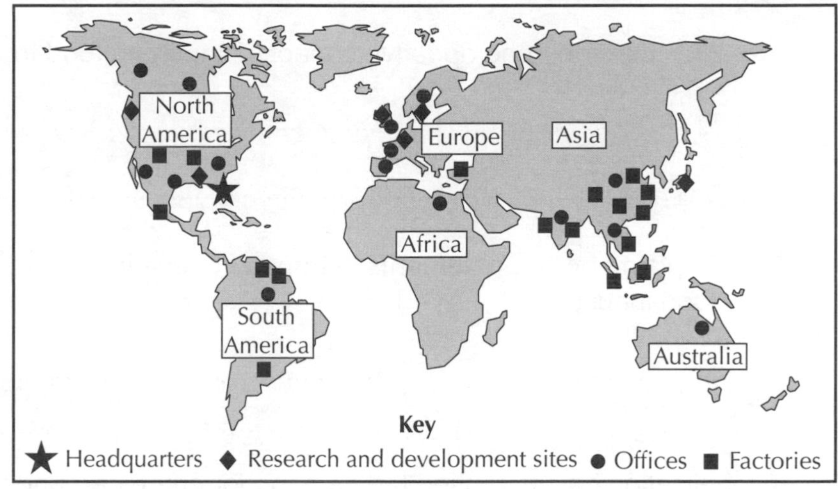

(b) Use **Figure 1** to describe and explain the distribution of Mega Lomania's sites.

Study the map carefully before you start writing.

Mega Lomania's headquarters, research and development sites and most of its offices are located in richer countries, e.g. in Europe. This is because there are more people with administrative and research skills in these countries. Most of Mega Lomania's factories are located in poorer countries, e.g. in Asia, because labour is cheaper so they can make more profit by locating them there.

(4 marks)

(c) How do TNCs like Mega Lomania increase globalisation?

They increase globalisation by linking countries together through the production and sale of goods.

(1 mark)

(d) For a named TNC that you have studied, describe the positive and negative effects it has had on the countries where it has located.

Make sure you cover the positive AND negative effects.

Wal-Mart is a retail TNC with headquarters in the USA. It has over 8000 stores located in various countries, e.g. Mexico, China and Canada. Wal-Mart creates lots of jobs in different countries, e.g. it employs over 150 000 people in Mexico. It also offers more skilled jobs in poorer countries, e.g. all the stores in China are managed by local people. It helps the economy of the countries it locates in as local companies and farmers supply goods, e.g. in Canada it works with over 6000 local suppliers. However, some companies that supply it have long working hours, e.g. it's claimed that workers at Beximco in Bangladesh (who supply clothing) regularly work 80 hours a week. Also, some studies suggest their stores force smaller shops nearby to shut, as they can't compete with the low prices.

(8 marks)

Exam Questions

1 In the last 10 years there's been an increase in the amount of food being imported by the UK.

(a) (i) What term is given to the distance food is transported to its market?

....

(1 mark)

(ii) Describe one negative impact of importing food from around the world.

....

....

(2 marks)

(b) Explain how improvements in transport have increased the globalisation of the food industry.

....

(1 mark)

2 Globalisation has increased the demand for energy around the world. Most of this increase in demand is being met by burning more fossil fuels.

(a) Explain why globalisation has increased the global demand for energy.

....

....

....

(2 marks)

(b) Describe and explain the environmental impacts of producing more energy from fossil fuels.

....

....

....

....

....

....

(6 marks)

(c) Some of the increase in demand could be met using renewable energy sources. Contrast the sustainability of renewable and non-renewable energy sources.

....

....

....

....

(3 marks)

Revision Summary for Section 13

Globalisation... not the most cheery of sections — but still kind of important for life, the future of the planet and all that jazz. Before you put it all behind you and move on to something more uplifting, check you've got the hang of the main issues with this useful bunch of questions.

1) What is globalisation?
2) How have improvements in ICT increased globalisation?
3) Why are call centres often based abroad?
4) Describe the multiplier effect.
5) Give two advantages and two disadvantages of TNCs.
6) What is industrialisation?
7) What are NICs? Name one NIC.
8) Give two reasons why TNCs move to NICs.
9) Why does deindustrialisation happen?
10) Give two impacts of deindustrialisation.
11) For an NIC you have studied:
    a) Describe how the economy has changed over the last 30 years.
    b) Give two reasons why manufacturing has increased there.
12) Give two reasons for the global increase in energy demand, other than globalisation.
13) Give a social impact of producing more energy.
14) Give an economic impact of producing more energy.
15) Give two reasons why food is imported into a country.
16) Give an environmental impact of importing food into a country.
17) Describe a political impact of producing more food.
18) What is sustainable energy production?
19) Describe two types of renewable energy source.
20) a) Name a country that uses renewable energy.
    b) How much of the energy used in that country comes from renewable sources?
    c) Give one positive impact on that country of using renewable energy.
21) What is the Kyoto Protocol?
22) How does a country get carbon credits?
23) Name an international agreement, other than the Kyoto Protocol, that aims to reduce pollution.
24) Globalisation has increased the amount of waste going to landfill. How can this impact be reduced?
25) Give one reason why buying locally produced food reduces the impact of a globalised food supply.

Growth in Tourism

Tourism is big business, and it's getting even bigger...

There's been a Global Increase in Tourism Over the Last 60 Years

Tourism's a growing industry — people are having more holidays and longer holidays.
Here are a few of the reasons why:

1) People have more disposable income (spare cash) than they used to, so can afford to go on more holidays.
2) Companies give more paid holidays than they used to. This means people have more free time, so go on holiday more.
3) Travel has become cheaper (particularly air travel) so more people can afford to go on holiday.
4) Holiday providers, e.g. tour companies and hotels, now use the internet to sell their products to people directly, which makes them cheaper. Again, this means more people can afford to go away.

Some areas are also becoming more popular than they used to be because:

1) Improvements in transport (e.g. more airports) have made it quicker and easier to get to places — no more week-long boat trips to Australia for a start.
2) Countries in more unusual tourist destinations like the Middle East and Africa have got better at marketing themselves as tourist attractions. This means people are more aware of them.
3) Many countries have invested in infrastructure for tourism (e.g. better hotels) to make them more attractive to visitors.

Cities, Mountains and Coasts are all Popular Tourist Areas

People are attracted to cities by the culture (e.g. museums, art galleries), entertainment (bars, restaurants, theatres) and shopping. Popular destinations include London, New York, Paris and Rome.

People are attracted to mountain areas by the beautiful scenery and activities like walking, climbing, skiing and snow boarding. Popular destinations include the Alps, the Dolomites and the Rockies.

People are attracted to coastal areas by the beaches and activities like swimming, snorkelling, fishing and water skiing. Popular destinations include Spain, the Caribbean and Thailand.

Tourism is Important to the Economies of Many Countries

1) Tourism creates jobs for local people (e.g. in restaurants and hotels), which helps the economy to grow.
2) It also increases the income of other businesses that supply the tourism industry, e.g. farms that supply food to hotels. This also helps the economy to grow.
3) This means tourism is important to the economy of countries in both rich and poor parts of the world, e.g. tourism in France generated 35 billion Euros in 2006 and created two million jobs.
4) Poorer countries tend to be more dependent on the income from tourism than richer ones, e.g. tourism contributes 3% of the UK's GNP, compared to 15% of Kenya's.

Tourism is booming all over the world

Now try to recite the reasons why tourism is on the increase backwards, whilst standing on your head. And don't forget — if an area is pretty or has tons of activities then it'll be a hit with tourists (which is great for the economy).

UK Tourism

You might not realise it on yet another rainy day here, but the UK is actually a top tourist destination.

Tourism makes a Big Contribution to the UK Economy

1) There were 32 million overseas visitors to Britain in 2008.
2) The UK is popular with tourists because of its countryside, historic landmarks (e.g. Big Ben and Stonehenge), famous churches and cathedrals (e.g. Saint Paul's cathedral), and its castles and palaces (e.g. Edinburgh Castle and Buckingham Palace).
3) London is particularly popular for its museums, theatres and shopping. It's the destination for half of all visitors to the UK.
4) In 2007, tourism contributed £114 billion to the economy and employed 1.4 million people.

Really popular areas are called honeypot sites.

Many Factors Affect the Number of Tourists Visiting the UK

1) Weather — bad weather can discourage tourists from visiting the UK, e.g. a really wet summer in 2007 was blamed for a drop in the number of overseas visitors.
2) World economy — in times of recession people tend to cut back on luxuries like holidays, so fewer overseas visitors come to the UK. It's not all bad though, as more UK citizens choose to holiday in the UK.
3) Exchange rate — the value of the pound compared with other currencies affects the number of tourists. If it's low, the UK is cheaper to visit so more overseas visitors come.
4) Terrorism and conflict — wars and terrorist threats mean people are less willing to visit affected areas. Tourism fell sharply after the London bombings on 7th July 2005.
5) Major events — big events can attract huge numbers of people. E.g. Liverpool was European Capital of Culture in 2008 and as a result 3.5 million people visited that hadn't been before. The 2012 Olympics are also expected to massively boost tourism.

The Tourist Area Life Cycle Model Shows How Visitor Numbers Change

The number of visitors to an area over time tends to go through these typical stages:

Number of visitors

Time

① Exploration: Small numbers of visitors are attracted to the area, e.g. by the scenery or culture. There aren't many tourist facilities.

② Involvement: Local people start providing facilities for the tourists, which attracts more visitors.

③ Development: More and more visitors come as more facilities are built. Control of tourism in the area passes from locals to big companies.

④ Consolidation: Tourism is still a big part of the local economy, but tourist numbers are beginning to level off.

⑤ Stagnation: Visitor numbers have peaked. Facilities are no longer as good and tourists have had a negative impact on the local environment, making the area less attractive to visit.

⑥ Rejuvenation OR decline:
Rejuvenate — if the area is rejuvenated then more visitors will come as they're attracted by the new facilities.
Decline — fewer visitors come as the area is less attractive. This leads to decline of the area as facilities shut or become run-down.

This model is also known as the resort life cycle model.

The number of tourists visiting a place is affected by many factors

The tourist area life cycle model applies to many seaside resorts in the UK. They were major tourism centres at the start of the 1900s but many stagnated, e.g. Morecambe, and declined. Some, e.g. Brighton, are now being rejuvenated.

UK Tourism — Case Study

The Lake District National Park has been a favourite with tourists since the early 1800s. Today, the huge number of visitors have to be carefully managed to preserve the natural beauty that's made it so popular.

*The **Lake District** is a **National Park** in **Cumbria***

The Lake District National Park gets around 15 million visitors a year.
There are several reasons it's so popular:

1) Tourists come to enjoy the scenery — for example large lakes (e.g. Windermere) and mountains (e.g. Scafell Pike).
2) There are many activities available, e.g. bird watching, walking, pony-trekking, boat rides, sailing and rock-climbing.
3) There are also cultural attractions, e.g. the Beatrix Potter and Wordsworth museums.

***Strategies** are Needed to **Cope** with the **Impact** of Tourists*

Tourists cause traffic congestion, erode footpaths and drop litter.
Here are a few strategies being carried out to reduce these problems:

1) **Coping with the extra traffic** — public transport in the area is being improved so people can leave their cars at home. There are also campaigns to encourage people to use the new services, e.g. the 'Give the driver a break' campaign. This provides leaflets that show the routes available and offers discounts at cafes and on lake cruises for people presenting bus or train tickets.

2) **Coping with the erosion of footpaths** — solutions include encouraging visitors to use less vulnerable areas instead, 'resting' popular routes by changing the line of the paths, and using more hard-wearing materials for paths. E.g. at Tarn Hows, severely eroded paths have been covered with soil and reseeded, and the main route has been gravelled to protect it.

3) **Protecting wildlife and farmland** — there are signs to remind visitors to take their litter home and covered bins are provided at the most popular sites. There have also been campaigns to encourage visitors to enjoy the countryside responsibly, e.g. by closing gates and keeping dogs on a lead.

*There are **Plans** to **Make Sure** it **Keeps Attracting Tourists***

1) The official tourism strategy for Cumbria is to attract an extra two million visitors by 2018 and to increase the amount tourists spend from £1.1 billion per year to £1.5 billion per year.
2) Public transport will be improved to make the Lakes even more accessible.
3) There's to be widespread advertising and marketing to make the area even more well known.
4) Farms will be encouraged to provide services like quad biking, clay pigeon shooting and archery alongside traditional farming — these should attract more tourists to the area.
5) Timeshare developments (where people share the ownership of a property, but stay there at different times) are to be increased, to help bring people into the area all year round.
6) The strategy also aims to encourage tourism in areas outside the National Park, like the West Coast, Furness and Carlisle, to relieve some of the pressure on the main tourist areas. E.g. there are plans to regenerate ports like Whitehaven and Barrow to make them more attractive to visitors.

15 million visitors a year has a big impact on the Lakes

Trust me, visiting the Lakes is a lot more enjoyable than learning about the area's strategies for coping with tourism — but the learning part's all you're going to get today (unless you're reading this whilst on a field trip to the Lakes, you lucky devil).

Mass Tourism

For me, 'mass tourism' conjures up images of sunbathing Brits in Spanish coastal resorts, but there's a bit more to it than that. It can have a big impact on the areas the tourists flock to.

Mass Tourism is Basically Tourism on a Big Scale

Mass tourism is organised tourism for large numbers of people.
For example, visiting Spain on a package holiday would count as mass tourism.
But, holidays where people organise it themselves or small group tours don't count.

Mass Tourism has Both Positive and Negative Impacts

	POSITIVE	NEGATIVE
ECONOMIC IMPACTS	• It brings money into the local economy. • It creates jobs for local people, and increases the income of industries that supply tourism, e.g. farming.	• A lot of the profit made from tourism is kept by the large travel companies, rather than going to the local economy.
SOCIAL IMPACTS	• Lots of jobs means young people are more likely to stay in the area. • Improved roads, communications and infrastructure for tourists also benefit local people. • Income from tourism can be reinvested in local community projects.	• The tourism jobs available to locals are often badly paid and seasonal. • Traffic congestion caused by tourists can inconvenience local people. • The behaviour of some tourists can offend locals.
ENVIRONMENTAL IMPACTS	• Income from tourism can be reinvested in protecting the environment, e.g. to run National Parks or pay for conservation work.	• Transporting lots of people long distances releases lots of greenhouse gases that cause global warming. • Tourism can increase litter and cause pollution, e.g. increased sewage can cause river pollution. • Tourism can lead to the destruction of natural habitats, e.g. sightseeing boats can damage coral reefs.

There are Ways to Reduce the Negative Impacts of Mass Tourism

Here are a few examples:

1) Improving public transport encourages tourists to use it, which reduces congestion and pollution.
2) Limiting the number of people visiting sensitive environments, e.g. coral reefs, reduces damage.
3) Providing lots of bins helps to reduce litter.

The Importance of Tourism Needs to be Maintained

Areas that rely heavily on tourism need to make sure the tourists keep coming.
Here are a few ways they can do this:

1) Build new facilities or improve existing ones, e.g. build new hotels.
2) Reduce any tourist impacts that make the area less attractive, e.g. litter and traffic congestion.
3) Advertise and market the area to attract new tourists, e.g. use TV to advertise in other countries.
4) Improve transport infrastructure to make it quicker and easier to get to the area.
5) Offer new activities to attract tourists that don't normally go there.
6) Make it cheaper to visit, e.g. lower entrance fees to attractions.

Tourism has economic, environmental and social impacts

Learning definitions for things like mass tourism is a good idea — they often pop up in exams. So do the pros and cons of tourism, and management strategies, come to think of it... which means you'll just have to learn it all.

Mass Tourism — Case Study

If watching lions devour a gazelle while on holiday is your bag, then Kenya is the place to go.

Kenya is a Popular Tourist Destination

Kenya is in East Africa. It gets over 700 000 visitors per year. There are a few reasons why people visit:

1) A fascinating tribal culture and lots of wildlife, including the 'big five' (rhino, lion, elephant, buffalo and leopard). Wildlife safaris are very popular.
2) A warm climate with sunshine all year round.
3) Beautiful scenery, including savannah, mountains, forests, beaches and coral reefs.

Tourism has Had a Big Impact on Kenya

	POSITIVE	NEGATIVE
ECONOMIC IMPACTS	• Tourism contributes 15% of the country's Gross National Product. • In 2003, around 219 000 people worked in the tourist industry.	• Only 15% of the money earned through tourism goes to locals. The rest goes to big companies.
SOCIAL IMPACTS	• The culture and customs of the native Maasai tribe are preserved because things like traditional dancing are often displayed for tourists.	• Some Maasai tribespeople were forced off their land to create National Parks for tourists. • Some Muslim people in Kenya are offended by the way female tourists dress.
ENVIRONMENTAL IMPACTS	• There are 23 National Parks in Kenya, e.g. Nairobi National Park. Tourists have to pay entry fees to get in. This money is used to maintain the National Parks, which help protect the environment and wildlife.	• Safari vehicles have destroyed vegetation and caused soil erosion. • Wild animals have been affected, e.g. cheetahs in the most heavily visited areas have changed their hunting behaviour to avoid the crowds. • Coral reefs in the Malindi Marine National Park have been damaged by tourist boats anchoring.

Kenya is Trying to Reduce the Negative Impacts of Tourism

1) Walking or horseback tours are being promoted over vehicle safaris, to preserve vegetation.
2) Alternative activities that are less damaging than safaris are also being encouraged, e.g. climbing and white water rafting.

Kenya is Also Trying to Maintain Tourism

1) Kenya's Tourist Board and Ministry of Tourism have launched an advertising campaign in Russia called 'Magical Kenya'.
2) Kenya Wildlife Service is planning to build airstrips in Ruma National Park and Mount Elgon National Park to make them more accessible for tourists. It also plans to spend £8 million improving roads, bridges and airstrips to improve accessibility.
3) Visa fees for adults were cut by 50% in 2009 to make it cheaper to visit the country. They were also scrapped for children under 16 to encourage more families to visit.

Most people visit Kenya for the wildlife

A walking safari in Kenya sounds dodgy — lions eat people and elephants can be pretty stroppy when they want to be. It's just one way of reducing the impacts of tourism though (which reminds me — check you know the impacts too).

Tourism in Extreme Environments

Some people aren't content with a week in the sun or a shopping spree in New York — they go on holiday to extreme environments, e.g. Antarctica, the Himalayas and the Sahara desert.

Extreme Environments are Becoming Popular with Tourists

There are many reasons why tourists are attracted to extreme environments:

1) They're ideal settings for adventure holiday activities like jeep tours, river rafting and trekking.
2) Some people want something different and exciting to do on holiday, which nobody else they know has done.

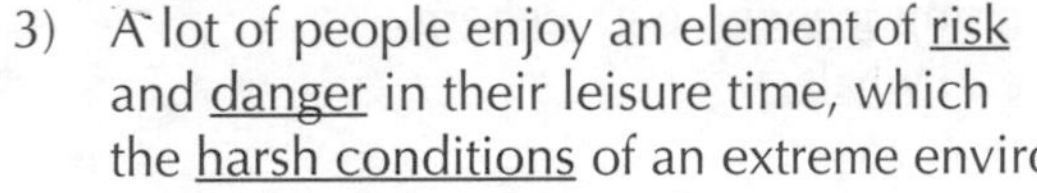

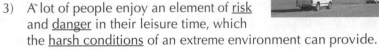

3) A lot of people enjoy an element of risk and danger in their leisure time, which the harsh conditions of an extreme environment can provide.

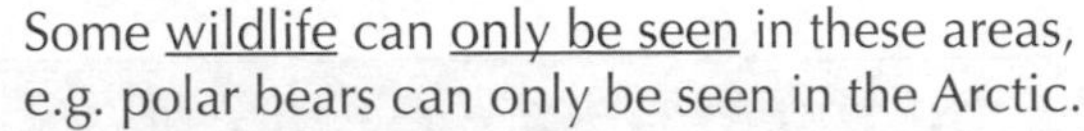

4) Some wildlife can only be seen in these areas, e.g. polar bears can only be seen in the Arctic.
5) Some scenery can only be seen in extreme places too, e.g. icebergs can only be seen in very cold environments.

There are also several reasons why tourism is increasing in extreme environments:

1) Improvements in transport have made it quicker and easier to get to some of these destinations. For example, the Qinghai-Tibet railway that links China and Tibet (an extreme mountain environment) opened in 2006. This increased tourism as Tibet was easier to get to.
2) People are keen to see places like Antarctica for themselves while they have the chance, before the ice melts due to global warming.
3) Tourism to extreme environments is quite expensive, but people nowadays tend to have more disposable income (spare cash), so more people can afford to go.
4) Adventure holidays are becoming more popular because of TV programmes and advertising.

Tourism in Extreme Environments can be Damaging

The ecosystems in extreme environments are usually delicately balanced, because it's so difficult for life to survive in the harsh conditions there. The presence of tourists can upset this fragile balance and cause serious problems. Here's an example of how tourism can damage the environment in the Himalayas:

1) Trees are cut down to provide fuel for trekkers and other tourists, leading to deforestation.

2) Deforestation destroys habitats.
3) Deforestation also means there are fewer trees to intercept rain. So more water reaches channels causing flooding.
4) Tree roots normally hold the soil together, so deforestation also leads to soil erosion. If soil is washed into rivers it raises the river bed so it can't hold as much water — this can cause flooding too.
5) The sheer volume of tourists causes footpath erosion, which can lead to landslides.
6) Toilets are poor or non-existent, so rivers become polluted by sewage.

Extreme environments have delicate ecosystems that are easily damaged

You might be asked to suggest reasons why people go to extreme environments, and answering 'because they're mad' won't cut it. So check you've got the reasons covered and have an extreme case study ready for 'em too.

Tourism in Extreme Environments — Case Study

Antarctica is the coldest place on Earth (it can get to minus 80 °C), making it an extreme environment. Despite this fact quite a few tourists brave the cold every year.

The *Antarctic* is Becoming *More Popular* with *Tourists*

1) Antarctica is a continent at the Earth's South Pole. It covers an area of about 14 million km^2 and about 98% is covered with ice.
2) The number of tourists visiting Antarctica each year is rising, e.g. there were 7413 in the 1996/1997 season, but 46 000 in the 2007/2008 season.
3) Tourists are attracted by the stunning scenery (e.g. icebergs) and the wildlife (e.g. penguins and whales).

Tourism has *Environmental Impacts* in Antarctica

Antarctica is very cold and doesn't get much sunshine in winter so the land ecosystems are very fragile — it takes a long time for them to recover from damage. The sea ecosystem is also delicately balanced. This means that tourists can have a massive impact on the environment there:

1) Tourists can trample plants, disturb wildlife and drop litter.
2) There are fears that tourists could accidentally introduce non-native species or diseases that could wipe out existing species.
3) Spillage of fuel from ships is also a worry, especially after the sinking of the cruise ship, MS Explorer, in 2007. Fuel spills kill molluscs (e.g. mussels) and fish, as well as the birds that feed on them (e.g. penguins).

There are *Measures in Place* to *Protect* Antarctica

(1) The Antarctic Treaty is an international agreement that came into force in 1961 and has now been signed by 47 countries. The Treaty is designed to protect and conserve the area and its plant and animal life. In April 2009, the parties involved with the Antarctic Treaty agreed to introduce new limits on tourism in Antarctica — only ships with fewer than 500 passengers are allowed to land there and a maximum of 100 passengers are allowed on shore at a time.

(2) The International Association of Antarctica Tour Operators also has a separate Code of Conduct. The code is voluntary, but most operators in the area do stick to it. There are rules on:

1) Specially Protected Areas — these are off limits to tourists.
2) Wildlife — wildlife must not be disturbed when being observed. E.g. when whale watching, boats should approach animals slowly and keep their distance.
3) Litter — nothing can be left behind by tourists and there must be no smoking during shore landings (to reduce cigarette end litter).
4) Supervision — tourists must stay with their group and each group must have a qualified guide. This prevents people from entering no-go areas or disturbing wildlife.
5) Plant life — tourists must not walk on the fragile plant life.
6) Waste — sewage must be treated biologically and other waste stored on board the ships.

The Antarctic Treaty and the IAATO Code of Conduct help protect Antarctica

Time to get your 'case study hat' on — I realise you might have been wearing it quite a lot throughout this section, but hey, we're on holiday. And oh, I wouldn't throw it away when you've finished this page either. Just a hint.

Ecotourism

As if UK tourism, mass tourism and extreme tourism weren't enough — it's time for ecotourism...

Ecotourism Doesn't Destroy the Environment

1) Ecotourism is tourism that doesn't harm the environment and benefits the local people.
2) Ecotourism involves:
   - Conservation — protecting and managing the environment.
   - Stewardship — taking responsibility for conserving the environment.
3) Ideally, conservation and stewardship should involve local people and local organisations, so that local people benefit from the tourists.
4) Ecotourism is usually a small-scale activity, with only small numbers of visitors going to an area at a time. This helps to keep the environmental impact of tourism low.
5) It often involves activities like wildlife viewing and walking.

Ecotourism Benefits the Environment, Economy and Local People

Environmental benefits:

1) Local people are encouraged to conserve the environment rather than use it for activities that can be damaging, e.g. logging or farming. This is because they can only earn money from ecotourism if the environment isn't damaged.
2) It reduces poaching and hunting of endangered species, since locals will benefit more from protecting these species for tourism than if they killed them.
3) Ecotourism projects try to reduce the use of fossil fuels, e.g. by using renewable energy sources and local food (which isn't transported as far so less fossil fuel is used). Using less fossil fuel is better for the environment as burning fossil fuels adds to global warming.
4) Waste that tourists create is disposed of carefully to prevent pollution.

Economic benefits:

1) Ecotourism creates jobs for local people (e.g. as guides or in tourist lodges), which helps the local economy grow.
2) Local people not directly employed in tourism can also make money by selling local crafts to visitors or supplying the tourist industry with goods, e.g. food.

Benefits for local people:

1) People have better and more stable incomes in ecotourism than in other jobs, e.g. farming.
2) Many ecotourism schemes fund community projects, e.g. schools, water tanks and health centres.

Ecotourism Helps the Sustainable Development of Areas

1) Sustainable development means improving the quality of life for people, but doing it in a way that doesn't stop people in the future getting what they need (by not damaging the environment or depleting resources).
2) Ecotourism helps areas to develop by increasing the quality of life for local people — the profits from ecotourism can be used to build schools or healthcare facilities.
3) The development is sustainable because it's done without damaging the environment — without ecotourism people may have to make a living to improve their lives by doing something that harms the environment, e.g. cutting down trees.

Ecotourism benefits local people without damaging the environment

Ecotourism is sustainable because it's something that can continue into the future — the area remains unspoilt, so tourists will continue to come and enjoy it. It helps give local people a better quality of life too.

Ecotourism — Case Study

I know you're a bit sick of case studies by now, but this is the last one in the section — I promise.

Tataquara Lodge is an Example of *Ecotourism*

1) Tataquara Lodge is on an island in the Xingu River in the Brazilian state of Para.
2) It's owned and operated by a cooperative of six local tribes of indigenous people.
3) The lodge has 15 rooms and offers activities like fishing, canoeing, wildlife viewing and forest walks.
4) The surrounding rainforest is home to a rich variety of wildlife, including many species of bat and tropical birds. There are also some endangered species in the area, such as the harpy eagle and giant river otter.

Para is in the Amazon rainforest.

The Lodge Has **Many Benefits**

Environmental benefits:

- The lodge was built from local materials such as straw and wood that was found on the ground — this means they didn't have to cut down any trees. These materials also make the buildings blend in with the natural environment so they don't spoil the scenery.
- It uses solar power to run lights, rather than burning fossil fuels to generate electricity, which is better for the environment.
- The food served in the lodge is all locally-produced. This means less fossil fuel is used to transport it than if it came from further away.

Economic benefits:

- The lodge is owned by a cooperative of indigenous tribes rather than a big foreign company, so the income it provides goes straight to the local economy.
- As the lodge uses locally-produced food, more money goes back into the local economy.

Benefits for local people:

- The lodge creates jobs for local people.
- People in nearby villages are encouraged to visit Tataquara Lodge to sell crafts and perform traditional songs and dances — this gives them an income and helps preserve their culture.
- Profits earned from the lodge are used to provide decent healthcare and education for thousands of people from the local tribes.

Tataquara Lodge **Helps** the **Sustainable Development** of the Area

1) Profits from Tataquara lodge are used to improve healthcare and education in the area. This helps the area to develop by increasing the quality of life for the local people.
2) The development is sustainable because the money to do it is generated without damaging the environment — local people don't have to find other employment that could damage the environment, e.g. logging or farming. Also, resources aren't used up, e.g. solar power is used to run lights instead of fossil fuels, so more resources are available for future generations.

Learn the details — where it is and what the benefits are

Tataquara is a bit of a mouthful to say, but it's a great example of how ecotourism benefits the environment and the local people. Check you can remember plenty of facts about it in case you get asked a question on ecotourism.

Worked Exam Questions

You know the routine by now — work carefully through this example and make sure you understand it. Then it's on to the real test of doing some exam questions yourself.

1 Study **Figure 1**, a graph showing the number of visits to the UK by overseas residents.

Figure 1

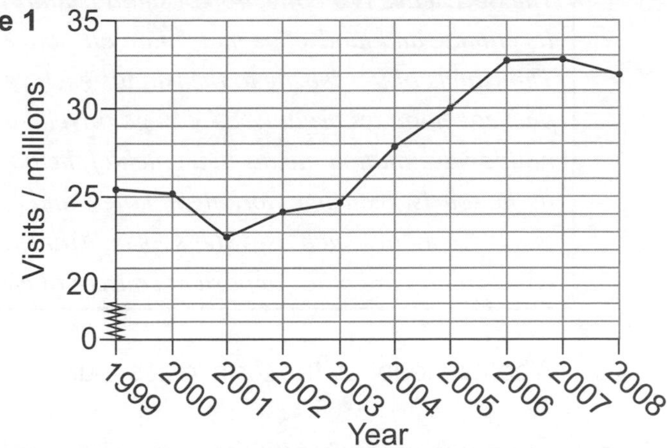

(a) (i) How many visits to the UK from overseas were there in 2005?

30 million

(1 mark)

Read off the scale carefully, and don't forget to include the units.

(ii) Use **Figure 1** to describe how the number of tourists visiting the UK changed between 1999 and 2008.

The overall number of tourists increased, from about 25.5 million in 1999 to about 32 million in 2008. The actual number of tourists fluctuated, with a slight dip in 2001 and a peak in 2006/2007.

Refer to the Figure in your answer.

(2 marks)

(b) Describe four factors that can affect visitor numbers to the UK.

Economic events, like a worldwide recession, can cause tourist numbers to drop as people can't afford holidays. Bad weather can discourage tourists from visiting the UK. A low exchange rate can make the UK cheaper for tourists, encouraging them to visit, so raising numbers. Terror threats can make tourists less willing to visit certain areas.

Numbers can go up or down, so the factors can be positive or negative.

(4 marks)

(c) The number of UK residents going on an overseas holiday each year has increased over the last 60 years. Suggest reasons for this trend.

More people are having holidays abroad because people have more disposable income than they used to so they can afford to go on more holidays. Holiday providers now use the internet to sell their products to people directly, which makes them cheaper so more people can afford them. Travel has become cheaper so more people can afford to go on holiday abroad. Improvements in transport have made it quicker and easier to get abroad, so people aren't put off by long journeys. Companies give more paid holidays so people have more free time to go on holiday. Also, countries in more unusual tourist destinations are marketing themselves as tourist attractions, so people are more aware of them and want to visit them.

(6 marks)

Exam Questions

1 Study **Figure 1**, which gives information about tourism in the Seychelles.

Figure 1

The Seychelles is a collection of small islands in the Indian Ocean. Its climate and landscape make it an attractive tourist destination. Thousands of tourists fly to the islands each year, many travelling there for package holidays organised by large travel companies. Its popularity as a holiday destination means that much of the population is directly involved in the tourist industry, working in hotels and restaurants, or offering leisure activities such as water sports. Transportation, fishing and construction are other important sources of employment.

(a) What is meant by the term 'mass tourism'?

....

(1 mark)

(b) Use **Figure 1** to describe the positive economic impacts of tourism on the Seychelles.

....

....

(2 marks)

(c) Explain how mass tourism might have a negative environmental impact on the Seychelles.

....

....

....

(3 marks)

(d) Describe the impacts of mass tourism on a named area and explain how any negative impacts are being reduced.

....

....

....

....

....

....

....

....

....

(8 marks)

Revision Summary for Section 14

It's that time again — just when you think you're all done and dusted with a section, another page of questions is sprung on you. This lot are all about going on your holidays though, so they shouldn't be too much of a strain. Give them a try, and then if there are any you struggle with you can go back through the section and pick up even more ideas for your next trip.

1) Why do cities attract large numbers of tourists?
2) What attracts tourists to mountain areas?
3) Why is tourism important to the economies of many countries?
4) How much money does the tourist industry contribute to the UK's economy?
5) Describe the six stages in the tourist area life cycle model.
6) a) Name an area in the UK that's popular with tourists.
   b) Describe what attracts tourists to the area.
   c) Describe the strategies used to reduce the impact of tourists.
   d) How does this area plan to keep attracting tourists in the future?
7) List three positive effects and three negative effects of mass tourism.
8) Give three examples of how mass tourism can be managed to ensure that an area keeps its appeal.
9) Give three reasons why tourism in extreme environments is increasing.
10) a) Name an extreme environment that is becoming popular with tourists.
    b) Describe the environmental impacts of tourism in the area.
    c) Describe the measures in place to limit the impact of tourism in the area.
11) Define ecotourism.
12) Explain one way that ecotourism can benefit the economy of a region.
13) Explain one way that ecotourism can benefit the environment of a region.
14) How can ecotourism help benefit local people?
15) a) What is sustainable development?
    b) Explain how ecotourism helps the sustainable development of areas.
16) a) Give an example of a successful ecotourism project.
    b) Explain how this project benefits the local environment, the local economy and the local people.

Answering Questions

This section is filled with lots of techniques and skills that will be useful in your exam. It's no good learning the content of this book if you don't bother learning the skills that will help you to pass your exam too. First up, answering questions properly...

Make Sure you Read the Question Properly

It's really easy to misread the question and spend five minutes writing about the wrong thing. Five simple tips can help you avoid this:

1) Figure out if it's a case study question — if the question says something like 'using named examples' or 'with reference to one named area' you need to include a case study.
2) Underline the command words in the question (the ones that tell you what to do):

Answers to questions with 'explain' in them often include the word 'because' (or 'due to').

When writing about differences, 'whereas' is a good word to use in your answers, e.g. 'the Richter scale measures the energy released by an earthquake whereas the Mercalli scale measures the effects'.

Command word	Means write about...
Describe	what it's like
Explain	why it's like that (i.e. give reasons)
Compare	the similarities AND differences
Contrast	the differences
Suggest why	give reasons for

If a question asks you to describe a pattern (e.g. from a map or graph), make sure you identify the general pattern, then refer to any anomalies (things that don't fit the general pattern).
E.g. to answer 'describe the global distribution of volcanoes', first say that they're mostly on plate margins, then mention that a few aren't (e.g. in Hawaii).

3) Underline the key words (the ones that tell you what it's about), e.g. volcanoes, erosion, migration, rural-urban fringe, population pyramid.
4) If the question says 'Use evidence from Fig. 2...' you need to refer to the figure in your answer, e.g. quote numbers from it to back up your points.
5) Re-read the question and your answer when you've finished, just to check that what you've written really does answer the question being asked. A common mistake is to miss a bit out — like when questions say 'use data from the graph in your answer' or 'use evidence from the map'.

Case Study Questions are Level Marked

Case study questions are often worth 8 marks and are level marked, which means you need to do these things to get the top level (3) and a high mark:

1) Read the question properly and figure out a structure before you start. Your answer needs to be well organised and structured, and written in a logical way.
2) Include specialist terms (geographical words), e.g. destructive margin, backwash, longshore drift.
3) Include plenty of relevant details:
   - This includes things like names, dates, statistics, names of organisations or companies.
   - Don't forget that they need to be relevant though — it's no good including the exact number of people killed in a flood when the question is about the causes of a flood.
4) Your answer should be legible (you won't get many marks if the examiner can't read it). You should use correct grammar, and everything should be spelt correctly (double-check jazzy geography words).

Answers to level marked questions should be well structured

It may all seem a bit simple to you, but it's really important to understand what you're being asked to do. This can be tricky — sometimes the differences between the meanings of the command words are quite subtle.

Describing Maps and Graphs

You might get maps and graphs in the exam, and often you'll have to describe what they show.

Describing Distributions on Maps — Describe the Pattern

1) In your exam you could get questions like, 'use the map to describe the distribution of volcanoes' and 'explain the distribution of deforestation'.
2) Describe the general pattern and any anomalies (things that don't fit the general pattern).
3) Make at least as many points as there are marks and use names of places and figures if they're given.
4) If you're asked to give a reason or explain, you need to describe the distribution first.

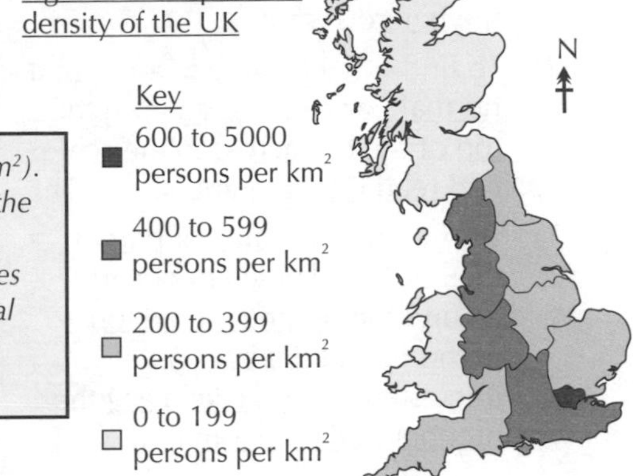

Figure 1 — Population density of the UK

Q: *Use Figure 1 to explain the pattern of population density in the UK.*

A: *The London area has a very high population density (600 to 5000 per km²). There are also areas of high population density (400 to 599 per km²) in the south east and west of England. These areas include major cities (e.g. Birmingham and Manchester). More people live in and around cities because there are better services and more job opportunities than in rural areas. Scotland and Wales have the lowest population density in the UK (less than 199 per km²)...*

Describing Locations on Maps — Include Details

You could be given two maps to use for one question — link information from the two maps together.

1) In your exam you could get a question like, 'suggest a reason for the location of the settlement'.
2) When you're asked about the location of something say where it is, what it's near and use compass points.
3) If you're asked to give a reason or explain, you need to describe the location first.

Q: *Use the maps to describe the location of the National Parks.*

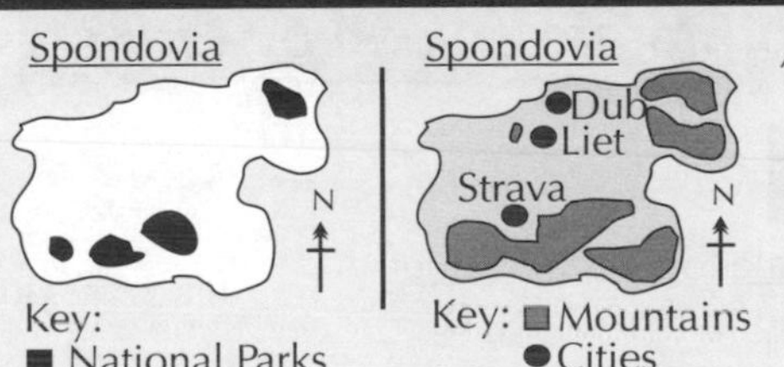

A: *The National Parks are found in the south west and north east of Spondovia. They are all located in mountainous areas. Three of the parks are located near to the city of Strava.*

Describing what Graphs Show — Include Figures from the Graph

When describing graphs make sure you mention:

1) The general pattern — when it's going up and down, and any peaks (highest bits) and troughs (lowest bits).
2) Any anomalies (odd results).
3) Specific data points.

If it's a scattergraph you can also talk about correlation — see page 227 for more.

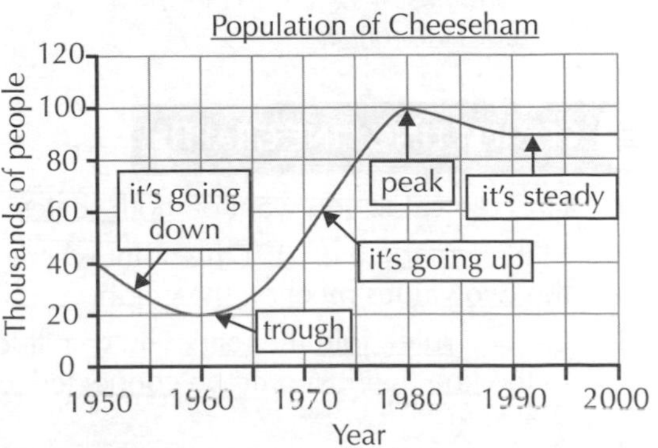

Q: *Use the graph to describe population change in Cheeseham.*

A: *The population halved between 1950 and 1960 from 40 thousand people to 20 thousand people. It then increased to 100 thousand by 1980, before falling slightly and staying steady at 90 thousand from 1990 to 2000.*

Don't forget to mention any anomalies when describing patterns on maps

The key to describing anything (whether it's a pattern, location or graph) is including plenty of relevant details, e.g. compass points, numbers from graphs, numbers from keys, anomalous numbers.

Charts and Graphs

The next four pages are filled with lots of different types of charts, graphs and maps. There are two important things to learn — NUMBER ONE: how to interpret them (read them), and NUMBER TWO: how to construct and complete them (fill them in). You might have to do it in the exam so pay attention.

Bar Charts — Draw the Bars *Straight* and *Neat*

1 READING BAR CHARTS

1) Read along the bottom to find the bar you want.
2) To find out the value of a bar in a normal bar chart — go from the top of the bar across to the scale, and read off the number.
3) To find out the value of part of the bar in a divided bar chart — find the number at the top of the part of the bar you're interested in, and take away the number at the bottom of it.

Q: How many barrels of oil did Oxo oil produce per day in 2008?

A: 500 thousand – 350 thousand = 150 thousand barrels per day

Oil production

2007
2008
Line across from 350
Thousands of barrels per day
500
400
300
200
100
0
Oxo oil
Gnoxo Ltd.
Froxo Inc.
Company

2 COMPLETING BAR CHARTS

1) First find the number you want on the vertical scale.
2) Then trace a line across to where you want the top of the bar to be with a ruler.
3) Draw in a bar of the right size using a ruler.

Q: Complete the chart to show that Froxo Inc. produced 200 thousand barrels of oil per day in 2008.

A: 150 thousand (2007) + 200 thousand = 350 thousand barrels. So draw the bar up to this point.

Line Graphs — the *Points* are Joined by *Lines*

1 READING LINE GRAPHS

1) Read along the correct scale to find the value you want, e.g. 20 thousand tonnes or 1920.
2) Read across or up to the line you want, then read the value off the other scale.

Q: How much coal did New Wales Ltd. produce in 1900?

A: Find 1900 on the bottom scale, go up to the red line, read across, and it's 20 on the scale. The scale's in thousands of tonnes, so the answer is 20 thousand tonnes.

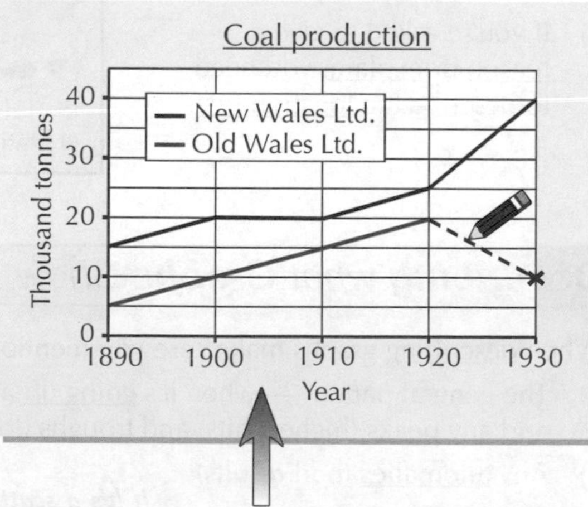

2 COMPLETING LINE GRAPHS

1) Find the value you want on both scales.
2) Make a mark (e.g. ×) at the point where the two values meet on the graph.
3) Using a ruler, join the mark you've made to the line that it should be connected to.

Q: Complete the graph to show that Old Wales Ltd. produced 10 thousand tonnes of coal in 1930.

A: Find 1930 on the bottom scale, and 10 thousand tonnes on the vertical scale. Make a mark where they meet, then join it to the blue line with a ruler.

Make sure your lines, bars and crosses are neat and legible

Something to watch out for with bar charts and line graphs is reading the scale — check how much each division is worth before reading them or completing them. It's easy to think they're always worth one each, but sadly not.

Charts and Graphs

Right, on to the next two types...

Scatter Graphs Show Relationships

Scatter graphs tell you how closely related two things are, e.g. rainfall and river discharge. The fancy word for this is correlation. Strong correlation means the two things are closely related to each other. Weak correlation means they're not very closely related. The line of best fit is a line that goes roughly through the middle of the scatter of points and tells you about what type of correlation there is. Data can show three types of correlation:

1) Positive — as one thing increases the other increases.
2) Negative — as one thing increases the other decreases.
3) None — there's no relationship between the two things.

Line of best fit

Positive Negative None

1 READING SCATTER GRAPHS

1) If you're asked to describe the relationship, look at the slope of the graph, e.g. if the line's moving upwards to the right it's a positive correlation. You also need to look at how close the points are to the line of best fit — the closer they are the stronger the correlation.
2) If you're asked to read off a specific point, just follow the rules for a line graph (see previous page).

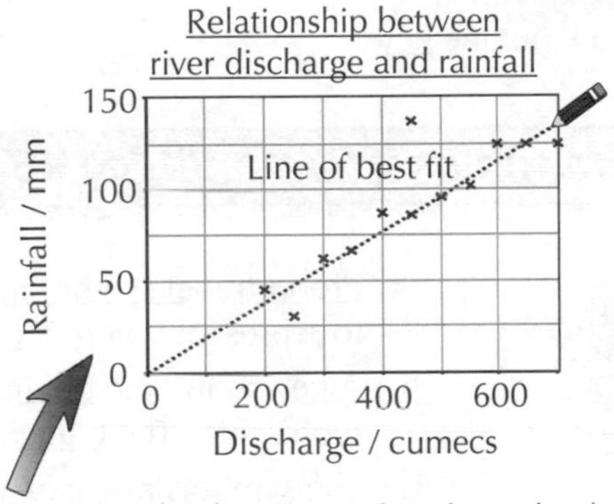

Q: Describe the relationship shown by the scatter graph.

A: River discharge and rainfall show a strong, positive correlation — as rainfall increases, so does river discharge.

2 COMPLETING SCATTER GRAPHS

1) You could be asked to draw a line of best fit — just draw it roughly through the middle of the scatter of points.
2) If you're asked to add a point — just follow the rules for adding a point to a line graph (see previous page).

Pie Charts Show Amounts or Percentages

The important thing to remember with pie charts is that the whole pie = 360°.

1 READING PIE CHARTS

1) To work out the % for a wedge of the pie, use a protractor to find out how large it is in degrees.
2) Then divide that number by 360 and times by 100.
3) To find the amount a wedge of the pie is worth, work out your percentage then turn it into a decimal. Then times the decimal by the total amount of the pie.

Q: Out of 100 people, how many used the bus?

A: 126 – 90 = 36°, so (36 ÷ 360) × 100 = 10%, so 0.1 × 100 = 10 people.

Pie Chart of Transport Type

0° 324° Bicycle 270° 90° Car Bus 126° 180°

2 COMPLETING PIE CHARTS

1) To draw on a new wedge that you know the % for, turn the % into a decimal and times it by 360. Then draw a wedge of that many degrees.

Q: Out of 100 people, 25% used a bicycle. Add this to the pie chart.

A: 25 ÷ 100 = 0.25, 0.25 × 360 = 90°.

2) To add a new wedge that you know the amount for, divide your amount by the total amount of the pie and times the answer by 360. Then draw on a wedge of that many degrees.

Q: Out of 100 people, 55 used a car, add this to the pie chart.

A: 55 ÷ 100 = 0.55, 0.55 × 360 = 198° (198° + 126° = 324°).

A line of best fit should go through the middle of the points

Hmm, who'd have thought pie could be so complicated. Don't panic though, a bit of practice and you'll be fine. And don't worry, you're halfway through this section now — only a few more pages to go.

Maps

A couple of jazzy maps on this page for you, both with complicated names — topological and proportional symbol. And a bit on isolines too.

Topological Maps are Simplified Maps

1) Some maps are hard to read because they show too much detail.
2) Topological maps get around this by just showing the most important features like roads and rail lines. They don't have correct distances or directions either, which makes them easier to read.
3) They're often used to show transport networks, e.g. the London tube map.
4) If you have to read a topological map — dots are usually places and lines usually show routes between places. If two lines cross at a dot then it's usually a place where you can switch routes.
5) As always, don't forget to check out the key.

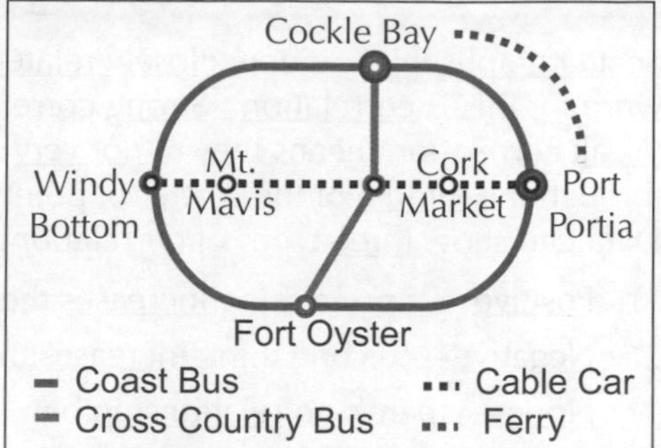

Q: How many different transport routes pass through Port Portia?

A: Three (bus, cable car and ferry).

Proportional Symbol Maps use Symbols of Different Sizes

Car Parks in Drumshire

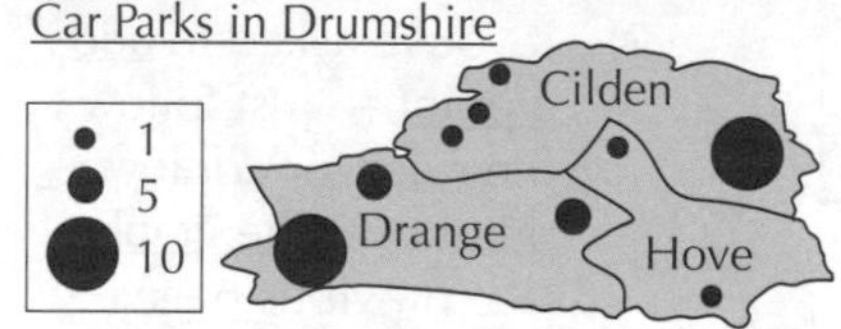

Q: Which area of Drumshire has the most car parks?

A: Drange, with 20.

1) Proportional symbol maps use symbols of different sizes to represent different quantities.
2) A key shows the quantity each different sized symbol represents. The bigger the symbol, the larger the amount.
3) The symbols might be circles, squares, semi-circles or bars, but a larger symbol always means a larger amount.

Isolines on Maps Link up Places with Something in Common

1) Isolines are lines on a map linking up all the places where something's the same, for example:
   - Contour lines are isolines linking up places at the same altitude (see p. 231).
   - Isolines on a weather map (called isobars) link together all the places where the pressure's the same.
2) Isolines can be used to link up lots of things, e.g. average temperature, wind speed or rainfall.

1 READING ISOLINE MAPS

1) Find the place you're interested in on the map and if it's on a line just read off the value.
2) If it's between two lines, you have to estimate the value.

Q: Find the average annual rainfall in Port Portia and on Mt. Mavis.

A: Port Portia is about half way between the lines for 200 mm and 400 mm so the rainfall is around 300 mm per year. Mt. Mavis is on an isoline so the rainfall is 1000 mm per year.

Average annual rainfall on Itchy Island (mm per year)

N
600
500
1000
600
500
Mt. Mavis
800
Port Portia
600
400
200

2 COMPLETING ISOLINE MAPS

1) Drawing an isoline's like doing a dot-to-dot — you just join up all the dots with the same numbers.
2) Make sure you don't cross any other isolines though.

Q: Complete on the map the isoline showing an average rainfall of 600 mm per year.

A: See the red line on the map.

Make sure you study the key for any map

If you have to draw an isoline on a map, then check all the info on the map before you start drawing. If you know where the line's got to go you won't muck it up. Make sure you do it in pencil too, so you can rub out any mistakes.

Maps

And now for some slightly weirder maps...

Choropleth Maps show How Something Varies Between Different Areas

1) Choropleth maps show how something varies between different areas using colours or patterns.
2) The maps in exams often use cross-hatched lines and dot patterns.
3) If you're asked to talk about all the parts of the map with a certain value or characteristic, look at the map carefully and put a big tick on all the parts with the pattern that matches what you're looking for. This makes them all stand out.
4) When you're asked to complete part of a map, first use the key to work out what type of pattern you need. Then carefully draw on the pattern, e.g. using a ruler.

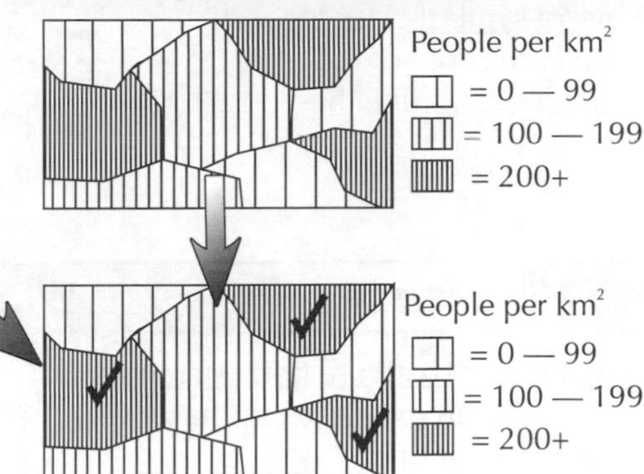

Flow Lines show Movement

1) Flow line maps have arrows on, showing how things move (or are moved) from one place to another.
2) They can also be proportional symbol maps — the width of the arrows show the quantity of things that are moving.

Q: From which area do the greatest number of people entering the UK come from?

A: USA, as this arrow is the largest.

Q: The number of people entering the UK from the Middle East is roughly half the number of people entering from the USA. Draw an arrow on the map to show this.

A: Make sure your arrow is going in the right direction and its size is appropriate (e.g. half the width of the USA arrow).

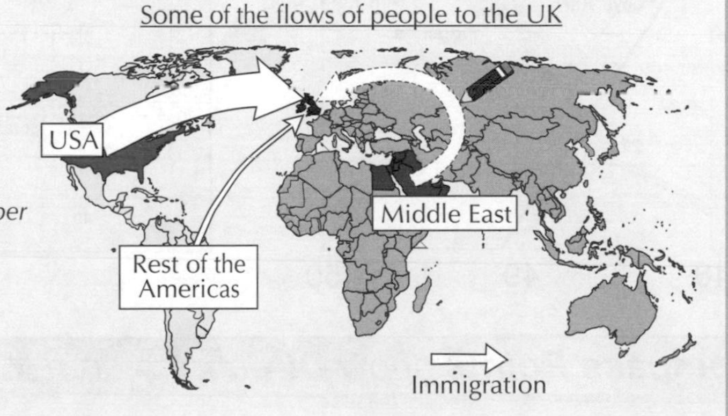

Desire Lines show Journeys

1) Desire line maps are a type of flow line as they show movement too.
2) They're straight lines that show journeys between two locations, but they don't follow roads or railway lines.
3) One line represents one journey.
4) They're used to show how far all the people have travelled to get to a place, e.g. a shop or a town centre, and where they've come from.

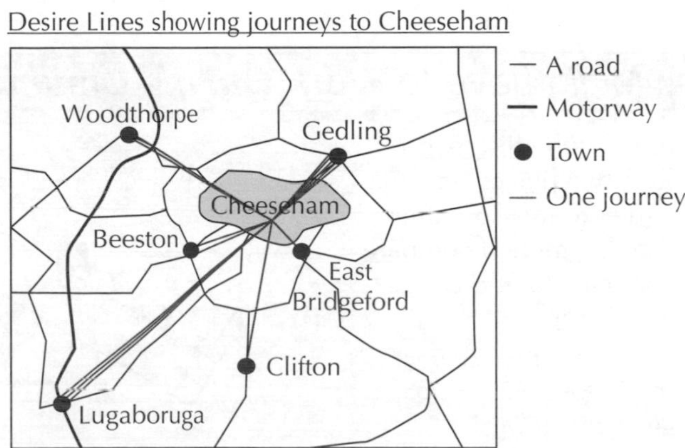

Learn how to read these three types of map

Flow line maps and desire line maps aren't that common in exams (choropleth ones are more common). Unfortunately I can't predict whether they will come up in your exam or not, which means you'll just have to learn them all.

Ordnance Survey Maps

Next up, the dreaded Ordnance Survey® maps. Don't worry, they're easy once you know how to use 'em.

There are a few Common Symbols

Ordnance survey (OS®) maps use lots of symbols. It's a good idea to learn some of the most common ones — like these:

- Motorway
- Main (A) road
- Secondary (B) road
- Bridge
- Railway
- County boundary
- National Park boundary
- Footpath
- Building
- Bus station
- **PO** Post Office®
- **PH** Pub
- Place of worship
- Place of worship, with a tower
- Church with a spire, minaret or dome

Grid References show you Where Things Are on a Map

Four figure and six figure grid references often come up in exams, so it's handy to know a bit about them.

Q: Give the four figure and six figure grid reference for the Post Office®.

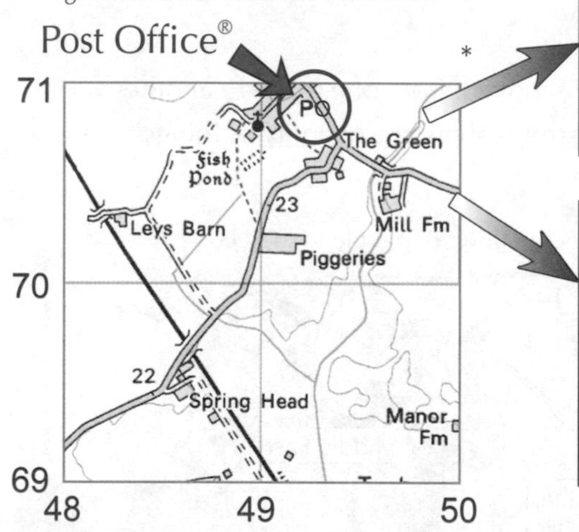

FOUR FIGURE GRID REFERENCE

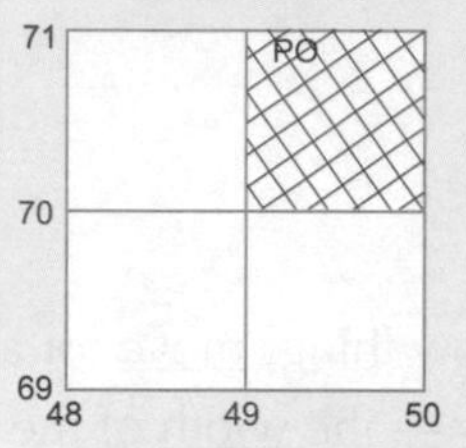

A: Find the eastings (across) value for the left edge of the square with the Post Office® in — 49. Then find the northings (up) value for the bottom edge of the square — 70. Write the numbers together with the eastings value first. So the four figure grid reference is 4970.

SIX FIGURE GRID REFERENCE

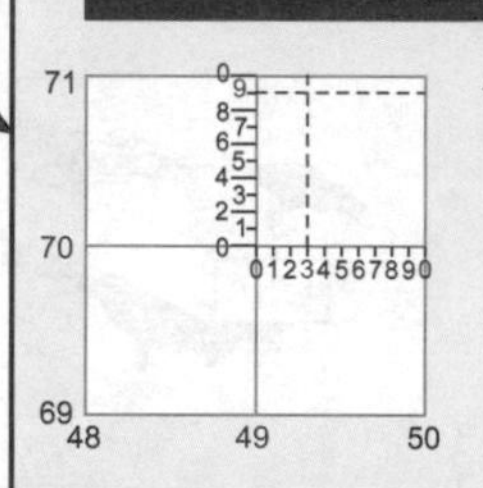

A: Work out the basic eastings and northings as above. Then imagine the square's divided into tenths. The eastings value for the Post Office® is now 493 (49 and 3 'tenths') and the northings is 709 (70 and 9 'tenths'). So the six figure reference is 493709.

Compass Points show Directions on a Map

The compass points are very useful in exams — for giving directions or understanding questions that say things like 'look at the river in the NW of the map'. Read them out loud to yourself, going clockwise.

OR

You Might have to Work Out the Distance Between Two Places

To work out the distance between two places on a map, use a ruler to measure the distance in cm then compare it to the scale to find the distance in km.

Q: What's the distance from the bridge (482703) to the church (490708)?

A: They're 2.2 cm apart on the map...

...which means they're 1.1 km apart in real life.

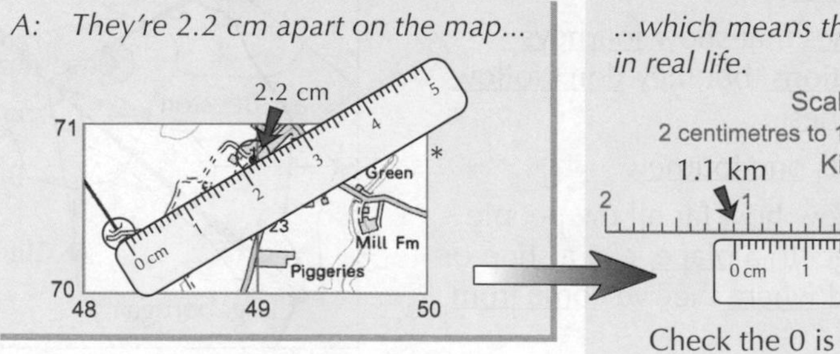

Keeping ramblers happy since 1791...

I told you OS maps aren't as bad as you thought. If a dodgy looking rambler who's been walking in the rain for five hours with only a cup of tea to keep him going can read them, then so can you. Get ready for some more map fun...

Ordnance Survey Maps

Almost done with exam skills now. Just this final page looking at contour lines and sketching from Ordnance Survey® maps or photographs to deal with.

The **Relief** of an Area is Shown by **Contours** and **Spot Heights**

1) Contour lines are the orange lines drawn on maps — they join points of equal height above sea level (altitude).
2) They tell you about the relief of the land, e.g. whether it's hilly, flat or steep.
3) They show the height of the land by the numbers marked on them. They also show the steepness of the land by how close together they are (the closer they are, the steeper the slope).
4) For example, if a map has lots of contour lines on it, it's probably hilly or mountainous. If there are only a few it'll be flat and often low-lying.
5) A spot height is a dot giving the height of a particular place. A trigonometrical point (trig point) is a blue triangle plus a height value. They usually show the highest point in that area (in metres).

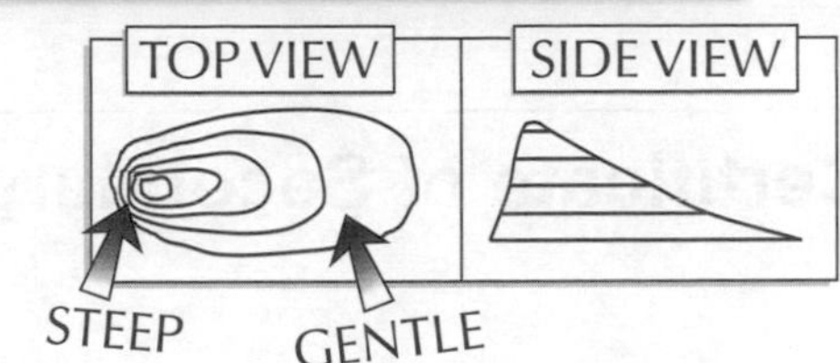

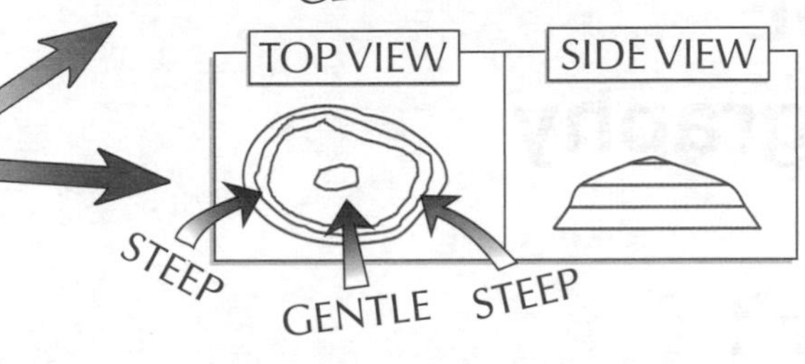

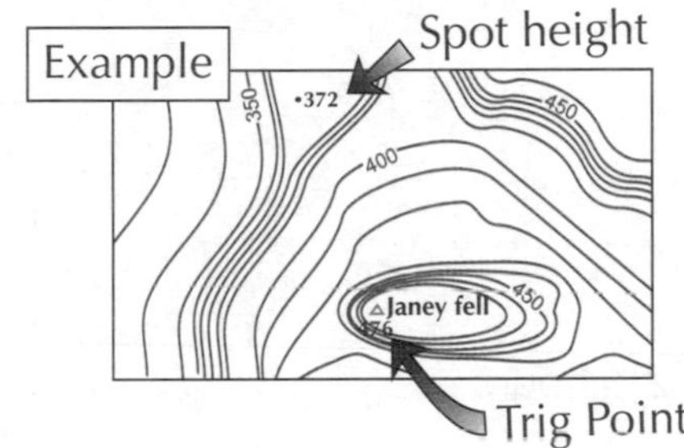

Sketching Maps — Do it Carefully

1) In the exam, they could give you a map or photograph and tell you to sketch part of it.
2) Make sure you figure out what bit they want you to sketch out, and double check you've got it right. It might be only part of a lake or a wood, or only one of the roads.
3) If you're sketching an OS® map, it's a good idea to copy the grid from the map onto your sketch paper — this helps you to copy the map accurately.
4) Draw your sketch in pencil so you can rub it out if it's wrong.
5) Look at how much time you have and how many marks it's worth to decide how much detail to add.

Q: Draw a labelled sketch of the OS map shown below.

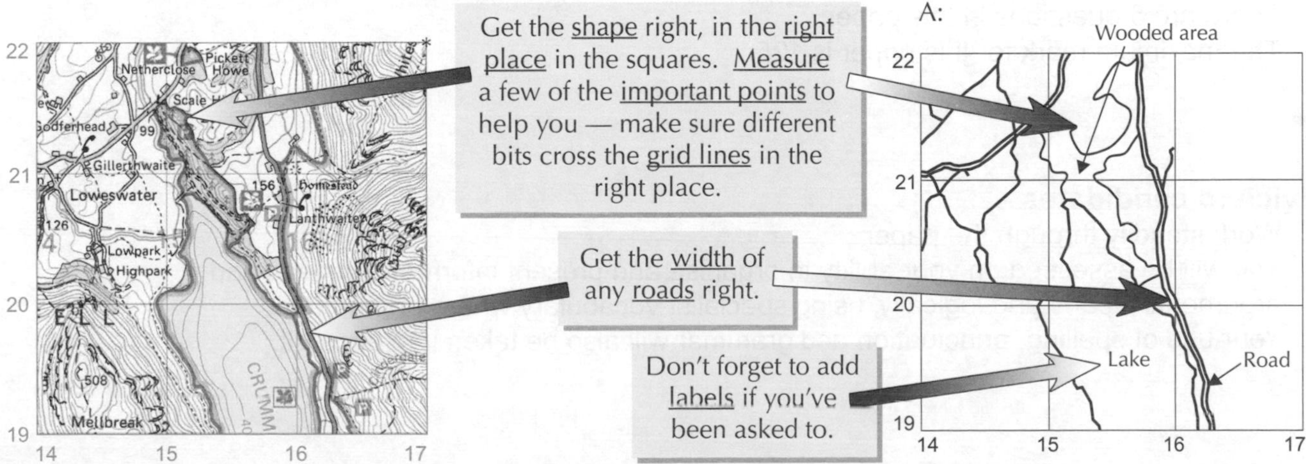

Sketch in pencil so you can rub out any mistakes

When you're sketching a copy of a map or photo see if you can lay the paper over it — then you can trace it (sneaky). And that my friends is the end of the exam skills section. Now go treat yourself to a practice exam.

Practice Exam

Once you've been through all the questions in this book, you should feel pretty confident about the exam.
As final preparation, here is a **practice exam** to really get you set for the real thing.

General Certificate of Secondary Education

GCSE Geography

Paper 1

Centre name					
Centre number					
Candidate number					

Surname
Other names
Candidate signature

Time allowed: 2½ hours

Instructions to candidates

- Write your name and other details in the spaces provided above.
- Do all rough work on the paper. Cross through any work you do not want marked.

Information for candidates

- The marks available are given in brackets at the end of each question or part-question.
- Marks will not be deducted for incorrect answers.
- There are 5 questions in this paper.
- The maximum mark for this paper is 125.

Advice to candidates

- Work steadily through the paper.
- You will be assessed on your ability to organise and present information, ideas and arguments clearly and logically, using specialist vocabulary where appropriate. Your use of spelling, punctuation and grammar will also be taken into account.

Leave blank

1 **Tectonic Activity**

(a) Study **Figure 1**, which shows the Earth's tectonic plates and the distribution of earthquakes.

(i) Describe the distribution of earthquakes around the world.

....

....

....

....

....

(2 marks)

Figure 1

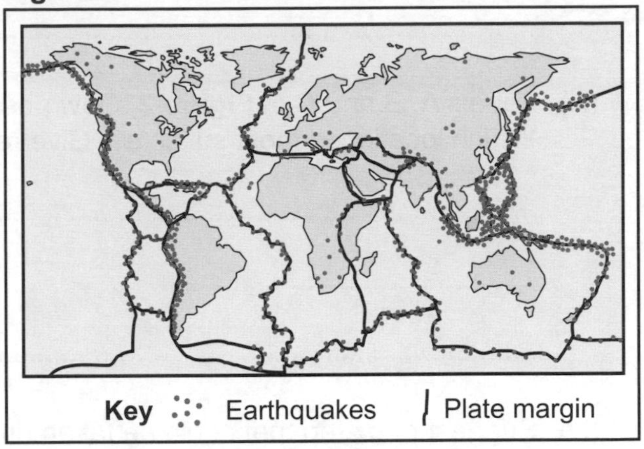

Key: Earthquakes | Plate margin

(ii) Explain how earthquakes are caused at destructive plate margins.

....

....

....

....

(4 marks)

(b) (i) Describe how earthquakes are measured using the Richter scale.

....

....

(2 marks)

(ii) The Richter scale is logarithmic. How much more powerful is an earthquake with a magnitude of 8 compared to an earthquake with a magnitude of 7?

....

(1 mark)

(c) Study **Figure 2**, a map of Burtona County, which shows the location of previous earthquakes in the region and the boundary between two tectonic plates. A new town is to be built in Burtona County.

(i) What kind of plate margin is shown in **Figure 2**?

....

....

(1 mark)

Figure 2

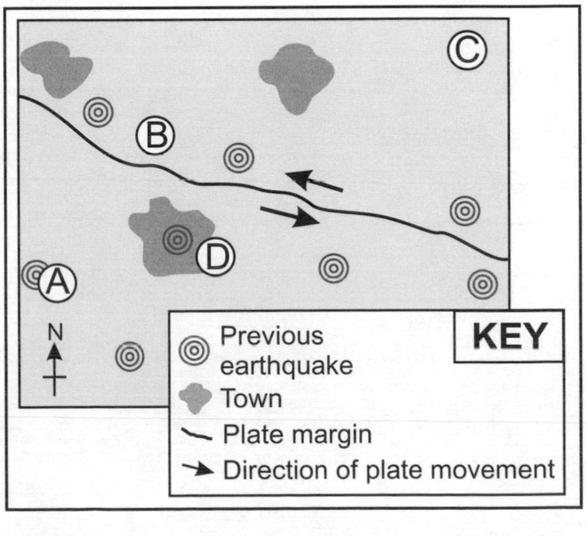

A
B
C
D
N
KEY
Previous earthquake
Town
Plate margin
Direction of plate movement

(ii) Suggest three possible primary impacts of an earthquake in Burtona County.

....

....

(3 marks)

(iii) Labels A, B and C in **Figure 2** show possible locations for the new town. Which location is most suitable? Give reasons for your answer.

....

....

....

(3 marks)

(iv) Suggest one step that could be taken during the planning and building of the new town to help reduce the impacts of any earthquakes that might happen.

....

....

(1 mark)

(d) Describe and compare the primary impacts of earthquakes in rich and poor parts of the world that you have studied.

....

....

....

....

....

....

....

....

....

....

....

....

....

(8 marks)

Leave blank

2 Rivers

(a) Study **Figure 3**, which shows how the velocity of a river varies along its course.

(i) Small gravel particles are transported by velocities above 0.1 m per second. At what distance along the river does the transportation of gravel start?

....

(1 mark)

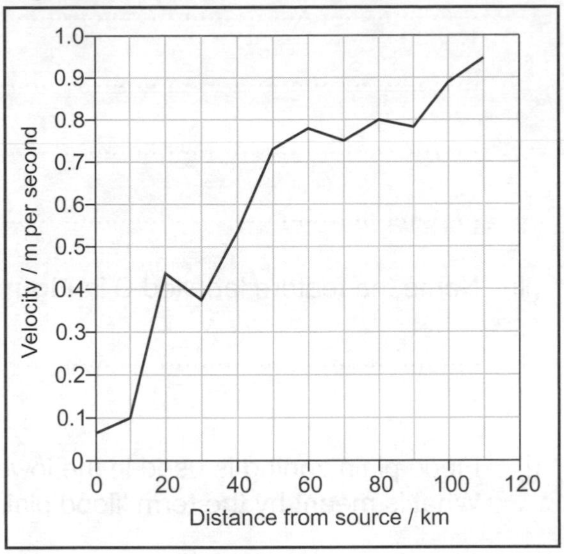

(ii) At 80 km along the river, pebbles are being transported. Give the velocity of the river at this point and name the process by which pebbles are transported.

....

....

....

....

(2 marks)

Figure 3

Velocity / m per second: 0, 0.1, 0.2, 0.3, 0.4, 0.5, 0.6, 0.7, 0.8, 0.9, 1.0

Distance from source / km: 0, 20, 40, 60, 80, 100, 120

(iii) Describe the four processes of erosion taking place in the river.

....

....

....

....

....

....

(4 marks)

(b) Study **Figure 4**, which is a photograph of a meander in the lower course of the river.

(i) Suggest a feature likely to be found at the part of the river labelled A in **Figure 4** and explain its formation.

....

....

....

....

....

....

....

(3 marks)

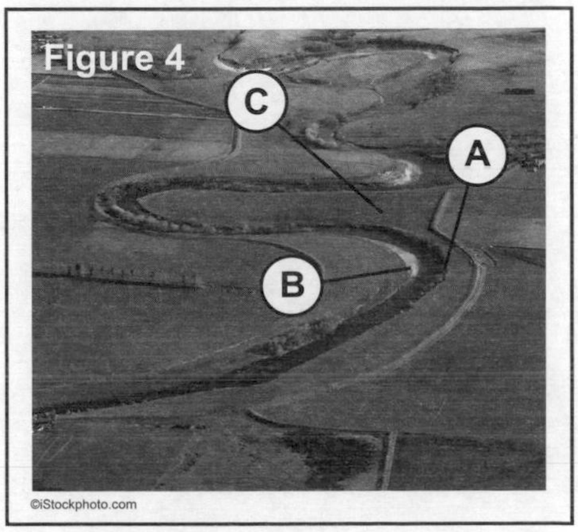

Figure 4

C

A

B

(ii) Suggest a feature likely to be found at the part of the river labelled B in **Figure 4** and explain its formation.

....

....

....

....

(3 marks)

(iii) Name the feature labelled C in **Figure 4**.

....

(1 mark)

(c) (i) Flood plain zoning is used in the lower course of the river. What is meant by the term 'flood plain zoning'?

....

....

(1 mark)

(ii) Name and describe one other soft engineering strategy that could be used to reduce the risk of flooding.

....

....

(2 marks)

(d) Describe and compare the primary and secondary effects of flooding in rich and poor parts of the world that you have studied.

....

....

....

....

....

....

....

....

....

....

(8 marks)

Leave blank

3 **Coasts**

(a) Study **Figure 5**, a photograph showing coastal landforms.

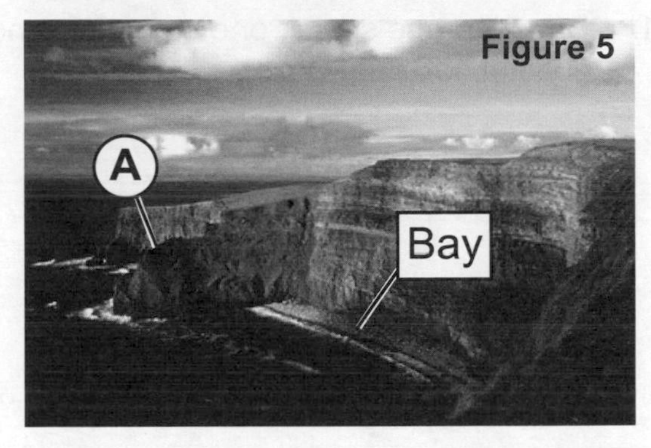

(i) Name the type of landform labelled A in **Figure 5**.

.... *(1 mark)*

(ii) Describe the characteristics of the landform labelled A in **Figure 5**.

....

....

.... *(2 marks)*

(iii) Explain how the landforms shown in **Figure 5** are formed.

....

....

.... *(3 marks)*

(b) Study **Figure 6**, an Ordnance Survey® map of a coastal area near Bournemouth.

(i) Hurst Castle is found at X on **Figure 6**.
Give the six figure grid reference for Hurst Castle. .... *(1 mark)*

* **Figure 6**

3 centimetres to 1 kilometre (one grid square)

Kilometres

2 1 0

(ii) State the distance between Hurst Castle and the end of the spit at 316905.

.... *(1 mark)*

(iii) Explain how a spit is formed.

....

....

....

....

....

....

....

.... *(2 marks)*

(c) Coastal flooding can cause problems in low-lying coastal areas.

(i) Describe one social, one economic and one environmental impact of coastal flooding.

Social ....

....

Economic ....

....

Environmental ....

....

(3 marks)

(ii) Name and describe two hard engineering strategies that can be used to protect coastlines from flooding and erosion.

....

....

....

....

....

(4 marks)

(d) Explain the benefits and costs of coastal management strategies used in an area you have studied.

....

....

....

....

....

....

....

....

....

....

....

(8 marks)

Leave blank

4 Population

(a) Study **Figure 7**, which shows world population for the years 1500-2000.

Figure 7

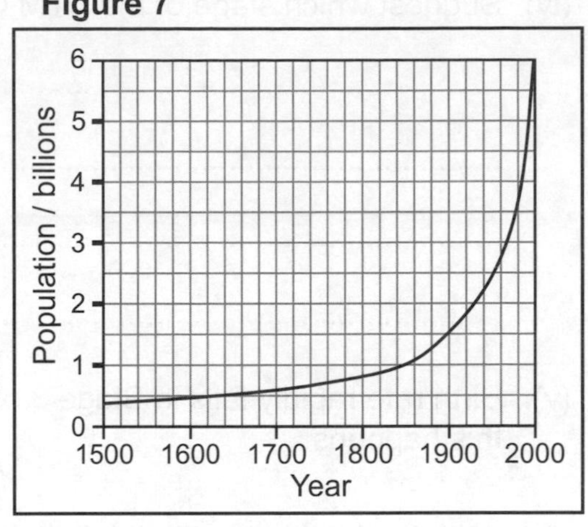

(i) What was the world population in 1900?

.... *(1 mark)*

(ii) How many years did it take for the world population to double from 1 billion to 2 billion people?

.... *(1 mark)*

(b) Study **Figures 8a**, **8b** and **8c**, which show population pyramids for countries A, B and C.

Figure 8a — Country A

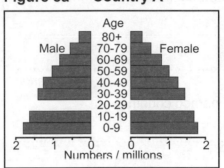

Age
80+
Male 70-79 Female
60-69
50-59
40-49
30-39
20-29
10-19
0-9
2 1 0 0 1 2
Numbers / millions

Figure 8b — Country B

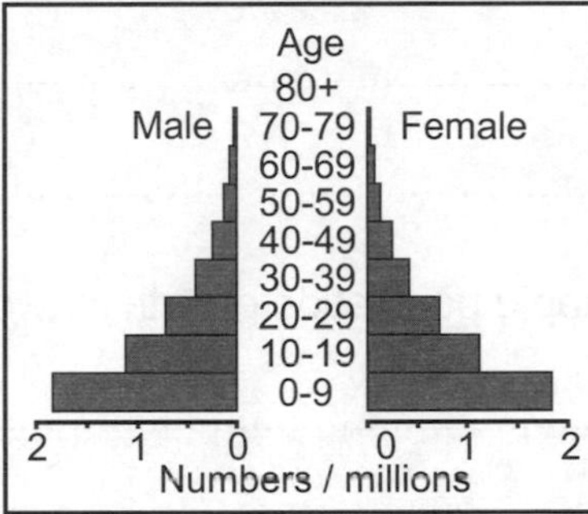

Figure 8c — Country C

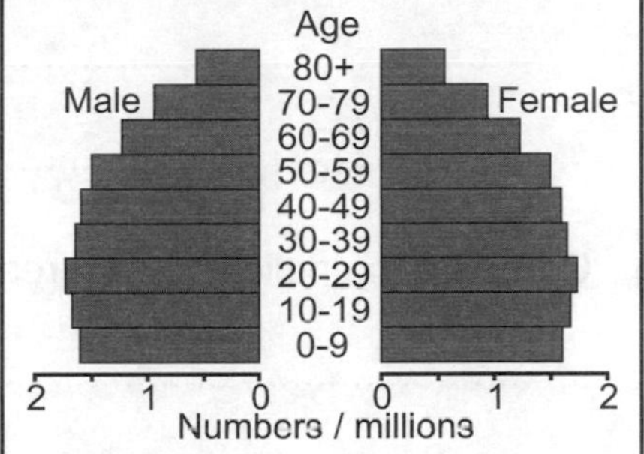

(i) What do population pyramids show?

....

.... *(2 marks)*

(ii) Complete **Figure 8a** to show that the population of Country A includes 1.6 million women aged 20-29 and 1.5 million men aged 20-29.

(1 mark)

(iii) Compare the population pyramids for Country A and Country B.

....

....

....

....

....

....

.... *(6 marks)*

Turn over

(iv) Suggest which stage of the DTM Country C is in. Give reasons for your answer.

....

....

....

....

(3 marks)

(v) Birth rate rapidly falls in Stage 3 of the DTM. Suggest reasons for why this happens.

....

....

....

....

....

(3 marks)

(c) Compare the policies to address rapid population growth in two named countries.

....

....

....

....

....

....

....

....

....

....

....

....

(8 marks)

Leave blank

5 **Development**

(a) Study **Figure 9**, which shows measures of development for two countries.

(i) Define birth rate.

....

....

.... *(1 mark)*

Figure 9

	Country X	Country Y
Birth rate	15.2	20.5
Death rate	25.2	42.3
Infant mortality rate	72.9	102.1
Literacy rate	83.9%	75.3%
Access to clean water	73.6%	54.7%

(ii) Using **Figure 9**, explain which country is less developed.

....

....

.... *(3 marks)*

(iii) Suggest why a low literacy rate could have a negative impact on development.

....

....

....

.... *(3 marks)*

(b) Study **Figure 10**, which shows life expectancy in Country X.

Figure 10

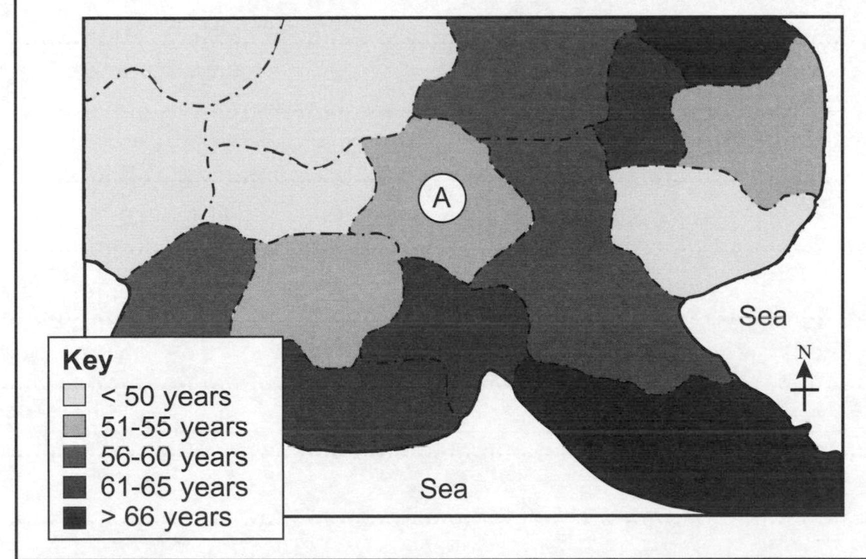

(i) Define 'life expectancy' and state what aspect of development it measures.

....

.... *(2 marks)*

(ii) What is the life expectancy of the region labelled A in **Figure 2**?

....

(1 mark)

(iii) Describe the distribution of regions with a life expectancy of less than fifty years.

....

....

....

(2 marks)

(iv) The north west of Country X has very low rainfall. Suggest how this may have limited the area's development.

....

....

....

....

(4 marks)

(c) (i) Country Y receives long-term aid from several other countries. What is meant by the term 'long-term aid'?

....

(1 mark)

(ii) Explain how a development project you have studied is benefiting the recipient country.

....

....

....

....

....

....

....

....

....

....

....

(8 marks)

Section 1 — Tectonic Activity

Page 10

1 (a) (i) The focus is the point in the Earth where the earthquake starts *[1 mark]*.

(ii) 17 km *[1 mark]*

(b) One mark for epicentre correctly labelled on the surface directly above the focus.

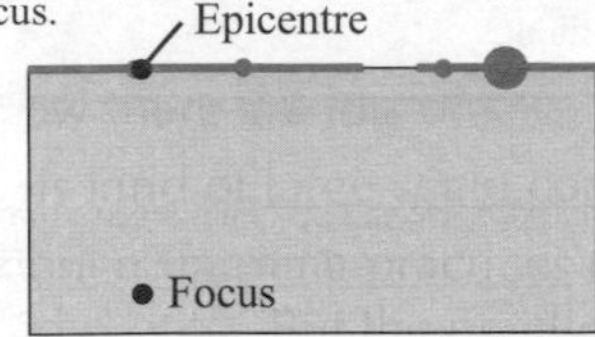

(c) The Richter scale *[1 mark]*.

2 (a) E.g. the earthquake triggered landslides *[1 mark]*. / Landslides blocked the roads, meaning that rescue teams could not reach some areas *[1 mark]*. / People were left homeless *[1 mark]*. / People were left without clean water *[1 mark]*. / People were left without medical aid *[1 mark]*.

(b) E.g. there is more low quality housing in poorer countries *[1 mark]*. Low quality houses are less stable, so they're more easily destroyed by earthquakes *[1 mark]*. / The infrastructure is often worse in poorer countries *[1 mark]*. Poor quality roads make it harder for emergency services to reach injured people, which leads to more deaths *[1 mark]*. / Poorer countries don't have much money to protect against earthquakes, e.g. by making buildings earthquake-proof *[1 mark]*, so more buildings are destroyed *[1 mark]*. / Poorer countries don't have enough money or resources (e.g. food and emergency vehicles) to react straight away to earthquakes *[1 mark]*, so more people are affected by the secondary impacts *[1 mark]*. / Healthcare is often worse in poorer countries *[1 mark]*. Many hospitals in poorer countries don't have enough supplies to deal with the large numbers of casualties after an earthquake, so more people die from treatable injuries *[1 mark]*.

(c) E.g. buildings can be designed to withstand earthquakes *[1 mark]*. This reduces the number of buildings destroyed by an earthquake, so fewer people will be killed, injured, made homeless and made unemployed *[1 mark]*. / Future developments, e.g. new shopping centres, can be planned to avoid the areas most at risk from earthquakes *[1 mark]*. This reduces the number of buildings destroyed by an earthquake *[1 mark]*. / Governments and other organisations can educate people about what to do if there's an earthquake (e.g. stand in a doorway) and how to evacuate *[1 mark]*. This reduces deaths *[1 mark]*. / Emergency services can train and prepare for disasters, e.g. by practising rescuing people from collapsed buildings and by stockpiling medicine *[1 mark]*. This reduces the number of people killed *[1 mark]*.

Page 18

1 (a) Vesuvius attracts lots of tourists, providing jobs in the tourist industry *[1 mark]*. The soil around Vesuvius is fertile so it's good for farming, which attracts farmers *[1 mark]*.

(b) E.g. people and animals may be killed or injured by pyroclastic flows, lava flows and falling rocks *[1 mark]*. / Roads and buildings may be damaged by pyroclastic flows, lava flows and falling ash *[1 mark]*. / Crops may be damaged by falling ash *[1 mark]*. / Water supplies may be contaminated by falling ash *[1 mark]*. / People, animals and plants may be suffocated by carbon dioxide *[1 mark]*.

(c) E.g. they could monitor changes in the shape of the volcano that happen before eruptions *[1 mark]*.

(d) Prediction is a sustainable strategy *[1 mark]*, because although it is expensive, it can be effective and is environmentally friendly *[1 mark]*.

(e) HINTS for answering this question:

- Start off by describing the volcanic eruption — include the name of the volcano, where it is and when it erupted, e.g. 'The Soufrière Hills Volcano in Montserrat erupted on the 25th June 1997'.
- Then describe the primary impacts. Make sure you include relevant details, e.g. 'Over 20 villages and two thirds of homes on the island were destroyed by pyroclastic flows'.
- Finish off by describing the secondary impacts, e.g. 'Tourists stayed away from the area and fires destroyed many buildings including the police headquarters and local government offices'.
- You'll probably include a lot of negative impacts, but you can include positive impacts too.

Section 2 — Rocks and Resources

Page 30

1 (a) One mark for each correct label.

(b) HINTS for answering this question:

- You need to start off by talking about the features of the rock, e.g. 'Granite has lots of joints that aren't evenly spread'.
- Then you can go on to talk about how the features you've mentioned result in the formation of tors, e.g. 'Freeze-thaw and chemical weathering wear down the parts of the rock with lots of joints faster because there are more cracks for the water to get into. Sections of the granite that have fewer joints are weathered more slowly than the surrounding rock, so they stick out at the surface, forming tors'.

(c) (i) Granite is an impermeable rock so granite landscapes are good places to build reservoirs *[1 mark]*. Granite landscapes have features like tors and moorland that are attractive to tourists *[1 mark]*. Granite areas can be used for rearing livestock *[1 mark]*.

(ii) HINTS for answering this question:

- Start off by describing the quarry and its location, e.g. 'Whatley Quarry is a limestone quarry in Somerset that produces around 5 million tonnes of rock every year'.
- You need to talk about both the advantages and disadvantages of the quarry.
- Make sure you include at least one economic, one social and one environmental advantage or disadvantage.
- Use specific details in your points, e.g. 'The quarry is one of the largest in the UK, it's around 1.5 km long and 0.6 km wide. This is an environmental disadvantage because lots of habitats have been destroyed to make way for the quarry'.

Section 3 — Weather and Climate

Page 40

1 (a) The temperature stayed between about 13.5 and 13.8 °C between 1860 and 1930 *[1 mark]*, and then rose fairly steadily to around 14.4 °C in 2000 *[1 mark]*.

(b) Global warming is the increase in global temperature over the last century *[1 mark]*.

(c) Rising temperatures and decreased rainfall will mean that some environments will turn into deserts *[1 mark]*. The distribution of some species may change due to climate change, and species that can't move may die out *[1 mark]*.

(d) HINTS for answering this question:

- State and describe three local responses. For each one, use an example to help your description, e.g. 'Congestion charging is where local authorities charge people for driving cars into cities during busy periods, e.g. in central London'.
- Then you need to explain how the response reduces the threat of climate change, e.g. 'Because it costs more to drive their cars, people will use them less, which reduces emissions'.
- Then do the same for the other two local responses, e.g. recycling and conserving energy.

Page 49

1 (a) (i) One mark for each correct label up to a maximum of four.

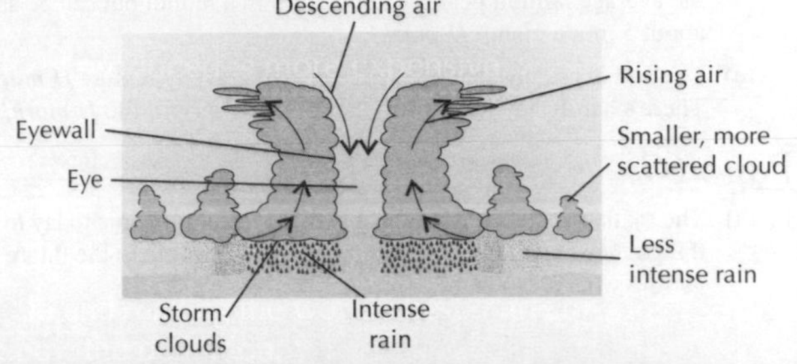

(ii) E.g. they have a circular shape *[1 mark]*. / They spin anticlockwise (in the northern hemisphere) *[1 mark]*. / They're hundreds of kilometres wide *[1 mark]*.

(b) E.g. they've always lived there, so moving away would mean leaving friends and family *[1 mark]*. / They're employed in the area. If people move they have to find new jobs *[1 mark]*. / They're confident of support from their government after a tropical storm, e.g. to help rebuild houses *[1 mark]*. / Some people think that severe tropical storms won't happen again in the area, so it's safe to live there *[1 mark]*.

(c) E.g. people are left homeless *[1 mark]*. / There's a shortage of clean water and a lack of proper sanitation, so it's easier for diseases to spread *[1 mark]*. / Roads are blocked or destroyed so aid and emergency vehicles can't get through *[1 mark]*. / Businesses are damaged or destroyed, causing unemployment *[1 mark]*. / There's a shortage of food because crops are damaged and livestock has died *[1 mark]*. / People may suffer psychological problems if they knew people who died *[1 mark]*.

(d) (i) Scientists can predict when and where a tropical storm will hit land by tracking the storm and using computer models *[1 mark]*. / Future developments can be planned to avoid the areas most at risk *[1 mark]*. / Emergency services can train and prepare for disasters *[1 mark]*. / Governments can plan evacuation routes to get people away from storms quickly *[1 mark]*. / Buildings can be designed to withstand tropical storms *[1 mark]*. / Flood defences can be built along rivers *[1 mark]*. / Governments can educate people about how to prepare for a tropical storm and how to evacuate *[1 mark]*. / People can be told how to make a survival kit *[1 mark]*.

(ii) It is sustainable *[1 mark]*, because it is effective and environmentally friendly *[1 mark]*.

(e) HINTS for answering this question:

- Start off by saying a bit about the tropical storms you've chosen — give the <u>names</u> of the storms, say <u>where</u> and <u>when</u> they happened, and state which is from a rich part of the world and which is from a poor part of the world. E.g. 'On 29th August 2005, Hurricane Katrina hit south east USA, a rich part of the world. On 2nd May 2008, Cyclone Nargis hit the Irrawaddy Delta in Burma, a poorer part of the world'.
- Then <u>describe</u> the <u>short-term</u> responses to one storm, and <u>compare</u> them with the <u>short-term</u> responses to the second. Include plenty of specific details, e.g. 'Immediately after Hurricane Katrina, about 25 000 people were given shelter in the Louisiana Superdome. After Cyclone Nargis, Burma's government initially refused to accept foreign aid, and aid workers were only allowed in three weeks after the disaster occurred'.
- Next, <u>describe</u> the <u>long-term</u> responses to one storm, and <u>compare</u> them with the <u>long-term</u> responses to the other storm, e.g. 'The US government has set aside over $34 billion to rebuild houses and schools, whereas Burma is relying on international aid to repair the damage and fewer than 20 000 homes have been rebuilt'.

Section 4 — The Living World

Page 58

1 (a) Seaweed *[1 mark]*

(b) Periwinkle / crab / octopus *[1 mark]*.

(c) Octopuses would have less to eat so some might die *[1 mark]*. Fewer periwinkles would be eaten so their numbers might increase *[1 mark]*. There might be more periwinkles to eat the seaweed so the amount of seaweed could decrease *[1 mark]*.

2 (a) 40 °C *[1 mark]*.

(b) E.g. Temperatures in the desert are extreme, being very hot in the day and very cold at night *[1 mark]*, e.g. Figure 2 shows that the difference between maximum and minimum temperature in January is about 20 °C *[1 mark]*. There is very little rainfall *[1 mark]*, e.g. Figure 2 shows that the average rainfall peaks at about 25 mm a month but can be as low as about 5 mm a month *[1 mark]*.

(c) The soil is usually shallow with a coarse gravelly texture *[1 mark]*. There's hardly any leaf fall so the soil isn't very fertile *[1 mark]*.

Page 67

1 (a) The management of forests in a way that allows people today to get the things they need *[1 mark]* without stopping people in the future from getting what they need *[1 mark]*.

(b) Selective logging can be used *[1 mark]*. This is less damaging to the forest than felling all the trees in an area because only a few trees are take from each area, so the forest will be able to regenerate and be used again in the future *[1 mark]*. New trees are planted *[1 mark]*, which means that there will still be trees available for people to use in the future *[1 mark]*.

2 HINTS for answering this question:

- <u>Describe</u> the <u>location</u> of hot deserts in richer countries and what they are <u>used for</u>, e.g. 'There is a hot desert in central and western Australia which is used for tourism and mining'.
- Do the same for the deserts in <u>poorer areas</u>, being as specific about the country or area as you can.
- Then <u>compare</u> the <u>rich</u> and <u>poor areas</u>, e.g. 'The deserts in poorer areas aren't mainly used for tourism whereas the deserts in the US and Australia are'.

Section 5 — Rivers

Page 79

1 (a) The map shows waterfalls, which are found in the upper course of a river *[1 mark]*. The land around the Afon Merch is high (around 500 m in grid square 6353) *[1 mark]*. The river crosses lots of contours lines in a short distance, which means it's steep *[1 mark]*. The river is narrow (shown on the map by a thin line) *[1 mark]*.

(b) Waterfalls form where a river flows over an area of hard rock followed by an area of softer rock *[1 mark]*. The softer rock is eroded more than the hard rock, creating a step in the river *[1 mark]*. As water goes over the step it erodes more and more of the softer rock *[1 mark]*. A steep drop is eventually created, which is called a waterfall *[1 mark]*.

2 Erosion causes the outside bends of a meander to get closer *[1 mark]* until there's only a small area of land left between the bends (called a neck) *[1 mark]*. The river breaks through this land, for example during a flood *[1 mark]*. The river then flows along the shortest course *[1 mark]*. Deposition eventually cuts off the meander *[1 mark]* so an ox-bow lake is formed *[1 mark]*.

3 (a) The wide valley floor on either side of a river which occasionally gets flooded *[1 mark]*.

(b) When a river floods onto a flood plain the water slows down *[1 mark]* and deposits the eroded material it's transporting, which builds up the flood plain *[1 mark]*. Flood plains are also built up by the deposition that happens on the slip-off slopes of meanders *[1 mark]*.

Page 89

1 (a) The frequency of flooding of the River Turb has increased between 1997 and 2008 *[1 mark]*, e.g. between 1997 and 2002 there were two floods, but between 2002 and 2008 there were 16 floods *[1 mark]*.

(b) The risk of flooding would be lower *[1 mark]* because more water percolates into the rock instead of flowing on the surface *[1 mark]*. This means there's less runoff and a longer lag time, so peak discharge will be lower *[1 mark]*.

2 (a) (i) Channel straightening *[1 mark]*.

(ii) Flood water is carried to Fultow faster, which may cause flooding or increased erosion there *[1 mark]*.

(b) Flood plain zoning prevents people building on parts of a flood plain that are likely to flood *[1 mark]*. It reduces the risk of flooding because impermeable surfaces aren't created, e.g. buildings and roads *[1 mark]*. It also reduces the impact of flooding because there aren't any houses or roads to be damaged *[1 mark]*.

3 HINTS for answering this question:

- You need to mention at least <u>two human factors</u> that can cause a river to flood, e.g. deforestation and building construction.
- First describe a factor, e.g. 'Deforestation is when trees are cut down. Trees intercept rainwater on their leaves, which then evaporates. Trees also take up water from the ground and store it'.
- Then explain why it can cause flooding, e.g. 'Cutting down trees increases the volume of water that reaches the river channel because less is intercepted and taken up from the ground. This increases discharge and makes flooding more likely'.
- Then do the same for another human factor.

Section 6 — Glaciation

Page 102

1 (a) (i) The output of water from a glacier as the ice melts *[1 mark]*. It mostly occurs in the lower part of the glacier (zone of ablation) *[1 mark]*.

(ii) HINTS for answering this question:

- Start by explaining what the glacial budget is, e.g. 'The glacial budget is the difference between total accumulation and total ablation over one year'.
- Explain what kind of glacial budget would cause a glacier to advance, e.g. 'A positive glacial budget is when accumulation exceeds ablation. The glacier gets larger, which causes the snout to advance down the valley'. Do the same thing for glacial retreat.
- Double check your answer to check you haven't got positive and negative glacial budgets, accumulation and ablation, and advance and retreat mixed up.

(iii) 10 km (accept 11 km) *[1 mark]*.

(b) HINTS for answering this question:

- There are six marks available so aim for three social impacts and three environmental impacts.
- Start with social impacts, e.g. 'Once a glacier has completely melted, the amount of meltwater decreases. Meltwater lakes are often used to generate hydroelectric power (HEP). Changes to the amount of water entering the lakes will mean disruptions to power supplies from HEP and could leave some people with an unreliable power supply'.
- Then move on to the environmental impacts, e.g. 'Glacial retreat is linked to an increase in natural hazards. For example, rapid melting can cause flooding, rockslides and avalanches. These hazards destroy habitats and disrupt food chains'.

Section 7 — Coasts

Page 113

1 (a) E.g. at 0 m, the beach was wider in 2000 than it was in 2005 *[1 mark]*. At 1000 m, the beach was narrower in 2000 than 2005 *[1 mark]*. The width of the beach varied less in 2000 than it did in 2005 *[1 mark]*.

(b) (i) Waves follow the direction of the prevailing wind, which means they usually hit the coast at an oblique angle *[1 mark]*. The swash carries material up the beach, in the same direction as the waves *[1 mark]*. The backwash then carries material down the beach at right angles, back towards the sea *[1 mark]*. Over time, material zigzags along the coast *[1 mark]*.

(ii) Spits and bars are both beaches formed by longshore drift *[1 mark]*. Spits stick out into the sea and are joined to the coast at one end only *[1 mark]*. Bars are connected to the coast at both ends *[1 mark]*.

(iii) Traction *[1 mark]* is when large particles like boulders are pushed along the sea bed by the force of the water *[1 mark]*. / Suspension *[1 mark]* is when small particles like silt and clay are carried along in the water *[1 mark]*. / Saltation *[1 mark]* is when pebble-sized particles are bounced along the sea bed by the force of the water *[1 mark]*. / Solution *[1 mark]* is when soluble materials dissolve in the water and are carried along *[1 mark]*.

Page 122

1 (a) (i) Schemes set up using knowledge of the sea and its processes to reduce the effects of flooding and erosion *[1 mark]*.

(ii) Beach nourishment / dune regeneration *[1 mark]*.

(b) (i) Rock armour *[1 mark]* involves piling up boulders along the coast *[1 mark]*. / Building sea walls *[1 mark]* involves creating walls from hard materials like concrete *[1 mark]*.

(ii) Rock armour — The boulders absorb wave energy and so reduce erosion and flooding *[1 mark]*. It's a fairly cheap method *[1 mark]*. Sea wall — It reflects waves back to sea, which prevents erosion of the coast *[1 mark]* and it acts as a barrier to flooding *[1 mark]*.

2 (a) The melting of ice on the land (e.g. the Antarctic ice sheet) causes water that's stored as ice to return to the oceans *[1 mark]*. This increases the volume of water in the oceans and causes sea level to rise *[1 mark]*. Increased global temperature causes the oceans to get warmer and expand *[1 mark]*. This increases the volume of water, causing sea level to rise *[1 mark]*.

(b) E.g. The high salt content of sea water can damage or kill organisms in an ecosystem *[1 mark]*. / The force of floodwater can uproot trees and plants *[1 mark]*. / Standing floodwater can drown some trees and plants *[1 mark]*. / A large volume of fast-moving water can cause increased erosion *[1 mark]*.

Section 8 — Population

Page 132

1 (a) 6 *[1 mark]*.

(b) There was rapid population growth *[1 mark]* / the number of people increased from 1.4 million people to 4.4 million people *[1 mark]* / in 2000 there were two cities with at least 1 million people *[1 mark]* / there were four brand new settlements with at least 100 000 people in 2000 *[1 mark]* / four settlements grew from populations of 100 000 to 500 000 *[1 mark]*.

(c) Two marks for two social impacts, e.g. services like healthcare and education might not be able to cope with the increase so not everybody has access to them *[1 mark]* / children may miss out on education if they have to work to help support a large family *[1 mark]* / people may be forced to live in makeshift houses or overcrowded settlements *[1 mark]* / health problems may arise if not everyone has access to clean water *[1 mark]* / there may be food shortages if the country can't grow or import enough food for the population *[1 mark]*.

Two marks for two economic impacts, e.g. unemployment increases because there aren't enough jobs for the number of people in the country *[1 mark]*. Poverty increases because more people are born into families that are already poor *[1 mark]*.

(d) E.g. birth control programmes *[1 mark]*. These aim to reduce the birth rate by having laws about how many children couples are allowed, or by offering couples free contraception and sex education *[1 mark]*. The policy helps to achieve sustainable development because reducing the birth rate means the population won't get much bigger *[1 mark]*, so people won't use up as many resources today and there'll be some left for future generations *[1 mark]*.

Page 139

1 (a) The movement of people into an area *[1 mark]*.

(b) (i) Economic migrants, so any two economic push factors, e.g. high unemployment *[1 mark]* / low average wages *[1 mark]*.

(ii) Unlimited numbers of immigrants are allowed to enter *[1 mark]* / or any economic pull factors, e.g. more work available *[1 mark]* / higher wages *[1 mark]* / good exchange rate *[1 mark]*.

(c) Migrant workers pay taxes that help to fund services *[1 mark]* / there is an increased labour force *[1 mark]* / there may be an increased demand on services, e.g. schools *[1 mark]* / locals may have to compete with immigrants for jobs *[1 mark]* / money earned by immigrants isn't always spent in the UK *[1 mark]*.

2 HINTS for answering this question:

- Start your answer by introducing the two countries you've chosen to write about and say a bit about why people are migrating.
- Then describe the economic, social and political impacts of the migration on the source and the destination countries. E.g. 'Most of the people who left Poland were young. This led to an ageing population in Poland. But the young people who left didn't need houses or jobs any more, which helped with the housing shortages and unemployment problems in Poland. One social impact in the UK was that some people were unhappy about the large numbers of Polish immigrants'.
- Finally, describe what is being done to manage the international migration. Write about any schemes that are in place to reduce the number of immigrants, or any border controls. E.g. 'After allowing unlimited migration from Poland, the UK Government has tightened the control of migration from some of the newer EU states, e.g. immigrants from Romania have to get permission from the Home Office to work in the UK'.

Section 9 — Urban Environments

Page 150

1 (a) (i) 1500 ***[1 mark]***.

(ii) 14 ***[1 mark]***.

(iii) The use of cars dropped dramatically ***[1 mark]***. / More people cycled and used public transport ***[1 mark]***. / Public transport options increased to include trams and hydrogen buses ***[1 mark]***.

(b) They're trying to tackle housing shortages by building 500 more new houses in 2005 than in 1995 ***[1 mark]***. They're trying to tackle an increase in waste by building 14 more recycling sites ***[1 mark]***. They're trying to tackle traffic congestion by improving public transport ***[1 mark]***. They're trying to reduce pollution by encouraging people to use more environmentally-friendly transport like trams, hydrogen buses and bicycles ***[1 mark]***.

2 (a) A settlement that is built illegally in and around a city by people who can't afford proper housing ***[1 mark]***.

(b) Because lots of rural-urban migration happens in poorer countries ***[1 mark]***. There is nowhere else for the poor migrants to go as they can't afford other housing ***[1 mark]***.

(c) E.g. site and service schemes are where people pay a small amount of rent for a site and borrow money to buy materials to build or improve a house on their plot ***[1 mark]***. The rent money is then used to provide basic services for the area ***[1 mark]***.

Page 159

1 (a) (i) 100% - 82% = 18% ***[1 mark]***.

(ii) It decreased from 150 hectares to 100 hectares ***[1 mark]***.

(iii) One mark for table correctly completed.

Year	Housing available	No. of people on housing list	Housing deficit
1992	9000	12 000	3000
2000	7500	23 000	15 500
2008	14 000	18 000	**4000**

(b) More housing is needed ***[1 mark]***. More jobs are needed ***[1 mark]***. More green spaces are needed ***[1 mark]***.

2 HINTS for answering this question:

- You need to <u>name</u> the example you're using and say where it is, e.g. Curitiba in Southern Brazil.
- You should include <u>lots of detail</u> about the different ways in which your chosen city is sustainable, e.g. '70% of rubbish is recycled in Curitiba. Residents in poorer areas where the streets are too narrow for weekly rubbish collection are given food and bus tickets for bringing their recycling to local collection centres'.
- You need to <u>conclude</u> your answer by saying how successful your example has been, e.g. 'More than 1.4 million people in Curitiba use the bus every day and there are over 200 km of bike paths in the city. The reduction in car use means that there's less pollution and use of fossil fuels, so the environment isn't damaged as much and fewer resources are used up'.

Section 10 — Rural Environments

Page 169

1 (a) One mark for filling in the diagram correctly.

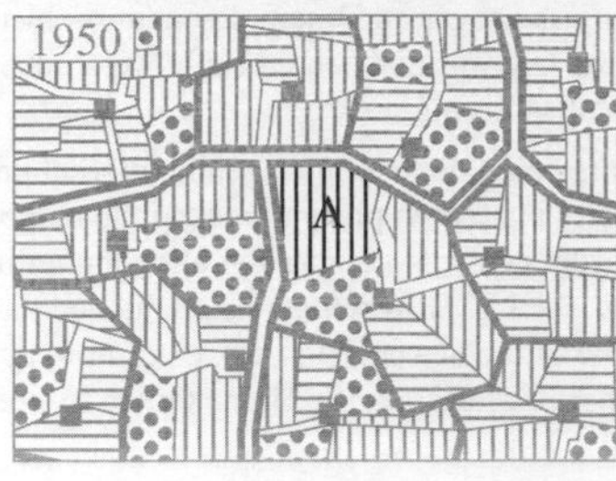

(b) (i) Farms have increased in size ***[1 mark]***, and are growing fewer types of crop ***[1 mark]*** in larger fields ***[1 mark]***.

(ii) Growing fewer types of crop reduces biodiversity as there are fewer habitats ***[1 mark]***. Removing hedgerows to make larger fields destroys habitats and increases soil erosion ***[1 mark]***.

2 (a) Farming where crops and animals are produced to be sold ***[1 mark]***.

(b) 1000 km^2 ***[1 mark]***

(c) Description:
The area of land used for commercial farming has steadily increased from 300 km^2 in 1960 to 1000 km^2 in 2000 ***[1 mark]***.
Impacts:
If subsistence farmers have their land taken over by big companies, they are likely to be forced onto poorer land where it's harder to grow food ***[1 mark]***. / If farmers depend on a single crop, and the price drops, they might not have enough money to buy food ***[1 mark]***. / Farmers will only have an income at harvest or slaughter time and could struggle for the rest of the year if they don't make enough money ***[1 mark]***. / Food has to be brought in from other areas, increasing food prices ***[1 mark]***.

Section 11 — Development

Page 179

1 (a) Nicaragua exports mostly primary products. Not much profit is made selling primary products so less money is made to spend on development ***[1 mark]***. The UK exports a much higher percentage of manufacturing products than Nicaragua, which make more profit so there's more to spend on development ***[1 mark]***.

(b) If a country has poor trade links it will be less developed ***[1 mark]*** because it won't make a lot of money so has less to spend on development ***[1 mark]***.

2 (a) Botswana's HDI decreased from 0.68 in 1990 to 0.63 in 2000 ***[1 mark]***. It then increased to about 0.67 in 2005 ***[1 mark]***.

(b) HINTS for answering this question:

- Start your answer by describing the effects of corrupt or unstable governments, e.g. 'Corrupt governments allow some people in a country to get richer by breaking the law, while others stay poor'.
- Build on your first points by explaining how these things affect development, e.g. 'The poorer people in the country have a low quality of life because they can't afford things such as good housing, healthcare and education....'.

Page 185

1 (a) (i) Bilateral [1 mark].

(ii) Long-term aid helps the recipient country to become more developed ***[1 mark]***. Also, the country will become less reliant on foreign aid over time ***[1 mark]***. However, it can take a long while before the aid benefits the country, e.g. because schools and hospitals take a long time to build ***[1 mark]***. Bilateral aid can also be tied, so the aid might not go as far as untied aid ***[1 mark]***.

(b) Sustainable aid is aid that helps a country to develop in a way that doesn't irreversibly damage the environment ***[1 mark]*** or use up resources faster than they can be replaced ***[1 mark]***. The aid described in Figure 1 is sustainable because it does not irreversibly damage the environment and doesn't use up resources except for money ***[1 mark]***.

2 (a) When part of a country's debt is paid off by someone else in exchange for investment in conservation ***[1 mark]***.

(b) It would have helped Bolivia develop ***[1 mark]*** because money made by the country could be used to develop rather than pay off debt ***[1 mark]***.

Section 12 — Industry

Page 197

1 (a) (i) There is no longer any secondary industry near to the coal fields ***[1 mark]*** or the city centre ***[1 mark]***.

(ii) Environmental reason:

E.g. secondary industry is less reliant on coal as an energy source because it can use electricity from the national grid ***[1 mark]***.

Social reason:

E.g. transport facilities may have improved so the work force can commute to areas outside of the city centre ***[1 mark]***. / Changing government policies encourage industries to settle in different locations ***[1 mark]***.

(b) E.g. the location is near an urban area, providing lots of customers ***[1 mark]***. There are green open spaces nearby to provide a pleasant environment ***[1 mark]***. There are good transport links, e.g. a train station nearby, so customers can get there easily ***[1 mark]***.

(c) This is a good location for the company ***[1 mark]***, because it is close to the university which will provide skilled and educated workers ***[1 mark]***. It also has good transport links to allow workers to commute, e.g. main roads and a train station ***[1 mark]***.

Section 13 — Globalisation

Page 210

(a) (i) Food miles ***[1 mark]***

(ii) E.g. imported foods have high food miles so transporting them, e.g. by plane, produces lots of CO_2 ***[1 mark]*** and this adds to global warming ***[1 mark]***.

(b) It's quicker and easier for companies to get supplies from all over the world ***[1 mark]***.

(a) Globalisation has increased the wealth of some poorer countries so people are buying more things ***[1 mark]***. A lot of these things use energy, e.g. cars, so this increases the global demand for energy ***[1 mark]***.

(b) HINTS for answering this question:

- Marks are only given for talking about the environmental impacts, so don't waste time with social or economic impacts.
- Make sure you explain each impact that you mention, e.g. 'Burning fossil fuels releases gases that dissolve in water in the atmosphere and cause acid rain, which can kill animals and plants. Using more fossil fuels to provide more energy will increase acid rainfall'.
- Include a variety of impacts, e.g. habitat destruction and oil spills.

(c) Renewable energy sources are sustainable and non-renewable sources are not ***[1 mark]***. This is because renewable energy sources don't cause long-term environmental damage ***[1 mark]*** and they won't run out, so the sources will be available for future generations ***[1 mark]***.

Section 14 — Tourism

Page 220

(a) Organised tourism for large numbers of people ***[1 mark]***.

(b) It brings money into the local economy because people spend money, e.g. on activities ***[1 mark]***. / It creates jobs for local people, e.g. in hotels and construction ***[1 mark]***. / It increases the income of industries that supply tourism, e.g. fishermen ***[1 mark]***.

(c) E.g. thousands of tourists flying to the island means lots of air pollution from planes burning fuel ***[1 mark]***. Many water sports use engine-powered boats, which may pollute the water ***[1 mark]***. Overfishing to supply food to tourists could cause stocks of fish to become depleted ***[1 mark]***.

(d) HINTS for answering this question:

- Don't forget to put the name of the area — use a case study you've learnt about.
- Describe both the good and bad impacts of mass tourism first.
- Include plenty of facts and figures to back up your statements, e.g. don't just say that loads of people work in the tourist industry, include facts like 'Around 219 000 people worked in the tourist industry in Kenya in 2003'.
- For the negative impacts you've included, explain how they're being reduced. E.g. 'Kenya promotes walking or horseback tours over vehicle safaris, to try to reduce the amount of vegetation being destroyed'.

Exam Paper Answers

(a) (i) Almost all earthquakes are found along plate margins ***[1 mark]*** but some (very few) occur in the middle of plates ***[1 mark]***.

(ii) Tension builds up ***[1 mark]*** as one plate gets stuck as it's moving down past the other into the mantle ***[1 mark]***. The plates eventually jerk past each other ***[1 mark]***, sending out shockwaves ***[1 mark]***.

(b) (i) The Richter scale measures the amount of energy released by an earthquake/the magnitude of an earthquake ***[1 mark]***. It's measured using a seismometer ***[1 mark]***.

(ii) 10 times more powerful ***[1 mark]***.

(c) (i) A conservative plate margin ***[1 mark]***.

(ii) E.g. many people could be killed or injured ***[1 mark]***. Buildings could be destroyed ***[1 mark]***. Roads could be damaged ***[1 mark]***.

(iii) Location C is most suitable ***[1 mark]***, because it is furthest away from the plate margin ***[1 mark]*** and has not experienced any earthquakes in the past ***[1 mark]***.

(iv) E.g. buildings can be designed to withstand earthquakes, e.g. by using materials like reinforced concrete ***[1 mark]***.

(d) HINTS for answering this question:

- For this question you need to describe the primary impacts of two earthquakes in two different countries — one in a poorer country and one in a richer country. Primary impacts are the ones that happen straight away due to the ground shaking, e.g. deaths, building destruction, homelessness. As well as describing them, you also need to compare the impacts in the two countries.
- The question says, '...in rich and poor parts of the world that you have studied', which means it's a case study question. So you need to talk about two earthquakes you know — start by describing them both, e.g. 'An earthquake measuring 6.3 on the Richter scale hit L'Aquila in Italy on the 6th April 2009'.
- Compare each impact as you describe it, e.g. for number of deaths, say what it is for one, then compare that to the other, e.g. 'The death toll in L'Aquila was around 290, whereas it was around 80 000 in Kashmir' (include loads of details for each one).

2 (a) (i) 10 km ***[1 mark]***

(ii) The river's velocity is 0.8 m per second ***[1 mark]***. Pebbles are transported by saltation ***[1 mark]***.

(iii) Abrasion — eroded rocks picked up by the river scrape and rub against the channel, wearing it away ***[1 mark]***.
Attrition — eroded rocks picked up by the river smash into each other and break into smaller, more rounded fragments ***[1 mark]***.
Hydraulic action — the force of the water breaks rock particles away from the river channel ***[1 mark]***.
Solution — river water dissolves some types of rock, e.g. chalk and limestone ***[1 mark]***.

(b) (i) A river cliff is likely to be found at A ***[1 mark]***. The current is faster on the outside bend of the meander because the channel is deeper ***[1 mark]***. This means there's more erosion on the outside bend, so a river cliff is formed ***[1 mark]***.

(ii) A slip-off slope is likely to be found at B ***[1 mark]***. The current is slower on the inside bend of the meander because the river channel is shallower ***[1 mark]***. This means material is deposited on the inside of the bend, so a slip-off slope is formed ***[1 mark]***.

(iii) The neck of the meander ***[1 mark]***.

(c) (i) It's when restrictions prevent building on parts of a flood plain that are likely to be affected by a flood ***[1 mark]***.

(ii) Flood warnings ***[1 mark]***. These warn people about possible flooding through TV, radio, newspapers and the internet ***[1 mark]***. / Preparation ***[1 mark]***. Buildings are modified to reduce the amount of damage a flood could cause and people make plans for what to do in a flood, e.g. they keep a blanket and torch in a handy place ***[1 mark]***.

(d) HINTS for answering this question:

- Start by naming the areas, rivers and dates of the floods you've decided to write about, e.g. 'The River Eden in Carlisle, England, flooded on the 8th January 2005'.
- Then describe the primary effects of the floods in each area and compare them, e.g. 'The floods killed people in both areas. Three people were killed by the Carlisle flood but a lot more people (over 2000) died as a result of the South Asia flood'.
- Next, describe and compare the secondary effects, e.g. 'One secondary effect of the floods in both areas was that children lost out on education. Although one school in Carlisle was closed for months, the impact on education was much greater in South Asia, where around 4000 schools were affected by the flood'.

3 (a) (i) Headland ***[1 mark]***.

(ii) Headlands have steep sides ***[1 mark]***. / They jut out from the coastline ***[1 mark]***. / They are made of resistant rock ***[1 mark]***.

(iii) Headlands and bays form where there are alternating bands of resistant and less resistant rock along the coast *[1 mark]*. The less resistant rock is eroded quickly and this forms a bay *[1 mark]*. The resistant rock is eroded more slowly, forming a headland *[1 mark]*.

(b) (i) 319898 *[1 mark]*.

(ii) 0.7 km (accept between 0.6 km and 0.8 km) *[1 mark]*.

(iii) Longshore drift *[1 mark]* transports sand and shingle past a sharp bend in the coastline and deposits it in the sea *[1 mark]*.

(c) (i) One mark for social impact — People can be killed by the floods *[1 mark]*. / People can be forced to move because their houses are damaged *[1 mark]*. / Salt from floodwater can pollute the water supply *[1 mark]*. / Jobs can be lost because businesses shut down due to damage to buildings and equipment *[1 mark]*.
One mark for economic impact — Flooding can cause tourist attractions to close and put tourists off visiting an area *[1 mark]*. / Repairing the damage caused by flooding is very expensive *[1 mark]*. / Salt from the floodwater can leave farmland unusable, so farmers may lose their income *[1 mark]*.
One mark for environmental impact — Ecosystems can be affected because seawater has a high salt content and increased salt levels can damage or kill organisms *[1 mark]*. / The force of floodwater can uproot trees and plants *[1 mark]*. / Standing floodwater can drown trees and plants *[1 mark]*. / A large volume of fast-moving water can cause increased erosion, destroying habitats *[1 mark]*.

(ii) Rock armour *[1 mark]* involves piling up boulders along the coast *[1 mark]*. / Building sea walls *[1 mark]* involves creating walls from hard materials like concrete *[1 mark]*. / Breakwaters *[1 mark]* are concrete blocks or boulders deposited on the sea bed off the coast *[1 mark]*. / Groynes *[1 mark]* are wooden or stone fences that are built at right angles to the coast *[1 mark]*.

(d) HINTS for answering this question:

- Start by giving the <u>details</u> of the area you have studied, e.g. 'The Holderness coastline is 61 km long and stretches from Flamborough Head to Spurn Head. Erosion along the coastline is causing the cliffs to retreat'.
- Then describe the strategies that are being used and <u>explain</u> their costs and benefits.
- Give your answer a <u>logical structure</u> — fully describe each management strategy and explain its benefits and costs before moving onto the next one.
- Include <u>specific areas</u>, <u>facts</u> and <u>figures</u> in your answer, e.g. 'Defences, including two rock groynes, were built at Mappleton in 1991. They cost £2 million and protect the village and a coastal road from erosion and flooding. However, the groynes are reducing the width of beaches further down the Holderness coast, which increases erosion down the coast, e.g. Cowden Farm south of Mappleton is at risk of falling into the sea'.

4 (a) (i) 1.5 billion *[1 mark]*.

(ii) 80 years (accept anything from 75 to 85 years) *[1 mark]*.

(b) (i) The population structure of a country — how many people there are of each age group in a country *[1 mark]* and how many there are of each sex *[1 mark]*.

(ii) One mark for both bars drawn correctly.

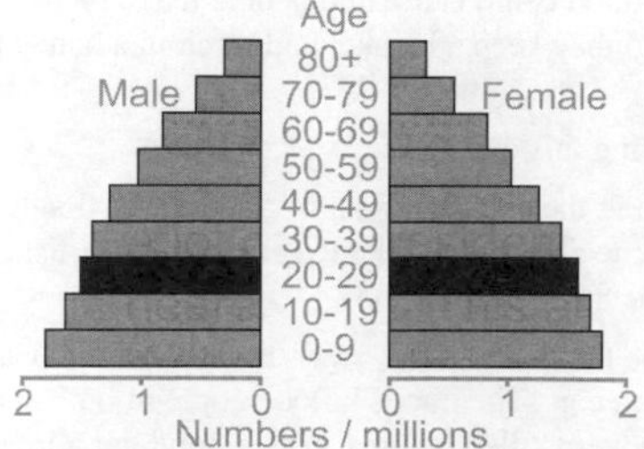

(iii) HINTS for answering this question:

- Look <u>carefully</u> at the two pyramids and the labels to make sure you understand what each pyramid shows.
- Write about the <u>similarities</u> and <u>differences</u> in the number of young people, old people and overall population numbers.
- Include lots of details and try to read some <u>figures</u> off the pyramids as accurately as you can. E.g. 'Country A has approximately 0.6 million people (0.3 million males and 0.3 million females) aged over 80, whereas the pyramid for Country B shows that no-one lives over the age of 79'.

(iv) Stage 4 *[1 mark]*, because there are a similar number of younger people and middle-aged people, which suggests a low birth rate *[1 mark]*, and there are many people surviving to quite an old age *[1 mark]*.

(v) Birth rate falls due to the emancipation of women *[1 mark]*. Better education and more widespread use of contraception means more women work instead of having children *[1 mark]*. The economy also changes from agriculture to manufacturing, so fewer children are needed to work on farms *[1 mark]*.

(c) HINTS for answering this question:

- <u>Decide which countries</u> you're going to <u>compare</u>. Pick ones that have really different policies, then you'll have lots to write about.
- Start off by explaining <u>why</u> the first country needs a population policy, then describe the policy. E.g. 'China has the largest population in the world, over 1.3 billion people. China introduced a 'one-child policy' in 1979, which very strongly encouraged couples to have only one child'.
- Compare this policy to another country's — <u>describe</u> the policy and <u>explain why</u> it's needed, and then <u>describe</u> how it's <u>different</u> to the first country's policy.
- Explain whether the policies have been <u>successful</u> and if they're <u>sustainable</u>. E.g. 'China's population growth rate was reduced, whereas Indonesia's policy only reduced the impacts of population growth. This means Indonesia's population is still growing too rapidly, so the policy in Indonesia isn't as sustainable as the policy in China'.

5 (a) (i) Birth rate is the number of live babies born per thousand of the population per year *[1 mark]*.

(ii) Country Y is less developed *[1 mark]* because it has a higher birth rate, death rate and infant mortality rate than Country X *[1 mark]*. It also has a lower literacy rate and percentage access to clean water than Country X *[1 mark]*.

(iii) A low literacy rate shows the country's population is poorly educated *[1 mark]*. If a country's population is poorly educated, they can't get good jobs so will have a lower quality of life *[1 mark]*. Having a poorly paid job also means they can't add much money to the economy, so the country will have less money to spend on development *[1 mark]*.

(b) (i) The average age a person can expect to live to *[1 mark]*. It's a measure of the quality of healthcare *[1 mark]*.

(ii) 51-55 years *[1 mark]*

(iii) Regions with a life expectancy of less than 50 years mainly occur in the northwest of the country *[1 mark]*. However, there is also one region in the east with a life expectancy of less than 50 years *[1 mark]*.

(iv) Low rainfall means it will be hard for the area to produce a lot of food *[1 mark]*. This can lead to malnutrition and people who are malnourished have a low quality of life *[1 mark]*. People also have fewer crops to sell, so they have less money to spend on goods and services *[1 mark]*. The government will get less money from taxes so there's less money for it to spend on developing the area *[1 mark]*.

(c) (i) Money or resources given to help recipient countries develop, e.g. to improve healthcare *[1 mark]*.

(ii) HINTS for answering this question:

- Begin this <u>case study question</u> by writing about the donor and recipient, e.g. 'FARM-Africa is a non-governmental organisation that provides aid to eastern Africa'.
- Then, explain what the aid project actually <u>does</u>, e.g. 'FARM-Africa funds several projects including women's empowerment schemes, prosopis management schemes, community development schemes and forest management schemes'.
- Finally, discuss the <u>benefits</u> for the <u>recipient country</u>, e.g. 'Prosopis is a pest plant that invades grazing land and makes farming difficult. Farmers are shown how to convert prosopis into animal feed. The animal feed is then sold, generating a source of income'.

Index

Index

Index